Unbuttoned

Unbuttoned

A History of Mackenzie King's Secret Life

CHRISTOPHER DUMMITT

McGill-Queen's University Press

Montreal & Kingston • London • Chicago

ISBN 978-0-7735-4876-3 (cloth)
ISBN 978-0-7735-4938-8 (ePDF)
ISBN 978-0-7735-4939-5 (ePUB)

Legal deposit second quarter 2017
Bibliothèque nationale du Québec

Printed in Canada on acid-free paper that is 100% ancient forest free
(100% post-consumer recycled), processed chlorine free

This book has been published with the help of a grant from the Canadian
Federation for the Humanities and Social Sciences, through the Awards to
Scholarly Publications Program, using funds provided by the Social Sciences
and Humanities Research Council of Canada.

McGill-Queen's University Press acknowledges the support of the Canada
Council for the Arts for our publishing program. We also acknowledge the
financial support of the Government of Canada through the Canada Book
Fund for our publishing activities.

$34.95

Library and Archives Canada Cataloguing in Publication

Dummitt, Christopher, 1973–, author
Unbuttoned : a history of Mackenzie King's secret life / Christopher Dummitt.

Includes bibliographical references and index.
Issued in print and electronic formats.
ISBN 978-0-7735-4876-3 (cloth). – ISBN 978-0-7735-4938-8 (ePDF).
– ISBN 978-0-7735-4939-5 (ePUB)

1. King, William Lyon Mackenzie, 1874–1950 – In mass media.
2. King, William Lyon Mackenzie, 1874–1950 – Public opinion. 3. Prime
ministers – Canada – Biography. 4. Politicians – Canada – Public opinion.
5. Political culture – Canada. I. Title.

FC581.K5S68 2017   971.063'2092   C2016-908162-1
                                                 C2016-908163-X

To Juliet and our tribe,

Rowan, Finlay, Gilbert, and Arthur

Contents

Part Five *The People Unfooled*

Illustrations

Preface

I'm going to tell two stories in this book. One is the story of how Canadians came to learn about the eccentric private activities that former prime minister William Lyon Mackenzie King had managed to keep secret while he was alive. The second story is about the transformation in Canadian culture from the 1950s to the 1980s that gradually allowed many Canadians to talk publicly and irreverently about the details of this former prime minister's secret life.

This book is a kind of narrative history where the argument is largely, though not entirely, developed through the unravelling of a series of events. It moves forward chronologically, retelling the stories of those figures who played an influential role in exposing King's secrets. It's a book, as the great Canadian historian Donald Creighton might have said, of characters and their circumstances. Readers looking for the usual sorts of things that one associates with peer-reviewed scholarly monographs – the review of the academic literature, the positioning of my arguments within theoretical debates, and an acknowledgment, in the text, of the many debts owed to the work of other scholars – will not find them here. This is not to say that the book doesn't rely extensively on the work of others (it does), nor that it isn't making an argument that interacts with this literature (it is). But in this book those debts and debates are largely confined to the endnotes.

In some academic circles, narrative history has come to seem old-fashioned. It is supposed to be insufficiently analytical. A postmodern critic might say that it creates an artifice in the form of a story, using realism to hide what it (and its author) doesn't know: history didn't really happen in "just that way" and to pretend otherwise is just an example of the historian trying to fool the reader and perhaps even to fool himself. These criticisms seem, to me, insufficient and unconvincing on the whole.[1] As any teller of stories, fables, or parables knows, it's very clear when a story has a point to make. Analysis and argument aren't precluded by storytelling but the writer often makes those points in different ways. As for the postmodern concern about truthfulness, I both concede to not knowing the whole truth and, more to the point, admit to the necessity of constructed and partial versions of the truth offered in any history.[2] I'm just not convinced that a more analytical style of writing that more obviously engages, in the text, with what other scholars are saying gets us any closer to the truth or its construction.[3]

It seems to me that the role of history is to make an earlier era come alive again in the minds of our contemporaries. It won't really be the past, to be sure, but this isn't essential. A map is never the place it represents. Yet the usefulness of history comes from the affinities and sympathy it inspires or the shock of difference it can evoke, even for a relatively recent historical era that used to be, but is no longer, our own. Perhaps a personal analogy can make clearer this point. As a father of four children I've relived the early years of parenthood again and again and again, each time realizing how little I remembered from the previous child, each time reliving in new ways what I had done before many times but had forgotten. And, of course, it is and is never just the same. This isn't quite what we do in history but it's similar. In reliving the memories of what the last child was like, in looking back to ask "Is this what a baby does now?" I'm forced to question what I think I know, to relive what I remember, and to experience it all again. By the fourth baby I've learned something, though it's nothing close to total recall. Nor would I say, because I'm a historian, I've avoided the fate predicted by that usual quotation we employ to justify our existence – "Those who forget the past are doomed to repeat it." Though (usually) I would hesitate to call parenting my "doom," I have indeed repeated the past. Perhaps because I remember what came before I am, sort of, prepared. This, it seems to me, is the most we can ask of history.

The real questions are these: How best to make this past come alive so that others today can relive and remember it in somewhat accurate and useful ways? How to make it poignant? How to make it (sort of) real, or at least allow us to catch glimpses of an earlier time in what can only be, at best, a kind of peripheral vision? My modest ambition is twofold: to eke out a place for narrative history as one legitimate answer to these questions; and to suggest that narrative history isn't just for popularizers or journalists or dead historians. It is possible, I hope, to write a story and to still make a contribution to scholarly knowledge.

⟨ॐ⟩

Having said all this and forewarned the reader about what will be coming in the book proper, I do want to make space here, over the next several pages, to explain more explicitly how this book does in fact engage with certain areas of contemporary scholarly literature. We're still in the Preface, so the story hasn't quite yet begun.

In his book on the posthumous memorialization of French explorer Jacques Cartier, historian Alan Gordon reminds us of how much "interpretations of the past ... reflect the common sense of their own times." A whole historical subdiscipline now devotes itself to the politics of historical memory and the way in which particular historical figures and events come to be written into history – by whom, when, and for what purpose.[4] This book benefits from these works, and certainly from the basic insight that historical memory is always rooted in a particular kind of political project and cultural situation. Yet the goal here is somewhat different. We are looking at only one relatively short period of time, from King's death in 1950 until the early 1980s. Because King was prime minister for so long, it is likely that he will continue to show up again and again in Canadian historical writing and in the broader culture, taking his place as someone whose life and career can speak to other kinds of concerns.

But this book addresses an accident – the fact that King died when he did and that he had secrets to reveal, and that these secrets were written in a diary that was ultimately opened up to the public at a propitious moment. It was a chance event, an example of a concept that historians prize almost above everything else: contingency. This book isn't concerned so much with the many changes in historical meaning of Mackenzie King as it is with the very specific meanings that a couple of generations of Canadians gave to King's secret life over the course of a few decades in the second half of the twentieth century.

My account primarily contributes to a scholarly debate about how best to characterize political and cultural change in North America from the 1950s to the 1980s. Here I lean on the work of those scholars who push us away from a decade-by-decade division of the era. Too much of the popular imagination of these years – and some of the scholarly debate – retells the story as a transition from the conservative and "quiescent" 1950s to the radical 1960s, and thence to the co-opted 1970s and the neo-liberal 1980s.[5] While there is some truth in these generalizations, the neat dividing lines of decades obscure longer-term trends and continuities. As we move farther away from this part of our recent past, it becomes clearer that, if we want a convincing explanation for what happened in these years, we need to avoid what Michael Dawson and Catherine Gidney call "decaditis."[6]

This book also takes the view that many earlier histories, written by partisans of one view or another, do the post-war years an injustice. Although the radical political movements and general rebelliousness of the 1960s clearly represented a rupture with what came before, the general direction of these changes was presaged by similar developments in the 1950s. And while some partisans see the 1960s as a failed revolutionary moment, to frame the era primarily in this way is to see history mostly as a Marxist and counter-cultural quest for revolution that has continually failed to arrive. The fact that capitalism was not overthrown and that bourgeois society didn't explode into oblivion in the 1970s may be one way of seeing this era but it surely is not the most helpful.[7] Politics did not end in the 1970s. Even if one sticks to the priorities of the political left, it was actually in the 1970s and afterward that a host of movements radically altered Canadians' political consciousness – from the women's and environmental movements to gay liberation and beyond. As the American historian Thomas Borstelman writes, the 1970s saw the rise of "a spirit of egalitarianism and inclusiveness that rejected traditional hierarchies and lines of authority, asserting instead the equality of all people, particularly women, gays and lesbians, people of color, and the disabled – that is, the majority of people." Borstelman concludes that for Americans – and the same could be said of Canadians – "'the 1960s' really happened in the 1970s."[8]

Yet even this reading of the transition from the 1960s to the 1970s doesn't go far enough – it simply points out continuities in radical politics. The key change under way in these years – the "thinning out" of social discourse in a wash of radical individualism – did not so neatly fit into ideological categories.[9] Instead, these individualizing metaphors were taken up by those on both the right and the left of the political spectrum, albeit in different ways. For instance, the rise of neo-liberal market ideas and an attack on the welfare state and social-citizenship ideals in the 1970s actually shared a good deal in common with the radical anti-authoritarian politics espoused by those on the left at the same time. In Canada, the welfare state had been slow in arriving. There had been a long, hesitant development of state programs to counteract the failures of capitalism and modern urban-industrial society to meet the needs of all – with programs for mothers' allowances, benefits for veterans, and old age pensions (initially means-tested and later universally based on citizenship). Only in the 1960s did the key universal welfare-state programs emerge, especially universal health care. In the early 1970s other programs were seemingly on the immediate horizon, including universal daycare and perhaps a guaranteed minimum income. Yet all of these programs, as well as the ability of the state to act within the economy, came under attack in the 1970s.[10]

The long post-war boom dramatically came to an end in 1973 as the OPEC oil embargo combined with an overall economic downturn and rising unemployment. Yet inflation continued at a rampant pace and the combination of stagnant economic performance and high rates of inflation created the newfangled crisis of the era, stagflation. Economists and government planners struggled to make sense of what was happening and how to fix it – or whether governments even could play a role in doing so. In this context, the regulations of government and the social-citizenship goals of the welfare state came under attack by those who thought that what was needed was to free markets and individuals.

While this has often been presented as one of the key factors in diminishing the radicalism of the 1960s, that explanation no longer seems complete. It's true that the economic downturn forced many to tighten their belts. It was at this time that the Baby Boom youth, who had played such a key role in 1960s radicalism, reached their twenties and were obliged to look for work in tougher circumstances, to form families and to take on the responsibilities of life that made the radicalism of youth harder to sustain. Yet there are clear continuities in the rhetoric and priorities between the 1960s and the 1970s and between those on the left and those on the right. The egalitarian impulse for individual rights and the desire to overturn social constraints like conventional morality and prejudice found its right-wing counterpart in the radical individualism of neo-liberalism. As Borstelman puts it, "while sometimes at odds with each other, egalitarian values and market values converged to form a purified version of individualism and consumer capitalism, one in which all were welcome as buyers and sellers, but the devil might take the hindmost."[11]

This book draws on the work of a range of scholars who try (in different ways) to make sense of this overall trajectory of change in a way that isn't directly tied to one political project or another. The American intellectual historian Daniel T. Rodgers's *Age of Fracture* is especially helpful. Rodgers explores the intellectual atmosphere of the 1970s and 1980s, pointing out the way in which certain terms and ideas, certain metaphors of freedom and choice, spread across the cultural landscape and were picked up by those on both the left and right. He argues that a language that "had been thick with context, social circumstance, institutions, and history gave way to conceptions of human nature that stressed choice, agency, performance, and desire. Strong metaphors of society were supplanted by weaker ones. Imagined collectivities shrank; notions of structure and power thinned out. Viewed by its acts of mind, the last quarter of the century was an era of disaggregation, a great age of fracture." Here Rodgers links schools of thought not typically associated with each other, from the neo-liberalism of the Chicago School to the postmodern thought of Michel Foucault and critical feminist and anti-racist thinkers. He points out that the deregulation of markets urged by neo-liberal economists actually shared affinities with the radical social deregulation urged by counter-cultural critics of the 1960s. As he puts it, "deregulation was a radical project before it became a conservative one."[12]

Also important are the works of several conservative American historians and political scientists including Francis Fukuyama, James L. Nolan, Gertrude Himmelfarb, and James Lincoln Collier. Like Rodgers, these scholars have been concerned with tracing the way the individual's relationship to society and state changed over the second half of the twentieth century. These scholars largely decry the kinds of changes that they identify. For Himmelfarb, what happened was a "demoralization of society" in which older cultural values were thrown aside in favour of a demoralized and anything-goes radical individualism. Collier titles his work *The Rise of Selfishness in America*. He sets out to answer a series of questions: "How in the course of about the sixty years from 1910 to 1970 did a morality that seemed fixed and permanent get stood on its head? ... How did the United States turn from a social code in which self-restraint was a cardinal virtue to one in which self-gratification is a central idea, indeed ideal? How did we erect a moral code which has at its center the needs of the self – in which self-seeking is not merely condoned but actually urged upon us by philosophers, schools, television pundits, even governments?" Fukuyama calls the overall period of change the "great disruption." By this he means the way in which a radical individualism undermined social values and constraints, from family values and deference to legitimate authority, that had girded social and communal life in America for generations.[13]

In the Canadian scholarly context, these kinds of conservative perspectives have had little influence and the end result has been a diminished ability of scholars to characterize adequately the nature of cultural change in this era.[14] In Canadian scholarship, the tendency has been to decry the lack of radical change over the whole period and to focus consistently on thwarted movements for liberation. What gets lost is a real sense of how much had changed and why – exactly the issues that so concern conservative scholars. So, instead of focusing on the incredible rise in drug use in the 1960s, one of the few books on the topic explains how marijuana was not legalized. Works on the history of censorship, instead of noting the ever-widening scope of what was considered publishable, emphasize the continuities in moral regulation. Histories of gay and lesbian activism, instead of underlining the growth of acceptance and equality, focus on continued regulation and discrimination. In each case (and in other similar instances) it isn't so much that these scholars are incorrect on the details as that they miss the wider picture. They don't see the historical forest because their attention is trained on chopping down the few remaining trees that obscure the vista of the world as they wish it to be.[15]

One key Canadian figure who has traced some of these changes, and to whose work this book is indebted, is the philosopher Charles Taylor. In *Sources of the Self* and *The Malaise of Modernity* especially, Taylor has traced the rise of a culture of authenticity in the modern West that values self-affirmation, choice, and freedom. Unlike American conservatives, Taylor does not lament the changes he surveys (though he does point out the many downfalls of such an individual-oriented idea of what is good and true). He points to the longer-term trajectory of change, arguing that the culture of authenticity that had become so prominent in Canada by the 1970s and 1980s actually had its roots in Western Christianity and the Enlightenment. Yet he also acknowledges how the decades after the Second World War saw a radical speeding up of this culture of self-affirmation where notions of the good were bound up in valuing the experience of ordinary life.[16]

Each of these very different scholars and groups of scholars, including the philosopher Taylor with his roots in the New Democratic Party, the conservative Americans like Fukuyama and Himmelfarb, and the newer historians of the 1970s and 1980s like Borstelman and Rodgers, are pointing to the complex way in which a culture and language of the self and individualism grew steadily from the 1950s to the 1980s. Without denying the differences between decades and across the whole period, my book takes the position that this broader trajectory of change is worthy of scrutiny.

How does this connect to William Lyon Mackenzie King and the oddities of his private life – his table-rapping seances and his guilt-ridden carnal confessions, scribbled out in his diary? That is the subject of the book itself. Mackenzie King died in the summer of 1950. Over the next several decades – over just the period discussed above – his secret life would be revealed ever more fully in newspaper stories and books and documentaries. As each new story and anecdote made it into print, and as year followed year, Canadians responded to King's secret life ever more irreverently and openly, delving into the full story of who King had been. In the story of King's secret life, in other words, we see one particular example of the rise of an individualistic, therapeutic culture of the self and the odd consequences it had for the reputation of a prime minister who just happened to die, and have his secrets revealed, at a moment in history where self-revelation mattered profoundly.

There is a lesson here of a kind: be careful when you die. And burn your diaries.

❦

Although I've already mentioned them, they need now to reappear and to come first in this place where I acknowledge those who have helped in the writing of this book: my children. To say that Rowan, Finlay, Gilbert, and Arthur helped with the book might seem odd if one thinks only about efficiency. There is no doubt that the book would have been finished years earlier if not for them. But to live with this book and with these children over the last nine years has been to live a rich life indeed. Although I love my work and still marvel at the privilege of getting paid to read and write books and to talk about them, I also love the time away from the books, at the end of the day, in the middle of the day or, alas, in the middle of the night – whenever being a parent requires me to pay attention to life now and to those I love. The book took longer, but the life has been better.

The children, though, have lived not with one writer but with two. And I owe Juliet more thanks than a few words here can convey. But in this instance, I can at least say how much her wise counsel, keen eye for literary and grammatical detail, sharp intelligence, and soft, bright spirit have meant. Mackenzie King was unwise to have remained a bachelor.

I first started working on this book while I was teaching at the Institute for the Study of the Americas (ISA) at the University of London. It wasn't until after I had taken my first trip to the archives that I stopped to read the small historical plaque that hung behind the front door to one of the Bloomsbury mansion houses the Institute occupied on Tavistock Square. I was then more than a little amused to learn that the building I was working in had once been the home to the Society for Psychical Research – that body of pseudo-scientific spiritualists who wanted to believe in the possibility of communing with the dead but didn't want the whole enterprise to be ruined by the quacks. Mackenzie King would not have seen it as a coincidence.

But certainly this was a good place to begin, and the scholarly friendships there and in Canada have helped immensely along the way. In London, Phillip Buckner was a mentor and very good friend (which he remains). James Dunkerley was a model of what good university leadership looks like, and my other ISA colleagues were immensely helpful and gracious to their token Canadian who didn't know enough about Latin American or American history and politics.

At Trent University, many of my colleagues have provided smart advice and good companionship as I worked on the project. Special thanks go to John Wadland, John Milloy, Julia Harrison, Kevin Siena, Finis Dunaway, Dimitry Anastakis, Caroline Durand, Janet Miron, Carolyn Kay, Keith Walden, Jim Struthers, T.H.B. Symons, Michael Eamon, and Jennine Hurl-Eamon. In 2014–15 and 2015–16 I had the great pleasure of teaching the core class in the joint Trent University and Carleton University PhD in Canadian studies. The students in these classes, through their range of experiences and sharp questions, taught me a good deal, and I greatly benefited as well from the knowledge, intellectual curiosity, and generosity of my co-instructor, Peter Hodgins.

In the summer of 2011 I was the visiting professor of Canadian studies (sadly the last to occupy the post) at the Freie Universität's John F. Kennedy Institute in Berlin. I owe a great debt both to Petra Dolata for initial help and especially to my host Frauke Brammer. She didn't entirely know what she was getting in this professor who showed up in Berlin speaking no German and with very young children. But she and the Institute were paragons of good intellectual citizenship and a poignant example of what was lost when the Harper government cancelled the Understanding Canada program.

A number of archivists have helped me track down documents for a book that both was and wasn't about Mackenzie King. My thanks to the many, many archivists at Library and Archives Canada who have assisted me on my many trips to Ottawa. The archivists dealing with prime ministers and political papers, Maureen Hoogenrad and Michael MacDonald, have been especially helpful. My thanks also to George Henderson at Queen's University, Brian Hubner at the University of Manitoba Archives and Special Collections, the staff at the University of Calgary Archives, the University of Toronto Archives, the Cork County Archives in Ireland, and the Dalhousie University Archives.

Very early on, and then again a few years later, H. Blair Neatby agreed to sit down with me and give me his recollections about being

Mackenzie King's official biographer. This was especially kind. I'm grateful, too, to Graham Fraser and to John Ferns and Pat Ferns, all of whom helped me to understand their fathers a little better. Lynn McIntyre also agreed to speak to me about the psychobiography of Mackenzie King that she wrote as a student at the University of Toronto. And Lucile McGregor kindly spoke to me of her recollections of her grandfather.

When trying to figure out the oddities of RCMP Security Service records and when trying to get hold of the Operation Featherbed files which were open but which Library and Archives Canada somehow could not locate, two people with a good deal more experience in working with these records than me came to my help. My thanks to Reg Whitaker and Jim Bronskill.

In the project's early days, Pauline Harder worked as a research assistant, and her work was invaluable. Daniel Simeone provided very useful technical assistance and I still owe him more than one beer at least. Heather Graham and Chris Marsh raided western Canadian archives with digital cameras in hand, hence saving me time away from my family. I am very grateful that this work and other parts of the project were funded by the Symons Trust Fund for Canadian Studies, the Frost Centre for Canadian Studies at Trent University, a Trent University SSHRC Operating Grant, and a Faculty Research Grant from Foreign Affairs Canada.

I am grateful to several people who read parts of the manuscript, including Erika Dyck and, in the form of an article, Bryan Palmer and Finis Dunaway. A few others agreed to read the whole thing and for this I can't thank them enough, except to say that I probably didn't improve the manuscript nearly as much as their comments should have allowed. Thanks to Dimitry Anastakis, Jerry Bannister, and Tim Cook. The three anonymous readers gave model reviews which genuinely improved the book. I have presented parts of the work here to audiences at the University of Waterloo, Dalhousie University, Trent University, the University of Alberta, Brock University, University College London, the Canadian Historical Association, the J.F.K. Institute in Berlin, the University of Toronto, and the British Association of Canadian Studies in London. Several people have graciously played host to my talks and I want to thank particularly Ian Milligan, Shirley Tillotson, Dominique Clément, Tony McCulloch, Frauke

Brammer, and David Wilson. My editor at McGill-Queen's, Jonathan Crago, has been a champion of the project from the very beginning.

Quite a few years ago I picked up a copy of C.P. Stacey's *A Very Double Life: The Private World of Mackenzie King*. It was summertime and I was on a cross-country road trip, a short break before I finished my PhD dissertation. As I drove across Canada, reading about Mackenzie King's oddities as a way of not thinking about the dissertation, it occurred to me that there might be a different way to tell the story of Mackenzie King's secret life. Too many years later, it now seems clear that one ought to be careful when selecting what is supposed to be light summer reading.

Part One

King, Then and Later

1

Changing Tastes

Canada's greatest prime minister was a mama's boy. Not only that, he was a sexually repressed, hypocritical, ghost-talking, spiritualism-practising, guilt-ridden, prostitute-visiting mama's boy. Or so Canadians learned in 1976.

That was Mackenzie King's *annus horribilis*, when the "Weird Willie" phenomenon reached a climax amidst a mounting din from books, documentaries, poetry, newspaper stories, and radio shows exposing King's secret life. "Weird Willie" King seemed to be everywhere and he looked nothing like the staid, boring bachelor William Lyon Mackenzie King who had so dominated Canadian political life as prime minister and Liberal leader for most of the first half of the twentieth century.[1] Mackenzie King was dead. Long live "Weird Willie."[2]

No man did more to expose King's double life than Charles Perry Stacey. He was an odd figure to play the role of sensationalistic muck-raking biographer. In 1976 Stacey was a septuagenarian professor of history at the University of Toronto whose memoirs, when published several years later, revealed almost nothing about his own intimate life. Stacey had grown up in – and imbibed the values of – "Toronto the Good," that city of Sabbath observance, propriety, and closed curtains. He was a man for whom restraint, not unabashed confession, was a virtue. Stacey was also a figure of the historical establishment, having served as the official historian of the Canadian Armed Forces during the Second World War. Nothing in his life beforehand would have pegged Stacey as the figure who would write the tell-all exposé of Mackenzie King's private and often petty particularities.[3] Yet that is exactly what he did in the spring of 1976. His book *A Very Double*

Life: The Private World of Mackenzie King became the informational centre of the gossip storm whirling around the former prime minister's reputation. There were many novelists, poets, historians, and others who delivered up "Weird Willie" to the public in the mid-1970s, and most of these selected their juiciest bits from Stacey's *A Very Double Life*. It was quite a transformation for the aging historian.

But this was 1976 after all. Neither politics nor society was what it had been. Maggie Trudeau, the flower-child wife of the current prime minister, was about to sneak off to New York to party with the Rolling Stones as her marriage to Pierre Trudeau fell apart in full view of the nation he governed. An American president, Richard Nixon, and his vice-president, Spiro Agnew, had been forced to resign in disgrace after reporters exposed their illegal and corrupt behaviour. It wasn't just politics. The culture of exposé made normal the outing of secrets and the baring of previously taboo desires. In the 1950s, the "girly magazines" like *Playboy* had bookended their snapshots of topless women with essays on high culture and literature, a veneer of respectability to get them past the censors. Yet in the 1970s *Hustler* magazine eschewed the facade of respectability and made no attempt to hide its masturbatory purpose. The two cultures of exposé came together nowhere more clearly than in the Watergate scandal that brought down Richard Nixon. The top-secret source who leaked information to the reporters at the *Washington Post* was code-named "Deep Throat" – a reference to pornographic film that had achieved mainstream notoriety in 1972 and, of course, to oral sex. Outing the secrets of the powerful and exposing the secrets of the bedroom – they were of a piece. The mighty had fallen. What was secret had come into the open. The personal was political.[4]

For quite some time, it had been clear that Canada's longest-serving prime minister was a rather odd duck. Shortly after King died in 1950 stories leaked out claiming that he had been a practising spiritualist. The full extent of his ghost-talking beliefs – including whether he relied upon ghostly advice to make political decisions – remained a question for years, always downplayed by those who had been close to him. New reminiscences from King's former mediums occasionally heightened the speculation. In the early 1970s, Mackenzie King's literary executors released a large number of volumes of his personal diary. These confirmed and added detail to the rumours. But until now, the details had been tantalizing but sporadic. In *A Very Double Life* C.P. Stacey promised to answer all of these questions. Here was a respected historian who had taken the theme of King's private life and explored it in full, replete with direct citations and thoroughness, not to mention stylistic wit. Finally, Canadians were to learn the true story of Mackenzie King.[5]

The version of Mackenzie King that Stacey offered up in *A Very Double Life* could not have fit more perfectly with the ethos of the age. Stacey gave to Canadians "Weird Willie," the prime minister who "inhabited two worlds." One was "the world of public affairs," the part of King's life typically found in the history books. Yet King also lived another life in "his private world" and this had been hidden from the public. In his private world, King was utterly unlike his public image. King's private world "was often emotional and sometimes irrational." It was a world "of the women and the spirits."[6] King was not the man he claimed to be. Just like the politicians of the 1970s, the Richard Nixons of the world, King had secrets. While Nixon's secrets were exposed on the infamous White House tapes, Stacey uncovered Mackenzie King's secrets on the pages of his diary, so recently released to the public.

Stacey's King was a man who had practised odd forms of spirit communication, believing that the knocks he heard on seance tables were the voices of ghosts. King appeared pathetic as a middle-aged bachelor who couldn't commit to other women but who devoted himself to his mother, smothering her with seventy-four kisses on her seventy-fourth birthday – a level of physical attention that seemed altogether less innocent in the Freud-soaked 1970s than it had in 1917 when King had delivered the kisses. Stacey showed King as a bachelor who had always seemed staid and almost asexual but who in fact had visited prostitutes again and again as a young man. He had even gone on a stroll of Ottawa's streets looking for a woman after speaking to a church group one Sunday. As for King's claim that he visited the prostitutes to save their souls and bring them to Christ, Stacey would have none of it. Those protestations were for a more innocent, and more hypocritical, age. *A Very Double Life* retold how King succumbed to his carnal urgings with these women, only to rush back to his bedroom at night and scratch out guilty admissions in his diary about nights and money "wasted" and "worse than wasted."[7]

Stacey didn't deny King's political genius. Instead he offered a double image of the great man. Like a Picasso painting in which perspective is ripped asunder so that viewers can simultaneously see the visible and what would normally be hidden, *A Very Double Life* painted into King's public image the lurid view of King's private side, insisting that we view all of Mackenzie King simultaneously. The other books on the best-seller lists in the summer of 1976 included Bob Woodward and Carl Bernstein's exposé of the Watergate scandal, Joel Kovel's *The Complete Guide to Therapy*, and the American satirist Tom Wolfe's send-up of the narcissistic "Me Decade" republished in *Mauve Gloves & Madmen*. Secrecy, politics, therapeutic analysis, and narcissism: you could read about them separately, or you could just buy *A Very Double Life* and get them all in one slim little volume.[8]

It hadn't always been so. A generation earlier, a book like *A Very Double Life* would never have been published in Canada. The Canadians of this earlier era might have been just as curious about King's private life. They might even have gossiped about it privately, the journalists among them snickering about the "medium" of King's communications in side-long remarks in newspaper columns. But for a respectable press to have published an entire book on the peculiarities of a statesman would have been unthinkable.[9] Stacey admitted as much as he talked to reporters when launching *A Very Double Life*. "Twenty years ago," he reflected, "I can't imagine myself having written a book like this." Yet he had done so. The world of 1976 made it possible. As Stacey put it, "tastes had changed."[10]

Gossip is eternal; its meaning isn't. Over the course of this book we will follow how the "changing tastes" of post-war Canada made possible the revelations of Mackenzie King's secret life.

The stops on our journey are various. We will watch as the popularization of Freud's ideas in the 1950s caused new terms and assumptions to seep across the pages of books, letters, and magazines.

The light soaking of the 1950s became a Freudian flood as the 1960s turned into the 1970s and a culture of introspection, self-analysis, and glorified inhibition increasingly challenged earlier Victorian-rooted ideas of morality and restraint. Freud was joined by other thinkers like Carl Jung or popular-science figures like Margaret Mead and her celebration in the press of the less inhibited, more open sexuality of the Polynesian peoples she studied. Parenting experts like Dr Benjamin Spock in the United States and William Blatz in Canada became conduits for a more psychological and less overtly moralistic view of human nature.

These kinds of ideas didn't just stick to their own realms. They spread from one area to another, from parenting advice to politics. They showed up in how people talked about Mackenzie King. Here the differences between different forms of psychological thought (whether Freudian or Jungian or otherwise) mattered less than the rising importance of the individual as the central feature of society and ultimate source of any claim to truth. The test of veracity increasingly became individualized – truth meant being true to yourself. This was spelled out nowhere more clearly than in a blockbuster film at the end of this era. In the 1980 film *The Empire Strikes Back*, the villain Darth Vader reveals that he is the father of Luke Skywalker. How is Luke to know if this is true? "Search your feelings, Luke," Vader tells him. "You know it to be true." The filmmakers may have mangled the sophistication of expert thought, but the gist of the change was clear. Truth resided not in tradition or authority but in the self and how one felt.[11]

We will also watch how the world of journalism changed and the small, clubby, more deferential Ottawa press corps of King's years was shaken up by the growth in the size of the media, the introduction of television with its facade of authenticity and immediacy, and the rise of investigative journalism with its egalitarian assumptions about the need to know what really happened behind closed doors. More generally, coarser, less deferential sensibilities slowly spread across the Canadian cultural landscape. A human-rights revolution transformed how Canadians thought about politics and how they were governed. By the early 1970s, every province had human-rights codes and by 1982 the country had a Charter of Rights and Freedoms in its constitution. Such developments added an assertiveness to the politics of the era that challenged those in authority to deal fairly and equitably with all kind of individuals and their rights.

These developments changed the kinds of stories that appeared in newspapers, the novels and poetry Canadians wrote and read, the jokes they told, and the television they watched. These broader transformations played out in King's own story. The nudge-nudge, wink-wink satire of the 1950s became edgier and more daring through the following decades. These were manifestations of a culture of individual rights: a more raucous and assertive questioning of authority that openly poked into what might previously have mattered only privately.

Each of these changes – the coarsening of public speech, the more demanding journalism, the rise of a culture of individual rights, the emphasis on authenticity and finding oneself, the spread of Freudian and psychological language – was part of a cultural shift in which a psychological and individualistic rights-based culture of the self came to exert greater force over how Canadians talked and thought from the 1950s to the 1980s. This pronounced individualism did not go uncontested. Some would argue that the 1980s witnessed a backlash against it. Yet if we look at the language of public speech – at the idea of what could and should be said publicly – in 1976 when Stacey published *A Very Double Life* and compare it to 1950 when King died, the change could not be more obvious.

Tastes had changed considerably and this book is an explanation of how this happened and why it came to matter both to the story of Mackenzie King and to Canadian politics more broadly.

Yet, if part of the story told here is this broader pattern of cultural change, the other story concerns King's diary itself. In order for Canadians to reassess King, they first had to learn about his bizarre life. The most damning evidence of King's double life came from his own hand, in the form of his diary. Ever since his days as a young student at the University of Toronto in 1893, Mackenzie King had kept a daily log of his thoughts and actions. With only a few breaks early in his life, King kept up the practice until three days before he died in the summer of 1950. For much of his life, King wrote by hand in a spidery script that is almost impossible to decipher. In 1935 the busy prime minister began dictating the diary to an assistant who would later type up the entries and place them in binders. From that point onward, the entries ballooned in size. The Mackenzie King diary spans fifty-seven years and runs to thousands of pages. It is probably the most complete record of a politician's life that we will ever possess. But how did we get it?

King's wishes in his final will and testament seemed clear: he dictated that the diary was to be destroyed except for those portions that he indicated were to be preserved.[12] At the time of his death, King had not specified in writing that anything be kept. The entire diary was to be destroyed. Yet it certainly wasn't. In fact, today, anyone in the world with an Internet connection can browse freely through the digitized version of its entire contents. Are you wondering what Mackenzie King did after dinner on 3 February 1901? Search by date and you can find out.[13] Perhaps you're curious about what Mackenzie King wrote about his political nemesis Arthur Meighen. A keyword search on this or any other topic will bring you what you want. It is all there to be read freely. How did this happen? How did King's secrets come to be exposed so fully?[14]

After King's death, a team of literary executors had to decide the fate of the prime minister's infamous diary as well as all of his papers. The literary executors were establishment figures and Liberals alike. They were the kind of pragmatic nation builders who helped create the federal civil service in the middle years of the twentieth century. Some of these men admired King. One called him a friend, while others had no fondness for him at all. Still they accepted the obligation and honour of overseeing access to the literary estate of Canada's longest-serving prime minister. None of them quite knew what to do with the diary in all of its bizarre variety.[15]

Over the course of the next two decades, these men would grapple with their obligation to King – both to his place in historical memory and to his desire for privacy. The bumps on the road were many. King's literary executors attempted to hush up former spiritualist mediums who wanted to expose King's ghost-talking ways; they attempted to catch someone who had stolen copies of the King diary and sold them on the black market; a pivotal copy of the King diary would go missing and end up being the subject of RCMP Security Service investigations into Soviet espionage and infiltration of the top levels of Canadian government in the Cold War. Two of the literary executors would die before their job was done. The official biography would become an ever longer and more drawn-out project after the death of one biographer and the tortuous path to publication taken by others. Ultimately the literary executors would open King's diary to the public and opt for preservation and not destruction. Yet the path to making this decision was a long and sometimes odd one. It might not have happened as it did. The story of King's secret life is, in large part, the story of how his diary eventually came to be opened for our scrutiny.

In July 1950, though, all of this was in the future. As the Canadian government led by Louis St Laurent debated whether to send the nation to war in Korea, former prime minister Mackenzie King had retired to his country home outside Ottawa for the last time. When news came over the radio that the former prime minister was ill, what did Canadians know and think of this man who had governed Canada for longer than any other? To his contemporaries, who was Mackenzie King?

2

Death of a Statesman

When a man is prime minister for almost twenty-two years, the nation cannot help but react to his death. As one newspaper put it, "he was Prime Minister of Canada for so many years that boys and girls grew up without realizing that conceivably somebody else could fill that post."[1] In our current age, when political leaders are selected and disposed of like T-shirts on the sale racks, it is hard to comprehend the longevity of Mackenzie King. The only man who has come even close to King's record in the last seventy years is Pierre Trudeau, a man who divided even as he united the country, and at whose death the population responded with sharply divergent sentiments, some with profound respect, others muttering their long-held resentments.[2]

Late on a hot July Saturday night in 1950, a sombre-voiced announcer came over the radio to inform the nation that Mackenzie King had died. Grant Dexter, the Ottawa correspondent for the *Winnipeg Free Press*, heard the news as he popped into a store. Looking at the other customers, he listened as they talked about King and noticed that they didn't seem to be criticizing anything about "his life or the things he had done." It could just have been the usual hushed deference for the dead, though he wondered if "perhaps it was something more favourable than that." Dexter didn't know. He just knew that they were calling him a "great Canadian."[3]

On Monday, when everyone went back to work, and the newspapers gave their first draft of history, this too was their assessment. Even Tory papers held in check their usual partisan ire and reflected on the significance of Mackenzie King as statesman. For this was an era that still believed in the idea of the statesman, the public leader who came from the people but who rose above them. This is how most papers across the country, east and west, French and English, chose to remember Mackenzie King, as "a great Canadian."

"Next to Confederation itself," intoned the *Globe and Mail*, "no single factor has been more significant" in the shaping of "national affairs" than the career of Mackenzie King.[4] The Tory *Ottawa Journal* admitted that "Mr. KING ... was actuated in all his public acts by a deep concern for the good of the Canadian people ... He was a great Canadian, a world figure, and a very human figure as well. He was MACKENZIE KING of Canada, and we shall not see his like again."[5]

Canada in 1950, at the end of the Mackenzie King era, stood higher in the world than it had a generation earlier. Five years after the end of the Second World War, a war in which Canadians had fought fiercely and with distinction, and a war which had been followed by economic boom and not recession, the nation found itself more confident and more assertive in its collective identity. The death of Mackenzie King made commentators look back and appreciate the national achievements since King had first entered office.

It mattered what others thought. The newspapers prominently re-published the praise of foreign dignitaries. What did the British prime ministers Winston Churchill and Clement Attlee have to say about the Canadian prime minister? What about the American president Harry Truman, or India's first prime minister, Jawaharlal Nehru? The favourite pictures to publish included the images of King as wartime leader: King with Roosevelt, or King with Churchill, or better yet King with Roosevelt *and* Churchill. One caption showing the leaders at the Quebec Conference of 1943 in the *Globe* read: "Mr King not only acted as host for the parley but took an active role in the discussions."[6] This stretched the truth considerably. In fact, King and the Canadian delegation had been little more than furniture for photo-ops at the conference. King showed up smiling to pose for the camera, then the American and British leaders sent him away while they decided strategy. King largely accepted Canada's exclusion from strategic talks, afraid of the international commitments that they might involve. Yet the truth remained hidden, and Canadians could peruse these images at the time of King's death as symbols of Canada's rising place in the world, oblivious to the real story.[7]

Numbers speak. And when it was announced that King would lie in state in the foyer of the houses of Parliament, Canadians came in

2.1 Mackenzie King lying in state.

large numbers. Over a little more than a day and a half, close to forty thousand lined up for hours in the midsummer heat for a chance to shuffle into the cool interior of Centre Block and past the former prime minister. King lay in an open coffin surrounded on four corners by a member each of the Navy, Air Force, Army, and RCMP. So many came that officials kept the building open later into the night so that no one would be turned away and everyone could have a chance to pay their respects. The prime minister arrived early to pay his respects along with a group of nuns. Yet the newspapers wanted it known that in the crowd that lined up to view King "there was no distinction of age or rank or occupation. Parents brought their children, some of them in arms. Teen-agers arrived in slacks. Laborers came from their jobs in their working clothes. Priests and clerics of all denominations mingled in that never-ending stream."[8]

2.2 Mackenzie King with Roosevelt and Churchill

What did these men and women, these boys and girls, think of as they walked past the still body of Mackenzie King? Even supportive journalists admitted that it seemed likely "there was no deep sense of personal loss." Yet there did seem to be "something else; a feeling of sadness over the ending of a life of public service."[9] One woman noticed that "people who for years had criticized, condemned and often bewailed his existence, suddenly pulled up short when he died … suddenly realized, perhaps for the first time, that there was a man who had poured himself out unsparingly for Canada; had held its destiny in his hands for years. They realized that Mr. King had become a symbol of nationhood."[10]

After King's funeral, crowds lined up to watch the political elite of Canada march in ceremony down Wellington Street past the Chateau Laurier and into Union Station. As the RCAF band filled the station with the sounds of "Nearer My God to Thee," that Protestant anthem of mournful, hopeful death, the song many believed to have been the last played on board the *Titanic* as it sank into the north Atlantic, Mackenzie King left Ottawa for the last time.[11] The dignitaries departed on a train for Toronto where King was to be buried alongside the scions of the Canadian elite at Mount Pleasant Cemetery. As the train travelled across eastern Ontario, "the people were standing at every station, crossroad, village and farmhouse, bare-headed paying their last respects."[12]

Critics privately sneered at the whole operation. Conservative Party leader George Drew thought, not without reason, that King had organized it all himself and called it a "revolting spectacle." King's former nemesis, Arthur Meighen, wrote privately how "the State funeral was put on with the same thoroughness and much the same purpose as a General Election."[13] Certainly King never left anything to chance, and had been known to fuss over the intricate details of many state occasions and dinners – flower arrangements and menus, seating plans and dinnerware. This was one of the reasons so many political men disliked him, or refused to take him entirely seriously. A statesman ought not to trifle with what they thought of as feminine trivialities. John Stevenson, the former London *Times* correspondent in Ottawa, thought that most of those who queued up to see King or to watch his funeral procession were American tourists. Certainly the "majority of them [were] women,"[14] he wrote, as if this somehow made their show of sympathy less significant.

Still, in public, it wouldn't do to be so impolite. The aftermath of death muffles dissent, beckons a soft reply. And then there was the fact that Mackenzie King had won all those elections. Never personally popular, Mackenzie King had nevertheless won the support of the nation and its parliamentarians more often and for longer than anyone else in history. Gossip and bitterness were for private conversations. In the pages of newspapers and on the radio, Mackenzie King was a statesman.

Yet who really was Mackenzie King? In 1950, when the newspapers recalled for the nation who Mackenzie King had been, what did they know and think about this former prime minister? Decades later, he would be "Weird Willie," the prime minister who, as Dennis Lee put it in *Alligator Pie*, "loved his mother like anything" and "sat in the middle and played with string." But in 1950, at the end of his long life, what did Mackenzie King mean to the Canadian public?

Mackenzie King was born to be a Liberal prime minister. At least, it could seem that way.[15] King was the grandson and namesake of William Lyon Mackenzie, the leader of the failed Upper Canada rebellions of 1837 and 1838. King wanted to recover the family reputation. Years later, he proudly hung on the wall of his office the offer of reward for his grandfather, traitor to Queen Victoria. When King, the rebel's grandson, became prime minister and a member of His Majesty's Privy Council, the family was redeemed. At the time that King entered politics, though, it's not clear how much this mattered to contemporaries. After all, almost a century had passed since the rebellions. Passion faded. Animosity and disrepute slipped away, leaving only the young Mackenzie King with the benefit of a name that was already mentioned in the history books.

Mackenzie King had been engaged in public affairs from a young age. During his lifetime several sycophantic biographies had been published by admirers and Liberals, sometimes secretly with King's direct aid. These presented the young King as an earnest and morally upright striver, a man born for a life of public service. He was a devoted Presbyterian who regularly attended church throughout his life. More importantly, he took seriously the moral strictures of late Victorian Canada that called on young men to be hard-working, abstinent, patient, self-denying, and disciplined. He volunteered his time reading to children in Toronto's Hospital for Sick Children. He attempted to rescue unfortunate "ladies of the night" by conversing with them earnestly, introducing them to the right companions, and extolling the message of the Protestant faith. King took an active role in student politics and was a key figure in a famous student strike at the University of Toronto. Or, at least, this was the version of his life portrayed in the early biographies.

King first made his mark in the wider world as a labour negotiator and expert on class turmoil. The turn of the century was a time of violent labour unrest and social tumult, when the massive transformations being wrought by industrialization seemed to be changing life in North America from the bottom up. Mackenzie King wanted to be at the forefront of responding to the crisis of class conflict and social need. After finishing his BA, he searched for the right future, finishing several university degrees in quick succession and going on to the University of Chicago to spend time at the famous Hull House, one of the birthplaces of modern social work. King rejected the radical arguments of contemporary socialists. Instead, he found his own thinking to be more shaped by Christian morality and moderate reform. He began a PhD at Harvard on these topics but would not finish the degree for a decade. The call of service to Canada interrupted his career.

While doing research in London, he received an offer from William Mulock, postmaster general in Wilfrid Laurier's cabinet and a King family friend. In 1900 the Laurier government intended to create a new Department of Labour, with Mulock as its first head. Mulock invited King to return to Canada and take up a post as deputy minister of the new department and editor of the newly created *Labour Gazette*. The young King had to decide between a scholarly life and the more immediate and practical career of public service. King chose to work in Canada's capital at the heart of power.

The young Mackenzie King soon made a name for himself as a competent and ambitious administrator. Criss-crossing the country by train, he waded into tense labour negotiations, armed with the message of conciliation. What was needed, King urged, was for labour and capital to come together in a process of open discussion alongside himself as the spokesperson for the government and wider community. Before any strike could occur, King believed, there should be a cooling-off period where both sides were presented with the facts of the situation by a neutral third party. His efforts in various strikes across the country led to government legislation mandating this kind of pre-strike conciliation.

In 1908 King left the civil service behind and ran for elected office, with the promise that, should he win, he would take up a seat in cabinet as minister of labour. He did win, and at the cabinet table Mackenzie King proved himself to be just as effective a junior minister as he had been a deputy minister. But in the government of Wilfrid Laurier, in power since 1896, other senior voices carried more authority. In 1911 the Laurier government mistakenly went to the people with a plan for reciprocity with the United States and went down to defeat. King found himself without a job.

King did not volunteer for military service during the Great War, and did not take up any kind of civilian posting connected to the war. His laudatory biographers tried to present what he did do as a form of service for the war effort. For King had accepted an offer in 1914 to go to the United States as a labour expert at the request of John D. Rockefeller, who found himself embroiled in controversy because of a violent strike at mines in Colorado owned by his family. At a time of massive labour turmoil, King applied himself to the task of achieving workplace peace. He earned a substantial salary but tried to protect himself from the charge that he served the moneyed interests by working for the charitable Rockefeller Foundation and not the Rockefellers directly. He was officially hired to conduct research into industry and labour relations in the modern world.

The war came to Mackenzie King anyway. King had insisted to the Rockefellers that he would not give up his political prospects in Canada. He secured the Liberal nomination in York North, the riding associated with his grandfather. Like everyone else, he watched as the war tore apart the political certainties of the nation. No issue hurt more than conscription. Farmers resented losing their sons to the dying fields of Europe. Labour unions complained about the conscription of labour when the state did not conscript capital. But as month followed month in the Great War, as the list of dead mounted, as the blinded, limbless, and disfigured veterans returned home, and still the war raged on with no sign of end let alone victory, the call for conscription came louder. Equality of sacrifice. If my son is to die, why does yours remain safe at home? That, and the rumours. Why did French Canadians not volunteer in the same numbers as English Canadians? The details did not matter – the fact that most who initially signed up had actually been born in Britain, or the inadequacy of recruitment staff in Quebec. Such statistical clarity, such reason, rarely found a place in the rhetoric of war.

The nation, and the Liberal Party, broke apart in 1917. The Conservative prime minister, Robert Borden, formed a Union government of pro-conscriptionists, inviting Liberals and Conservatives alike to join him in a coalition that would wage the war to the fullest. The election of 1917 was fought over the issue and it left Laurier leading a small rump of a party and most of Quebec isolated and unrepresented in government. The federal government sent its police across the country, into towns and villages, knocking on doors, traipsing through woods and fields, hunting men who fled conscription. The worst moment came on Easter Sunday 1918, a year after the battle for Vimy Ridge, as anti-conscriptionists rioted and clashed with Canadians troops at home. A race war. Everything Canadian governments had for years tried to avoid. And ultimately the Conservative Party would pay the price.

In the short run, the Unionists won and Mackenzie King went down to defeat in York North. Yet loyalty was rewarded. When Wilfrid Laurier died in 1919, and with the war over, the Liberals decided to hold the then untested process of a convention for the purpose of selecting a new leader. Although the Unionist Liberals were now back in the party, the animosity of their wartime departure had not disappeared. King ran for the leadership. His anti-conscriptionist record meant that he could present himself as someone who had stayed true to Laurier. That, plus his youth and his expertise in conciliating labour issues, a key issue in 1919, made him an attractive candidate. With significant support from Quebec, King ultimately triumphed against his main opponent, W.S. Fielding, who had joined the Union government.

In 1921 King came to power, defeating the Conservatives under the leadership of Arthur Meighen, the man who bore the brunt of the public's disgruntlement about the wartime government. In the early 1920s the country was divided as never before. A farmers' movement had taken off in the midst of the war, rooted in resentment against high tariffs and a general distrust of the political system and main-stream political parties. Farmers' governments took power in Alberta (1921) and Ontario (1919). In 1921, under the loose banner of the Progressives, the farmers took fifty-eight seats in Canada's House of Commons, the second most seats of any party – though because the Progressives derided the political system they refused to take on what they saw as the sullied role of Official Opposition.

For Mackenzie King, the task was to unite the country under the banner of the Liberal Party. He had no patience for Conservatives, whom he viewed, as he did throughout his life, as the enemy. But the Progressives he saw simply as Liberals who had temporarily gone astray. His governments of the 1920s tried to bring the Progressives, and the Canadians they represented, back into the Liberal fold. These governments were known for their modest efficiency – competent if unambitious. King had promised much in the Liberal Party platform that came out of the 1919 leadership convention, heralding the creation of a host of welfare-state programs. In office, King's Liberals proved more tentative, concerning themselves with balancing the budget and paying off the debt.

King's great achievement of the 1920s came in international affairs. In later years, King could claim to have asserted Canada's independent stance on the world stage as a part of the British Commonwealth of Nations yet not as a subservient partner to Britain itself. Canada had achieved responsible government in domestic affairs as far back as the 1840s. In fact, King believed that his own grandfather had played no small part in this development by leading a rebellion whose intent was Canadian control over Canadian affairs. When Mackenzie King came to power in 1921 he took up the family fight for Canadian autonomy, but this time in international affairs.

This is the story of Canada's rise from "colony to nation," as one textbook of the 1940s had it. It is a complicated tale, fascinating to some historians but rarely to others. It is a story of pragmatism and compromise, of halfway measures and divided loyalties, a story of two steps forward and, it often seemed, two steps back. The highlights included John A. Macdonald's efforts to participate in British treaty negotiations, the Laurier government's decision to build a tiny Canadian navy, and the separate Canadian signature on the Treaty of Versailles that ended the Great War (even if Canada signed not as a fully independent nation but in a small rubric set off under the British signatures).

When Mackenzie King came to power, then, he grabbed a baton of national self-control that had already been passed from hand to hand, Conservative to Liberal and back again. The race he ran over the next three decades pushed the colony ever farther on the road to nationhood. Many commentators, on both left and right though especially in the centre, and particularly in Quebec, gave King credit. Arthur Lower, author of *Colony to Nation*, called King "the architect of Canada's present position of national independence."[16] *Saturday Night* editor B.K. Sandwell thought this had been one of the constant impulses in King's career, his conviction "that the colonies of the United Kingdom could not continue to be colonies, and that the only alternative was that they should become nations."[17]

How did King push Canada into nationhood? If the ending seemed heroic, the route travelled often gave little indication of impending glory. There was King's refusal to commit Canadian troops in the Chanak Crisis of 1922 when it appeared that Britain might go to war against Turkey. There were the negotiations in the imperial conferences of 1923 and 1926 that ultimately led to the equality and independence of the dominions within the British Commonwealth of Nations. The Statute of Westminster in 1931 made law what King had pushed for in the Balfour Declaration that followed from the 1926 Imperial Conference. The Balfour Declaration put it thus: that the British dominions like Canada and Australia were "autonomous Communities within the British Empire, equal in status, in no way subordinate one to another in any aspect of their domestic or external affairs, though united by a common allegiance to the Crown, and freely associated as members of the British Commonwealth of Nations."

In this story of Liberal-led Canadian autonomy, the King-Byng controversy of 1926 symbolized how King stood up for Canada's newly independent status. In the 1925 election King was returned with fewer seats than the Conservatives but he clung to power with the tenuous support of a much diminished number of Progressives and a few Labour MPs. Governor General Byng believed that King should resign and let Arthur Meighen, the man whose party controlled the most seats in the House of Commons, try to form a government. King refused to step down and managed to govern for several months with the help of the Progressives. Eventually, though, as claims of corruption relating to customs officials swirled around the government, King was forced to resign or face the censure of Parliament. King wanted to go to the people in an election but the governor general would not allow it. He claimed that Meighen should now have his chance to govern. King reluctantly handed over power to Meighen and then did everything possible to make sure that Meighen's position was untenable. This proved to be the case as Meighen's government lasted only a few days. Byng then acceded to Meighen's request to dissolve Parliament and hold an election.

In that election of 1926 King brilliantly campaigned on the issue of British interference in Canadian affairs. He charged that the governor general had picked sides, allowing the Tory Meighen but not the Liberal King to dissolve Parliament and call an election. It was the battle of responsible government all over again, the fight King believed his grandfather had led in the rebellions, and King masterfully (if dishonestly) turned the issue into a winning strategy. The constitutional issue obscured what had seemed to be the more pressing concern about corruption in his own government. He was returned to power with a majority government, holding office until 1930 when, just as the harsh realities of the Depression were sinking into the Canadian consciousness, he was defeated by R.B. Bennett.

Nine years is a respectable length of time at the helm of any country and political parties in our era would think it sufficient. When R.B. Bennett trounced the Liberals in 1930, any contemporary party would have sent its leader packing, and most leaders would have known this and resigned before being forced out. Not Mackenzie King; not in 1930. King held on to office during the Bennett years, even enduring a humiliating scandal when it was revealed that his party had accepted huge donations, and King himself large personal gifts, from a business syndicate trying to win government favours. King called this his "Valley of Humiliation." But he stayed on his feet and walked through the valley and out into the sunshine of the hill beyond in the form of the 1935 election. Overturning a sitting government in the midst of the Great Depression was not altogether a difficult task and King's Liberals accomplished it. Several new smaller parties splintered the popular vote, leaving Mackenzie King's Liberals with much the same support they had garnered in 1930 but this time with a majority government.

In the second half of the 1930s, the King government tried to drag Canada out of the economic doldrums, only very belatedly turning to a tentative form of economic stimulus based on the ideas then being touted by the British economist John Maynard Keynes. By 1937, it had also become clear that Europe was headed yet again to war and King hesitantly braced the nation for what this might mean, especially on the front of national unity. Like British Prime Minister Neville Chamberlain, King hoped that appeasing Hitler would work. But he also vowed that, should it not, Canada would be at Britain's side. This time, however, it would be Canadians themselves, in the form of Canada's Parliament, who would decide when or whether the nation would go to war.

When Hitler invaded Poland in the autumn of 1939, Canada declared war and King, who was then sixty-six years old, became a wartime prime minister. King won re-election in March 1940 on a commitment to fight a limited war with no overseas conscription. However, with the German advances in the spring of 1940 and the fall of France, everything changed. Britain and its Empire alone stood against Hitler's Germany. The neutral Americans remained to one side, unwilling to commit. The King government quickly put Canada on the path to total war, mobilizing all of the resources possible to support Britain in its fight. Yet, on the old issue of conscription, King was faced with a potential political crisis that could have ruined him.

In the family of Canada as it was at mid-century, there were a few topics guaranteed to disrupt and perhaps spoil any holiday dinner. One, the proper proportion of British pepper and American salt in the Canadian dish, Mackenzie King handled with expert ease. The second, and even more volatile, topic was the relation between French- and English-speaking Canadians – what many in the first half of the twentieth century called the "race question." For many, King's handling of French-English relations, especially in relation to conscription, proved his political genius.

This bitter feud between French and English Canadians over the issue of conscription in the Great War had greeted King as he became leader of the Liberal Party. King won the leadership in no small part owing to his loyalty to Laurier and his stance against conscription. The issue had divided the party but the Liberals also made sure that it helped them to win elections. Part of the reason the conscription issue threatened to be so dangerous again in the Second World War is that Quebec Liberals made sure, at every election in the 1920s and 1930s, that voters didn't forget it. This was easy in the elections of 1921, 1925, and 1926. For who led the Conservative Party but Arthur Meighen, the *diable Anglais* himself, the man in the Borden cabinet responsible for the conscription law? The journalist André Laurendeau later recalled that, even in the elections of the 1930s, Liberal politicians hit the hustings calling Bennett simply another Empire-loving Tory like Borden or Meighen. The memory of conscription still burned in the mind of the Quebec voter. As Laurendeau put it: "How, moreover, could he have forgotten, when he was reminded of it at every election?"[18]

Mackenzie King probably knew very little of the details of electioneering in Quebec. He soon came to trust his Quebec lieutenant

Ernest Lapointe, who represented the King government in the province. When Lapointe died in late 1941, King lured the corporate lawyer Louis St Laurent to Ottawa to take his place. On issue after issue, King avoided new policies that might have been viewed with disfavour in Quebec – holding back on social policy lest it interfere with provincial jurisdiction, not disallowing the infamous and illiberal Padlock Law of Maurice Duplessis.

In 1939 King promised the nation that he would not impose conscription, and he made the same promise again in the federal election of March 1940. Yet the fall of France in 1940 forced King to qualify this promise. The government passed the National Resource Mobilization Act (NRMA), registering all Canadians fit for military service, but with one important caveat. If called upon, conscripts would serve only within Canada. Yet this promise could not hold.

The bifurcated nature of the French-English Canadian reality is probably nowhere more clear than in the conscription crisis of the Second World War. The crisis refers to different events in Quebec than in the rest of Canada. When André Laurendeau wrote *La crise de la conscription*, he saw the height of the crisis as the events of 1942, when the King government held a plebiscite asking to be released from its promise not to impose conscription for overseas service. A series of events in late 1941 and early 1942 had transformed the nature of the war. Internationally, the bombing of Pearl Harbor and other American and British bases in the Pacific by the Japanese made the conflict truly global. It brought the Americans into the war, and it also exposed Canada's west coast to attack. Domestically, Ernest Lapointe, the voice of Quebec in the national government, had recently died. At just this point, the Conservative Party coaxed Arthur Meighen to come back as leader. He and other Conservatives went on a national campaign calling for a unity government of all parties and the imposition of equal sacrifice through conscription.

King responded by calling a national plebiscite. The question, awkwardly and indirectly worded as most missives were from King, asked Canadians if they would release the government from its pledge not to impose conscription. This is the conscription crisis in the public memory of Quebec – the moment when the King government went back on its word – on King's repeated promises not to impose conscription for overseas service. The results of the plebiscite showed

2.3 Mackenzie King inspecting the troops.

a nation divided. It revealed, as Lord Durham wrote about the Canadas of the 1830s, "two nations at war in the bosom of a single state." Quebec voted overwhelmingly against releasing the government from its pledge (79 per cent) while the other provinces voted overwhelmingly to allow the government the freedom of action to impose conscription.

King now became as cunning as he would ever be. He held off calls from within his government to see the plebiscite results as a clear mandate for conscription. Instead, he modified the NRMA to allow for overseas service of conscripts, but only if the government and Parliament deemed this necessary. As yet the government did not deem it necessary. It was then that King uttered the words for which he has become best remembered: "not necessarily conscription, but conscription if necessary."[19] For a Quebec nationalist like Laurendeau, it was only a matter of time until the final blow came and the government imposed conscription. Still, King managed to find a middle ground. No conscript had yet been sent overseas.

In English Canada, the height of the conscription crisis came two years later in the autumn of 1944. Until this point in the war, Canadian involvement in actual combat hadn't been extensive enough to challenge the voluntary system. With the June 1944 D-Day landings, though, came the heaviest and most intense combat in Europe. The push northward through France and into Belgium exacted a heavy toll. Defence Minister J.L. Ralston visited the troops in the autumn of 1944, and he came back to Ottawa with reports from his generals that the forces needed to be replenished and that the number of volunteers would not be sufficient. The final push at the end of 1944 and into 1945 would bring even more casualties. Already, units were fighting under-strength, making them not only less effective but endangering the lives of soldiers. Now, Ralston said, conscription really was necessary.

Mackenzie King resisted this advice almost unto the end. When the cabinet met, King insisted that the government try yet again to get more volunteers. Ralston agreed to this but wanted it guaranteed that, should the recruitment drive fail, the government would impose conscription. The issue threatened to bring down the government.

Years later, when some of King's cabinet ministers and political journalists said that King could be ruthless, they usually had in mind this moment. When Ralston demanded his guarantee, King drew forth a letter of resignation that Ralston had penned two years earlier – in 1942 – in the midst of the last crisis. King had rejected Ralston's resignation offer then, but he had kept the letter. King quietly but firmly said that he now accepted Ralston's resignation – a resignation Ralston had not in fact offered.

To take Ralston's place, King had secretly recruited General Andy McNaughton, the former head of the Canadian Army overseas, a man whose commitment to the "boys overseas" no one could question. The men at the cabinet table sat in stunned silence. No one had seen this coming. King had essentially just fired one of the most important figures in the Canadian government, and the man most responsible for its war effort.

What would Ralston do? Did he shout in anger? Did he threaten to begin a revolt of the pro-conscription Liberals and form a Union government? The fate of the government and the nation hung on his next moves. If he had decided to do so, it is very likely that he could have toppled King's government and, along with the Conservatives, formed a coalition government. Ralston did none of this. He quietly rose from his seat, shook hands with the other men around the table, and left the room. The man who could have broken the government, the man whom, as many of his colleagues saw it, Mackenzie King stabbed in the back, did not flinch. The Christian gentleman, for the good of his party, and the nation, turned the other cheek.

Despite all of Mackenzie King's cunning, though, neither he nor his newly recruited defence minister could convince enough NRMA men – "zombies" as the public called them – to switch from reserve duty to active service. Within two weeks, General McNaughton reported to King that he didn't have the numbers. It was exactly as Ralston had said. At this final juncture, Mackenzie King conceded defeat – and just in time. Other ministers in cabinet had been meeting to prepare letters of resignation and to topple the government. Canada, in the second great war of the twentieth century, decided once again to force its citizens to serve in combat for their country.

As awkward and stumbling as King's policies seemed day by day, in retrospect they came to be seen as his greatest legacy. Only one cabinet minister resigned, and the government carried on. The country did not fall apart. There was no repeat of the Easter riots from the Great War. King had kept the nation united. The praise of King always came in half-measures, with qualifications, but praise it was. "As a war minister," Arthur Lower said of King, "he did well, but plenty of other men would have organized the country better; some might have inspired it; few [would] not have divided it."[20] On conscription, Blair Fraser put it succinctly, "Neither side liked it; both put up with it."[21]

During the war King had led a government of able ministers, balancing the conflicting interests and needs of the country. Taxation had never (and has never since) been higher. The government controlled wages and prices. Much of the entire economy revolved around the government, whether directly through the one million Canadians who worked at some level in the military (out of a total 1939 population of 13 million) or in the scores of industries that serviced the military, building tanks and planes, sending supplies to Europe. It is little wonder that the socialism promised by the Co-operative Commonwealth Federation (CCF) came to seem like a more popular option in these years. Who could argue for private enterprise when the wartime economy had never been stronger, and it all depended upon government initiative?

The King government held in check such utopian hopes and the political challenge from the left. The Liberals planned for the post-war return of soldiers and resolved to stave off the feared post-war recession. In 1945 King's plan of benefits for veterans and social-welfare programs, notably the Family Allowance (the "Baby Bonus"), was enough to win him just enough seats to hold onto power. Even as the more renowned Winston Churchill in Britain went down to defeat, Mackenzie King's Liberals proved their electoral adroitness, scraping up sufficient seats to form another majority government.

The King government managed the potential economic crisis of reconstruction, fending off the post-war recession. It also negotiated Canada's place in the new United Nations, with the country taking up a non-permanent seat on the Security Council. As the Cold War became a reality, and the Gouzenko scandal revealed that the Soviets even had an active spy ring in Canada, King pushed Canada ever closer to its traditional allies. With Britain's power fading under the heavy debt load built up by the war, King found a new balance between Britain and the United States in the north Atlantic triangle.

Still, Mackenzie King was now well into his seventies and he increasingly seemed like someone from another era. A trip to Europe in the autumn of 1947 had him laid up in a London hotel, too sick to take part in diplomatic meetings. When he returned to Canada he slowly began putting in place plans for his retirement. His chosen successor, Louis St Laurent, was selected by a heavily stage-managed Liberal Party convention in the summer of 1948. King gave up his leadership of the party but held onto his role as prime minister until the autumn. Then, and only reluctantly, did Mackenzie King step down as prime minister of Canada. He had governed for almost twenty-two years, not only longer than any other Canadian prime minister but longer than any other prime minister in the Commonwealth. No parliamentary leader then or since has ever been as successful as Mackenzie King of Canada.

Such a career in the nation's highest and most demanding post commanded attention even if the man who filled it did not. Almost everyone agreed that Mackenzie King was not an impressive figure, nor popular. He didn't look the part. In an age before anxiety over obesity, commentators slipped in references to King as pudgy or tubby or just plain fat. His long-time valet once quietly muttered to another aide, after a particularly long and embittered attempt to fit King into his evening suit, "Well, I can dress him but I can't make him look like a gentleman."[22]

King had aged in the post, and so had his style and personal taste. In an era before television and before personal assistants who construct the image of a politician down to their choice of tie or sweater-vest, King had largely been left to his own devices. He maintained the style of dress that he considered proper and fitting. This meant that, even as the age of flappers gave way to wartime restraint and then to post-war casualness, King continued to look like an upper-class and uptight Edwardian gentleman. His starched collars erased his short stubby neck. When in public, it was usually the more old-fashioned bowler hat and not the fedora that graced his head. Some found King's fustiness reassuring. Here was a man who did not change, who at least looked serious and respectable. His looks and style, though, didn't inspire the nation.

Neither did the way he spoke. Eloquence was not a Mackenzie King trait. His speeches seemed designed to hide rather than reveal. He refused catchy slogans, or colloquialisms, seeing in them political danger. More than one assistant frustrated themselves to no end in trying to spice up his speeches. It just wasn't King's style. And yet for all of King's failures, his inability to inspire or to look the part of the great statesman, there was still the real success of Mackenzie King: his election victories and all those years in office. As the journalist Douglas How put it, "there was no way to reconcile the way Canadians talked and acted about Mr. King and the way they voted."[23]

When King died, commentators puzzled over this contradiction. Enigmatic, they called him. Arthur Lower stated that King was the "most unpopular man in Canada."[24] A tad strong perhaps. But it does get to the heart of the jokes about Mackenzie King – the ones people whispered and snickered over in private but didn't put into print. It wouldn't have been polite, to speak ill of the dead, and so soon. One joke had it that a drunkard boarded a Toronto streetcar and stumbled about the car threatening to shout the two most horrible words in the English language. The passengers implored him not to do so – for the sake of the women and children. As the drunk exited the car he finally let loose. "That's it," he shouted "I will say them … Mackenzie King."

King was indeed an enigma. Popular and unpopular, successful and a joke, the target of ire, animosity, and yet also respect. Years later, historians would credit King as a founder of the welfare state. Others would come to laugh at his oddities. Yet at the time of his death commentators largely saw King as a statesman of the nation. He had led Canada to an ever more autonomous place within the world, and he did so even as he brought Canada through the war united. He was many things but, above all, he was Mackenzie King of Canada.

Part Two

Keeping Secrets (or Trying to)

Psychic Newsflash

It took only a few weeks for one of King's occult friends to expose him. In mid-August 1950 an obscure British publication called the *Psychic News* published an article on its front page headlined "Mackenzie King Sought Spirit Aid in State Affairs." The piece was based on the stories of an acquaintance of King, the Duchess of Hamilton, an aristocratic woman known for her eccentric views. The duchess recalled that she had introduced King to many reputable spiritualist mediums when he had visited England. Her initial introductions had led to many later meetings between King and British spiritualists. She even told a story of how King had been responsible for bringing back to England a watch that Queen Victoria had given to a spiritualist medium and which had since been removed to the United States. The ghost of Queen Victoria apparently wanted the watch returned to her homeland and King allegedly took on the task of Anglo-American spiritualist rapprochement.[1]

The duchess didn't want anyone to think the worse of the Canadian prime minister. Quite the opposite. She cautioned that, of course, she had led King only to "reputable mediums." King himself knew that messages from the spirit world could be "coloured," she said, as they passed through the minds of even the purest mediums. According to the duchess, the former prime minister had been a rigorous thinker and practitioner of psychic research. In true scientific fashion, he had consulted more than one medium, sifting the information they delivered to him from beyond the grave. On the same day that the *Psychic News* broke the King story, it also reported on its front page about the dangers of fraudulent mediums. This was, the paper claimed, always a danger. The community of reputable mediums needed to root out these imposters lest spiritualism's reputation be tarnished. When your own beliefs are so far outside the realm of normal, it always helps to have someone else who seems even crazier.[2]

News of the story leaked back in private letters to Canada. King's partisan enemies privately snickered, loving the embarrassment that this allegation could cause Liberals and other King-defenders.[3] Finally, a few months later, in October 1950, a Canadian newspaper decided to break the story on this side of the ocean. The *Ottawa Citizen* reprinted the *Psychic News* article, albeit without the headline specifically saying that King had relied upon the advice of mediums in state affairs. The *Citizen* story inspired a series of similar reports in papers across the country in the autumn of 1950. Mackenzie King had been "outed" as a ghost-talker.[4]

How to respond to this stunning news? William Lyon Mackenzie King, the bachelor prime minister in the fussy suits, the man of careful speech, of practicalities and pragmatic politics, the man who ran an efficient if unexciting government, who turned his back on any kind of wild ideas, who made his reputation by refusing to be riled, by keeping his head when all about lost theirs – this man had sat down in darkened rooms to speak to spirits? Perhaps with ouija boards and a crystal ball? It all seemed too much, too far-fetched.

Years later some historians would try to rejuvenate King's reputation by claiming that spiritualism was much more common in his own day and age. King was odd, but understandably odd – like the Duchess of Hamilton who posthumously outed him. The historian Michael Bliss asked contemporary Canadians to recall that King's had been a much more religious era. "Surely," he claimed, we can recall "the force of the belief in the immortality of the spirit, and how it led millions of lonely people into intense efforts to communicate with the souls of loved ones who had gone before." If spiritualism sometimes seemed silly, still "there was also a serious interest in life after death." Such has been the sympathetic recent historical interpretation of Mackenzie King's ghost-talking.[5]

This laissez-faire approach to the spiritual is a product of our own relativistic age. It's true that the much more church-going and Christian world of late-nineteenth- and early twentieth-century Canada helps explain why King believed what he did. Most Canadians did indeed believe in life after death, and in fact this idea was part of the public culture of the nation. But slight differences mattered. To shift from theology to tarot cards, from the catechism to psychic research as King called it, meant taking a step outside of what was respectable. If these differences can seem less significant in our own age, we shouldn't mistake the varieties and hierarchies of belief in King's own day.

While a belief in the spirits is long-standing, the modern version of spiritualism as a kind of communication between the living and the dead traces its history to the period of religious revivalism in mid-nineteenth-century North America. The Fox sisters of upstate New York claimed to be able to communicate with the ghosts of the departed who took over the girls' bodies and communicated through a series of raps. Although the women admitted later in life that the whole thing had been a hoax, in the meantime the movement was picked up by many others and spread across the United States, Britain, Canada, and elsewhere. The methods of communication grew and diversified, and different mediums sprang up to promise that they could be the ones who would put you in touch with spirits from the other side of the grave. Yet, while the movement spread widely, it remained a minority taste and retained a whiff of the taboo. Especially in Britain, it found a home in upper-class circles and there were even semi-mainstream associations established such as the Society for Psychical Research whose purpose was ostensibly to test mediums and their claims scientifically. Such researchers, however, were often found to be less than scientific in their real desire to believe it was all possible. The mainstream churches officially shunned spiritualism and anyone who openly practised it invited sanction or ridicule.[6]

Especially after the Great War and the many deaths that rent apart families, some privately turned to spiritualism in the hope of reaching out to loved ones lost too soon. There were also many stories of those who hunkered over a ouija board, almost as a joke but hoping still for some kind of sign. Yet, contrary to the claims of some historians, there is no evidence of "millions" of Canadian sympathizers. In reality, only a small number of Canadians seem to have been spiritualists in any significant sense. We need only look to other figures who "outed" themselves as practising spiritualists to see why King kept this part of his life hidden. The most famous case was the Reverend Benjamin Fish Austin, the Methodist educator and thinker who became convinced of the need to search for truth in spiritualism. Austin had been a respected educator, principal of a girl's college in St Thomas, Ontario, for more than twenty years. The Methodist church even conferred on him a doctorate of divinity in 1897. But when he turned to spiritualism and preached the need to be open to its truths, his church expelled him. He may have gone on to become a renowned spiritualist, but this was a hollow success. His position in society generally would never be the same. Others learned from this and other international examples. A few prominent Canadians dabbled in spiritualism, and others drew inspiration from them. But for most, and especially for a politician, the costs of believing openly were too high.[7]

King himself had always kept his spiritualistic activities a closely guarded secret. Over the years, he would occasionally say something to a colleague or a friend about the life beyond this one, about the survival of the human personality. And sometimes he went too far, remarking on how he had been speaking to someone long dead. When King let this slip, his listeners raised an eyebrow, perhaps thinking that they hadn't heard him right.[8] Did he just say that he had spoken to FDR? The dead president? No, that couldn't have been right. Such slips, though, were just that: lapses. King did not advertise his interest in matters psychical beyond a small circle. He guarded his privacy because he feared the consequences of revelation. The risk was not worth it. King's assistant Frederick McGregor later wrote to King's English confidant Violet Markham that "the spiritualistic cult has not achieved in Canada the degree of acceptance which it seems to have done in the Old Country."[9]

What did Canadians in 1950 make of the allegation that King had been a devotee of this "spiritualistic cult"? Some of King's opponents thought it a gift. The *Globe* columnist J.V. McAree wrote up the whole story for Torontonians, detailing the Duchess of Hamilton's revelations and the bizarre stories of King and his English mediums. McAree treated King's spiritualism as part of a larger problem. After King's funeral, the executors of his estate had released the news of King's gift to the Canadian public of much of his estate. But this had made public the fact that Mackenzie King had died a very rich man. For McAree, the spiritualism news fitted into this revelation, showing "that Mr. King was not quite the sort of man he had been generally supposed to be."[10]

Still others remained uncertain. The editor of the *Victoria Times* claimed that "it is hard for us to believe that he waved his small hands [and] ... sent his imagination into overtime as a slave of the occult." Surely it wouldn't be right to think that King ventured "into the realm of table-tapping and the weird happenings in the darkness where only the ouija board holds sway." King was a "practical man" and "a good man. Leave the rest." A letter to the *Toronto Star* thought the story an "unfair attack," and a fifty-year subscriber to the *Globe* demanded that McAree "kindly try and refrain from slurring [Mackenzie King's] good name when he cannot defend himself." For many, the old adage kept its power: do not speak ill of the dead.[11]

With only this one allegation, and no confirmation as to its truth, King's defenders could pretend that King had been a spiritual leader, but not a spiritualist. The Liberal *Toronto Star* thought it all a "curious discussion." In truth King could "more aptly be described as a mystic." The paper quoted extensively from his speeches during the Second World War, showing that "he believed in Satanic forces at large in the world; spiritual not military forces, although they found expression in military aggression. He believed in powers of evil which take possession of men's minds; the minds of nations as well as individuals." This wrapped up King's beliefs in the kind of acceptable Christian common sense that he himself had always publicly expressed.[12]

To know more of King's private beliefs probably wasn't possible. *Time* magazine published a short article on the allegations but concluded, "Chances are that no one would ever know whether in the privacy of his study, Mackenzie King actually tried to communicate with his dead mother or whether his spiritualist experiments had any effect upon his conduct of the country's affairs." The truth might be in King's personal diary but that documentary trove was "ordered destroyed after his death under the terms of Mackenzie King's will."[13] Perhaps Canadians would never know the full story.

It really all depended on what became of that diary.

4

The Official Story

Mackenzie King always meant to be the person who wrote the full story of his life. When he finally retired late in 1948 he told everyone around him that he was going to write his memoirs. After all, Churchill had done it, proving himself to be both a statesman and a man of letters. King dearly would have liked to equal if not best his contemporary. Everyone seemed to expect it. "What a story he could write!" exclaimed the editor of the *Ottawa Journal*. Even if King did not have it in him to write monumental history and biography, "just the things from memory" would suffice, "recollections that would make old scenes and controversies live again – the sort of thing that so many British statesmen, their armour put off, did so well about memorable happenings at Westminster."[1]

King privately claimed that he had already written his story. It was all there in his diary, just waiting to be revised and presented to the public. While he lived he would bring down a volume of his diary for a specially honoured guest and read them a passage. Look at the detail, the accuracy, he would say. All he had to do was put it in order.[2] It is a mistake many writers make. A book in your head, and a book in draft, is not a book on the page. So Mackenzie King found out. Even if his health had not deteriorated, he quailed at the sight of his own papers. One of the few people who could be called King's good friend, Violet Markham, recalled visiting him in the autumn of 1949. He was supposed to meet her on the American eastern seaboard for a holiday but his bad health meant that she came to him in Ottawa instead. She found him fretting about his will and estate and especially his memoirs. King led her down to his basement and showed her the shelves and filing cabinets stuffed with papers. "As he showed me the material," she later wrote, "I was conscious of the nervous tension with which even the sight of the papers filled him."[3]

Still, there was no shortage of help. His old friend John D. Rockefeller was alive and the Rockefeller Foundation offered the help of its vast resources. Perhaps what King needed was a team of assistants, two or three top people from the civil service or universities and a small cadre of stenographers and office assistants. The Foundation, along with the president of McGill University, Cyril James, made the arrangements, and in early April 1949 the Rockefeller Foundation announced its largest grant of the year (amounting to $100,000) to fund Mackenzie King's memoir project. Rumours had leaked out suggesting that the American foundation was buying King's papers, essentially exporting vital documents of national historical importance. King quickly released a statement quieting such concerns. The papers would be donated to the National Archives.[4]

A small team of assistants began to sort through the mountain of material. His long-time colleague Fred McGregor, who long ago had served as his secretary when he worked for American companies and when he came to Ottawa first as opposition leader and then prime minister, returned to him once again to help him with this, the last of his books. But it was not to be. Throughout the winter and spring of 1950, King's health deteriorated. A team of nurses came to care for him, with someone present in his home at all times. He hoped that the move to his summer home at Kingsmere would help him feel better. Instead, it was there that he died toward the end of July. The memoirs would never be finished. Others would take charge of his papers, his diary, and his secrets.

It is unclear what he himself would have revealed about his private life and his belief in spiritualism. After King died, it became commonplace for journalists and academics to say what a shame it had been that Mackenzie King never lived long enough to finish his memoirs. It was the journalistic equivalent of saying "I'm sorry for your loss" or "He will be greatly missed." But the hints we get from the documents King left behind suggest that this was wishful thinking. Perhaps, to put it charitably, we could say that King's memoirs would have been much like his public speeches: significant as much for what they didn't say as for what they did, tales of omission and purposeful obfuscation.

We would have learned a great deal about all the good things other people said about Mackenzie King. One of King's first tasks in his memoir project was to have an assistant compile an extensive list of all the honours he had received. The enterprising assistant kept it all in a neatly organized binder with its own index. Entries included "Clubs, messes, etc. (honorary life membership in or honors from)" and "Freedom of City, honorary citizenship, etc." An astonishing number of Greek cities named streets and parks after King and the prime minister had kept a record of each. He even recorded those honours he had declined.[5]

King left a plan for the biography, an outline of what he thought it could offer to readers.[6] Under four headings, King broke his story down into the inspirational, the informative, the philosophical, and the secret of his success in government. King felt his story might inspire readers because of how it showed that "privilege in the form of birth, wealth, position, etc., [was] not essential to success in public life." He failed to mention that, while he may not have had the wealth of a Rockefeller, his family connections were of fundamental importance in his career. Indeed, in other documents, King confessed how his early successes depended heavily on his father's friends on the University of Toronto's Board of Governors. This brought him into the orbit of figures like Willison of the Toronto *Globe* and William Mulock, postmaster general in Wilfrid Laurier's government and the man who later recruited King as the youngest deputy minister in the federal government.[7] It was not clear how the son, let alone the daughter, of a Cape Breton coal miner or an Oshawa autoworker might have been inspired by King's rise from what may have felt to King like, but what really was not, a very humble station.

But King also thought his story compelling because it showed that "the path to success lies along lines of *being true to certain teachings and right activities*, e.g. integrity, good-will, initiative, disinterestedness vs. self-seeking." This last reads especially oddly because King had been an incredibly ambitious young man, a networker of shameless proportions who rarely failed to seek out powerful and influential potential friends. Later, on his trips to England as prime minister, he was known to arrive unannounced and uninvited at the country homes of the British aristocracy. Even King's friendly biographers in later years noted King's ambitious self-seeking.[8] King's own memoirs, if finished, would have suggested something much more modest and, frankly, untrue.

The only mystical side trip would have been King's belief in the pattern of his life. He believed that, when his life was examined as a whole, it showed what he called "the perfect round." This is a subject that interested others, though it fascinated King more than most: the generational shift from rebel grandfather to prime ministerial grandson. King's rhetoric could be a trifle lofty, calling this "God's covenant fulfilled." But for him it mattered that Queen Victoria had put a bounty on his grandfather's head, and that another monarch had greeted King himself, the grandson, as head of the Dominion of Canada. The monarch had bestowed on the grandson the Order of Merit, the highest honour possible. (No doubt King's memoirs would have glossed over the irony that, in accepting the Order of Merit, King in fact went against a measure he claimed to have been so proud of, the outlawing of Canadians' accepting British titles and honours.) Perhaps even better, when Mackenzie King was unwell in London, the monarch personally visited him at his sickbed. This was, for King, "evidence of divine guidance and direction ... The ever-widening circle. The perfect round."[9]

It's quite possible that, so long as King lived, he would have gotten away with this level of cursory treatment of his life. The other biographies that had been published of King had not attempted to delve deeply into his personal life, and barely scraped the surface of the controversial public decisions he had made. A combination of deference, behind-the-scenes control, and censorship put King out of the reach of many critics. The first biography of King had been written back in the 1920s by Owen Ernest McGillicuddy, a journalist out for an opportunity. His choice of biographical subjects seemed more to do with commercial success than partisan considerations given that he later wrote a biography of R.B. Bennett. His book on King, *The Making of a Premier*, couldn't have been friendlier. *Saturday Night* thought it verged on propaganda and would find a suitable place on the bookshelves of Sunday schools. The book could really have been called *How Virtue Was Rewarded*. King emerges in its

pages as "an ideal school-boy, an exemplary undergraduate, an efficient public servant, a good son and a fond brother, an assiduous
worker – strong, unselfish, clear-headed, compassionate – how else
could he be fittingly rewarded but by the premiership?"[10]

Another biography of the 1920s, written by John Lewis of the
Toronto Star, was clearly partisan. Lewis was later promoted to the
Senate by King. In 1935, in advance of the general election, it seemed
a good idea to release another book on King; King went back to the
Lewis volume but this time hired Norman Rogers of Queen's University to update it. What neither King nor Rogers admitted publicly
was that Mackenzie King himself was reading and even writing sections of the book himself. It is little wonder that the volume gives a
sympathetic explanation of all the tricky parts of King's past. Rogers
himself ran as a Liberal candidate in the 1935 election and after winning soon found himself in the Liberal cabinet. It paid to write or update an homage to the chief.[11]

The language of deference and statesmanship found in Rogers's
book is worth noting. It appealed to the idea that, when Canadians
were finding out about a politician's life, they were looking for examples of his character. It was political biography as Victorian fiction,
looking to see what kind of Dickensian character King came out as.
"There has been little opportunity for the younger generation of
Canadians to become acquainted with the early life and public service
of Mr. King," wrote Rogers. "It is more important, perhaps, that
Canadians generally should be made familiar with these qualities of
character, training and experience which have given him an excep-
tional education and equipment to meet that challenge of a new era
in Canadian history." Statesmen like King were different from ordinary mortals. As the introduction put it: "A modern biographer has
said of statesmen that they lay upon posterity the duty of understanding them." And so it was of King.[12]

The London *Times* reporter in Ottawa, John Stevenson, had wanted
to pen a critical biography of King. Drafts of it still survive in his
private papers deposited with Library and Archives Canada in Ottawa.
However, they come with a note attached to the front: "Suppressed at
request of the London *Times*." His bosses didn't think it was politic
to have their man in Canada printing something that could make
enemies in Ottawa during the war. Apparently, the publishing houses

in Canada went along with this, though the editors themselves were happy to read Stevenson's work personally. It was one thing to snicker in private, but quite something else to deride a statesman in public.[13]

When deference didn't work, King and the Liberals resorted to more strenuous means of ensuring that the public received what they considered to be the proper image of the prime minister. Robert Rumilly, a French refugee living in Quebec during the war, wanted to write a biography of King. While he initially intended it to be praiseworthy, he changed his mind when he learned that another author, Emil Ludwig, was granted access to the prime minister though Rumilly was not. Rumilly turned against King. He added a final scathing chapter to his draft and negotiated with a publisher for the book to be printed in Quebec. When the Liberals learned of the book and of its unfriendly final chapter, they made sure no one would see it. They approached Rumilly and his publisher with an offer they couldn't refuse, buying up all 15,061 of the printed copies of the book as well as all rights to its further publication. The wartime public only ever saw Emil Ludwig's small romantic volume on King as a heroic, gentle, thoughtful wartime leader.[14]

Even when King's secrets were out in plain sight, the Canadian public seemed unwilling to pry. In 1949 H. Reginald Hardy, at the time a reporter for the *Ottawa Citizen*, wrote a full-length biography of Mackenzie King. The former prime minister was retired, and this could have been an opportunity to pry into the more controversial aspects of his life. But this wasn't what Hardy had to offer. In fact, he consulted with King and even omitted certain sections that had concerned him. These had to do with King's friendship with Joan Patteson, the woman closest to him during his time as prime minister but also the wife of Godfroy Patteson, a local Ottawa banker. The section itself was innocuous but, even in raising the relationship, King no doubt felt that it opened him to gossip.[15]

Even more telling of the deference of the age: Hardy's biography actually exposed King's interest in psychic research and yet he did so in a seemingly innocuous fashion that no one deemed fit to follow up on. Midway through the biography Hardy addressed what he called the "King legend." By this he meant the stories that his contemporaries told of King, especially by the late 1930s, after King had been in office for a number of years. "The stories they told!" enthused

Hardy. "They left no corner of his public or private life unexplored." This may have been true, but the way they told the stories mattered a good deal and Hardy is a case in point. A few pages later Hardy addressed King's "religious side," which, he said, was "highly developed." Hardy went on to explain how King began each day in contemplation, reading the Bible or some inspiring text. "King's views on life, death, and the hereafter are very definite and clear," wrote Hardy. King very much believed in life after death and in the "survival of the human personality."

Yet it went beyond that, though Hardy was slightly coy in explaining how much further. He discussed how King's connections with loved ones who had departed this life was closer than for others, perhaps because King never married and never had children. King firmly believed that the departed continued to influence his life. The book writes of King's interest in "psychic research," stating that, in his view, it is a "branch of scientific study which ... cannot be overlooked by any thinking man." Hardy then notes King's connection to the late Oliver Lodge, a noted spiritualist. This could have raised eyebrows. So too could the subsequent extended quotation from a biography of the late British prime minister Arthur James Balfour, who had been a member of the Society for Psychical Research. This explained how Balfour had been drawn toward questions of eternal life but also, revealingly, toward the possibility of being recognized by those on the other side. Hardy quotes King as saying that "my interest in psychical phenomena and my views on life after death couldn't be better expressed."[16]

In other words, even while King still lived, a friendly biography had already exposed King's interest in psychic research. It would not have taken much for a slightly more inquisitive and less deferential journalist to take the same information and write an altogether different account, one that questioned the prime minister's spiritualistic activities. Yet this never happened, at least not yet. For the moment, deference reigned. King could keep his secrets, even if this meant that they remained hidden in plain sight.

King's literary executors prided themselves on their judgment. Good Liberals all, they represented the apotheosis of what sound government in Canada had become at mid-century – sound Liberal government, that is. They came from the top echelons of the Canadian civil service. "Ottawa Men," some would later call them.[17] They represented an era in Canadian government when the civil service grew in size and reputation as never before. During the Depression and then especially during the Second World War, the government took on more and more complicated tasks, controlling everything from the price of butter to social-welfare programs and even what products private factories could produce. Sitting atop this growing heap of possible government chaos, smart, competent, ambitious men tried to ride the Canadian state in the right direction. They had pushed aside the partisan appointees who usually staffed the civil service and in their place tried to create an efficient government of experts.

Of the literary executors, only Fred McGregor could have been called King's friend. McGregor had worked with King decades earlier as a private secretary. He had gone on to a career of his own, managing the industrial-relations bureaucracy in Canada. By the end of the 1940s, McGregor chaired the Combines Commission, a Mackenzie King–inspired creation that regulated business competition. When King retired and looked about for someone to organize his papers, he turned to his old secretary. McGregor was loyal and efficient, even if he was rumoured to once have angrily thrown a book across the room at his boss. McGregor had just the kind of quiet, self-effacing personality that King demanded.[18]

J.W. Pickersgill was the most political choice. No man blurred the line between the civil service and partisan politics more than Pickersgill. Jack, as he was known to friends, joined External Affairs in 1937 after finishing first overall in the national civil-service entrance exams. Mackenzie King immediately seconded this former Rhodes scholar and historian to work on his own staff. King was both prime minister and his own minister of external affairs, and he had a habit of cherry picking the best and brightest from the foreign service, although not many lasted. King demanded much, and friends told Pickersgill that he would be back in his department soon.[19]

Instead, Pickersgill soon became King's most trusted adviser. He had a knack for knowing just what King wanted. Perhaps it was what

4.1 Frederick McGregor

the historian Harry Ferns called his "chameleon character," the way he took on the mannerisms of those around him. Even in his days at university, the student paper presciently referred to him as "the power behind the throne." By the time of King's death, Pickersgill had switched over easily into the St Laurent administration. The advice in Ottawa was to "clear it with Jack" before proposing an idea to the prime minister. Most days he could be found lunching with one cabinet minister or another, and many said that Pickersgill was at least as powerful as anyone in Ottawa save the prime minister himself.[20]

Another literary executor, Norman Robertson, managed to wed himself more skilfully to the civil-service ideal. When Robertson first entered External Affairs in 1929, he, too, was seconded by King to the prime minister's office, but only for a brief time. Robertson returned to External Affairs, eventually heading the division as under-

4.2 J.W. Pickersgill

secretary in 1941. King trusted Robertson and in 1948 made him clerk of the Privy Council, the senior civil servant in the government. The tall, lanky Robertson shared many of King's beliefs, though like many he respected King far more than he liked him. Still, when King named Robertson a literary executor, Robertson carried out his duties with all of the careful efficiency that he took to his other posts. Indeed, he would eventually be the literary executor most concerned with guarding King's privacy.[21]

It was only logical that King also chose W. Kaye Lamb, the new national archivist. Hailing from British Columbia, Lamb was a scholar-administrator who already impressed observers. He would go on to shape profoundly the national archives and library, dramatically expanding the collections and leading the move to the impressive new building on Wellington Street in a monumental row

4.3 Norman Robertson and Mackenzie King

alongside the Supreme Court and Parliament. As King's papers were destined for the archives in the end, Lamb would have much to do with them anyway.[22]

These, then, were the four men King relied upon to guard his literary legacy: Ottawa men and, after their own fashion, Liberals. To them went the task of determining what later generations of Canadians would see of King's private and public world. They had a dual job – to reveal and to hide, to open up some parts of Mackenzie King's great life and to suppress others, albeit quietly. Like theatre promoters, they put together the show that would be the life of Mackenzie King, statesman. But, as with all such productions, a great deal happened at the edge of the curtains that the audience was not supposed to see.

4.4 W. Kaye Lamb

These men were not radicals and they were not likely to reinvent the methods of public remembrance for a man like King, who, after all, was not one for radical change himself. Their first and main job consisted of erecting the proper monument for King. In his will, King left a great sum of money and property to the government of Canada, including his residences in Ottawa and at Kingsmere in the Gatineau hills just outside the capital, both of which would be turned into museums. The literary executors turned their attention to erecting what is often the most enduring monument to a public man, the few inches of space devoted to him on bookshelves in libraries and private homes across the country. It is the biography, a thick hard-backed tome of steady prose and careful research, often simply called "The Life." If Mackenzie King couldn't write his own version, this left his literary executors with the task of deciding what kind of a life would be written, who would write it, and what secrets it would and would not reveal.

The list of potential biographers they considered reads like a who's who of Canadian men of letters at mid-century. It included the nation's great journalists Bruce Hutchison and Blair Fraser, the writer Hugh MacLennan, literary critic E.K. Brown, historians like Arthur Lower and Frank Underhill, and the political scientist Robert Mac-Gregor Dawson. Everyone agreed that the ideal candidate would be "a Canadian of the stature of John Morley or Robert Sherwood." John Morley had written a biography of King's idol W.E. Gladstone. Indeed, King's own copy of Morley's *Gladstone* was well-thumbed. The playwright Robert Sherwood had just won the Pulitzer Prize for *Roosevelt and Hopkins*, a dramatic and intimate account of Roosevelt's foreign policy during the Second World War. A Canadian like this would be ideal but, McGregor lamented, "Where shall we find him?"[23]

They seriously considered the prose dynamo Bruce Hutchison. The author of *The Unknown Country*, Hutchison would have written a compelling book. (Indeed, as we will see, he didn't give up the idea of writing on King.) But the literary executors chose safely. They selected MacGregor Dawson, a serious scholar, a Nova Scotian transplanted to Ontario, and a thoughtful middle-of-the-road liberal intellectual. Dawson's book *The Government of Canada* wasn't titled to inspire, but, as the *Montreal Star* reported, it displayed "a lightness of touch and a trace of somewhat sardonic humour." Dawson could be trusted, and he could at least inject his prose with the kind of wry wit appreciated by the Ottawa Men themselves.[24]

The *Montreal Star* considered Dawson a lucky man, winning what it called "the most entrancing job of his generation." In this they weren't far wrong. He would be paid an annual salary of $10,000, almost twice what he had earned at the University of Toronto. He would be helped by a team of research assistants and stenographers. But the paper couldn't have been more mistaken on how long the job would take, predicting that Dawson would finish in about two years. In fact, Dawson would work for the next eight years before dying in 1958, several months before publication of the first volume. Two more official biographers would take over after he died. Several more books would be published over the next two and a half decades, the last one in 1976. Even then, King's official biography would never be finished.

That, though, was all in the future. By late 1950, the literary executors had selected their man. Then began an even more difficult task: figuring out what to do with King's papers.

Mackenzie King didn't throw things away. He left his house stuffed with letters and notes, memoranda and reports. Whole rooms in the basement of Laurier House, his Ottawa residence, now a museum, were devoted to filing cabinets. He never seemed to have even thrown away a Christmas card. Then there was his diary. Volume after volume sat on shelves to be either read or destroyed. King had first taken up his diary as a young student at the University of Toronto in 1893. He wrote in purpose-made diary books, the kind that contained useful bits of information at the front and back, important facts about Canada like the names of all the members of the House of Commons. Each day had a short space in which to write. Soon King was filling up the entire allotted space and writing along the edges in between. Few diarists had King's stamina. There were only a few years in his life where he lapsed from his daily ritual. Every day, for almost fifty-seven years, King recorded his life. In the mid-1930s, back as prime minister after the R.B. Bennett interregnum, he found that he had so much to say he wanted a secretary to take it all down. He began dictating his diary, and his accounts and confessions ballooned in size. There was so much to say, so much to record, of matters high and low, of policy and daily minutiae. The diary books, kept in binders, found their place on the shelves next to the earlier bound volumes. In all, the diary comprised almost thirty thousand pages and spanned more than half a century from 1893 right up until three days before his death in July 1950.

For King's official correspondence and other government records, the team from the Public Archives were already at work and could simply carry on as they had while King still lived. But the private papers and correspondence were another matter. These had their complications, including correspondence with his family and with a number of women friends that might have contained surprises for the public. The biggest surprise would have been King's records detailing his psychical research. No one outside a tiny circle either knew or at least publicly spoke of this. There was a great deal of these records – binders full of transcripts, books on occult matters, correspondence with mediums and fellow believers. All required some kind of decision, and likely destruction.

As for the diary itself, King had seemed to decide its fate. The newspapers reported on the sections in King's will that said the diary was to be destroyed except for the portions he specifically indicated should be preserved. When journalists enquired about this last clause, they heard from sources at Laurier House unofficially that King had not indicated that any parts of the diary were to be kept. Too bad, some said. A lost opportunity to get to know the inside story of Canadian politics, and the real life of Canada's longest-serving prime minister.[25]

Except it wasn't quite so straightforward. It all depended on the meaning of the word "indicated." Behind the scenes, the literary executor Fred McGregor and King's former private secretary J. Edouard Handy (to whom King had dictated his diary) weren't so sure. Both knew just how extensive King's diary keeping had been. They also knew just how valuable it would be to anyone trying to write the biography of the former prime minister. It would be a shame if they were forced to burn these vital historic documents.[26]

Handy and McGregor went to the other executors with their ideas. They claimed that, even though King had not managed to mark in writing which sections of his diary he wanted preserved, he had spoken his wishes to them. Some entries could not be made public or preserved, particularly where he had written down discussions with other heads of state. The same applied to entries that would hurt the feelings of someone who still lived. Handy thought that there weren't too many of these, but nonetheless, they should be suppressed. Then there were the purely private matters, things only King could have cared about, including his interest in psychical research. Such diary entries, they said, would have to be handled with a great deal of care. But, aside from these delicate matters, would it be possible to preserve the rest of the diary, at least for the writing of King's official biography?

4.5 Mackenzie King with his secretary Edouard Handy

To seek advice, the literary executor Jack Pickersgill wrote to Prime Minister Louis St Laurent asking if the Department of Justice could provide an interpretation of the law regarding literary executors and the specific way in which the instructions from the deceased could be interpreted. St Laurent agreed and, within a matter of weeks, the deputy minister of justice had written back with a detailed assessment on the legal precedents. Most importantly, the Department of

Justice thought the meaning of the word "indicated" could be interpreted liberally to include verbal instructions.[27] Essentially the literary executors could use their own judgment based on what they broadly understood King's wishes to be. In other words, if you want something destroyed, do it yourself before you die.

The legal advice opened the door, but it remained to be seen whether King's literary executors would walk through it. Not everyone was pleased with the idea of seeming to go against King's written instructions. King's closest friend, Joan Patteson, thought that the executors should destroy the diary books. She said that King had made her promise to ensure that the executors "burned them without reading – and while I saw the need perhaps of reading them, the dying request was very sacred to me."[28] Patteson might not have read the diary herself, but aside from Handy she would have known more than anyone else what it might contain. Norman Robertson, too, considered King's written instructions sacred. As the executors sat down to decide what to do, it was Robertson who kept urging caution. It might very well be, as Fred McGregor kept pointing out, that King had planned to use the diary to write his memoirs. Robertson, though, wanted some more precise indication by King, perhaps to be found in the diary, before he would concede that it should be preserved forever or used in and quoted from in the official biography.[29]

For this was the debate now upon them. McGregor, with Handy at his side, pointed out the great value to history and to the nation of King's papers. Against them was the argument of caution and privacy, of keeping to King's strict advice. The executors debated back and forth through the early 1950s and onward. In the short term, though, they reached a compromise. Robertson gave his assent to allowing McGregor and Handy to begin to transcribe parts of the diary for use by the official biographer. They initially hoped to separate out the sections of the diary that King would have wanted to be kept from those that he would have wanted to remain private. It didn't help that King's handwriting was so difficult to read. Fred McGregor was one of the few to manage the task. So he set himself up, with a Dictaphone, in a room on the second floor of Laurier House. Handy would also help, and they employed a stenographer. They would try to create a sanitized version of the Mackenzie King diary.

It soon became clear that they couldn't manage to keep apart the public and the private King, the diary that he would have wanted others to read from the one he would have wanted to be secret. They removed some sections from the diary, leaving a note in each instance. They claimed, though, that it soon became almost impossible to divide the diary in this way. What they did omit, they said, was inconsequential, although no one has ever gone through the different versions of the diary to be sure.

In a room beside theirs on the second floor at Laurier House worked Robert MacGregor Dawson, the official biographer. Around them, King's old house had become a museum whose curator was J. Edouard Handy himself. Handy helped McGregor with the diary transcription and otherwise oversaw the museum. It made for an odd mix. A team of King's assistants was secluded on the second floor working on the Official Life while visitors shuffled respectfully through the rest of the house, peeking into corners and learning about the curios on display in the private home of a very public man.

5

Striking an Unhappy Medium

King's literary executors might have hoped to carry out their work with minimal fuss. Get the biography started, sort out what to do with King's papers, and watch as the government took over control of King's former homes. This is how government was supposed to work in 1950s Canada – efficient administration carried out by experts. Yet being a literary executor of Mackenzie King brought surprises. There was the odd case of someone calling herself Mary Mackenzie King. The manager of Eaton's had rung to check her story. She had ordered an exorbitantly expensive $1,450 scarf and asked it to be billed to King's estate. She claimed to be the widow of the man everyone knew to be a bachelor prime minister. The Eaton's manager thought the shipping address was for an insane asylum in southern Ontario. Mrs Mackenzie King persisted. Over the next few years, she ordered expensive jewellery and a fur coat, always insisting that the shop owners bill the Mackenzie King estate. Wasn't she, after all, King's widow? Her letters hectored King's executors, demanding they recognize their obligation to her. She even eventually created her own official letterhead scribbled out in messy slanted pencil writing, elevating herself to the aristocracy as the Duchess of Innisclare.[1]

More worrisome was the case of Geraldine Cummins. When Edouard Handy brought them the letter from Geraldine Cummins, King's literary executors were only just learning the extent of the kinds of secrets the former prime minister had once kept. Handy explained who she was, what she was. King had twice met with Geraldine Cummins and her assistant on his visits to London in 1947 and again in 1948. Now it seemed that Geraldine Cummins, the medium who claimed to speak for the spirit world, was not finished with Mackenzie King.

5.1 Geraldine Cummins

Cummins asked politely after the fate of her own papers in King's records. King had apparently promised to return copies of what had transpired between them – transcripts of his conversation with ghosts. She had read in *The Times* that his papers were to be destroyed but she thought that this couldn't be right. Cummins radiated sweetness and sympathy, yet she said something that worried the literary executors. "He told us," she wrote, "that he had every intention of publishing in his MEMOIRS, his interest in the matter about which he saw us, and of similar investigations he had made."[2] This meant King's psychical research. What were they to do?

King did seem to have taken the documents Cummins now wanted returned. They searched through his correspondence and saw that he had promised to send copies back to her once he had the time to have a secretary make copies for himself. Yet King himself had stressed the need for privacy. He had only one secretary to whom he could entrust the job and this was Handy. Death intervened and King never returned the documents. Even though the executors couldn't agree on how much they would let the official biographer use for his task, they were certain that some documents, exactly the ones Cummins requested, were the kinds of things the public should not see.

Geraldine Cummins had other plans. She professed not to care if others believed in her psychical research. She claimed that she was no missionary for the spiritualist cause. Yet in fact she published book after book on the subject, detailing what she thought of as her research. The modern world needed what she called a new Magna Carta for freedom of thought. In a more blessed age, Queen Victoria had held sittings with mediums. Two British prime ministers, Gladstone and Arthur Balfour, joined the Society for Psychical Research, an organization that, even if it did debunk phony mediums, also took seriously and openly the possibility of communicating beyond the shadow of death. The modern world of the 1950s had turned its back on this freedom. Was this any different, she wondered, from Soviet totalitarianism? "When will the western nations learn in their struggle for peace and freedom that psychical research and 'Spiritualism' are not things of shame to be hidden and suppressed?" she asked. "Tolerance, gentlemen, tolerance, please."[3]

King had been impressed. He had sat beside her as she picked up a pen, foolscap paper on the table in front of her, while she descended into a trance and her hand began to write. "Most remarkable" is how King described the results. It had to be true, remarked David Gray, the wartime American ambassador to Ireland. The words poured onto the page, with a speed "beyond normal powers of composition." It seemed to Gray "to constitute a supernormal phenomenon of first importance."[4] Perhaps he needed to meet more writers with a tight deadline, but clearly her mediumship impressed some.

In her memoirs Cummins recalled some of the different occupations she had taken up over her life: novelist, short-story writer, playwright, agricultural labourer, and even athlete. She omitted to mention spy, yet the Irish classical scholar E.R. Dodds recalled how Cummins told him that she had been a spy during the Second World War. With Ireland neutral in the war, she put herself at the service of the British government, reporting on pro-German elements in Ireland. "I believe[d] her," he said, "the courage, the deviousness, and the necessary skill in 'fishing' were all of them in character."[5]

Her psychical research perhaps helped with this too. At the outset of the war, with the United States still neutral, Cummins met for a session with David Gray. Gray wasn't only ambassador to Ireland. He was also related to Eleanor Roosevelt, the president's wife, and hence in a potentially useful position to influence American policy. It was quite the coincidence that, in a seance with Cummins, the spirit of Roosevelt's dead mother chose to come through Cummins to send a message to the American president. What message did she have? Did she miss her son? Perhaps. But the spirit message that Cummins passed on had more to do with current affairs. It urged the American president to "throw down the gauntlet" in the present war.[6] It was certainly the message the British government would have wanted delivered to the American president.

If Cummins professed that the spirits spoke through her, she did not entirely diminish her own role. The question of who wrote the words that came from Cummins's pen was never more clearly tested than in a court case in 1926. In the mid-1920s Cummins transcribed the scripts of a series of seances featuring a ghost purporting to be from the time of Jesus. She published these as *The Scripts of Cleophas*. But a very unchristian feeling came over one of her sitters, an architect named Bligh Bond. He thought that he owned the scripts. As he saw it, he had been the sitter and the scripts were addressed to him. Moreover, although Cummins wrote out the scripts in long form, he typed them and corrected the grammar. If anyone should profit from the sale of the book, Bond thought that it should be him.

The conflict travelled to the courts, where a judge had to decide whether spirits enjoyed copyright protection. He sidestepped the issue, which would have set a unique legal precedent. Instead, his judgment ordered that if "these writings were the composition of a spirit the brain of Miss Cummins was used to 'interpret and write' the composition. So it belonged to Miss Cummins." Cummins kept the scripts and the copyright, and British law escaped from a tight scrape with the paranormal.[7]

This meant, though, that Geraldine Cummins was well aware of her rights when she wrote to King's literary executors. She knew whose papers these scripts really belonged to. Still, she kept up her cordial correspondence with King's literary executors for the time being.

The *Psychic News* story gave Geraldine Cummins an idea. She wrote to Fred McGregor to say how much she agreed with him that the *Psychic News* story had been in bad taste. "Too much care and discretion cannot be exercised in making such matters publicly and widely known," she wrote.[8] But this did not mean hushing up the story of King's psychical research. It only meant that someone should tell the whole story properly.

As luck would have it, Cummins was just then completing her memoirs. "In view of the publicity that Mr. King's connection with mediumship has now received," she wrote, she had decided to add King's story as an appendix to her book. McGregor needn't worry, she wrote. Her account would "put the facts in their true perspective, *free from all sensationalism.*"[9]

King had told her that he did not consult mediums about affairs of state. Even if he had, she knew him to be a rigorous investigator who "analysed everything in the critical spirit proper to psychical research." She assured McGregor that her books reached "a good class of people all over the world and are not of the vulgar, sensational kind." In case he was interested, she enclosed a leaflet for an earlier book, festooned with dignified commentary from reputable aristocrats and pseudo-scientists. The leaflet announced, no doubt in an attempt at reassurance, "No cheap edition of this book will be issued."[10]

It was left to King's former secretary Edouard Handy to reply. He was the one contact that the Irish medium had actually met. He tentatively asked to review the part of the memoir dealing with King ahead of publication. "It might be," he offered, "that I could make some suggestions that might prevent the kind of comment that both you and I would like to avoid."[11]

The appendix arrived at Laurier House in January 1951. The little furor over the *Psychic News* story from the autumn had finally subsided. When McGregor read Cummins's appendix he recoiled in horror. Here was a document that threatened to bring it all back up again, but in a far more sensationalistic fashion. For Cummins presented the actual words of one of King's mediums, showing how convinced he had been by the truth of his experience with her. In this book, vague stories became eyewitness testimony.

By chance, two men closely connected with the literary executors were to be in London in a matter of days. Duncan MacTavish, King's lawyer and an executor of his estate, was leaving by ship directly. Leonard Brockington, a former King speechwriter and another executor of the estate, was already in London. They went directly to meet with Cummins, appealing for discretion. Ideally, she would agree to delete the appendix altogether. McGregor scribbled some notes of instruction for the two men. Remember to emphasize, he wrote, that King had "kept everything so secret – nobody knew – [not] even his family." Then there was the matter of his Roman Catholic friends, to whom spiritualism was anathema. To speak of these things publicly would diminish his stature in Canada, McGregor noted. In time, the men were to say, his literary executors would deal with everything. It could even be dealt with in his official biography, but later, and in the way King would have wanted.[12]

They offended Cummins almost at once. She lived in London with someone she referred to as her investigator, Beatrice Gibbes. The two unmarried women had lived together for decades, Gibbes handling the practicalities of life for the medium. She researched the significance of Cummins's findings and kept the public at bay, arranging all of Cummins's meetings with her sitters. King's men came to their Chelsea home to be greeted by Gibbes and led in to an audience with Cummins.

Gibbes was not impressed. "I have never been so insulted in my own drawing-room," she said later. "We were treated as though we were criminals in the dock." It seems that King's representatives were a little heated in their appeals to the women. None of the literary executors were spiritualistic sympathizers themselves. McGregor urged the men who were negotiating with Cummins not to get "contaminated!" "We have to live with you for a while yet," he wrote. One of the men later said about his meeting with Cummins and Gibbes that "never in his life had he had a greater desire to strike a happy medium."[13]

Some of this must have been evident when they implored Cummins to delete the appendix. Wasn't the relationship between a medium and her sitter, they asked, like that "between solicitor and client or between priest and parishioner or between doctor and patient"? Gibbes asked the men to leave.[14]

They didn't give up. Over the next several days, telegrams went back and forth across the Atlantic as the executors tried to fix the problem. The women suggested that the most they could do would be to make the appendix anonymous, leaving out King's name. At first, the executors thought this would be worse. It would only heighten the mystery. People would wonder about the real identity of the mysterious Commonwealth statesman. They would quickly see through the ruse. There was also the delicate matter of payment. The book had been sent to the printers and it cost money to interrupt a printing and reset the type. On this the executors offered to help, but when they received an exorbitant bill from the printer, they recoiled. Telegrams again went back and forth across the Atlantic, haggling over how much of Cummins's printing costs Mackenzie King's estate would pay.[15]

Eventually, McGregor and the executors accommodated Cummins's proposal of making the references to Mackenzie King anonymous. McGregor tried to smooth relations with Cummins. He wrote to apologize for any offence given to her, and to tell her a bit about the sterling character of the men who had managed to upset her. He hoped that all would be forgiven between those who, they all agreed, had King's best interests at heart.

※

Maclean's magazine gave Canadians an early Christmas present in December 1951. Blair Fraser's article "The Secret Life of Mackenzie King, Spiritualist" was an in-depth account of the former prime minister's spiritualistic activities. For anyone who had doubted the rumours about King's dalliances with the occult, this article showed them to be true. Mackenzie King really had been a spiritualist. Blair Fraser, the trusted, middle-of-the-road, and, some would have said, Liberal journalist, confirmed it.

In each issue of *Maclean's* Blair Fraser took Canadians on an inside tour of national politics.[16] His column was the most popular feature of the magazine in the 1940s and 1950s. *Maclean's* was meant to be different from a daily newspaper and Fraser was part of that difference. The magazine came out fortnightly. The distance

5.2 Blair Fraser

from the daily bustle and hurly burly was supposed to matter. There was time for reflection, gentle analysis, and consideration.

Fraser knew all the politicians. He felt particularly close to the civil-service mandarins, the Ottawa Men, the kind of people King had chosen to be his literary executors. Fraser and the Ottawa Men shared a view of what Canada and the national government could do, should do. They wore the same suits and went to the same clubs and parties. They lunched and fished and canoed together. Martinis in hand, they cultivated a North American version of Oxbridge style, a "wry wit, relaxed nature and subtle manner," and they frowned on enthusiasm.[17]

Fraser's crowd distrusted partisans and doctrinaire thinking. Pragmatism served them better. They had ideals and, in a way, this distrust of ideological rhetoric was its own ideal. They were generally progressive liberals, committed to freedom and liberty and in sympathy with the little guy. Fraser had a social conscience, pushing for a broader view of English-French relations in Canada and penning sympathetic accounts of labour strikes. As the economic boom of the 1950s spread over the country, why couldn't these sympathies coexist with a realization that the country was at least moving in the right direction?

If Fraser was part of the Ottawa establishment, he also refused to firm up his allegiances and considered himself an "independent" liberal. He had friendships, networks of contacts, informants who could trust him. He might criticize the government but he mostly wanted to give constructive criticism. Why push when a gentle nudge would do?

Some stories, though, were just too good to overlook. Someone tipped him off, but it isn't clear who. In the summer of 1951 Fraser got hold of a copy of Geraldine Cummins's new memoir, *Unseen Adventures: An Autobiography Covering Thirty-Four Years of Work in Psychical Research*. In the fall he flew to London and was knocking on the door of the book's author. He claimed that he already knew that the book's anonymous Commonwealth statesman, "Mr. S," was really Mackenzie King. To the women in London, with their recent memory of unpleasant Canadian visitors, Fraser must have seemed a pleasant guest. Good journalists know how to listen. Cummins and Gibbes invited him in and told him their story.

It was only a starting point for Fraser. He spoke to the editor of the *Psychic News* and tracked down another of King's mediums in Scotland, Helen Hughes. Back in Ottawa, Fraser showed up at Laurier House with a draft version of his article: Did the people crafting the official version of King's life care to comment? Backed into this corner, Fred McGregor agreed to talk, as did King's closest friend, Joan Patteson, feeling it was better to control misinformation than to say nothing at all.[18]

Anyone who had taken much of an interest in the career of Mackenzie King would have known that King made no secret of his special fondness for his mother. She was, in a way, the woman in his life. A bachelor, and certainly one who seemed not to be a ladies' man, was almost expected to be especially devoted to his mother, and to her memory, as King had been. Early biographies of King extolled him as a dutiful son. Even the trenchant critic John Stevenson, who had tried and failed to publish a scathing biography of King, had said it was to the young King's "credit" that he had spent so much time with his mother when she was alive.[19]

Yet sometimes as you peek around a corner, the glimpse you catch is partial in a particularly misleading way. Look longer, take in just a few more details, and the meaning of everything shifts. A chaste kiss becomes the prelude to a longer embrace. A smile turns to a sneer. So it was with Mackenzie King and his mother, and the rest of King's private life.

Fraser's article began with a full-page picture of King and his mother – or rather, King in devotion before a portrait of his mother. The picture had been seen before. From this point on, it would begin to take on a new meaning and become one of the most reproduced images of King. The soft light from a lamp glows on her portrait. The dutiful son gazes lovingly at her image. He is now almost as old as she had been when the portrait was made. "In Laurier House King kept a light burning before this portrait of his mother," *Maclean's* announced. "In England he 'talked' with her through mediums." The article promised to reveal these and other details of King's belief in spiritualism: "the best-kept secret of Mr. King's amazing career."[20]

Blair Fraser exposed King's dealings with British mediums, how he turned to them to talk to the ghosts of his mother and other close relatives, to his deceased friends like Franklin Roosevelt and Wilfrid Laurier. He even conducted seances in the third-floor library of Laurier House. Only a small group of intimates knew of King's psychical research, and they had kept it a secret until now.

For those who might not know anything about mediums and seances, Fraser explained the different kinds of mediums King had consulted. There were automatic writers like Geraldine Cummins, who went into a trance and whose hand began to pen messages from

MACLEAN'S
CANADA'S NATIONAL MAGAZINE

In Laurier House King kept a light burning before this portrait of his mother. In England he "talked" with her through mediums.

THE SECRET LIFE OF MACKENZIE KING, SPIRITUALIST.

By BLAIR FRASER
MACLEAN'S OTTAWA EDITOR

For twenty-five years Canada's famous Prime Minister was a practicing spiritualist. He believed that, through mediums, he had communicated with his mother, Franklin D. Roosevelt and even his dog Pat, after they had died. Here, for the first time, is revealed the best-kept secret of Mr. King's amazing career

LONDON

ONE WET Saturday afternoon in October 1948, William Lyon Mackenzie King lay ill at the Dorchester Hotel in Park Lane. His visitors were few and uniquely eminent—King George VI, Winston Churchill, Prime Minister Nehru of India—so the London press was keeping a close watch on the hotel lobby.

Reporters were amazed when two plainly dressed women came in, asked for Mr. King's suite and were shown up immediately. The two women did not reappear. They were ushered out by a side door (they couldn't understand why at the time) and the reporters never did find out who they were—Geraldine Cummins, well-known medium and author of m—— on spiritualism, and her friend and collaborator Beatrice Gibb——

That was as close as any outsider ever came, in Mackenzie K. to the best-kept secret of his career—the fact that the Pr——

5.3   "Mackenzie King, Spiritualist"

the spirits. Helen Hughes was a "clairaudience" medium, someone to whom the spirits spoke, sometimes when she was in a trance, and who then reported back what was said. Most remarkable perhaps was Mrs Etta Wriedt, a "direct voice" medium. Wriedt used a silver trumpet which would roll up to a sitter and through which a spirit could speak. A friend of King's recalled: "I remember the thing rolling up to me and giving me quite a rap on the shin ... The voice that came out did sound very like a person I knew who had died. However, I was a bit shaken when she got hold of somebody who was supposed to be French. That trumpet spoke very bad French."

Fraser didn't shy away from these more ludicrous aspects of spiritualism, though he usually let the sources do the speaking. Perhaps the revelation that later damaged King's reputation more than any other was that he had communicated with the spirit of his beloved dog Pat. Even for those sympathetic to King, this seemed a step too far.

Despite the shocking revelations of the article, Fraser remained remarkably respectful. He went along with the testimony of the mediums and King's friends that King had never sought advice in matters of state. Fraser repeated again and again the words of those who said King hadn't wanted "advice about public affairs." King had been a lonely man. His mother and father and then two siblings had died, leaving the bachelor King very much alone. In the spirit world, King sought solace and comfort. Fraser emphasized the secrecy and caution of King and those around him. His English visits were coordinated by Miss Mercy Phillimore of the London Spiritualist Alliance, one of the oldest such institutions and "regarded in spiritualist circles as a pretty careful investigator of mediums' claims."

What is striking in retrospect is that the commentary was so restrained. The safest thing for a 1950s journalist or editor to do was to just report the facts, reporting what King was said to have done or believed without editorializing. There were hints that, in private, many told jokes at King's expense. Over the next few years references to King and the spirits showed up in papers and even in the House of Commons in a sly fashion, rarely directly. What people said privately differed from what made it into print or was said on the air.[21]

Other journalists took it on faith that King did not govern the country at the behest of the spirit world. Denys Paré in *La Patrie* wrote soberly of King as "A great reader. And his research in the field of spiritism was equally serious." He remained content to say that "spiritism was perhaps more than a hobby, but it concerned only his private life and in all likelihood had nothing to do with matters of state." The editor of the *Windsor Star* seemed to be confessing personal knowledge of King's beliefs when that paper said that, of course, King had "occasionally consulted mediums," and with more frequency over the years. But it insisted that King was simply a "mystic" and explained his beliefs within the range of acceptable Christian ideas of belief in life after death. Even the Tory *Ottawa Journal* came to King's defence, repeating the line about King not consulting the spirits about affairs of state. The *Journal* reported that King's "friends were indignant at the suggestion Mr. King had made contact with the spirit of his dog, the Irish terrier Pat. They said Mr. King, much as he loved this venerable animal, would not have it claimed it had a soul like mankind."[22]

The letters *Maclean's* received about the Fraser article give a sense of the fine line that journalists trod in discussing the odd private life of this very public man. Some writers clearly thought that Mackenzie King was bonkers. Ada Hayner wrote from Mindemoya, Ontario, to complain that "there is little wonder we are faced with such chaotic conditions as exist today" if "those who have been entrusted with the highest position that the Dominion has to offer should resort to the ravings of a medium." An Alberta man exclaimed: "No wonder Canada is debt-ridden when men of King's position are allowed to spend the taxpayers' money to gallop all over the world to talk to dead dogs."[23]

Still, if King's bizarre behaviour angered some readers, others found the whole exposé itself to be "in very bad taste." "Surely a new journalistic low," wrote one man from St Catharines. "You might at least have left out his mother." Another wanted the magazine to know "that at least one of its readers did not approve of this effort to cast dubious reflections on the private life of Canada's greatest Canadian." Some of this talk no doubt came from Liberal supporters. Overlaying it, though, was the idea that public men reflected the nation. If you criticized someone like King, you criticized Canada.

Back in 1926 Mackenzie King's Quebec lieutenant, Ernest Lapointe, had faced scandal when a Conservative MP claimed that Lapointe had gone on a binge cruise of women, drink, and music aboard the government ship *The Margaret*. The story made headlines in the midst of the election, but the political class had largely closed ranks around Lapointe and he was vindicated in a hastily arranged and closed-to-the-public inquiry. Simply by raising such an unseemly topic, the Tories seemed to have sullied themselves. If the allegation were true, Lapointe's behaviour would have been "contrary to the dignity of public men" yet the allegation itself was also seen as improper and undignified.[24]

Twenty-five years later, Fraser still trod on dangerous territory. If public men had secrets, the common sense of the early 1950s left doubts as to whether these could or should be talked about openly. Did it matter now that King had done these things, especially after he had died? Different Canadians came up with different and opposing answers. Journalists moved carefully in the murky area of contemporary public speech.

⟨⟩

For Geraldine Cummins, the story did not end with Blair Fraser's outing of Mackenzie King. A short time after her meeting with the *Maclean's* journalist, Cummins had a rather special Canadian visitor. It was the spirit of Mackenzie King himself. According to the transcript that Cummins kept of this ghostly prime ministerial conference, King wanted to reassure Cummins that she had done right in telling his story. In fact, he confessed to feeling "remorse" for leaving the decision about his papers and his psychical research up to his literary executors. They were "good but ill-advised friends."[25]

King had one further message. This was for the person who had tipped off Blair Fraser and sent the journalist her way. Cummins doesn't record who this was, only referring to the person as "X." She does record King as saying that this individual had given "devoted service" to him in his life. The person had "in the journalistic phrase 'given my story away.'" For this he was grateful: "I have obtained my freedom and my peace through his action." It is impossible to know for certain who this "X" was, yet the most likely candidate would have to be J. Edouard Handy. He had been King's devoted assistant in the latter years of his life. It was Handy who transcribed

King's diary entries each day. No one else knew more about King's dealings in the occult.

How did Fred McGregor and the literary executors react to Blair Fraser's exposé? Day by day, McGregor continued to pore over King's diary, transcribing this important private document into a form that the official biographer could use. He worked toward making the proper respectful monument for King the statesman.

McGregor remained guarded. "Fraser has his facts right as far as they go," he wrote to a close friend of King's, "but even he has not realized the extent and intensity of Mr. King's interest in establishing direct communication with the spirits of the departed."[26] King had a great many more secrets. And in the early 1950s it still seemed possible that these could either be kept secret or handled discreetly in such a way as to preserve the old chief's dignity.

Part Three

No One Could Fool the People So Long

6

Statesman or Politician?

In the summer of 1952 an *Ottawa Citizen* reader wrote to complain to the paper: "It seems as if no one may mention the name of the late Prime Minister, the Rt. Hon. W.L. Mackenzie King, without bringing forth a violent diatribe from Mr. Eugene Forsey."[1] The reader wasn't wrong. In the middle years of the twentieth century, if you went looking for criticism of the former prime minister in any newspaper or magazine across the country, you would probably find Eugene Forsey. At the time Forsey worked as research director of the Canadian Congress of Labour but the former McGill University professor was also coming to be considered one of the nation's foremost constitutional experts. Not surprisingly, Forsey replied to the disgruntled reader. He admitted to being a perennial corrector of Mackenzie King myths but he also pointed out that the reader hadn't suggested that any of Forsey's criticisms were actually wrong.[2] For Forsey, this mattered most of all: the truth.

When revelations emerged about King and his relations with mediums, Forsey privately guffawed like the rest.[3] But Forsey did not think that revealing King's spiritualism would truly expose the prime minister for who he had been. For Mackenzie King's most persistent critic, the question of who the former prime minister really was and the secrets he kept from the Canadian public had almost nothing to do with his personal oddities. The damning evidence against King wasn't peculiarity but lack of character. King's great secret was his dishonour. The real truth of Mackenzie King was that, although he had pretended to be a statesman, in fact King had merely been a grubby politician.

In the early 1950s, in the years just after Mackenzie King died, it appeared as if getting to the truth of Mackenzie King's legacy might mean sorting out exactly these kinds of issues. Forsey would have agreed with King's literary executors about the importance of retaining a sense of the dignity of the nation's public leaders. He simply disagreed on whether King had himself lived up to those high standards. The real secrets of Mackenzie King, according to a critic like Eugene Forsey, lay with those parts of his political actions that he had kept hidden from the public. In taking on Mackenzie King's record so relentlessly, Eugene Forsey put to the test whether the statesman ideal still held sway in Canadian politics. Forsey would expose King for who he really was. And Canadians would have to judge if it mattered whether one acted as a statesman or merely as a politician.

※

The young Mackenzie King might have liked Eugene Forsey. As Canada's youngest deputy minister of labour, King had seen himself as Galahad, engaged in a quest for the grail of labour peace. He sat up nights in the apartment he shared with his friend Bert Harper reading Tennyson's *Idylls of the King*. This was the Mackenzie King who led a campaign to erect a statue when this same friend Bert Harper died in 1902. Harper had thrown himself into the Ottawa River in an effort to rescue a woman who had fallen through the ice at a skating party. "What else can I do?" Harper had said as he slipped to his heroic death.[4]

Life gets murky, especially for the ambitious. As a politician King learned that he couldn't always follow where his ideals led. Still, King was always, in his heart, the aspiring Galahad. Even as he acted duplicitously, told lies, and evaded the truth, he wanted to believe that he did right.[5]

In Eugene Forsey, King met the man he might have become had he stayed true to his ideals – a man who believed in the possibilities of politics and in the dignity and worth of the statesman. If it wasn't inevitable that Eugene Forsey came to be Canada's leading constitutional expert, it wasn't altogether surprising either. Forsey grew up in his maternal grandparents' home in Ottawa, steeped in daily lessons on government, parliamentary procedure, and politics. His maternal grandfather started work as a clerk in the House of Commons in 1855 and retired in 1915 as chief clerk of votes and proceedings. Forsey

6.1 Eugene Forsey

knew the faces of every prime minister in the country since 1894 save for Charles Tupper. He went to McGill in the 1920s and then off to Oxford as one of two Rhodes scholars from Quebec in 1926.[6]

Like a small but significant number of young men his age (and like the young Mackenzie King), he didn't smoke or drink or gamble. At Oxford a man living next to him once convinced him to join a game of bridge being played for money. Forsey reluctantly agreed but then, when he and his partner won the game, Forsey fretted about what to do with his ill-gotten gains. His friends jokingly suggested that he could give his winnings to missionaries. For Forsey it wasn't a joke. He promptly did just that.

But a straight moral back didn't mean he couldn't take risks. It was Oxford, he later recalled, that made him a socialist. He left Montreal a Conservative but came back determined to socialize the economy. His second stay in Montreal was bumpier than the first. He became involved in political and radical circles, the kinds of intellectual gatherings that led to the formation of the League for Social Reconstruction and the new socialist political party, the CCF. Forsey ran as a candidate for the party several times, always in ridings that didn't offer him much of a hope of winning. For Forsey, in this and in so much else, it was the principle that mattered.

His socialism didn't endear him to his employer, the McGill University Board of Governors. McGill only barely tolerated the activism of its few left-wing professors like Forsey and his friend, the radical poet and lawyer Frank Scott. While Scott managed to hold on to his position, the university ultimately forced Forsey out of his job. The official reason given was that Forsey had not yet earned his doctorate, but Forsey claimed it had much more to do with his stern willingness to stand up for principle even when it inconvenienced those in authority.

Still, Forsey landed on his feet. The upstart radical Canadian Congress of Labour hired him to be its research director, a position he held for more than two decades and from which he launched himself into national discussions of politics across the country. Later in life, Forsey would come to be known as Canada's pre-eminent writer of letters to the editor. It was an odd achievement, and one that Forsey made into a unique and dignified post of a kind. In an age before the press regularly published op-eds by leading intellectuals, Forsey used the "Letters to the Editor" sections of magazines and newspapers to carve out the same kind of space for himself.

Journalists and editors respected and feared him. A letter from Forsey could unzip them from top to bottom. The *Maclean's* journalist Blair Fraser once privately wrote to Forsey, plaintively asking: "Would you consider accepting a small bribe to discontinue your subscription to *Maclean's*?" The *Globe and Mail*'s obituary writer Don Downey recalled that Eugene Forsey was the only man, aside from the paper's owner, who had been asked to read his own obituary. Forsey responded by saying he had found "a few minor errors" and then attached seven pages of corrections.[7]

The public myths around Prime Minister William Lyon Mackenzie King also needed a few corrections. Forsey did end up finishing his doctorate and based on that work he published, in 1943, his book *The Royal Power of Dissolution of Parliament in the British Commonwealth*. The title was somewhat misleading. In fact, much of the book centred on the King-Byng dispute that had played such a central role in the 1926 national election. In it, Forsey exploded the Liberal interpretation of the King-Byng dispute of 1926. Some saw the timing of Forsey's book as an attack on the Liberal government. After all, Mackenzie King was a sitting prime minister. This was wartime, and here was an upstart socialist academic undermining one of the central pillars in the Liberal story of Canada's rise from colony to nation and Mackenzie King's place in that achievement. He was also doing so in the same year that the Conservative Party had brought back Arthur Meighen, King's nemesis from 1926, as party leader in an attempt to undermine King's wartime government.

The King-Byng crisis is now only barely remembered, and probably for the assonance of the name rather than anything else. In the middle years of the last century, though, the incident gleamed brightly amidst other gems of Canada's emerging constitutional and national story. King-Byng baked together all of the classic ingredients of the colony-to-nation struggle: a haughty British aristocrat, an out-of-touch and arrogant English Canadian Tory, and a defiant Liberal determined to stand up for Canada's independent status. That, and a happy ending. The country fought an election over the issue. And Mackenzie King and the Liberals won. Or, at least, this is how it went according to one version of the tale.[8]

In 1926 the governor general had denied Mackenzie King, the Canadian prime minister, his request that Parliament be dissolved and an election called. Byng had instead turned to the Conservative leader, Arthur Meighen, to see if he could form a government. Yet a short time later, when Meighen's government lost the confidence of the House of Commons, Byng granted Meighen a dissolution of Parliament and Canadians went to the polls anyway. How could Byng have granted the dissolution to Meighen when he denied it to King? For Mackenzie King and the Liberal version of history, this was a gross manifestation of Canada's still colonial status and an example of British (and aristocratic) interference in Canadian democracy. Canadian voters seemed to agree and they elected King's Liberals to a majority government in the 1926 election.

Writing in *Maclean's* in 1949, Lister Sinclair neatly encapsulated this popular reading of King-Byng, saying that "the Governor-General ruled in Canada until 1926 as even the King did not rule in England." It was only the King-Byng controversy that finally up-ended this state of affairs. "That year," Sinclair wrote, "Governor-

General Byng rejected Prime Minister King's recommendation to dissolve Parliament and King instantly resigned. Lord Byng then sent for Arthur Meighen who in a few days offered the same advice, which was accepted this time. In the election King was decisively supported, and a hurried Imperial Conference made the constitutional position of the Governor-General absolutely clear."[9]

Or did it? Eugene Forsey's book put the whole issue into the context of British parliamentary democracy and how it was supposed to work. King and the Liberals had put themselves forward as fighters for liberty and the rights of the people. In Forsey's analysis, King's logic showed itself more and more as a smokescreen – a politician claiming one thing and appealing to popular prejudice as a ruse. In reality, Forsey argued, King's actions had systematically belittled the essence of parliamentary democracy.

Forsey went through the argument with an eye for detail that few could muster. He dissected the arguments and the precedents and, one-by-one, showed the faults in the Liberal logic and evidence. Even King, Forsey pointed out, had acknowledged that a governor general had the right to refuse a prime minister's request to dissolve Parliament. As to the question of British interference in Canadian politics, Forsey showed that it had been King himself who wanted British interference when he thought it would help his case. King had written to the governor general urging him to get advice from the Colonial Office in London. Yet this letter had only emerged after the 1926 election, and after King had campaigned on a nationalist platform that would have derided such British interference. There were other details, dull with the intricacies of parliamentary governance (on the "broken pair" that had brought down the Meighen government, for example), yet the overall thrust was clear and deadly. The whole Liberal story of King-Byng was a sham. Far from being a nationalist hero, Mackenzie King had actually acted against the interests of Canadian democracy. In subsequent years, Forsey has largely been proven right on many of these details, but the nationalist mythology has been hard to dislodge.

Although Forsey acted on principle, there was also a personal element to his dislike of King. In preparing the manuscript of his book, Forsey had earlier sent copies of two draft chapters to Arthur

Meighen, the Conservative prime minister with whom King had battled. Meighen responded warmly and with detailed comments. After the publication of Forsey's book, Meighen and Forsey drew closer. They would correspond regularly, sometimes almost daily. "From then on," Forsey later recalled "Meighen was perhaps my closest friend."[10]

Meighen and Forsey's friendship didn't make sense: a Tory and a socialist; a scion of the Bay Street country-club establishment and a radical proponent of labour rights and the nationalization of banks. Forsey even ran as a CCF candidate in 1947 and again in 1948 against the then current Conservative leader and aspiring prime minister George Drew. Conservatives lambasted Forsey as a radical, accusing him of being a communist. After Forsey was defeated by Drew, the *Ottawa Journal*, whose editor Grattan O'Leary was a Meighen friend, wrote a glowing story on the strange friendship of Forsey and Meighen. This embarrassed both of them. "I suppose our friendship is a mystery to most people in our respective parties," Forsey wrote to Meighen. Still, Forsey claimed that he found it "a trifle hard to understand why people think it so extraordinary when I reply to lies about you. I can't see it has anything to do with your being my friend. It's a matter of common decency and fair play that when a distinguished public man is shamefully misrepresented, people who know the facts should state them."[11]

For the rest of his life, Forsey continued to set the record straight on the King-Byng dispute, long after the publication of his book and after King's death. Again and again, he set out the case for the way Meighen had been wronged in the King-Byng dispute and how the accepted version of events was nothing more than "the fables of the Liberal party propaganda."[12] But Forsey didn't simply leave it at King-Byng. He also wrote about King's legacy on Canadian constitutional politics and on politics in general, including the way in which King's policies had hurt the possibilities for stronger central government action on social welfare, on the lack of attention to civil liberties, and other matters. In his book and then again in articles and letters throughout his life, but especially in the 1940s and 1950s, Forsey unmasked Mackenzie King. The case was detailed and intricate, often difficult to follow or even understand. As Forsey complained: "You can tell a lie in three words; to expose it may take twenty." Forsey quoted Keir Hardie: "The lie goes round the world while truth is putting on her boots."[13]

The strength of the critique, though, emanated from its moral basis in a code of honour. Politics ought to be a gentleman's game, a place not just of that ambiguous figure, the politician, but of that much abler, noble creature, the statesman. If a politician could survive by cunning and manipulation, a statesman persevered with integrity, adhering to principle and truth. In showing King to have lied and deceived, Forsey essentially exposed him as someone with no honour.

⚜

What was the truth of Mackenzie King? For Forsey, the answer was clear. Yet did any of this really matter to Canadians? The moral code of statesmanship that Forsey appealed to depended upon others agreeing to its significance. But did they?

We don't often speak of statesmen any more. The term is reserved for truly outstanding public officials, perhaps a Nelson Mandela or a Mahatma Gandhi. Indeed, as the Google Ngram shown in figure 6.2 demonstrates, the term "statesman" rose to prominence in the early years of democratic government in the English-speaking world in the early twentieth century but came to be used much less frequently in the more rambunctiously democratic and egalitarian context of the post–Second World War decades.[14] The elusiveness of this term in our own era seems to reflect our own changed attitudes toward politics and political leadership. It shows the decline of an older notion of democracy that was both more idealistic but also hierarchical. In the nineteenth century and into the early decades of the twentieth century, the idea of the statesman occupied an important place in democratic politics.[15] These were figures who stood above the rest, representatives of the people but allegedly in the best sense. Their elevated status in public discourse rested on social, political, and economic hierarchies which put certain men above others (and usually men above women), and on a belief in divisions between what was public and private that allowed these figures to seem to be essentially public men and to hide certain aspects of their lives that would have

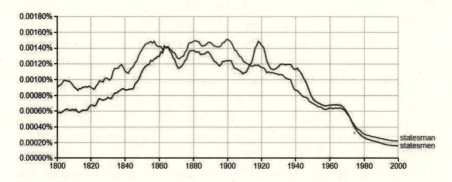

6.2 Graph showing shifting use of the terms "statesman" and "statesmen" in the Google Books library of books digitized and searchable (in English).

complicated such idealistic characterizations. They seemed better because we knew less about them. And we knew less about them because of a deference rooted in Victorian notions of propriety. Even as systems of government in Canada became more open, allowing for universal male suffrage and then universal female suffrage (with important lingering racial exclusions), the ideal of the statesman provided a continuing aristocratic tinge to the political scene.

Early democratic reforms in Canada and elsewhere aimed to bring others up to the idealistic elevated status of the statesman. Democracy seemed to demand the best of citizens. This was the hope of universal education, that it could create these kinds of ideal citizens. The same hope was at the basis of the desire to make electioneering more rational through reforms like the secret ballot. It lay behind the discourse of those who gathered together in civic organizations to create a public sphere via intelligent discussion in newspapers and in local meetings. All of these initiatives were inspired by liberal notions of individual uplift. There was also, of course, the concomitant fear and assumption that certain people couldn't be lifted. This was at the heart of the various exclusions of women or racial groups that persisted so long – rooted in racial, class, and sexual prejudice.[16]

Still, this idealistic notion of democracy hoped for a better political self that could act in the public sphere. The best expression of this public self was supposed to be the statesman. That all politicians didn't match this ideal was clear. And disagreements about who exactly did achieve such a status were often violently partisan. But the ideal itself has been a significant feature of modern democracy. It hasn't altogether disappeared though hopes have dimmed. Expectations lessen.

These liberal-democratic ideals fuelled the criticisms of Mackenzie King in the years just after he died. To criticize the public record of Mackenzie King after the fashion of Eugene Forsey was to assume a notion of politics as a high form of public service. Those who truly excelled at politics deserved to be lauded for their achievements. The test of whether someone excelled at politics mattered and it mattered in precise detail. Forsey's critique was based in these older traditions of parliamentary conduct and notions of the honourable behaviour needed of citizens in the public sphere.

It is hard now to resurrect the full meaning of what honour meant to an earlier Canada.[17] Yet honour used to matter a great deal to Canadian political culture and social life. Honour shaped the language, though, of course, not always the practice, of politics. The prime minister was and still is "Right Honourable." Members of Parliament speak of themselves and their colleagues as the "Honourable Member" from such and such a riding. The rules of decorum in the House and Senate are meant to add dignity and ritual to its proceedings, shared ceremony and titles embodying virtues and relationships. We can translate honour partially into modern parlance by replacing it with respect or self-respect, yet this loses some of the intricacy and hierarchy implicit in the older idea. Honour was meant to be a code that impelled action. Honour could be lost, and once lost, it was utterly gone. It was the male equivalent of feminine virtue. The reverse of honour is not just less honour but shame, humiliation, and disgrace. Even if it is held and acted upon individually, honour is a communal idea. It depends on a collective set of understandings of right action that are then internalized. Honour is most readily seen in small groups, among an elite, a family, a small community or ethnic group, a sports team, or a military unit. It also can be seen in politics and especially among the small group of those who occupy political office. The question of whether these small-group hierarchical notions of honour could survive into the era of democratic, universal-rights mass politics remained open at mid-century.

Today parliamentary ritual and etiquette appear Byzantine and foreign. Yet in the nineteenth century they did not so clearly contrast with everyday life nor with ideals about what democracy ought to be. Political relations between local citizens and their representatives resembled those between patron and client, a system that one historian has called "clientelism."[18] Voters put forward their local bigwig, a man (always a man) with local connections and status, someone who might also hold or have held local office. The system of patronage worked to cement these relations. Many voters could expect to receive something back from their vote, not simply a voice in Parliament but perhaps a job or a contract for themselves or a relation. Governments kept lists of reliable or trusted businesses who could receive contracts, even newspapers that would receive government advertising. The local member of Parliament played a direct role in the minutiae of this kind of patronage and connection with his riding. With a much smaller electorate, and the open ballot (until 1877), voters and their representatives knew who was on their side. The party systems of the late nineteenth century cemented these mutual ties of obligation and support.[19]

The society of nineteenth-century Canada was also much more obviously formal in its outward relations. This included everything from relations between the sexes (one needed to be introduced to a woman before speaking to her) to formal modes of address: to use someone's Christian name implied familiarity, something to be earned not assumed. As soon as pioneering families could manage it, they built homes that reserved a room, the parlour, for public socializing. Kept meticulously clean and proper, and usually out of bounds for day-to-day activities, the parlour represented the formality of nineteenth-century life in domestic miniature. Part of the home, and yet not entirely of it, it sat often empty, a depressurization chamber between the public and the private. In a society such as this, the codes of parliamentary behaviour were not entirely foreign even if they differed in kind from how most Canadians went about their daily business. Respectability mattered even if it could not always be achieved at home or in public life.[20] Indeed, the facade of respectability mattered most when private behaviour undermined publicly shared values. Politics and family life could often be tumultuous, violent, and messy yet that only made the public face of respectability all the more important.

This is not to say that political debate was not partisan and bitter. Indeed, quite the opposite. The level of partisan vitriol in a nineteenth-century newspaper along with the liberal dose of vituperative Dickensian insult can often seem shocking to those more accustomed to the neutral tone adopted by most newspapers in the twentieth and twenty-first centuries.[21] Yet these attacks coexisted with a more widespread sense that the act of politics itself mattered and ought to be held in high regard. The insults meant so much because they were contrasted with an exalted ideal.

When Eugene Forsey attacked Mackenzie King, he appealed to the moral force of this culture of virtue and honour among the small club honoured to have been selected to sit in Parliament. The truth ought to have mattered. A statesman was supposed to hold himself to higher standards, at least in public and at least when it came to publicly defending his actions. To act in a forthright manner, all could agree, was the ideal position of the statesman.

Yet the moral code that gave force to Forsey's arguments was crumbling under the social and political changes of the twentieth century. The change in politics was clear. The clientelist model of politics, with its strong role for individual members of Parliament, was only a shadow of its former self. Although political parties still doled out patronage, they did so in different ways that often excluded or at least minimized the role of a local MP. Some spoke, for example, of welfare-state programs like the Family Allowance as new forms of patronage that went directly to citizens. The creation of the Civil Service Commission in 1907, and then frequent reforms to it over the years since, removed much of the power of the MP to control patronage directly and to dole out positions to local supporters. Political parties still used government contracts to win support and get money from companies, but this increasingly happened at a more centralized level, perhaps with the assistance of regional cabinet ministers. In other words, the material rewards of clientelism diminished.[22]

Moreover, the expansion of different forms of commercial entertainment, from cinema to radio to the automobile and beyond, meant that Canadians had many more ways of amusing themselves. Politics had always been partly about socializing. It mattered because it was one of the only shows in town. Like the mainstream churches in the same years, political parties struggled to keep the attention of Canadians. As Norman Ward wrote of a slightly later period, "the day is over when local political enterprise provided the major form of social activity outside religion, with few alternate sources of entertainment."[23] Pierre Trudeau had not yet said that as soon as an MP was fifty yards away from Parliament Hill he was a nobody, but the long slow decline of parliamentary prestige was well on its way.

Culturally, the 1950s sat on a precipice of change, teetering in both directions, from the more to the less formal. Many English Canadians still admired the monarchy, for example. To read letters from the era is to go back into a period when the slightest variations in address still carried great weight. When King's literary executor Fred McGregor got to know the official biographer Robert MacGregor Dawson better, the shift in their correspondence from Dear Mr Dawson to Dear Dawson to Dear Bob intimated much.[24]

Yet the signs of a less formal, more democratic sensibility bubbled everywhere. In so many areas of life, formalism retreated – in dining with the barbecue, in architecture with the California-style bungalow and its easy shift from inside to outside. Journalism and writing changed, throwing up Ernest Hemingway and Morley Callaghan as exemplars of the new style. To write well was to write shorter, punchier sentences, to throw off punctuation and extraneous phrasing even as some threw off the constrictions of Victorian clothing and values. Even fonts threw off serifs. In communication, radio embodied this trend, as did, in more dramatic fashion beginning in the early 1950s, television. They brought public figures and politicians into the open. For both mediums, little change was evident at first – their daily fare was heavily scripted speeches and announcements. But soon the media responded to immediacy and even intimacy, to sheer presence. Old traditions and codes of conduct meant for small quarters looked old-fashioned and stodgy, out of date and maybe even irrelevant.[25]

The codes of honour and morality that Forsey appealed to, in other words, were themselves being transformed in the middle years of the century. The idea of the upright statesman who spoke the truth and led with dignity still carried weight. Many read Forsey's articles and were inspired and convinced. But there were other ways of thinking about politicians and political life emerging in these years, and the differences did not just depend on partisanship – they did not just pit Liberals against Conservatives, Tories versus Grits. The material basis for the statesman ideal, rooted as it had been in clientelist patronage politics and a society of moral Christian respectability and small-town life, diminished. At the same time, Canadians turned away from politics as one of their main areas of entertainment and socializing. As Canadian culture grew slowly less formal, the stiff formalities of Parliament became an ever more distant and archaic ritual – less real and thus less relevant.

Yet in the 1950s it still seemed as if the old formalities could hold out, at least for a while longer. Stiff formalities could pass themselves off as necessary respectability; the long-winded speeches of Parliament might not yet seem pompous – or not necessarily so. Eugene Forsey could deride the lack of statesmanship of the country's most successful prime minister, and insist that the details did, in fact, matter.

Blame Freud

Different truths, though, matter to different people. In the early 1950s, another book came along that promised to tell unsuspected truths about Mackenzie King. It wasn't a disreputable book by a mudslinging, politically motivated detractor. Nor was it an academic treatise. Instead, Bruce Hutchison's *The Incredible Canadian: A Candid Portrait of Mackenzie King* was about as middle of the road as you could imagine. Yet the book promised to tell "the amazing story of the man, Mackenzie King, not as the public knew him, but as he really was."[1] It raised King up with one hand – as the greatest prime minister – and brought him down with the other – as a chubby, petty little man. *The Incredible Canadian* presented King as an enigma, highlighting the mismatch between King's small personal stature and his record of public greatness. An effeminate man who acted on intuition, who was dominated by his mother, yet one who understood the needs of his country as no other. It was a candid portrait indeed.

The Incredible Canadian came out in the autumn of 1952, just in time for the Christmas book-buying season. It made a huge splash. *Maclean's* published three large instalments in advance to whet the public's appetite. The titles came as bold exclamations, like the excited announcement in films of the time about "Technicolour!" or "Cinemascope!": "Mackenzie King and the Revolt of the Army" – "How Mackenzie King Won His Greatest Gamble." Newspapers across the country widely reviewed the book, many favourably. It would go on to win various awards including the University of British Columbia Award for Biography.[2] There was clearly a market for a certain kind of truth-telling about the former prime minister.

This is because Bruce Hutchison's desire to get an authentic version of the great public man spoke to a burbling cultural current of ideas that supported just this sort of thing. It didn't just mean looking at King's public record (though that counted too). It also meant thinking about his personality and the inner truths of the man. Hutchison was willing to take this curiosity only so far. Others would go farther in following decades. But in the early 1950s, it seemed that there were some rumblings about the need to look to the inner workings of public men.

⚇

Blame Freud. The rise to prominence in the 1950s of psychoanalytical and therapeutic ways of thinking put a premium on revealing what was hidden in the unconscious mind. Freudian ideas were popularized in these years in a mishmash of loosely Freudian metaphors and terms.[3] The trend indicated the mid-century public's fascination with the hidden secrets that often underlay the facade of respectable life.

It is hard to overestimate the novel excitement generated by Freudian ideas in 1950s Canada. Although Freud died in 1939, his ideas came to dominate psychiatry in the 1940s. Freudian ideas also spread throughout North American popular culture, forming a kind of common sense about the importance of childhood sexual experience in later psychological development. These ideas had been taken up by the urban middle class of Europe in the early twentieth century and had become more popular in the immediate aftermath of the First World War and especially after the arrival in North America of psychoanalysts fleeing Nazi Germany in the 1930s. American historian of psychiatry Nathan G. Hale calls the period after the Second World War the "Golden Age" of Freudian and psychoanalytic popularization.

Freudian psychoanalysis came to be the dominant paradigm within the psychiatric profession in the United States and Canada, though there were certainly alternate perspectives, and Freud dominated most in urban areas.[4] The Canadian psychiatrist (and historian of psychiatry) Joel Paris noted that Freudian ideas made psychiatry itself seem significant, with large numbers of medical students (more than later in the century) wanting to specialize in psychiatry. "Becoming a psychiatrist," Paris recalled, "was seen as the only way to become a physician who cared about the mind and the soul." The public fascination was flattering. "Analysis was believed to provide access to the

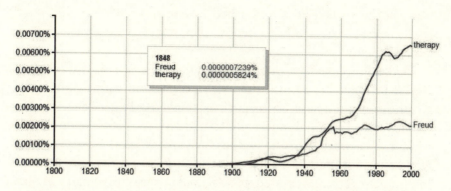

7.1 Graph showing shifting use of the terms "Freud" and "therapy" in the Google Books library of books digitized and searchable (in English).

unconscious mind. While this claim was never backed up by data, the general public was in awe of the technique's purported capacity to understand the psyche. Psychiatrists or psychiatric residents [could] be asked at parties whether they could read other people's minds."[5] As historian of psychiatry Edward Shorter puts it, "for a brief period at mid-twentieth century, middle-class society became enraptured of the notion that psychological problems arose as a result of unconscious conflicts over long-past events, especially those of a sexual nature."[6]

The mid-1950s saw the centennial of Freud's birth and the celebrations combined with new translations and reissues of his works put Freudian ideas into circulation as never before. A three-volume biography by Ernest Jones, published between 1953 and 1957, gave English speakers a Freud that was both personal and profound. The reviewer in the *New Yorker* called it "the greatest biography of our time." Most importantly, Freudian ideas came to North Americans via magazines. Beginning during and just after the Second World War, journalists worked to popularize – and vulgarize – Freud for readers across the continent. Freudians added new words to the English language and gave new meanings to old terms: penis envy, Oedipus Complex, transference, Freudian slip, psychosomatic, erogenous zone, obsession, fixation. Freudian ideas slipped into the common sense of North America: the idea that dreams reflected the workings of the unconscious, and the very idea of the unconscious as a part of one's personality where certain desires and impulses bubbled away beneath the surface, the unfinished business of ongoing childhood conflicts that were ready to expose themselves at awkward or random moments.[7]

Publications like *Life*, *Scientific American*, *Newsweek*, and *Reader's Digest* brought Freud into the living rooms and waiting rooms of North America. These US magazines enjoyed a larger readership in Canada than Canadian ones, and Canadians, too, became fascinated with, if not always believers in, the new psychological insights. Hollywood played its part as well. The period from the mid-1950s through to the mid-1960s represented its own golden age of psychiatry in film. Just as many working in the industry went through their own analysis, psychiatrists and psychoanalysts never looked better as a profession than they did on the screen.[8] In other words, the popularizing of Freudian ideas in Canada was part of a broader trend of Americanization in these years when American capital and American cultural products flooded into Canada, propelling the post-war boom.

The rise of Freudian psychiatry was also part of a wider push toward environmentalist explanations of human behaviour in the middle of the twentieth century, and away from biologically determinist views. For Freudians, mental illness and mental health existed on a continuum. The difference between the severely mentally ill and run-of-the-mill neuroses was only a matter of degree. Everyone was "a little bit schizophrenic or a little bit manic-depressive."[9]

In this democratic version of mental health, psychiatry became not just something for the severely mentally ill or for those in asylums. Everyone could benefit from an understanding of how the mind worked and the role of unconscious conflicts in our lives. Not coincidentally, the psychiatric profession came in these years to move out of the asylums and into private practice and to focus on a broader, more common, range of mental illnesses, often understood as neuroses. The concept of mental illness was becoming ever more inclusive.

What this meant in practice is that social conventions that seemed to proscribe or inhibit the self opened themselves up to scrutiny. The rise of psychoanalytical ways of thinking provided the language whereby these earlier values could be labelled as repressed – a pseudo-scientific gloss to explain why older values should no longer reign. Freud gave North Americans permission to look more frankly at their desires and their impulses. As Robert White put it in *Scientific American*, Freud was a hero "for many thoughtful people because he dared look steadily at the dark forces within us and ... held out hope, however cautiously, that they might be better governed." The rise of a psychoanalytic view of human impulses opened the door to a more relativistic assessment of them, although, at mid-century, Freudianism did not necessarily condone these dark places and impulses. Instead, it offered a modern, scientific moralism shorn of Christian theology. These ways of thinking represented a shift away from a Victorian moral code around issues of sexuality and respectability, but Freudian psychology retained the aura of a moral code nonetheless – a moral code translated into scientific, psychological language.[10]

Perhaps the best-known Canadian Freudian was Brock Chisholm, who had become famous in 1945 for telling Canadian parents that they were laying the seeds of future wars by lying to their children about the existence of Santa Claus. While journalists and politicians ridiculed and lambasted Chisholm's ideas, he represented the wave of cultural change that was to come. He led the way in setting up psychological testing in the Canadian military. He rose to public prominence through his Santa Claus remarks in the aftermath of being awarded the Lasker Award for 1946 (the Lasker being an attempt to create an American Nobel). The first Lasker had gone to American psychoanalyst popularizer Karl Menninger. Chisholm fitted well into this company. In the speech he gave on receiving the award, and in others subsequently, he decried the way that contemporary morality skewed the actions of individuals in contemporary society. Modern North Americans needed to develop new and rational ideas of right and wrong. They needed to throw off the yoke of cultural baggage, especially the sort stemming from the traditional churches, that led to neurotic impulses like aggression, guilt, desire for power, and other psychological causes of war and turmoil. Here was a man who demanded a truer and more frank assessment of the real patterns at work in post-war Canada.[11]

Freud did not reign unchallenged in these years. Indeed, many psychiatrists and psychologists offered alternate methodologies and explanations for human behaviour. Because of the unwillingness of Freud and then his daughter Anna to bend and modify the field's original tenets, the history of psychoanalysis is like the history of Christianity in the Protestant Reformation, with new sects splintering off in all directions. A series of influential thinkers including Carl Jung, Alfred Adler, Fritz Perls, and Wilhelm Reich would emphasize different explanations for neuroses and offer slightly different methods for treatment. Yet collectively they represented the flowering of a therapeutic culture of self-awareness by mid-century. The importance of one field of psychiatry or psychology mattered less than the overall rise of a perspective that saw ultimate truths in revealing what was essential or authentic in the individual self.

In this sense, Freud was a symbol as much as an agent of change. Freudian ideas matched other developments across the culture that pushed for a more authentic and frank expression of what an older morality would have wanted to hide or condemn. For example, beginning in the 1930s but picking up steam in the post-war decades, Alcoholics Anonymous radically changed how North Americans thought of drunkenness. Alcoholics Anonymous called for those with drinking problems to admit to themselves and to others who they truly were: alcoholics. The process was a hodgepodge of religious inspiration (admitting your powerlessness before the Creator), psychotherapeutic practices (group-therapy meetings), and pseudo-science (seeing the drinker as an addict).[12] The truth of problem drinking didn't rest with alcohol (and so prohibition was not the answer) but in the individuals themselves, and the need to admit who they really were.

In other fields, the trend was similar, pushing toward an acknowledgment of what was really on the inside. By the 1950s, progressive child-centred education was making inroads in most Canadian schools (with some regional variation, notably in Quebec where the Catholic system was a holdout). There were many critics of these developments, including historian Hilda Neatby, whose 1953 book *So Little for the Mind* crystallized the popular conservative worry over changing cultural priorities. When Eugene Forsey read Neatby's book, he wrote to Arthur Meighen, aghast at a school system that would raise a student's grade from 29 per cent to 50 per cent because of a grade curve. For Forsey, this was a sad example of a wider "flood of nonsense, stupidity, ignorance and mendacity."[13] But what for Forsey might have been evidence of decline could also be described as a progressive development. Schooling experts in the 1950s increasingly pushed for a more democratic classroom that centred on the needs of the child and where the usual need in schools to maintain authority was "tempered by the doctrine that too much authority was danger-ous."[14] In the post-war schools, teachers needed to worry not only about curriculum and discipline but also about the child's personality and self-esteem.

This could be both prosaic and profound. The main currents of high art in the 1950s were also predicated on the unvarnished truths that could be found within the self if only one could do away with re-strictions of social convention. The idea of the artist who let out her real self in her work has a long history, but it reached new heights with the rise of abstract expressionism in these years. Perhaps the best Canadian exemplar of the new school was the artist Jack Bush, whose friendship with the influential American critic Clement Greenberg put him at the centre of these cultural currents. Bush himself began psy-choanalysis in 1947 and started a regular diary in part based on this analysis in 1952. His analyst urged him to use his art as a kind of therapy, as a way to work through the emotions that still lingered from childhood trauma. It was essential for Bush and for other painters of this era to paint in a free and flowing style, eliminating the censor of the conscious brain and letting the truth that burbled within emerge on the canvas.[15]

Other cultural and intellectual developments pushed in the same direction. Margaret Mead became a popular figure for writing about Polynesian peoples and their more open, frank sexual practices. The popularization of her research moved mainstream North American culture toward a more relativistic assessment of sexual and moral stan-dards. So too did the Kinsey reports on human sexual behaviour, pub-lished in these years – the volume on male sexuality appearing in 1948 and the volume on women in 1953. Here was a seemingly scientific, not moral, accounting of what people allegedly actually did in their sexual lives – and all of it presented in public.[16] Better out than in.

All of this can seem at some remove from politics – Freud, high art, educational philosophy, frank scientific talk about sexual prac-tices. But when Bruce Hutchison's publishers promised Canadians a "candid" biography, they cannily locked into these broader develop-ments. It certainly wasn't that Hutchison wrote a Freudian biography of King – for he did not. But the culture of the early 1950s was ripe for this kind of seemingly more authentic version of the self – even the self of the nation's longest-serving prime minister.

⚉

It didn't hurt that Bruce Hutchison was a dazzling writer.

This was partly why Mackenzie King's literary executors had seriously considered asking Hutchison to be the official biographer and why they ultimately opted against him. They knew he could bring dramatic zeal and excitement to the task, but they opted for the safer academic choice of Robert MacGregor Dawson. Still, they had been tempted by the possibility of a Bruce Hutchison biography of Mackenzie King.[17]

As one of Canada's pre-eminent journalists and writers, Bruce Hutchison scribbled the history of twentieth-century Canada as it happened.[18] His trademark humility obliged him to say that he watched from the sidelines, but really he stood at the centre. As one of the country's few national political columnists, and a man tied by inclination and friendship to the Liberal Party, Hutchison knew all of the key politicians who controlled Canada's national fate from the 1920s to the 1970s. He came of age as a journalist in the 1920s and 1930s, working for newspapers in Victoria and Vancouver. In the 1940s, he impressed John W. Dafoe, the heralded Liberal editor of the *Winnipeg Free Press* (and one of Eugene Forsey's nemeses), who lured him into the orbit of the *Free Press*. From then on, even when he was far from Ottawa as editor of the Victoria *Times Colonist*, he played a role on the national political stage alongside other *Free Press* liberal journalists like Grant Dexter, George Ferguson, and the owner of the paper, Victor Sifton.

Hutchison could do it all. Even those who didn't much like his politics couldn't help but wonder at his way with words. Hutchison could make any subject come alive. He wrote columns not just on politics and international affairs but also gardening, a subject he loved, and any other light and humorous subject that struck his fancy. He wrote short stories for popular American magazines like *Saturday Evening Post* and *Collier's Weekly*. Most importantly, he wrote books: ruminations on the state of Canada like his Governor General Award–winning *The Unknown Country* (1942) and the follow-up

Canada: Tomorrow's Giant (1957); descriptions of his home province, as in *The Fraser* (1950); and accounts of Canadian politics like his history of Canada's prime ministers or his biography of one prime minister in particular, William Lyon Mackenzie King.

The Liberal Party had no more able and loyal friend than Bruce Hutchison. Hutchison and the *Free Press* had stood with the King government in the conscription crisis of the Second World War. In Louis St Laurent, Hutchison saw a father figure whom he admired more than any other. With Lester Pearson, Hutchison had a friend, someone of his own generation for whom he wanted the best of things. If he had asked for it, the Liberals would have given him a safe seat in Parliament, and almost certainly a seat in cabinet. They tried to convince him to run on several occasions. He always turned them down. But he remained loyal, even writing speeches for Pearson.[19]

This loyalty and friendship is no doubt partly why King's literary executor Jack Pickersgill took Hutchison aside and suggested that perhaps the great journalist could write his own biography of the chief, one that, unlike the official biography, could be popular and engaging. The spark of the idea flared in the kindling of Hutchison's imagination. He would write a biography of King. It would be a book not only about King but also about Canada and the era in which he had governed. He thought that the literary executors had been wise to pass him over for the official position of biographer since he would "only [be] interested in a portrait which paints the great man warts and all." The book would be "fair" but it also needed to be "utterly candid." For it had to "try to answer that fascinating question which haunts all my contemporaries, namely how a man so essentially small in most of his human aspects was yet able, with these ingredients, to erect such a large corpus of public achievement."[20]

It was a good time for candid biographies. By mid-century, a few other voices dared to ask why Canadians had been so ill-served in the biographies of its political figures. "It seems to me," lamented one critic in the *Ottawa Journal*, "that when a Canadian sets out to write about another Canadian he puts on his cleanest shirt and Sunday tie and dusts off his typewriter lest the keys bear any worldly dust as they make their imprint." No matter the real-life differences, the characters appearing in such biographies blurred into a national sameness: "We get a little parchment fellow who was born of Scotch-Canadian parents and always ran errands for his mother until he worked his way through university and won a scholarship in philosophy which brought him into business or politics wherein his sterling character at length but inevitably broke through to public recognition and left its beneficent rays on all with whom he came in contact." The respectable biography recoiled from the passions – beautiful, dirty, or anything in between. It stepped gently over "rows" and rarely admitted ambition. If the subject did well in life (as, of course, he did, hence the biography), his "advancements must always be ascribed to plain reward forced upon an unwilling victim."[21] If the journalist had been specifically describing the biographies so far published of Mackenzie King, he couldn't have been more spot-on.

Surely Canadians were ready for more insightful and authentically individualistic fare. Victorian-era biographies had been thoroughly deferential, eschewing scandal and intimacies. Such biographies were "constrained by a mania for good taste, respectability, and decorum." In England, of course, Lytton Strachey had begun writing exactly the opposite of these virtuous Victorian volumes a generation earlier. Canadian writers and publishers read Strachey but only belatedly copied him. In Canada, the debunking style of Strachey biography had been admired by some but, as Carl Berger notes, the Canadian versions were more "tepid and limited." Historians had tended to turn away from biography altogether and to look for the real patterns of history in economic forces. Yet by the 1940s some Canadian writers were looking to return to biography as a form of writing which was more human and direct, and which showed the real lives of individuals and their ability to influence their worlds. When the historian Donald Creighton set out to write his monumental biography of John A. Macdonald in the late 1940s, he complained about how "Canadian biographies have a formal, official air, as if they had been written out of the materials of a newspaper morgue." In such biographies, the human being at their centre "remains an important Public Personage – in capitals – dwarfed by the circumstances of his 'Times,' which are portrayed in great chunks of descriptive material, pitilessly detailed, and among which he drags out an embarrassed and attenuated documentary existence, like an unsubstantial *papier-maché* [sic] figure made up of old dispatches and newspaper files." Readers find it hard to resist the "uncomfortable sensation that one is reading about one and the same man."[22]

As good a Liberal as Bruce Hutchison was, he had no intention of giving Canadians a starched and respectable biography of Mackenzie King. If he didn't have access to King's private papers (reserved for the official biographer), Hutchison still had his sources. He drew informants from those who had been close to King. Jack Pickersgill, King's former assistant and current literary executor, gave him stories as someone loyal to King and a civil servant close to the action. For the secrets of the cabinet, Hutchison relied principally on two ministers, Chubby Power and T.A. Crerar. Both men had been at the highest reaches of the King government, but both remained skeptical of the King mystique. Both helped Hutchison on the assurance of anonymity. Power even gave Hutchison access to a diary that he had kept in the midst of the conscription crisis of 1944. Many other individuals pitched in to give Hutchison a sense of what had really happened in some of the key moments of King's life.

From this base, Bruce Hutchison gave Canadians a published version of Mackenzie King's life unlike anything published before. *The Incredible Canadian* presented King as a great prime minister but it did not do so by draping him in sentiment, high intentions, and noble action. Hutchison did believe King's vision for the country to have been great. But he also exposed King's often devious, manipulative, and self-serving actions. Hutchison wanted to show how politics really worked, the behind-the-scenes manoeuvring that really mattered. Ultimately, he generally approved of King's actions and he happily bathed them in the light of retroactive glory and claims of far-sightedness. Yet his detailed reconstructions of events on Parliament Hill had a vivid action that was new.

On the King-Byng crisis of 1926, Hutchison actually presented much of the evidence of King's misdeeds, though he did still repeat the Liberal story of the crisis as a moment of national evolution. What is intriguing about Hutchison's account is the way he happily transforms the story of the King-Byng dispute into a tale of political cunning and chance. The title of the excerpt in *Maclean's* gave the flavour, "How Mackenzie King Won His Greatest Gamble." In other words, King-Byng was not primarily a constitutional achievement (*pace* the traditional Liberal story) nor was it an example of moral perfidy (as Forsey had it). Instead, it was a perfect example of King's political skill.

When Mackenzie King goes to the governor general to ask for a dissolution, this comes after repeated attempts to get his government out of the danger of being defeated in Parliament. Hutchison has King trying on many disguises – Uriah Heep, Galahad, Sherlock Holmes, and Machiavelli – as he tries to navigate the crisis. In Byng's refusal to grant the dissolution, and Meighen's acceptance of the premiership, Hutchison has King finding a way to survive. Hutchison claims that King showed "fantastic adroitness" in burying his government's problems under the weight of this constitutional issue of a governor general refusing a Canadian prime minister's request to dissolve Parliament. He repeats many of the elements of the Liberal story about the memory of the fight for responsible government and the importance of King as a defender of Parliament (even when, as Forsey would say, he was trying to escape its verdict). Overall, though, King-Byng is turned into a story of political calculation – strategy over substance, luck over morality.[23]

Hutchison could not have picked a more certain way to offend Eugene Forsey. Forsey wrote extensively about the book, in private letters, in letters to the editor, and in a long article published in *Saturday Night*. The *Ottawa Citizen* even published a satirical poem by Forsey, mocking Hutchison's over-the-top prose style.[24] Forsey did not fall for what he saw as the trickery of Hutchison's realism, his bare-bones, politics-as-it-really-was, account. Forsey admitted that King did not come off unscathed in Hutchison's account but he nonetheless saw the danger that lurked underneath this "nasty, slippery, clever job." For, while Hutchison did not entirely overlook all of King's misdeeds, he also removed the whole event from the calculus of right and wrong. What truly offended Forsey was "the calm identifying of proficiency in mendacity and utter lack of honour or scruple with 'political genius.'"[25]

Forsey didn't disagree with everything Hutchison wrote. He thought that Hutchison did show the secrets of King's success: lying, support in Quebec, luck, strong ministers, an effective civil service,

The fantastic events of 1926 showed Mackenzie King as a true political genius. With cunning, courage, wild chance and pure Canadianism he steered the sinking Liberal ship through a major scandal, a fight with the Governor-General and defeats in the House

This bonus-length feature is condensed from Bruce Hutchison's new book, The Incredible Canadian, to be published later this month by Longmans, Green. In the next issue a final excerpt — Hutchison's personal appraisal and assessment of Mackenzie King — will be published.

GOVERNOR-GENERAL BYNG thought a promise was broken.

PRIME MINISTER KING played Machiavelli and Galahad.

How Mackenzie King Won His Greatest Gamble

A MACLEAN'S FLASHBACK

By BRUCE HUTCHISON

7.2 "How Mackenzie King Won His Greatest Gamble"

and, most importantly, being "unhampered by principles." But this could not excuse the Liberal journalist's refusal to cast judgment. How could you see and not find fault? This seemed to be the Liberal way. It demonstrated how the King era continued to bleed into the St Laurent Canada of the 1950s. As Forsey said, Hutchison "dislikes Mr. King. He denounces his foreign policy between the two wars ... He is highly critical of a lot of other things. But, like so many of our 'intelligentsia,' he just can't get over those elections. It is perhaps Mr. King's most enduring monument that for a whole generation he made the winning of elections the final test of statesmanship." In the same vein, Forsey wrote in a letter to *Saturday Night* that the version Hutchison gave of King's "double fraud" in King-Byng said a good deal about Hutchison himself: 'If a political manoeuvre succeeds, it doesn't occur to him even to question its morality; or that if it does, the standard Liberal answer to everything is enough: 'We won the election.'"[26]

Forsey wasn't any happier with Hutchison's account of the conscription crisis of the Second World War, also excerpted in *Maclean's* and the subject of much discussion in publications around the country. It was one thing to admire King's Machiavellian tactics in the distant case of King-Byng, but when Hutchison turned to the explosive issue of conscription during the Second World War, he ventured into a territory littered with still-active moral landmines. Hutchison claimed to have a secret to tell, a revelation that he clearly hoped would see him through this treacherous landscape.

The *Maclean's* headline boasted of a tale of "Mackenzie King and the Revolt of the Canadian Army."[27] The magazine promised to tell readers about "the most critical thirty-five days in the political life of Mackenzie King and perhaps in the life of the Canadian nation." Many might think that they knew this story. But Hutchison had a great secret to reveal. He claimed that in the final days of the conscription crisis, as the cabinet threatened to divide and break apart the government and the Liberal Party, an event that would have had terrifying consequences for the nation, Mackenzie King was worried about another crisis, one that no one, until this point, knew about. The details were vague, and even Hutchison admitted that he couldn't be sure how to reconcile the conflicting accounts. What he could say was that "King either saw, or thought he saw, or pretended to see, the Canadian Army on the verge of seizing political power through a sit-down strike or an open uprising." Hutchison proceeded to tell the tale, which reads "like the stage directions of a play, with an ending almost beyond belief."

It is not clear who was Hutchison's source for this story, though the most likely candidate would be the King literary executor and Hutchison friend Jack Pickersgill. No one else close to events during the war or after gave the story of the "Revolt in the Army" any credence.[28] Allegedly, King received a telephone call from General Andy McNaughton after he had been made minister of defence and in the short period when McNaughton was still trying to prove that the voluntary enlistment system could get more recruits quickly in the autumn of 1944. McNaughton had just been to a meeting with the Army brass. They insisted to him that the recruitment system was not working and would not work. More so, he said that "I have terrible news for you, Chief! What I must tell you will come as a body blow." When the call was over, King "hung up the telephone knowing, he said, that he no longer faced a political crisis, or even a racial schism, but the disintegration of the army, a military uprising, which might seize the civil power, a state of national anarchy, nothing less." Or so the source close to King told Hutchison, and so Hutchison reported.

When Hutchison was researching his book, he ran the story of the revolt past everyone he knew who was close to events at the time of the crisis – cabinet ministers, Army officers. They all thought the story was nonsense. Chubby Power, one of Hutchison's sources for other parts of the book, and the man who had been minister of air, joked to Angus McDonald, his predecessor in the post, that "it would have been great fun, had your loyal and intrepid Navy turned its guns on Laurier House from its armoured rowboats, in Dows Lake."[29]

The revolt story also continued Hutchison's account of politics as a kind of spectacle. Ultimately, King reversed his position. Even though he had fired Ralston for supporting conscription, three weeks later he adopted the same policy himself. For many in English Canada, this amounted to betrayal of the worst kind. In the writing on conscription in this era, Ralston plays the role of martyr. He died in 1949, and even then King refused to honour him in Parliament. As the *Winnipeg Daily Star* put it, "a less great Canadian than Mr. Ralston could have split the Liberal Party down the middle. It is to Mr. Ralston's credit, having seen the government finally take action, that he did not take any step that would interfere with the country's war effort. His patriotism came before his personal position."[30] This clearly contrasted with King's behaviour. King and his allies professed that King acted for the best of the country. But it is difficult to believe that the three-week delay before conscription was implemented truly mattered. King faced defeat, threw aside a rival, and then adopted the policies of that rival.

In the face of this conduct, Hutchison professed to see only King's higher intentions and, when these weren't enough, his political skill. King acted out of daring, and brutally. A leader needed to behave like this. Or such was the impression left by Hutchison. Privately, where Hutchison was less concerned about protecting the party's interests, he admitted that even King's official documents might not help in substantiating the revolt in the Army story because "the documents will be constructed to support the theory." He also admitted that he even doubted whether McNaughton's papers would "substantiate the suggestion that the military were about to launch some form of up-rising. Nevertheless, Mr. King used this fantasy, if such it was, with remarkable cunning."[31]

Eugene Forsey initially thought that Hutchison's account of the conscription crisis left "King naked and shivering before the bar of history. It throws a good deal of light on some of the secrets of his power: ruthlessness, callousness, utter lack of principle, infinite capacity to wear opponents down by sheer weight of irrelevant talk and, of course, sheer mendacity."[32] Yet this was not the whole story. Yes, Hutchison exposed King's brutal methods, but he also wrapped this up in a tale of how King tried to keep the nation together – how his tough tactics aimed at the better Canadian national good. The ends justified the means. Forsey saw only the double-handed duplicity, the absence of honour, but it's not clear that this was enough to bring down a politician's reputation. There were other kinds of truths to be told.

In the early 1950s, in a North American context that gave new values to being frank about hidden truths, Bruce Hutchison offered Canadians a story of Mackenzie King as he really had been, and politics as it really was. This didn't just apply to events in Parliament. Hutchison also wanted to give an unvarnished account of Mackenzie King the man, a frank assessment from someone who admired Liberal policies but also thought it important that the warts and blemishes mark the page every bit as much as the accomplishments. The book offered up a dual version of King, indeed almost a schizophrenic King.

The book parallels Hutchison's approach to Canada itself. His 1942 best-seller *The Unknown Country* began with a dark, poetic account of the nation and its unknown character. There, Hutchison had written: "No one knows my country, neither the stranger nor its own sons." Ten years later in *The Incredible Canadian*, Hutchison sang the same tune. "The mystery of William Lyon Mackenzie King is not the mystery of a man. It is the mystery of a people. We do not understand King because we do not understand ourselves."[33]

Hutchison promised to change all that, to give Canadians the real Mackenzie King. It was a mangled reproduction of a mixed-up man whom Hutchison admired – though not without reservations. Hutchison matched King to the nation, for bad and good. "Just as Canada, built against all logic, the laws of geography, the forces of economics and the accepted theories of politics, became larger than the sum of its parts," Hutchison wrote, "so King built a personal achievement incomparably larger than himself." One needed to admit King's private faults. "By the public measurement of statesmanship," Hutchison argued, "King was the greatest Canadian. By the private measurement of character, by the dimensions of the man himself, his two predecessors [John A. Macdonald and Wilfrid Laurier] tower above him."[34]

Throughout Hutchison's writing on King and Canada, he kept coming back to this idea of the hidden and unknown interior, the dark or important point that couldn't be seen from the outside. "Outwardly the dullest, he was inwardly the most vivid." This is King as an enigma, a mystery, someone whose public persona is as much "shadow" as substance. Canadians never understood this, they "never divined his infinite variety." For King played many roles – the politician as actor. He was philosopher and historian, "devious party manager," "supreme court of his party," friend to small people, a hard employer to secretaries, a "passionate social reformer," a "crafty autocrat," and "under all this ran a sense of humor too deep for the public to suspect!" Really, he had been a better actor than Roosevelt or Churchill for he put on the "drab impersonation of the common man – the last thing he ever was."[35]

The politician as actor and impersonator: Hutchison upended the moral reading of this idea. Back in 1949, the King biographer Reginald Hardy had claimed that King had been putting on a "show" in 1926. Hardy said King had "learned how to put on a show when the occasion demanded one" and talked about how King gave a "studied performance" of "righteous indignation" at Meighen's temporary government in 1926. Eugene Forsey laughed in delight at this characterization. "It doesn't seem to have struck him," Forsey wrote to Meighen, "that this is about as damning a thing as anybody has ever said about King. Even you and I could hardly say worse, and if we had said this, King would probably have sued us for libel."[36] Forsey's laughter made sense in a culture where character defined the man. But what about in a culture of personality? Personality was the newer psychological slippery concept. It implied that, in a sense, everyone put on an act. The outward appearance of a man was always an imposition.

Hutchison took Canadians into King's home, but he didn't do so, as an earlier biographer had instructed, because Canadians had a duty to know the statesman. Instead, Hutchison presented the private King as not much of a man at all, at least according to the standards of the day. King stuffed his house with bric-a-brac, like a fussy Victorian housewife. He could be petty and mean. He treated his employees terribly, showing little sympathy for their needs, certainly not when they conflicted with his own desire for immediate and constant service. King had no great skill as an orator, no charm with the people.

Yet Hutchison merged these personal criticisms with a sense of King's larger achievement. "The mystery grows, the fascination deepens and the enigma retreats farther from our clutch when the private man emerges and suddenly is overstopped by the public shadow. That single fact, more than any other, explains the mystery of King and his Canada – he, like the nation, was bitterly aware of his own stature, he was determined to be larger than his nature ordained and, in the affairs of this world, he and the nation succeeded." It was all an incredible act – the clothes of personality that King donned in order to do his job, to achieve what he so desperately wanted to achieve. "The Canadian people never divined this infinite variety. They saw only his set public act, the round little figure with hunched shoulders, the flat and homely face, the wisp of hair on the bald head, the antique collar and cuffs, the delicate hands, the bouncing, cautious gait of one walking on invisible eggs." Yet what an achievement it all really was.[37]

Ultimately, Hutchison threw up his hands at the disjuncture between petty man and great statesman. He called it a mystery, just as Canada itself was a mystery – and just as Freudians were telling Canadians that the human psyche was a mystery. The swirling passions and desire of the id, the inner child as it would later be popularized, never went away. They thrust and prodded and threatened to erupt constantly. But on top of this, the super-ego kept a lid on things. Social sanctions and morality, lessons of respectability, the hallmarks of civilization, ensured that the id could not ultimately rule. Sometimes, bad things might happen. An individual might erupt in passion. At other times, these passions could be sublimated in another direction. The animal drives of mother-love could be turned to a mature love of a mother-substitute. Such was the Freudian logic, which in the 1950s was only just becoming common sense. And such is the image of Mackenzie King and Canada that Bruce Hutchison gave Canadians: a man driven personally by the pettiest and silliest of intentions but who, through determination and skill, yet managed to achieve great things politically: a sublimation that ultimately benefited the nation at large.

What to make of Bruce Hutchison and his candid biography?

Many Liberals just didn't know. They knew that *The Incredible Canadian* sparkled with fine writing and drama and more excitement than any typical Canadian political biography. The *Globe*'s literary critic William Arthur Deacon half-joked that the "excitement injected into the character and career of William Lyon Mackenzie King constitutes the greatest feat of magic yet performed by any Canadian writer." The book sold thousands of copies and was a Canadian publishing success. Many commentators noted that MPs and others in political circles read it avidly. People approached Arthur Meighen and Colonel Ralston's son Stuart, on the street, to talk about it.

When ex-cabinet ministers travelled the country, the book was the top subject of conversation. Chubby Power declared that the extracts from Hutchison's book published in *Maclean's* were read widely even in Quebec. Clearly, Hutchison had done something right. And yet one critic later remarked that official Ottawa greeted the book with an "ovation of silence."[38]

Liberals just didn't know what to think of this book, so "full of treacle, [yet] laced with vinegar."[39] The safest thing to do was to say very little at all. Chubby Power, ensconced in the Senate, and close to but well above the fray, chuckled at the reaction of the "courtiers" in Ottawa. Whenever *The Incredible Canadian* "is mentioned by these gentlemen," he said, "there is first of all a look off the shoulder to see who is listening, and then a sort of a contemptuous shrug but no commitment. Apparently word is being awaited from on high as to whether it is to receive the imprimatur or not. There is some thought that the Party may be injured in some vague kind of a way. People outside the inner circle have varied and usually strong opinions – all the way from those who think that an injustice was done to the old man, to those who strenuously maintain that he was not damned half enough."[40]

Privately, the literary executor Fred McGregor wondered what had got into Hutchison. He couldn't "understand the tone of personal bitterness which is so evident." He knew "that Bruce was no worshipper … but why should he feel it necessary, in referring to the man, to use words such as despicable, flat and homely face, plump, round and spiritless, pale and bookish little man, flabby scholar, tiny creature?" It didn't make sense. Only one MP spoke out publicly, though. George Murray, the representative for Cariboo, British Columbia, put his displeasure on the record in the House. "One would almost think [Mackenzie King] was a monster from reading the book," Murray declared. This for a man whose record showed him to be "great humanitarian," "a stout defender of the poor, a diplomat, a negotiator; a modest man, simple in his habits." One citizen wrote to the *Ottawa Journal* to denounce Hutchison. All of this story about King being a mystery was pure nonsense, the writer declared. Canadians "protest when one of our great leaders is misrepresented." Someone, he wrote, "should write the true story of Mackenzie King's life, leaving out the sarcasms, the exaggerated phrases, the half-truths. Above all, do not attempt to represent Mackenzie King as a man of mystery. Definitely he was not that ... His life was an open book. A good clean book."[41]

With this last line one could almost imagine the letter writer going on to speak on temperance and the evils of the white slave trade, so redolent of a Victorian moral common sense. That was the world that Hutchison's book threatened. Not because Hutchison was a radical. He was an ideological liberal but middle of the road in most of his views. The culture was roiling around exactly these kinds of issues: whether to be more open and frank about our less than exemplary passions and secrets, and hence what to make of politicians and their own secrets. Some revelled in the freedom to see a politician as he really was. Frank Underhill didn't agree with everything in *The Incredible Canadian* but he loved the complex human picture it gave. The book, Underhill exclaimed, "makes you feel what an exciting, inspiring, disgusting, broad-minded, selfish creature a first-class politician really is."[42]

But this was just the point: the frank assessment of politicians, the open look into what makes them tick, neither hagiography nor partisan philippic, threatened the very idea of the statesman. One Liberal wrote to Fred McGregor to wonder what would be done about Hutchison: "To ignore is to condone and that is declaring an Open Season on every future Leader upon ending his Term of Office."[43]

Thomas Crerar had known King as well as anyone. The Canadian senator had once been the leader of the Progressive group in Parliament. But he had been drawn into the Liberal Party and into Mackenzie King's cabinet. Crerar didn't entirely agree with Hutchison's dual portrayal of King – as pathetic little man and greatest prime minister simultaneously. King didn't have the long-term vision that *The Incredible Canadian* claimed for him. Still, this didn't mean that Crerar thought it wise to portray the private King as such a "pitiable figure." "Hund[re]ds of thousands of Canadians believed him to be a great statesman and a great man," Crerar wrote to Hutchison. "You strip him completely of that." Crerar "doubt[ed] the wisdom" of writing this kind of book. "Without question," he claimed, "there has been a great loss of faith in public men in this country and in the institutions of Government." By his portrayal of the King in *The Incredible Canadian*, Hutchison might lead, "in some degree at least, [to] a furthering of that loss of faith." "Nothing is more important," the old politician wrote, "than to maintain as strongly as possible in the minds of our people a faith in their institutions and in the character and quality of their public men."[44]

Old men often complain that the world is declining around them. They aren't always right to think that the next generation will mind the changes, but they often do see the direction of what is changing. So it was with Crerar. The language of politics was changing. In *The Incredible Canadian* Hutchison opened up the idea of the statesman to a kind of frank and honest scrutiny that posed a threat to public men everywhere.

8
Ferns and Ostry

There is a boundary between being frank and being rude, between plain speech and just plain crass. Bruce Hutchison's candid biography of King walked the respectable side of the line, his Liberal credentials and his admiration for King as the great statesman keeping him safe. Two young radical academics, Harry Ferns and Bernard Ostry, offered their own candid biography of Mackenzie King in the mid-1950s but they did not fare as well. The publication of Ferns and Ostry's *The Age of Mackenzie King: Rise of the Leader* led to a scandal in Parliament and claims and counter-claims of censorship by the government and the Canadian Broadcasting Corporation (CBC). If all publicity is good publicity, then this should have helped book sales. It didn't. Partly, Ferns and Ostry suffered because their critique of King veered too far to the left. But it was also their youth and insouciant irreverence that made their perspective on King seem just a little too frank. In the mid-1950s, despite a growing appreciation for frankness and a waning support for the statesman ideal, the politics of deference retained a great deal of power. The age of Mackenzie King wasn't quite over yet.[1]

Harry Ferns had a history with the Liberal establishment; indeed, if not for his outspoken nature, he might have become one of them. In the mid-1930s, like many of the brightest minds in Canada, Ferns took the civil-service entrance exams, finishing third in the country. When war broke out in 1939, he tried to enlist in the Army but was refused on medical grounds. Instead, he took up a position in External Affairs. From there, the prime minister cherry-picked the bright young man to come and work in the prime minister's office.[2]

Harry Ferns did not fit in. He would never be someone to mould himself to his surroundings, to blend in. Ferns had grown up in the north end of Winnipeg, a boy from a poor Anglo-Saxon family in an immigrant neighbourhood where being Anglo-Saxon put you on the outside. From a young age, Ferns was already an odd kind of standout. He pulled himself up by hard and brilliant work. He scraped together the money to put himself through university in the midst of the Depression, an achievement of its own. After he got his BA, the next step for any ambitious colonial was to go abroad, perhaps to Oxbridge. He knew, though, that his lack of physical prowess meant he could never win a Rhodes scholarship. Instead he tried for an Imperial Order Daughters of the Empire (IODE) scholarship, though here too he recognized the limits of his upbringing, travelling to Queen's University for an MA because he considered the University of Manitoba not prestigious enough a location from which to win a scholarship. He won the IODE and went on to Cambridge where he ultimately earned a first, a rare distinction especially for Canadians.

The ship to England afforded the luxury of days spent in contemplation and conversation. It was in one such conversation that Ferns was won over to communism. Its material no-nonsense logic appealed to him. He had already been attracted to the newest trends in economic history in Canada. The works of Harold Innis and Frank Underhill took Canadian history out of the world of sentiment and morality, and explained Canada's development as the result of trade and resources. In the mid-1930s, with the inevitable logic of capitalism so obviously frayed, Ferns made the move to a radical critique of the economic and social status quo. He later claimed that he never officially joined the Communist Party at Cambridge, but he actively organized other Commonwealth students in groups that critics would later call "fronts" for communism. They challenged the British government on international issues – calling for independence for India and for action against the fascists in the Spanish Civil war. In the early Cold War, that kind of politics would be called "premature anti-fascism."

None of this seemed to matter to the Canadian government when Ferns returned to Canada to take up a position in External Affairs and then eventually in the prime minister's office.[3] Ferns worked, ultimately disconsolately, at the heart of Canadian power for several

8.1 Harry Ferns

years. The word on him was that he didn't have "good judgment." This likely meant that he stuck by his principles, and spoke them loudly – not the kinds of attributes that push you up the civil-service hierarchy, certainly not in Mackenzie King's government.

He went back to External Affairs in 1943, chewed up and spat out from King's staff like many others. The next year, a conflict with Deputy Minister of External Affairs (and later Mackenzie King literary executor) Norman Robertson drove Ferns to resign altogether. He returned to academic life at United College Winnipeg where his contract was not renewed after two years. Moving to the University of Manitoba, he found that there, too, his academic colleagues could respect his intellect but not appreciate his political views or outspokenness. When workers at the *Winnipeg Free Press* went on strike in the late 1940s, he thrust himself into a venture to create a citizens' newspaper. Ultimately, this is what pushed him out of academic life in that city. University boards of governors in the 1940s, a time when academic freedom was more a wish than a reality, did not respond well to academics on the left who publicly spoke their politics aloud.

Worse was to come for Ferns in 1949. He had applied for and won a job at the new Canadian Forces college, Royal Roads University, on Vancouver Island. Ferns had made all the arrangements to move his family and start his new job in the autumn of 1949. It was not to be. The letter arrived in August 1949. "The Department of National Defence has now indicated that your services are not acceptable." The Civil Service Commission informed him that it had "no alternative but to delete your name from eligible list 69,891."[4]

A more bureaucratic and less helpful letter would be hard to devise. It meant that Harry Ferns was not going to start work at Royal Roads the next month. One day he had a job, the next day he was unemployed. Ferns found it almost impossible to get an explanation as to why this might be the case. He wrote to the Civil Service Commission. He wrote to Brooke Claxton, the minister of national defence.[5] No reply.

He had his suspicions. This was late 1949. The Cold War search for subversives within every area of life, whether in the government or in Hollywood, was well under way. If the American witch hunts drew more publicity, Canadian officials still carried out their own quieter mole hunt, and Ferns would have known that his sympathies created suspicions. Hadn't he given a speech to the Canadian-Soviet Friendship Council as recently as 1947?

At this point, Ferns and his wife decided to move to England, to go back and finish his PhD and attempt to make his way in a country where he had once achieved so much. On their way out of the country, Ferns stopped in Ottawa to try his luck one last time – to get some redress for his poor treatment. It helped that he had connections, friends with whom he had served in the prime minister's office and who now helped him get meetings with the relevant deputy ministers. He demanded to know why he had been fired, why the government had broken its contract, and he demanded compensation. The government gave no explanation, but it did ultimately opt to compensate Harry Ferns in the amount of $2,000, though only if he stayed silent. Needing the money, Ferns agreed, but not without a final retort. He would accept the money "as a measure of compensation for a gross breach of contract and for the anxiety and financial loss arising out of this." As for the rest, he wrote, "I am content to leave the actions of Mr. Claxton and his associates in the Department of National Defence to history and their own consciences."[6]

It's perhaps not surprising that the sting of rejection stuck with Harry Ferns. Never quite fitting in, rarely of the right background to match those more privileged folk whose accomplishments were similar to his own, Ferns could sense, perhaps too readily, when someone did not show him the proper respect. Here was a clear situation where he suffered at the hands of those who didn't know the true facts. The irony of Ferns's treatment in Liberal Ottawa in these years is that he would ultimately turn out to be the exact opposite of a communist spy. In his later years, Ferns would become a right-wing ideologue, attacking the welfare state and acting as an intellectual avant-guard spokesman for Thatcherism in Britain. But in the early 1950s, when he turned to writing a biography of Mackenzie King, that transformation was in the future. Of only one thing was he then certain: he saw his book on Mackenzie King "as a blast on Joshua's trumpet which will, I hope, bring down the walls of the Liberal Jericho." Anticipating the response to his attack on the Liberal prime minister, he hoped that Liberal insiders like those he had battled in the prime minister's office or those responsible for his last beating – people like Jack Pickersgill and Brooke Claxton and Norman Robertson – would live to "regret the day they kicked Henry Ferns out of his native country and branded him a red."[7]

The idea for the biography came to him very soon after Mackenzie King died in July 1950. Ferns was in England completing his PhD thesis on Anglo-Argentinian relations and was about to take up a job at the University of Birmingham. He read the articles about the great statesman Mackenzie King and found them to be "sycophantic" and "drivelling guff." Surely Canada had matured to the point where its leaders could withstand mature scrutiny. Surely there was room for a more critical and truthful account of political leadership, warts and all. Ferns's ambitions resembled those of Bruce Hutchison. Ferns, though, was not a Liberal. Nor was he (yet) a Tory. His sense of the truth, of the real story of Mackenzie King and his power, owed more to Marx. At the time of King's retirement in 1948, Ferns had written several articles in the left-leaning periodical *Canadian Forum*. He decided to embark on a more enduring book-length effort.[8]

How to do it, though? With young children, and a new job and a PhD to complete, how could he have the time or resources to pull it off? The answer was near at hand. His name was Bernard Ostry.

Bernie Ostry could charm a shoe. With his classic dark handsome features, his expensive suits, his sports car, and his fine art collection, he was not exactly a typical graduate student. Ostry had studied under Harry Ferns back at the University of Manitoba. In the early 1950s he had arrived in England to pursue a graduate degree at the London School of Economics. Ostry was a young, ambitious Jewish Canadian from Flin Flon, not exactly attributes that pushed one to the top of the social circle in the late 1940s. But his family had made a good deal of money, starting in the dry-goods business and later expanding into other investments. By the time that Ostry had arrived in London, he was already very well-to-do, investing in companies in his spare time, borrowing $10,000 dollars from his father for one particular venture, and occupying the post of vice-president in two holding companies that were meant to make the eventual transfer of money from father to son less subject to succession duties.[9]

Material prosperity, though, wasn't what really mattered to Ostry. Above all, he wanted to "make it" socially and politically. He collected friends and connections just as he collected art, and he had excellent taste in both. He made himself well connected on the left of the Labour Party in early 1950s London. He even won himself a position as assistant to V.K. Krishna Menon when this stalwart of inter-war socialist London became representative of the newly independent India at the United Nations.[10]

It was hard not to like Bernard Ostry. Women found him attractive. His correspondence in the early 1950s is littered with letters from admiring female acquaintances. The New York literary agent Julie Medlock (and publicist for Bertrand Russell), a friend of Ostry's, wrote of him: "Your brief visits are like bolts of lightning. There you are – looking young, handsome, intelligent, debonair." When the conservative journalist Patrick Nicholson interviewed Ostry for CBC radio, he introduced him thus: "All, especially the ladies, [will] be interested to know that in addition to a sharp intellect and a keen

8.2 Bernard Ostry

sense of humour the professor is blessed with a considerable personal charm." Years later, on an episode of the CBC radio program "Cross Country Check-up," the otherwise professional female host gushed and giggled as she and Ostry spoke to callers. Ostry just had that effect on people. Medlock said that, when Ostry was at the United Nations with Krishna Menon in the early 1950s, the word was that he was likely a future prime minister of Canada.[11]

For this to be true, Canada was going to have to change. For different reasons, Ferns and Ostry had little time for what they considered the stodgy cultural and political status quo of 1950s Canada. At the coronation of the new queen in 1953, they listened to the events on the radio, guffawing at the ludicrous costumes and pomposity on display. In Canada they saw a Liberal Party that dominated the nation and yet was led by old men with old ideas. Most of the senior cabinet ministers in St Laurent's government hailed from the Mackenzie

King era. They had only reluctantly shifted their laissez-faire liberalism to accommodate the Depression and war. Now Ostry connected himself to those on the left of the party, such as Paul Martin, or to those in the CCF, such as Tommy Douglas, Alastair Stewart, or the MP for North Winnipeg, James Bryson. He corresponded with Pierre Trudeau in Quebec, seeing in the *Cité Libre* editor the kind of man needed for a new Canada.

The letters friends wrote to Ferns and Ostry give some sense of the cultural malaise that they felt. Julie Medlock wrote from New York: "I am so out of sympathy with what is going on here – I literally cringe every time I hear a radio commercial, and the unconscious materialism of this society and its moral perversions are just things I can no longer live with." Another friend wrote to Ferns saying how she was so looking forward to visiting with him in England. "We should have some long pleasant evenings of good conversation without the distraction of television. Everybody here is completely mesmerized by television. The art of conversation is completely and totally lost. Whenever one visits friends these days, the first thing one is handed is a drink, then the television set is turned on, and that's the end of a promising evening. I've gotten to the point now where I can't speak in more than two syllable words." The historian W.L. Morton, certainly not a radical, complained of "the growing stodginess of Canadian life. The boom, the American crusade against Communism, the provincialism of a great and struggling country, the conformist disposition of our best minds ... are stronger now than ever. Inevitably the demagoguery which results from the decay of intellectual and political principle is growing apace."[12]

The mix of resentment and dissatisfaction was complex, tied as it was to new technologies, the downside of prosperity, the complacency of the post-war boom, and the sense that something had to or should change in the political sphere. Ferns and Ostry determined to set one stone in motion by taking on the legacy of Mackenzie King, the man who seemed to have created Liberal Party fortunes in the twentieth century. They divided the job between them. Ferns was tied to Birmingham and his job and family. He would write the book itself. Ostry, with his money and ability to make connections, would head back to North America and do most of the research. He would scour collections to see what kinds of previously overlooked letters

and documents could be found. Ostry would also befriend prominent men who might be willing to open their own private collections
to him – Tories with no love for King like Arthur Meighen, and Liberals with a grievance (especially because of the conscription crisis),
such as T.A. Crerar, Angus Macdonald, and Chubby Power. Even if
King's literary executors shut off access to King's own documents,
Ferns and Ostry might be able to recreate a good deal of King's correspondence, and the key events in recent Canadian history, by other
means. They kept their purpose relatively secret. Ostry was dispatched
to Ottawa to see what kinds of documents were available. Together, he
and Ferns hid their true intent, saying that Ostry was to be engaged
upon a study of Canadian politics in the early twentieth century.
That was vague enough not to raise suspicions but precise enough to
get access to the right sorts of papers. For Ferns and Ostry weren't so
sure that their book would be welcomed in Canada.

⚉

It happened one day in January 1953. Bernard Ostry was going
through the Wilfrid Laurier papers in the Public Archives in Ottawa,
searching out references to Mackenzie King. When he left for lunch,
the papers were on his desk; when he returned they weren't there.
Where did they go? The archives employees gave him a vague answer:
the papers were no longer available.

Ostry went for advice to a friend of Ferns from his time in the
prime minister's office who suggested that Ostry visit Jack Pickersgill,
the clerk of the Privy Council. Pickersgill was Canada's top civil servant, the man who worked with cabinet to act as the voice between
the political and administrative forms of government, and it wasn't
clear why he should have anything to say about access to the papers
of a long-dead prime minister now housed in the Public Archives.
Ostry suspected the worst but arranged an appointment. On meeting
Pickersgill, he demanded to know why he was refused access to the
papers of Wilfrid Laurier. He threatened to go to his MP and raise the
issue of whether the clerk of the Privy Council was an appropriate
person "to determine who should and who should not look at the
Laurier Papers." Pickersgill could give no adequate explanation. He
responded with bureaucratic politeness, the kind that rarely leads to

satisfaction. Ostry would not get an answer here. He left the office but when he got back to the archives, the Laurier Papers were once again, without any explanation, open for him to inspect.[13]

This incident reinforced in Ostry and Ferns a sense that there were forces out to get them. "I am gathering the impression very quickly that there is developing in Canada a King cult designed to prevent any effective, well documented reconsideration of his role in Canadian life," Ferns wrote. The incident in January 1953 was the first of several. The archives lost track of certain papers they were supposed to send to Ostry in England; they didn't accept that he had permission to view other papers; they first reported that they could copy some papers onto microfilm and then later, when Ostry had returned to England, stated that they couldn't make copies. In each case there was a logical, if sometimes befuddled, explanation. It was especially awkward when Ostry was not sent papers because they had been removed by those working on the official biography of King. "What is the status of the Laurier House organization?" Ostry asked the chief archivist. "Can they come into the Archives and disorganize or organize material for their own purposes in a way which makes it difficult for a member of the public like myself to make use of public facilities?"[14]

The chief archivist, W. Kaye Lamb, couldn't adequately answer Ostry's questions. How could he? The man in charge of the Public Archives, the man who made decisions about which papers were open, which ones could be consulted, was also one of Mackenzie King's literary executors. Lamb no doubt thought he could play both roles successfully. He was an able, competent, and likely fair administrator. His own documents suggest that he saw Ostry as a too-assertive intrusion into the life of the archives, but also as a source of potential embarrassment and someone to be handled carefully. There is no direct evidence that there was any conspiracy to keep documents from Ostry.[15] Nonetheless, Lamb's dual status only reinforced the idea that official Ottawa was also Liberal Ottawa. It didn't help that later in the year Jack Pickersgill was parachuted into a safe Newfoundland riding to join the Liberal government and the cabinet as secretary of state. He was widely rumoured to be a potential successor to Louis St Laurent and future prime minister. It was becoming a well-trod path – from the senior civil service into the Liberal cabinet – the same path that Lester Pearson and Mackenzie King had followed.

When it came to finding a publisher for their book, Ferns and Ostry thought that no Canadian firm would have the guts to take it on so they sent it to the British company Heinemann's, which operated in Canada under the name of British Book Services. From the very beginning, Ostry and especially Ferns were fearful, almost paranoid, that Liberal interests would quash the book. One of King's literary executors, Norman Robertson, had moved on to be Canadian high commissioner in London. Ferns interpreted this to mean that the King defenders had a man on the ground. A visit to the United Kingdom by Bruce Hutchison also had them wary. "Hutchison & the Liberals obviously have good connections over here and we don't want them to start obstructing us." This was only the beginning of Ferns's worries. He found out that, when Heinemann's sent their manuscript to assessors in the United Kingdom, at least one reader had begged off from reading the text, which Ferns interpreted as being due to political timidity: "It seems to me that these fellows are afraid to go out on a limb which they think may be sawn off." Worse was yet to come. Alan Hill of Heinemann's had sent a copy off to the firm's Canadian branch. Ostry had specifically asked the publisher not to do this. "Now the manuscript has gone to Canada to be placed into the hands of god knows whom," Ferns complained. "As things are now it looks like our book is going to be spread from one end of Canada to the other."[16]

When the readers' reports arrived, they confirmed Ferns's and Ostry's fears. The Canadian report, from Peggy Blackstock at British Books, found that the book "reflect[ed] an attitude of mind which seems to be a combination of the 'pure Canada' cult, which has been developing recent years, and the left-wing political economist who reduces society to strata, racial and pressure groups. It is anything but objective." She was particularly offended by what she saw as derogatory comments about Canadians of Loyalist stock, the position of the governor general, and the state of parliamentary democracy. Hers was an Ontario Tory response – proud of Canada's British traditions. In fact, Blackstock had no great love for Mackenzie King. She had supported her sister Judith Robinson in her attempt with

Eugene Forsey and Jack Farthing to write a book about the British tradition in Canada and the way the Liberal Party was destroying it.[17] Yet the manner in which Ferns and Ostry went about attacking King, and especially their lack of respect for British Canadian traditions, offended her.

Another report, which didn't pick up on Blackstock's Loyalist hurt, nonetheless took a political angle. It was this angle that would continue to appear in connection with the book. This reviewer found the book to have "much first class material and some vigorous if rather bitter passages of analysis." But ultimately, the report said the book had two main faults. First, there was a "naïve and tiresome Marxist rhetoric ... woven throughout the manuscript." The reviewer felt that the authors' "description of each of the many strikes in which Mackenzie King was involved reads like *Daily Worker* reporting." Second, they displayed a "bitter animosity" toward Mackenzie King which "sadly mars a powerful and largely justified indictment of his shortcomings." Some of King's early ideas of labour relations, the reviewer suggested, were actually ahead of his time. If Ferns and Ostry did not give Mackenzie King credit for this, the reviewer warned, "the reader must feel 'How can I trust them later on?'" Similarly, regarding a cursory account of another strike, the reviewer complained: "One gathers this incident does not fit into the picture of Mackenzie King as traitor to the working classes. We are therefore told no more about it and the authors rush on in search of other evidence with which to pillory the diabolical Mackenzie King."[18]

Their editor at Heinemann's, Alan Hill, set to work on them and eventually managed to get them to agree to change the first four chapters of the book to make it more sympathetic to King. Ferns and Ostry thought that Hill had agreed, in turn, to get the book out by 1 July 1954. But 1 July would come and go, the first of several deadlines to pass with the book still not out. As the deadlines came and went, Ferns and Ostry became increasingly suspicious. They threatened to take the book elsewhere, at one point even raising the possibility of suing Heinemann's. Hill somehow managed to mollify though not please them despite more delays. He insisted that the book be sent out to Canadian and English lawyers to check it for libel.

Meanwhile, his Canadian office, notably in the person of Peggy Blackstock, kept being offended by the disrespectful tone of the book and called for more revisions.[19]

It's unclear if anyone exerted pressure on Heinemann's to delay the book, but the publisher was certainly being extremely cautious to cover itself before it went to print. For Ostry and especially Ferns, all of the delays and changes raised the spectre of political interference. Certainly, Ferns, having already suffered at the hands of those trying to ferret out radicals, was overly paranoid about any criticism of the book or its message. Writing in the context of Cold War anti-communism, in the stultifying atmosphere of post-war academia, he and Ostry couldn't help but wonder if someone was trying to prevent this book from seeing the light of day.

Ferns and Ostry needed friends, important friends. This was Ostry's job. He spent much of 1954 and 1955 visiting and corresponding with a range of political figures in what might be called the anti-Mackenzie King forces of 1950s Canada. These included prominent Tories like the journalist John Stevenson and the former prime minister and Mackenzie King nemesis Arthur Meighen. They also included senior English Canadian Liberals who had known King and who were, for various reasons of which the legacy of conscription was paramount, disaffected with Mackenzie King – Senator T.A. Crerar, Montreal Liberal A.K. Cameron, and Stuart Ralston (a judge and the son of the man King was seen to have betrayed during the conscription crisis, Colonel Ralston).

In part, of course, Ostry was digging up sources for further volumes of the biography. The current manuscript took King only up to 1919. But even more than sources, Ostry wanted credibility and connections. He was himself much more aligned with socialist thinkers and young CCFers. These weren't the kind of friends who would get the book advertised. Prominent Tories and Liberals might do just that.

At several points in their difficult relationship with Heinmann's, Ostry and Ferns considered trying to use these men to pressure the firm. When the book seemed to be bogged down in mid-1955 and there were suggestions of political interference, John Stevenson told Ostry: "I believe money could be found in Canada to finance [the book's] publication." "I talked to [a] prosperous friend, who loathed King, and he said that he would be willing to put up as much as $3000 in this good cause. Arthur Meighen would I feel sure give some money and could raise more."[20]

Ostry played to the egos of men like Meighen and Crerar, who were aging, no longer quite in the thick of things, thinking as much about their place in history as about the present. Meighen especially still carried the grudges of lost battles. Ostry acted the role of keen young admirer. His money didn't hurt either. He sent gifts – cigars for one, liquor for another – and remembered birthdays and anniversaries. He played up to their sense of history and duty, using a language of honour and chivalry that was wholly absent from his more flippant and jovial letters to closer, younger friends. Ostry visited the men on his travels in Canada in 1954 and 1955, following up with letters thanking them for their "kind hospitality" and fondly recalling the time they spent together – sitting down rye in hand and talking politics with the Liberal organizer A.K. Cameron, enjoying Meighen's company in his home. Ostry did occasionally assert his own views. More often, though, he was a fawning admirer, noting just how unsurpassed each man's knowledge was, and how valuable were their documents to the Canadian historical record.[21]

It was these men to whom Ostry turned in the summer and autumn of 1955 when it finally looked as if the book would be published. He had a grand publicity campaign planned but he need their help to pull it off. The first salvo was an article that he and Ferns wrote on Mackenzie King's activities during the Great War that was published that summer in the *Canadian Historical Review*. This was an academic article in a staid academic journal. Even granting that there might have been greater public interest in Canadian history in these years, it still seems incredible that Ferns and Ostry would think to use this article as a way of generating publicity. And yet they did. And, in part, it worked. Articles appeared in the *Winnipeg Tribune* and the *Vancouver Province*.

The allegations in the article were serious. Ferns and Ostry painted King as a pro-American, anti-labour advocate, someone who stuck for too long to a position of neutrality in matters relating to the war. "He possessed neither consistency of understanding nor consistency of emotion in relation to that great political event," they wrote. A friend reported that the article "fluttered the dovecotes in Ottawa & the copy in the Parliamentary Library was in great demand – Liberals reading it with anxiety – others with glee." With more than a modest level of pluck, Ostry sent copies not only to friends and Tories but also to Bruce Hutchison, Paul Martin, Lester Pearson, and other Liberals.[22]

Ostry wanted controversy. Articles began to appear about the upcoming biography on Mackenzie King. The Conservatives' *Progress Report* interviewed him and gave him top billing in its autumn 1955 issue. Ostry wasn't entirely satisfied. He complained to Meighen that the Tory papers weren't reporting nearly enough of the article's revelations. "If the Conservative Party and its leading members in the profession of journalism fail to see the real political value in something like this article," he complained, "we have reached a sorry state of affairs." Meighen wrote back to console Ostry, saying that what he said was no doubt true. He had taken up the issue with the editor of the *Globe and Mail* and he told Ostry to be patient; when the book arrived, the Tory press would deliver.[23]

⚙

Despite the many delays and bickering between its authors, *The Age of Mackenzie King* did finally arrive in Canadian bookstores on 4 December 1955. Given the success of Bruce Hutchison's book, the publishers had high hopes for this even more daring and candid biography. *The Age of Mackenzie King* was a different kind of book, certainly, but it, too, could find its place. A friend of Ostry's wrote in late November to ask when the book was coming out. He may have been doing some friendly exaggerating when he said that "everybody's been hanging around the bookstores waiting to grab the first copies," but the book was certainly hotly anticipated. A Mackenzie King executor, and friend of Harry Ferns from his time in the prime minister's office, Leonard Brockington, informed Ferns that "there is a great demand for [the book] in Ottawa. Grattan O'Leary [editor of the *Ottawa Journal*] told me a couple of days ago that [the Ottawa bookseller] Hope's sold seventy in one afternoon."[24]

The *Age of Mackenzie King* presented Canadians with a controversial version of Mackenzie King. Ferns and Ostry wanted to get to the truth of Mackenzie King, to give a version of King that went behind the myth the Liberals had created for him. Theirs was a work of demystification. They did this in a witty, sarcastic manner which was itself out of keeping with the stately volumes one expected from academic biography. The chapter titles conveyed their biting critique, each with its own double entendre: "Working on the Railroad Workers," "For Hire," "The Powerful and the Glory." The main thrust of the book was to present King as someone who was an expert manipulator. They admitted that King had incredible skill and foresight. He had, they claimed, discovered the importance of class relations to Canadian politics before any other mainstream politician. He had recognized the changing landscape around him as he grew up and watched Canada become an industrial nation. They even provocatively compared him to Lenin, noting that both shared the same view that the class struggle was at the heart of a new version of politics in industrial capitalist societies.[25]

Mackenzie King, however, came to very different conclusions from Lenin as to what was to be done. Central to his position was the idea of conciliation, which he developed early in the century and then elaborated on in his book *Industry and Humanity*. He had trumpeted this idea successfully in his work for the new Department of Labour. When he became the minister of labour, relied on it as his touchstone during his time with the Rockefellers, and used it as a key part of his ascension to power in 1919 at the Liberal leadership convention, as a new man with fresh but safe answers for a modern age. Ferns and Ostry pointed to all of the holes in King's application of what they saw as his muddled ideas. They showed how, in strike after strike where King was called in to conciliate, he actually worked against the real interests of working people. His attempt to find the soft compromise sapped the power of workers whose only real power came from the threat of industrial conflict. Similarly, they pointed out that, when King was called in to deal with the "Oriental problem" in British Columbia, his high-sounding language of compromise actually masked and justified racist immigration policies.

A friend wrote to Ostry in January 1956 to say that the book had "really jolted many Canadians. It is one of the most discussed books since its appearance on the bookstands. It has shocked many people who have even remotely been associated with King. Many people don't deny the truth of its portrayal of King but the reaction seems to be disapproval that these truths are written for everyone to read."[26] In other words, it wasn't so much what they said as the fact that they published the book at all. This is exactly the kind of book about King that Liberals had tried to suppress while King was still alive. Moreover, it was also written with a Lytton Strachey–like irreverence that was out-of-character for Canadian publishing until this point.

One common response was to say that the book wasn't even a biography at all. It didn't really get to the heart of its subject, as had, for example, the other great biography published that year – the historian Donald Creighton's biography of John A. Macdonald. In an unparalleled literary style, Creighton brought Macdonald to life as few biographers have ever done for any Canadian subject. He tried to capture Macdonald the man and the politician. There were certainly gaps in his approach, and the biography had a pronounced political angle to it, but the bias wasn't obvious on the surface. Against this, and dealing with a more recent period in which many of the protagonists were still alive and the partisan lines still clearly drawn, Ferns and Ostry didn't stand a chance.[27]

The review by Charles Bruce, republished in more than a dozen papers across the country, was typical. He argued that the book "loses impact, for the reader interested in objective fact, by reason of the sarcasm with which the authors have seen fit to treat not only their central subject but nearly everyone else." Alan Morley in the *Vancouver Province* complained that "in the five years since his [Mackenzie King's] death he has been 'debunked' more ruthlessly than has any modern leader of comparable stature." This, it seemed, is what Ferns and Ostry were offering – more criticism and from a radical-left perspective. "While they nowhere state the standards against which they judge Mr. King," Morley went on, "what they do regard as an unchallengeable moral code is nothing more or less than the economic-political dogma of the Socialist intellectuals of the British Labor Party." *Canadian Business* agreed, noting that the authors "are apt to do more to obscure the man's real character and stature than anything else unless they are soon counteracted by a more objective study." As an example of what was wrong with the book, the reviewer wrote that "there is more than a suggestion that the authors scorn Mr. King's advocacy of conciliation in labor disputes because they believe labor disputes should be heated up rather than cooled down." This, of course, is exactly what Ferns and Ostry argued in the book, so the review was at least honest if politically opposed. The *Winnipeg Tribune* found fault on more humanistic grounds, suggesting that the book couldn't get at the man himself. The early chapters portrayed King "in an uncharitable spirit," the reviewer claimed. Worse, "King is presented as resembling a crypto-fascist." Ultimately, the main problem was that "one side of King's personality is revealed in this book, but the man himself, the "poor naked fork'd thing," is not discovered. This is not biography, but dissection."[28]

The Tory press chewed only the morsels it found tasty. Grattan O'Leary of the *Ottawa Journal* skipped the Marxist analysis and went straight for the Liberal jugular. The most shocking revelation, from a Tory standpoint, came in the letter that Ferns and Ostry had discovered written by Mackenzie King to then American Secretary of State William Jennings Bryan in 1914. In it, King seems to be urging the Americans to maintain their neutrality in the early months of the war and to deny war loans to France. In other words, it seemed to show King working against the interests of Britain and Canada in the Great War. It was one thing for King not to have served during the war, something that many Tories held against him, but for King to have advocated American neutrality was an astonishing revelation. "It is tremendous to speculate," O'Leary declaimed, "upon what might have happened to Mr. King's subsequent political fortunes and to the whole course of Canada's political history had this letter become public."[29]

There were other similar allegations that reverberated in mid-1950s Canada. Ferns and Ostry alleged that King had not been Laurier's choice as Liberal leader, as was sometimes said. They also alleged that King had flirted with joining the Union government during the war, thus disproving the loyalty to Laurier which had been such a huge factor in King's winning the Liberal leadership in 1919. Ostry himself knew that these were the features of the book that would "sell" to the mainstream in 1955 and he highlighted them when he spoke to the press. He certainly got O'Leary's attention. "Some will say that authors Ferns and Ostrey [sic] fail in objectivity, that they

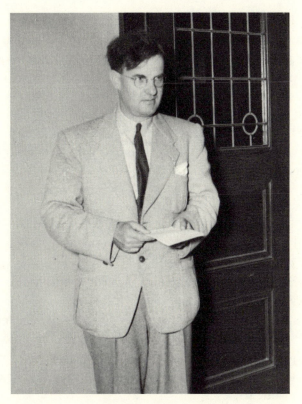

8.3 Grant Dexter

are too much the able prosecutors with a criminal in the dock,"
O'Leary noted. "The claim will not lack wholly validity; yet if this
volume is more an essay in impeachment than an objective biography, at least it can be said for it that its selected facts, arrayed often
with scorn and satire, and perhaps a touch of malice, are documented
adequately; that the writers state clearly what their evidence is and
where it can be found."[30]

The most vitriolic attack came from the Liberal Grant Dexter at
the *Winnipeg Free Press*. Dexter called the book a work of "unquali-
fied denigration." "It is doubtful," he predicted hopefully, "if this
book will have any wide audience in this country. It will be plain to
every reader ... that the authors are so obsessed by their antagonism
to King that they cannot be objective." Like others at the time, and
echoing the accolades showered on the former prime minister after

his death, Dexter linked King to the nation itself. What would it say if Ferns and Ostry's version of King were true? What would it say about Canada and Canadians? Some might be anxious about this but Dexter was contemptuous. It simply couldn't be true, for this very simple reason: "As everyone will agree, no small conniving, selfish man could ever be the prime minister of this country for more than 20 years." Here it was clearly spoken. A prime minister just couldn't have these kinds of secrets. Dexter put it this way: "No one could fool the people so long."[31]

On a mild day in early February 1956, with fresh snow on Parliament Hill and clear skies above the Peace Tower, an MP rose to clear the air inside the House – this time with respect to Mackenzie King. Hugh Bryson of the CCF had put a question on the order paper: "Why was the discussion on the book 'The Age of Mackenzie King' cancelled by the C.B.C.?"[32] On the surface, it was an innocuous and innocent question – about the scheduling of a TV program – yet it would set off one of those mid-term mini-scandals that so often rock sitting governments.

James McCann, minister of national revenue (with oversight of the CBC), claimed that it was all a misunderstanding. The CBC had considered running a program on this book but "on consideration it was not thought to be a good basis for such a discussion."[33] The CBC, he claimed, "has full authority and sole responsibility for all program decisions," so this really wasn't a matter for Parliament.

The government's answer hadn't satisfied opposition MPs. Bryson pointed out that, in fact, the CBC had advertised such a discussion program about *The Age of Mackenzie King* in its promotional materials and scheduled it for the evening of 20 December 1955. The advertisement even drew viewers' attention to the fact that "the book is said to be highly controversial."[34] The program had been scheduled. It certainly seemed to have been cancelled. And the book was controversial. There was the rub.

The Conservative broadcasting critic Donald Fleming found the Liberal explanation highly suspicious. Fleming knew that this book by "two eminent Canadian scholars" was "to say the least ... not complimentary to the late Mr. Mackenzie King or to the record of the Liberal party." Newspapers across the country had reviewed this undeniably important book. One of the authors, Bernard Ostry, had already pre-recorded an introduction to the panel discussion. Everything was, as far as he was concerned, set to go. Then, the cancellation. When Ostry asked why, he was told only that the decision came from Ottawa and from something called "the directorate." It all sounded very Orwellian.[35]

In fact, this was exactly the kind of controversy Bernard Ostry wanted to stir up. He returned to Canada in January 1956 to publicize the book and to do more research on future volumes. The abrupt and mysterious cancellation of the program meant to discuss *The Age of Mackenzie King* fell into his lap and he decided to use it to promote the book. There were other mysteries to solve, other reasons to think that someone was trying to prevent their book from getting the right kind of attention. One of these was sales. *The Age of Mackenzie King* sold more than two thousand copies in the few weeks before Christmas. This was a great start, but after that, sales fell off. It is a not uncommon fate for a book and even the sale of two thousand copies was excellent. It may simply have been the usual post-Christmas lull and the usual drop-off from sales after release. It may have been the bad reviews. It might, though, have been something else.[36]

Friends of Ferns and Ostry wrote to say that they couldn't get the book. A department store in Montreal claimed that it was sold out and that it would take three weeks to order a copy. The clerk seemed reluctant to put in an order. The book had been in store windows before Christmas; now it was nowhere to be seen. Ferns didn't know what to think but he remained suspicious. His suspicions were heightened by his dealings with *Saturday Night* magazine. The magazine commissioned him to do an article on the book and Mackenzie King. They sent him a cheque for $75 and he sent them the article. It never appeared. Later in the spring, the editor wrote to say that there hadn't been space for his article, and that it had by this point lost its "topicality" anyway. Ferns could, though, keep the cheque.[37]

Was someone attempting to suppress their book? Did the Liberal establishment have that kind of weight? Ferns thought so, and we know that the Liberal Party had done this before, though in that case the author and publisher were bought off. For Ferns, the important thing was to maintain his sense of scholarly dignity. His reading of Canadian society in these years was that controversy would kill the book. They had to present themselves as objective scholars. Ostry was a different man and his approach differed in kind. He approached friends in the CCF and that was what sparked the questions in the House of Commons.

Ostry was right to think that the book had upset official Ottawa. Former cabinet minister Brooke Claxton picked up *The Age of Mackenzie King* soon after it was published. He privately complained that "almost worse than its malicious distortions of everything having to do with Mr. King is the tiresome emission of communist venom on every page." The book was "nauseating" and Claxton had to "struggle hard to keep on with the exercise" of reading it. What effect, he wondered, would this have on King's reputation? What effect would it have on the party? At the Rideau Club during the holidays, three out of a total of six men at his table were reading the book. Among themselves, the men agreed that the book was "self-condemning." But Claxton worried whether this would "be the view generally held by" those whom he called "the less enlightened people who have not the good fortune to live in Ottawa."[38]

Claxton considered his options. "The thought occurred to me," he wrote to Jack Pickersgill, "that it would not be a bad thing if quite a few people across Canada sent letters ... to the newspapers. That, however, would start a controversy. The best thing to do is to let the matter die. Most effective of all would be not to buy or read the book." The latter really would be best – if it could be accomplished. "Neither the authors nor the publishers should be given the satisfaction of having the book purchased or read," he wrote to an academic at Queen's. But would it be possible? How could you silence a book? How best to ensure that it faded into obscurity?[39]

We don't know the full extent of what Claxton or other Liberals might have done, but it is clear that Claxton was the one behind the cancellation of the CBC program. One day Claxton had received a telephone call from the CBC that he regarded as an affront. The broadcaster was planning to run a panel-discussion program on the new book by Ferns and Ostry. The format would be simple. One of the authors had already recorded a five-minute spot in which he outlined

8.4 Brooke Claxton

the main themes of the book. Then a panel of four or five King experts, a mixture of academics and politicians, would review the book. The caller wanted to know if Claxton, as someone with such an intimate knowledge of Mr King and with so much political experience himself, would be kind enough to participate. Claxton loudly told them no, that he would not. He would also mention the matter to his friend "Dave." This was Davidson Dunton, chairman of the CBC.

Claxton said that he "could not conceive of Dave passing on this." He ran into Dunton later that day and asked him about the program. It seems that Dunton hadn't heard of it. The CBC was a big operation and he couldn't be aware of every little detail. Yet Dunton made it his business to find out and he decided to kill the program. Despite the pre-billing, there would be no CBC discussion program on

The Age of Mackenzie King. For someone like Claxton and no doubt for Dunton, it made sense. The book just wasn't worth it. As far as Claxton was concerned, and possibly Dunton too, that was the end of it.[40] The questions in the House of Commons brought it all out into the open.

"Can the minister inform me what medium the C.B.C. will use to review the book on Mackenzie King?" asked the CCF MP Alistair Stewart. Many of the papers picked up on this jibe; nothing else needed to be said, since everyone knew of King's interest in spiritualism. This was exactly the kind of humour usually used to poke fun of King in these years – slyly suggestive. Jack Pickersgill, now in government as a cabinet minister, managed to ensure that the opposition did not have all of the fun. When the Conservative Donald Fleming asked why the CBC had cancelled the program, he shouted out, "They probably read the book."[41]

The papers that could be expected to become irate did so – notably the *Toronto Telegram*, whose editor Ostry met with. But so too did some papers that didn't like the book itself but who disbelieved the government's explanation of the cancellation – that the book "did not merit" television treatment. The *Saskatoon Star Phoenix* set the tone, demanding that "Canadian taxpayers should be informed and soon, exactly why the Canadian Broadcasting Corporation cancelled two carefully prepared and scheduled programs which were to deal with a supposedly controversial biography of the late Prime Minister Mackenzie King." So far, it claimed, the government's answers had been "exceedingly woolly and confusing" and the public could "hardly fail to suspect the worst." The Canadian branch of Ferns and Ostry's publisher stirred things up by writing a public letter that was published in a number of papers. The editor gave Ostry's account of the cancellation and claimed to be concerned about this "matter which might appear to be a violation of or interference with one of the fundamental democratic freedoms."[42]

Grant Dexter spoke for the Liberal press when, under the heading "No Ostry-cism," he claimed: "It seems difficult to establish that democratic freedom involves a right to have a book discussed on a television program." A few weeks later, when the issue refused to go away from newspaper headlines, Dexter returned to the Liberals' defence. "Nobody has questioned the rightness of the decision not to proceed with the broadcast," he claimed. "It is pretty well agreed that there was no case for a CBC program."

Then Dexter set about giving the background to the story, telling how Claxton had been asked to be on the program and had angrily refused. But more importantly, Dexter claimed, "Mr. Dunton, the chairman of the Board of Governors of the CBC, had just finished reading the book and had reached the same conclusion as Mr. Claxton. After consultation with his colleagues, the review of the book was cancelled." Dexter ended the story claiming that "the most careful inquiry [the one he had just done] indicates that there was no political interference." Blair Fraser of *Maclean's* agreed. The main point was, he claimed, that "no member of the government had anything to do with the cancellation of that program project." This was an important technicality. It may have been true that Claxton was prominent in Liberal circles, that he was looked to for advice, and that in the next election he would take a lead role in shaping the future of the party, but he wasn't technically part of the government.[43]

The CBC knew of the disapproval of an important Liberal former cabinet minister. This man was a good friend of the chairman of the CBC and had voiced his displeasure loudly. But responsible journalists in the 1950s believed that the CBC had acted on its own. One might have speculated about the friendships that crossed boundaries when these men dined at their clubs. One might have speculated about the forming of a consensus, rooted in a single political way of seeing the world, in which it became common sense to decide that *The Age of Mackenzie King* "did not merit" public discussion. But Fraser, Dexter, and other Liberals didn't credit such wild accusations. They hoped that the "less enlightened people" wouldn't either.

In the mid-1950s, this Liberal common sense still carried weight. In the particular case of *The Age of Mackenzie King*, it helped that Bernard Ostry and Harry Ferns couldn't stand each other. The two men had been bickering at a steadily nastier rate month by month as the book moved toward publication and after. With so much anxiety over whether their book was being censored or not, it might only have been natural that the two came to suspect each other as well. It didn't help that Bernard Ostry was the one in Canada who handled the publicity. When articles began appearing that claimed Bernard Ostry was the sole author and gave him the title of professor no less, Harry Ferns became irate. These were the mistakes of sloppy journalism, but they rankled.

The final straw was when Ostry was quoted in the *Financial Times* boasting, "My next volume will be much stronger. I have in it a lot about people who are still living. There will also be a tale of corruption the like of which never occurred in Canada since the Pacific scandal." Ferns hadn't even known about the CBC program, let alone its cancellation. Now Ostry was busy creating more scandal, and dragging the name of Harry Ferns through the mud in the process. On 29 February he wrote to the *Financial Times* to dissociate himself publicly from statements made by Ostry. On 20 April, he went further and released to the press a statement in which he dissociated himself entirely from his co-author. "There will be no further volumes of *The Age of Mackenzie King*," he wrote. "I am satisfied that there is insufficient evidence available to the public at the present time to write a truthful and adequate account of Mackenzie King's life going beyond the year 1919." When Ostry wrote his own public letter, vowing to continue the biography on his own, Ferns responded with more than a trace of sarcasm: He claimed to be "delighted" that his former co-author would carry on to write his own book: "Such an enterprise will be a new and valuable experience for Mr Ostry." In the short run, it was all heartwarming for Canada's Liberals. The *Winnipeg Free Press* couldn't help but comment that "Mr. Ferns thus appears to have written an advance review of Mr. Ostry's next book."[44]

There never was another volume of *The Age of Mackenzie King*, though the book would be reprinted in the middle of the 1970s when the whiff of scandal would be a selling feature. Not so in the middle of the 1950s. As one commentator later wrote about the book, it "landed in the complacent liberal Canada of 1955 with all the social aplomb of a dirty joke at the Governor General's levy. It was treated by polite society like any other such faux-pas, it was coldly and pointedly ignored."[45] Partly it was the left-wing critique that irked Liberals. But it was also Ferns and Ostry's insouciance toward King the statesman, their derisive questioning of his motivations.

For the moment, at least, it was still possible to believe that the kinds of things Ferns and Ostry had to say about Mackenzie King couldn't be true – that no prime minister could be so fundamentally different from his public image. After all, as Grant Dexter of the *Winnipeg Free Press* had put it, "no one could fool the people so long."

Official Secrets

Even as critics like Ferns and Ostry or Bruce Hutchison or Eugene Forsey battled away in the newspapers and on the radio, King's literary executors worked quietly to create the official life of the former prime minister. As year followed year in the 1950s, they struggled with just how much to reveal about the whole life of Mackenzie King. Some of their troubles came from disagreements about what should or shouldn't be private, but, at other times, unexpected events threatened to take the power out of their hands completely. King's official biographer, MacGregor Dawson, had his own difficult task to create the official life, and he, too, felt obliged to make sense of King's personal peculiarities.

Shortly after they hired King's official biographer, the literary executors agreed to let him see the typed portion of the diary that was being created by Fred McGregor and Edouard Handy. But the ultimate decision of how much he could use of it, and whether he would be able to cite from the diary in the book itself, had remained an unanswered question. Initially, the literary executors had hoped simply to allow Dawson to consult the diary but not to quote from it. Over the years Dawson had kept up a steady campaign to change their minds. In this he was helped by King's long-time friend Violet Markham. She spoke to Norman Robertson when he went to England as Canada's high commissioner. He was the executor who most wanted to restrict access to the diary. Other executors had more liberal views.[1]

Fred McGregor knew more about the diary than anyone. He spent almost four years of his life, from 1951 to the end of 1954, reading the handwritten version aloud into a Dictaphone. For McGregor, the diary had "unparalleled historical value." He felt that the executors had been "completely right" in the decision not to "destroy" it. Moreover, he thought that "without access to this source-book, no historian could come to a fair appraisal of the complex nature of the man, the value of his contribution to Canada, and the forces that have acted and reacted in the determination of Canadian domestic and foreign policies." The national archivist, W. Kaye Lamb, came to have the same view. "The more I see of it," Lamb wrote in 1955, "the surer I am that it is one of the great political documents of our time."[2]

The executors signed an agreement handing over control of most of King's papers to the Public Archives but excluding King's diary from the agreement. They also excluded a series of binders containing King's detailed notes on his seances, treating these as a diary as well. They came up with the agreement late in 1954 and announced it publicly in May 1955. Even then, though, they maintained control of King's papers, with extended deadlines as to when control would eventually pass over to those at the archives. The papers would remain completely under the control of the executors until 1964, after which time the executors would still make decisions about who could access the documents. It wasn't until 1975 that the archives would gain full control of these records. By that time, the archivists would have organized all of King's papers and destroyed what was to be destroyed. Most importantly, the executors would have set restrictions on which documents could be consulted and when. In the end, many of King's most private papers, including his spiritualism correspondence and some of his financial records, remained closed until the next century, more than fifty years after his death. By mid-1955, then, the literary executors had come to an initial and temporary decision on what to do with King's papers but no decision had yet been made on how, when, or whether to destroy King's diary.

⚕

Surprise came in the form of a troubled employee of the nation's Public Archives. Only months after King's literary executors announced the plans for the preservation of some of King's papers – and the possible destruction of King's diary – they learned that their control over the diary was not as complete as they had thought.

Jean-Louis Daviault occupied low positions in high places. He probably never knew Mackenzie King personally, though in the late

1930s and 1940s he would have seen him up close on an almost daily basis, for Daviault worked as a page in the House of Commons at the end of the 1930s and again after the war for several years before he earned a job in the Library of Parliament.[3]

In September 1939, at the very outset of the Second World War, Daviault volunteered for the Canadian Navy, with the rank of able seaman. In 1941 tragedy struck when the corvette he was serving on crashed into another ship in the North Atlantic. The fog was so thick you couldn't see more than twenty feet in any direction. Daviault was on anti-aircraft duty, peering out through the mist to try to spot any incoming danger. He didn't see the other ship approaching. The collision jolted his own ship, causing two of the boilers to explode, blasting people and metal in all directions. Daviault found himself in the water, amidst streaks of oil and wreckage, swimming for his life. He and some of his fellow sailors found a lifeboat that had been thrown clear of the ship. They managed to get themselves in and keep the leaking vessel afloat until a merchant marine ship saved them. Twenty-four of his shipmates weren't so lucky. The Ottawa papers told Daviault's story in the same terms as they did many other such stories at that stage of the war – finding heroism in mere survival and persistence.[4]

Off the news pages, Daviault was not doing so well. He never really recovered from the disaster at sea. He deserted his post over Christmas in 1942. Then, late on a night in November 1943, he lost his cool and struck a superior officer. When another officer confronted him, Daviault grabbed a sten gun and shoved it in the officer's face, a vicious and potentially deadly confrontation that the bureaucratic language of the military forms only hint at. Nothing more happened. But that was enough. The Navy put Daviault in the stocks while they decided what to do with him. The Navy doctor recommended that the punishment not be too severe. He blamed the whole thing on the trauma of the sinking of Daviault's ship. It was an emotional storm. Daviault needed a break, at least six months inland. This seems to have been what he got, but even then it wasn't enough. Daviault later requested that he be discharged. The Navy ultimately agreed, thinking that it had got what it could out of him and could get nothing more.[5]

Despite the fact that a psychiatrist called Daviault a "constitutional psychopath of the aggressive type," Daviault was able to come back to Ottawa and take up a post again as a messenger in the House of Commons. From there he must have picked up some training as a photographer. By 1951, now with a wife and child, he had taken up a job at the Public Archives in its photography section. It was a fateful career choice.

As a photographer in the archives, Daviault had access to rare, secret, and potentially valuable material. Workers in this section photographed not just historical documents but also important government records. Each week, a courier from the Privy Council Office hand-delivered the latest batch of cabinet minutes to be copied and returned. Starting in 1953, Daviault also received a new assignment: making photographic copies of Mackenzie King's diary. The literary executors felt that they needed to make extra copies to ensure that they were preserved until Dawson finished the official biography. They still left open the possibility of eventually destroying all of the diary but in the meantime one couldn't be too careful.

Daviault seems to have seen an opportunity in his new task. He was an intelligent, bilingual federal employee, working in Ottawa, spending many of his off-work hours at his local club, the Institut Canadien Français (ICF). Admittedly, most of his time there was spent drinking beer, but the ICF was also about promoting French Canadian culture in the capital. He would have known about the general curiosity aroused by King's diary and whether it was to be destroyed or not. As someone who had lived through the war, and who had spent most of his adult life around Parliament, he, too, was perhaps curious about what secrets this diary contained. Now was his chance to peek inside and perhaps to make some money.

Daviault was often hard up for cash. He made a modest income at the archives, nothing like the large salary of the official biographer but more than others lower down the chain of command in his office. He liked betting on the races, even though he tended to lose more than he won. He frequently "borrowed" money from others at his club and then "forgot" to repay the loans. He never seems to have recovered from his traumatic wartime experiences. In 1954 he went on extended leave, suffering from "nervous exhaustion." Returning to work, he again took up his job making microfilm photographs of historic documents and of the Mackenzie King diary. That seems to be when he decided to make extra copies of the King diary for himself.

Looking for buyers, though, turned troublesome. It seems that Daviault began shopping the stolen copies of the diary to Tory newspapers. He called the offices of the *Toronto Telegram*, the Liberal-hating Toronto daily owned by John Bassett. The reporter on the other end of the line couldn't believe what he was hearing. Hanging up the phone, he rushed out of the offices saying, "I'm on to something big." Wherever they met, it must have been somewhere private, for Daviault hooked up a projection machine so that he could show samples of what he was selling. Later in the night the reporter called another journalist at the *Telegram* to give him the news. "This is crazy," he said. "I've just been offered a chance to buy some of Mackenzie King's private diaries. I had a look at some of them – how King made up his mind to fire Ralston and about that damn dog of his, Pat." Daviault claimed to have access to ten years of King's diary. He wanted $1,000 for the parts of the diary that he had that day. The reporter could take it right then. There would be more to come. The *Telegram*'s owner, John Bassett, was at that time planning on publishing the first Sunday edition paper in Toronto. What better way to mark this new daring move in Canadian journalism than by exposing the hidden secrets of the late Liberal prime minister? Ultimately, though, the *Telegram* opted for caution. The legality of the whole enterprise remained dubious.[6]

When Daviault approached another media tycoon, Jack Kent Cook, he ran into greater difficulties. For one of Cook's lawyers was none other than Duncan MacTavish, president of the National Liberal Federation and also one of the executors of Mackenzie King's estate. When MacTavish heard about the documents, he recognized their significance immediately. He advised Cook not to buy them because they were almost certainly stolen goods. To traffic in them himself would undoubtedly bring legal trouble. But MacTavish wasn't only obliged to help Cook. He felt that he had to warn his friends. But how to do so without breaking the legal necessity of secrecy between himself and his client?

MacTavish called Fred McGregor, who, aside from being one of King's literary executors, was also an executor of King's estate along with MacTavish. He told McGregor that a client had approached him about the legality of purchasing what seemed to be copies of King's diary. He couldn't tell McGregor who the client was, or who was doing the selling. But he could give some details about what was being sold – that they were microfilm copies of the 1941 diary, that more copies would be delivered in batches covering two to two and a half years' worth of the diary, and that the copies now being offered for sale were typewritten but had corrections in small handwriting in the margins. That was enough. McGregor knew what he was dealing with. These were copies of the diary that he and Handy had so laboriously transcribed.[7]

McGregor met with two other literary executors, Norman Robertson and Jack Pickersgill a few days later. They determined that the leak could not have come from one of them. At that point the executors had never been sent copies of the 1941 diary that were now being sold. Who, then, had done it? W. Kaye Lamb had been out of the country, but the investigation began in earnest when he returned. By mid-October 1955, it was determined that the culprit had to be someone in the photography section at the Public Archives. This was the person who had the access and the means of making the copies. Lamb wrote officially to Colonel L.H. Nicholson, commissioner of the Royal Canadian Mounted Police (RCMP), to file a complaint. Lamb wasn't just concerned about King's diary. Given that the photography section dealt with highly sensitive materials, copying not only historic documents but also the documents of the Privy Council, the danger seemed clear. If someone in the archives was selling copies of King's diary, what else were they selling? In the mid-1950s, in the midst of the Cold War, with fears of public-servant espionage rampant, this was a major concern.[8]

Fingering the likely culprit seemed fairly easy. The Mounties focused on Daviault quickly but proving his guilt definitively was more difficult. The investigation stretched on, and still they could not get definitive proof. Ultimately, Lamb called Daviault into his office. He told him that they suspected him of copying documents and selling them. They couldn't prove it. But, even so, Daviault had no future at the Public Archives. He had better look elsewhere for a job.[9]

At this point, no one else in the Public Archives knew about the investigation. The story didn't make it into the newspapers or onto the radio. Lamb and the other executors had kept the whole matter a secret. To make the matter public would only invite criticism. It would lead to questions and to controversy, exactly the things to be avoided. Daviault himself appears not to have been cowed. To Lamb, he pleaded ignorance and claimed that he was being "ill used." This was part of his persona. Another archives director later recalled that Daviault was a "man who always appeared to have some big deal on the go." At a time when formality still mattered, he would deal frankly with those of a higher rank, talking to them on a first-name basis. Tellingly, Daviault made no rush to leave the archives. It wasn't until 8 May 1957 – more than a year and a half later – that he finally left his job.[10]

After Daviault left the archives to set up his own used-furniture business, he continued to call Lamb, threatening him and complaining of his ill treatment. He also made another threat, one that would resonate in the years ahead. For when Daviault left, he seems not to have gone empty-handed. The RCMP and the executors never found proof of Daviault's misdeeds, which meant that they also never recovered the stolen copies of the diary. Daviault claimed to have kept these – a kind of insurance policy. He could threaten Lamb that he would sell them.[11] Lamb and the other executors, moreover, feared what he would do with them. Would they fall into the wrong hands? What if Daviault modified the diary, changing the record to make it seem as if King had thought or said or did something horrible? In the mid-1950s this remained a danger known only to the literary executors yet the issue of the stolen material would still come to play a role in the diary's fate.

Of more immediate concern was the question of whether the official biographer MacGregor Dawson could quote directly from King's diary. The executors let the matter simmer, but in the end they allowed Dawson to cite from King's diary and his personal letters to and from members of his family.

The first volume of the Mackenzie King biography was a long time in the making. The initial grant of $100,000 from the Rockefeller Foundation ran out at the end of 1953 and the literary executors were able to win another grant to cover all of the costs up to the end of 1956. But even after six years, Dawson wasn't even close to finishing the biography. The Rockefeller Foundation had given all it could, so the literary executors looked elsewhere for support. Rival media companies bid to get the rights to publish serialized extracts from the biography before it was published. *Maclean's* offered $60,000 but the executors opted for the more lucrative $90,000 offer from *Weekend* magazine. *Weekend* was a glossy magazine that appeared in the Saturday edition of papers all across the country, giving it a readership even wider than *Maclean's*. All told, the King biography was funded to almost $300,000 and this figure does not even include the money spent by the Public Archives in arranging King's papers. By the scale of academic funding today, let alone in the 1950s, the sum was enormous.[12]

Even so, the sheer amount of material must have been daunting. It seems as if the huge resources at Dawson's disposal made his task even more difficult. He had too much to work with, too much information to take in. The executors arranged for research assistants to help with the job, hiring various scholars to write research memos on topics of their expertise. These included the Queen's historian Frederick Gibson, the political scientists James Eayrs and Donald Worster, and H.J. Walker from the Department of Labour. The literary executor Fred McGregor also did some of this work. The task of organizing even the memos written by these research assistants would have been enormous. By mid-summer 1955, the assistants had written thousands of pages of memos on such topics as cabinet formation and external affairs. Some of this could simply be slightly modified and incorporated into the biography.

Dawson himself seems to have been overwhelmed by it all. He took to returning to his home in Nova Scotia during the summer, taking some work with him but also clearly needing a rest. He wrote to one executor that "just to keep my conscience quiet, I peck away in desultory fashion at some of the diary – off and on" but joked that he was presently "engaged on much more important things than a mere biography, and you will be pleased to hear that my garden flourishes."[13] This was in 1956. By the end of 1957, his health was much worse and the executors were growing impatient. They decided to hire extra help. They took on the young historian Blair Neatby to assist Dawson. Or at least this is how they put it to Dawson. To Neatby they said that they wanted him to finish the story of King's life up to 1939. The literary executor Jack Pickersgill would help

Dawson with King's story from 1939 onward. It was only just in time. Dawson died in the summer of 1958, a few months before publication of Volume One.[14]

Dawson's book appeared in stores in the autumn of 1958 and sold a respectable four thousand copies in the first two months. The next spring, Dawson would posthumously receive a medal for best biography of the year. *Weekend* magazine published extracts of the book that were sent to millions of newspaper subscribers across the country. While Dawson was no longer alive, his wife was offended on his behalf. She found the extracts in *Weekend* magazine to be tawdry. There was the official biography of a Canadian prime minister, a work to which her professor husband had devoted the last years of his life, printed alongside advertisements for Milkbone Dog Food and Castoria laxative. And, of course, the magazine had published the most titillating sections, those about Mackenzie King's brief dalliance with a Chicago nurse.[15]

The first volume of the biography was always going to be tricky for Dawson. He was a political scientist. Nothing he had previously published resembled anything like what he needed to deal with in writing this first part of King's biography, which, moving chronologically, covered Mackenzie King's youth, family upbringing, and education. Once the book reached the years of King's public life as a political figure, Dawson was on surer ground. At that point, the biography moves through the records of parliamentary debate and the decisions of cabinet formation just as previous biographies of statesman had done so before. Yet, because this volume centred on King's youth, Dawson couldn't help but delve into the childhood experiences that had shaped King the man. The abundance of source material made it all possible. And the growing mainstream influence of Freudian ideas that argued for the importance of childhood experiences in later personality development made it seem logical.

In 1958 some readers could remember clearly the early years of Mackenzie King's public life, but even for them the book offered a never-before-seen look at King's younger years. Readers were getting their first, intimate look at King in his own words. They learned of King as a schoolboy – a hellion at times, but a serious one. So although Dawson subtitled his book, "a political biography" and much of the book focused on King's public life, it was the private King that sparked the most interest. Readers saw King develop into an earnest adolescent and university student, someone who took seriously – perhaps too seriously – the moral strictures of the day concerning temperance, chastity, self-denial, and probity.[16]

Dawson carefully and not uncritically showed how the young Mackenzie King struggled to find safe passage between his own ambition and his desire to act selflessly. When dealing with King the private person, the tone of the biography is very much like a work by Lytton Strachey – critically sympathetic, poking pins into King's hypocrisy and the way the young man would not truly own up to his own base nature, especially his ambition. Readers learned about King's failed romances, including the serious dalliance with the Chicago nurse Mathilde Grossert, which *Weekend* magazine had so publicized in its excerpts. Given that most Canadians would have known nothing about the bachelor King's private life, even the suggestion that he had been in love seemed fascinating. King had always been a symbol of the sexless, sober public figure whose private life was entirely private and not for public consumption. Dawson's volume was nothing like Stacey's *A Very Double Life* yet readers still lapped up the few intimate details on offer.

J.B. McGeachy in the *Financial Post* especially appreciated the "candid" account of King's youth – in particular, the smothering attention from his mother. The "glimpse of King as boy and adolescent … is warmly recommended … as Canadian history and as a psychological study of political genius in embryo," he wrote. The account was almost unprecedented in Canada for the way it paid "almost equal attention to King's private mental experiences, so unusual as to be called eccentric, and his public career." McGeachy was probably not alone when he concluded that "to me, and perhaps to others, the more fascinating subject is the man's inner life for here is something one knew little about while he lived." Certainly, the *Globe and Mail* reviewer was fascinated by the hints of romance in King's life and ended wanting more, wishing that the "biographer had been permitted, or permitted himself, to reveal more of the human interest in the diaries and letters."[17]

Still, Dawson was sometimes at a loss for how to approach his subject. His research notes show that he read the main Freudian popularizers of the day – Karl Menninger and Karen Horney. Dawson never cites them in the final manuscript, but his notes make clear that he was trying to figure out King's psychological quirks, especially the way that what King said and professed to believe often did not match what he actually did and desired to do. This is a slightly more complicated version of the kind of issue that Bruce Hutchison struggled with in *The Incredible Canadian*. Dawson isn't only trying to make sense of the disjuncture between the private and the public King. He also recognizes that King himself could be blind to his own inner troubles.[18]

In his research notes Dawson underlined the psychiatrist Karen Horney's comments on "aggressive personalities," especially the kind of man whose "attitude is sometimes quite apparent, but more often it is covered over with a veneer of suave politeness, fair-mindedness and good fellowship." As Horney went on to write, "this 'front' can represent a Machiavellian concession to expediency. As a rule, however, it is a composite of pretenses, genuine fe[e]lings, and neurotic needs. A desire to make others believe he is a good fellow may be combined with a certain amount of actual benevolence as long as there is no question in anybody's mind that he himself is in command." This description aptly captures the kind of private man that Dawson discovered in the King diary. He found King to be someone who wanted to put on a public pretence of good-natured amiability but then found it difficult to admit to himself when he put these ideals aside to satisfy his overweening ambition and desire to get his own way.[19]

Dawson also needed to make sense of King's relationship with his mother. This would always have played some role in the biography, since King had made no secret of his devotion. The revelations about King conversing with her dead spirit, and the pseudo-shrine he established to her in his upper-floor library at Laurier House, made the issue pressing. But it mattered even more because psychiatrists and their popularizers were radically changing what to make of some men's relations with their mothers. This had to do, of course, with the Oedipus Complex.

In the late 1950s and early 1960s, Canadians were learning (or at least beginning to believe) that the mother-son relationship could be sinister. Freud and his popularizers warned of the dangers of excessive mother-devotion. What did it mean when young men did not learn to transfer their affections to other women? What happened when men were dominated by their mothers? At a time when psychiatry was dominated by psychoanalysis, which argued that the roots of mental illness were to be found in childhood, it wasn't surprising that motherhood became such a fascinating topic. Philip Wylie had warned of "momism" back in his popular 1942 book, *A Generation of Vipers*. These ideas, and the therapeutic techniques that flowed from them, spread throughout the culture. To appreciate how pervasive they were, one need only look at some of the most important films of the era, Nicholas Ray's *Rebel without a Cause* (1955), Alfred Hitchcock's *Psycho* (1960), and John Frankenheimer's *The Manchurian Candidate* (1962). Each film played on the idea of sons who become psychologically warped after being dominated by their mothers – and always with an uncomfortable sexual connotation.[20]

It must have seemed to Dawson that King's life was made for the age: there can rarely have been a man who was so devoted to his mother. His closest friend, Violet Markham, considered his mother-fixation a tragedy. In her memoirs she wrote of how she hesitated to "hold Mrs. King responsible for the cult into which her son's love developed … But in the jargon of the psychiatrists, it is undeniable that the mother-complex was a misfortune for Mackenzie King."[21] Like others, Markham blamed King's mother-love for the fact that he did not marry and have children. Markham herself was sympathetic but others could take the analysis further, wondering how his mother-devotion was a kind of neurosis and fitted into the Freudian idea of the Oedipus Complex.

Dawson took notes on Karl Menninger's book *Love and Hate*. So popular were Freud's ideas about the Oedipus Complex that Menninger claimed, "Nearly every individual of this type who comes to a psychiatrist announces that he has 'a mother fixation' or 'a mother complex.'" But Menninger insisted that most people misunderstood this complex to mean it involved some kind of sexual attraction. Instead, he said, it really is a combination of "dependence" on the mother, and, at the same time, "hostility" toward her for this dependence. Then Menninger went on to describe a kind of person who looked a great deal like Mackenzie King. "Such men have no sexual attraction, in the adult sense of the word, to their mothers or to any other woman; if they consort with women at all, it is with women who are much older or much younger than themselves, and these are treated either as protecting mothers or as inconsequential childish amusements."[22]

This image echoed strongly with MacGregor Dawson, as it would to anyone who knew of King's intimate relations. Not only did King never marry, but his closest relationships in his adult life were with two older married women. In his various attempts to find a wife, King rarely revealed any kind of sexual attraction to them. In fact, in his relations with Mathilde Grossert that Dawson wrote about in Volume One, King clearly became disturbed when she showed physical affection toward him. In other words, King's life matched up all too well with the mother-fixated neurotic. In an earlier age, even his critics could regard his devotion to his mother as something that was at least honourable. But by the time of Dawson's biography in the late 1950s, the spread of psychoanalytic ideas was transforming how people understood intimate relations, especially between sons and mothers.[23]

Yet Dawson held back. Even though the psychiatrists clearly informed his own thinking on King, his would not be a psychobiography. Certainly, when one now reads Menninger's ideas about the mother-fixated man, the way they so closely match King's own life is eerily familiar. But in the late 1950s, for a serious scholar like Robert MacGregor Dawson who was writing an official biography, it was still safer not to probe too deeply. He himself, and the reviewers of his book, found the private Mackenzie King fascinating. But they weren't yet ready to dive fully into all of his oddities. Volume One gave readers an intimate portrait of King's youth, yet it was still very much in the tradition of other biographies of statesmen. Readers might have been fascinated by the private King, but the book would soon move on to the real business: King's political career. A misprint on the dust jacket, though, raised anew the whole question of what kinds of secrets King might have and which ones the literary executors were going to allow the public to see.

☙

The University of Toronto Press screwed up. Someone at the press no doubt thought it would make the book seem all the more exciting if the public learned that the only way they would ever see Mackenzie

King's diary was in the form of excerpts in this biography. The dust jacket alerted readers that King's "diary has never been opened to the public, and, indeed, Mr. King directed that it be destroyed on completion of the biography."[24] In other words, if you wanted the real inside story of Mackenzie King, this book was the only place to get it. The dust jacket wasn't entirely wrong – King's will did dictate that the diary was to be destroyed, and although there was some wiggle room in this declaration, the literary executors hadn't decided yet exactly what to do.[25] But they also didn't want untoward publicity.

The note about the diary's destruction blew up a flutter of articles in publications across the country about the rights of public men to guard their private secrets. There was no settled opinion, but the issue clearly spoke to growing concerns of the age. The values of openness and authenticity, of the need for transparency, and the question of whether one could trust those in authority not to hide their dirty secrets: these had become issues in themselves.

Maclean's took the old common-sense approach. If King had ordered that his diary be destroyed, then, "the answer is painful, maddening, contrary to the public interest – and, alas! beyond dispute. Mr. King's wishes must be obeyed." Even *Maclean's*, though, questioned the right of politicians to destroy their public documents – those documents they created in the midst of conducting their public affairs. "What right has a politician, a statesman or a military leader," the magazine asked, "to keep his official and semi-official documents under lock and key while he's in office, pack them up when he leaves office, burn such of them as he'd like to have forgotten, and then turn the rest over to a chosen biographer or use them as the material for a book or books of his own?"[26] *Maclean's* had a very simple answer: none.

Some took this logic and applied it to the diary itself. Diaries could be private, true. But the *Ottawa Journal* made the point that King's privacy could be respected only so long as he didn't make the diary public himself. By allowing his private diary to be used for the official biography, King (or his literary executors) had made it a public document. Once certain parts of the diary were used in the official biography, the public could only ask the reasonable question: What else had been left out? The literary executors were no doubt professional men but, "no matter what their intellectual integrity or their impartiality or objectivity was," wouldn't it be reasonable to place them "under suspicion of selecting or interpreting what Mr. King wrote to create a favourable public image of him?" King's diary now simply had to be preserved and eventually made open to serious researchers. If not, it would only create cynicism. This kind of history would prove Napoleon right – that history was "a lie agreed to."[27]

In the *Globe and Mail*, Harry Ferns wrote in with his own opinion. "It is perfectly true ... that the public has no right to examine any man's diary," Ferns admitted. "If it was the wish of the late Right Hon. W.L. Mackenzie King that his diary be destroyed then most certainly his last will should be carried out." Yet this wasn't the case with Mackenzie King. "Unfortunately, but characteristically," wrote Ferns, "Mr. Mackenzie King wanted to have it both ways."[28] He couldn't use parts of the diary to present one kind of image of himself but then claim that others, who might come to different conclusions, could not examine the diary to check the veracity of that image. Of course, Ferns had been concerned for some time about excessive control over King's papers by the literary executors. Back in 1955 when he and Bernard Ostry published *The Age of Mackenzie King*, they drafted a bombastic "Note on Sources" that their publisher ultimately convinced them should not be included in the book. In that draft, they attacked political control over historical documents. "We are of the impression that political influences are at work in the study of historical data in Canada, and that the surest ticket of admission to public facilities for scholarly study is a clean bill of health from some Liberal political commissar." They went on to argue that "Canadians should be as free to fish and hunt in the National Archives as they are free to fish and hunt in the lakes and forests of the Dominion during an open season. They should also be allowed to shoot."[29]

Not all agreed. One man wrote into the *Globe and Mail* to complain that it was all just "another example of the pernicious tendency of the age to invade human privacy." Yet there did seem to be a good deal of support for the need to look more closely into the lives of public men. As the *Toronto Telegram* put it, "an ordinary man's private life is his own. But a national leader's life is not." After all, the paper argued, in the case of a public figure, the "deepest secrets of his private life have a bearing on his public life. His personal reactions can explain some otherwise inexplicable act of public policy. His personal problems influence the way he attacks public problems. Surely the nation has the right to the lessons of history, as they are revealed only in his personal record of events and personalities."[30]

It certainly gave the literary executors something to consider. Francess Halpenny of the University of Toronto Press wrote to apologize for her part in generating the controversy. Still, the literary executor W. Kaye Lamb reassured her that at least it "has perhaps served a useful purpose, as it has prompted quite a lively discussion on the question as to whether or not prime ministers have any *right* to have their diaries considered private, and to have them destroyed!"[31]

By the end of the 1950s, with the publication of the official biography and with the need to decide the ultimate fate of King's papers, those with the control over King's secrets found themselves facing the arguments of those who wanted to tear down older boundaries between public and private. The literary executors had their own opinions, differing from each other on matters of principle and pragmatic interest. But the rising tide of curiosity about what had been private could not be denied. What wasn't yet clear was whether the literary executors could hold out against it – or whether they would even want to.

Part Four

On the Precipice

End of an Era

Perhaps there is no better representation of the shifting mood in the late 1950s than the changed fortunes of poet and lawyer F.R. Scott.[1] A son of the Anglican bishop of Quebec, Scott was born into the anglo establishment and yet he became a radical critic of politics and society in Quebec and Canada in the middle years of the twentieth century. He won a Rhodes scholarship that took him to Oxford University in 1920, coming back eventually to teach law at McGill University. Like his friend Eugene Forsey, he became a leading socialist thinker in inter-war Canada, helping to found the CCF. Unlike Forsey, he was able to stay on at McGill even though his viewpoints were often a source of contention with the university's authorities and with the members of the Montreal elite who sat on its Board of Governors. Long overlooked for promotion to the deanship of the Law School despite his seniority, Scott nonetheless made his own reputation as a political thinker, legal expert, and poet. By the later years of the 1950s, he had been fighting to reform the politics and culture of his country for decades.

In 1957 he published a poem about the legacy of Mackenzie King – a *cri de cœur* of exasperation and a call for change. Scott's poem "WLMK" would go on to become one of the most widely cited and remembered of Canadian poems, showing up again and again whenever attention turned to Mackenzie King. "WLMK" was published in *Time* magazine and then again in two different books in 1957 (a collection of Scott's poems and an anthology of satirical verse). "How shall we speak of Canada, Mackenzie King dead?" Scott asks. It was the essential question for those who cared about politics and the nation after more than two decades of uninterrupted Liberal rule. Scott was not optimistic. Mackenzie King, said Scott, "blunted us":

We had no shape
Because he never took sides,
And no sides
Because he never allowed them to take shape.

...

The height of his ambition
Was to pile a Parliamentary Committee on a Royal Commission,
To have "conscription if necessary
But not necessarily conscription,"
To let Parliament decide –

Later.

King had left Canada an unfinished country, a jelly of a nation, with no shape, barely any substance. This might, as some then and since have argued, be a recipe for success. But Scott skewered the idea that the Mackenzie King style of leadership could be anything other than self-serving, allowing the status quo to endure for a little while longer. If this was what political success meant in Canada, thought Scott, pity the nation.

The poem is a candid assessment of King but also of the Canada of the 1950s – a nation that still had many who honoured King and his successors. The final lines speak to the Canada of this era as much as they do to King himself:

Truly he will be remembered
Wherever men honour ingenuity,
Ambiguity, inactivity, and political longevity.

Let us raise up a temple
To the cult of mediocrity,
Do nothing by halves
Which can be done by quarters.

A friend wrote to Scott that, in reading the satirical poems that Scott published that year, she "breathed a most welcome, astringent air: a fresh breeze in the somewhat debilitating atmosphere which tends to smother the day-to-day existence of the average individual."[2] In this case, the poet really did lead the people. Scott would eventually become dean of the McGill Law School and would live to see many of his previously radical ideas become a new common sense.

&

In the mid-1950s, Canadian politics exuded a misleading feeling of calm. The Liberal Party had governed uninterrupted for twenty years. When Mackenzie King retired in 1948, he handed power over to Louis St Laurent, who won majority governments in 1949 and again in 1953. The Liberal Party had become the governing party, its values seeming to seep across the landscape, filling in the cracks of opposition and keeping down the dust of controversy and discontent. The onset of the Cold War had dampened criticism from the socialist CCF, opening it up to attacks of communist subversion and leading those on the left to purge communists from their ranks. It helped that the Liberals presided over an era of unprecedented economic growth with unemployment at record low levels. Although inequality was in no way eradicated (and would re-emerge as a political issue in the 1960s), economic depression did not return after the war. The bounties of modern life, long promised but often reserved for the better off, came within reach for many. Shiny new things like refrigerators and televisions filled up Canadians' houses and the latest models of automobiles covered the roadways in a country where car ownership was becoming the norm. Progress could be gauged by the small fundamentals that we now overlook, things like indoor plumbing, which finally became a reality for almost all Canadians, and the spread of electricity to even remote rural areas. The expansion of unions across the blue-collar work world led to the standardization of the forty-hour week for many. This meant that, increasingly, Canadians could look forward to the time of leisure called the weekend.[3] When critics took on the legacy of Mackenzie King, St Laurent, and the Liberals, then, they were taking on those who had shaped what had come to be the bountiful harvest of modern Canada.

Yet decades in power can lead to arrogance. Certainly, arrogant is how the Liberals seemed. A series of scandals in the mid-1950s

10.1 Louis St Laurent and Mackenzie King

showed their weaknesses. The debate over the construction of a national gas pipeline in 1955 pitted the Liberals against both opposition parties and a large chunk of the media in a David and Goliath confrontation that made the Liberals appear both arrogant and undemocratic. The Liberals also came to seem too pro-American in their support of American capital and in their lack of deference for Canada's British connections. In these battles, the media gave space to the Liberal and Mackenzie King critic Eugene Forsey. His letters to the editor were read into Hansard and published in papers across the country. Forsey decried Liberal anti-democratic arrogance. If the Liberals were so willing to shut down parliamentary debate, "Why not dispense with Parliament altogether?" he asked. "Why not assure now, to us and our posterity, the full blessings of arbitrary power and untrammelled despotism?"[4]

The Liberals' response to Forsey and their critics revealed the problem. Brooke Claxton, the man who had been so critical of the Ferns and Ostry biography, was amazed at how the pipeline debate had been turned into "the greatest sensation since Confederation." He couldn't believe how "irresponsible" the media was behaving in giving Forsey and this line of argument any credence. Yet, while Claxton "felt that the conduct of the Opposition was so outrageous that there would be a heavy swing of public opinion in favour of the government," he had to admit that it hadn't happened yet, except in what he regarded as "more informed quarters."[5]

The Liberals survived the pipeline controversy but not its wider implications. The post-war era may indeed have been exceedingly prosperous but Bruce Hutchison was wrong to say that "no government can easily defeat itself, however it tries, under these conditions."[6] By the time Canadians could buy Volume One of the Mackenzie King biography and could read the newspaper debates about a public man's right to privacy, the political world in the country had been turned upside down. John Diefenbaker, the small-town lawyer from the Prairies, upset the St Laurent Liberals in the 1957 election, winning a minority government. The next spring, when the too-confident Liberals forced an election, Diefenbaker's Progressive Conservatives won a decisive majority government, taking 204 of the 265 seats in the House of Commons and 53.7 per cent of the popular vote, the largest majority ever recorded. The Mackenzie King era finally came to an end.

Yet the changes afoot in the late 1950s went beyond political parties. Politics is only ever partly about the subjects covered in parliamentary and journalistic debate. There were also other, subtler social and cultural changes that coincided with the downfall of the Liberals in the late 1950s. The moral landscape of Canada was changing. Attitudes toward practices previously unrespectable – or at least the subject of debate as to their respectability – softened. More tolerant views of the pleasurable aspects of life and self-expression became increasingly common. These changes in the culture of the self showed up usually only obliquely in speeches in the House of Commons or in the editorials of prominent newspapers. Yet they were political in a wider and cultural sense. In retrospect, it is easier to see how the shift to a more psychological- and rights-based model of the self was beginning to undermine the kinds of assumptions politicians could make about citizens and vice versa.

None of the political parties completely understood what was happening because the changes weren't directly partisan. They were tied to the affluence of the period and represented the spread of a culture of the self and individual rights that was slowly unravelling the tight grip of Victorianism on Canadian morals. By the end of the 1950s, as these cultural changes bubbled underneath the surface, the Liberal Party that was the inheritor of Mackenzie King's mantle would learn that the seemingly solid foundation of common sense was cracking everywhere around it.

⟨8⟩

The 1950s might be the most misunderstood decade of the twentieth century. In hindsight, the era has appeared conservative and quaint, something either to be derided as old-fashioned, sexist, and racist or longed for nostalgically as an era of family togetherness and political quiescence. Next to the radical social revolutions of the 1960s – with the youth revolt, Front de libération du Québec (FLQ) terrorism, and feminism – the earlier decade can't help but seem black and white. This view is only further reinforced by the fact that so much of the decade later came to be seen through the prism of the Baby Boom generation which grew up at that time. This was, to them, a period of youthful innocence to be succeeded by something more radical, tumultuous, and (depending on your viewpoint) exciting and progressive. None of this does us any favours in our attempts to figure out the dynamics of social change that were busily at work transforming everyday life and values throughout the decade.

Ironically, one man who understood what was happening at the end of the 1950s was seventy years old and a relic of many Liberal governments under both Mackenzie King and Louis St Laurent. Charles Gavan Power, or "Chubby" as he was known to most, was a politician entirely unlike Mackenzie King. From a family that took hockey as seriously as it did politics, Power represented the riding of Quebec South from 1917 until he went to the Senate in 1955. As he admitted himself, he didn't give much truck to the place of ideals in politics. An old-school politician of tactics and handshakes, of deals and pragmatism, he had survived in politics longer than most. King had hesitated in putting Power into the cabinet because of his fondness for drink – an issue that many in Liberal circles were loath to make public.

But in the aftermath of the Liberals' humiliating 1958 defeat, Power sought to explain to his fellow Liberals what was happening in the country. To his friends in the Liberal Party who wanted to push the party back to laissez-faire liberalism, with its emphasis on individualistic restraint and probity, he urged caution. Writing to his friend and fellow Senator Thomas Crerar, he told him that those (like Crerar) who wanted the party to take that path were out of touch with the realities of Canada in the 1950s. The welfare state was here to stay, he wrote. Those who argue against it, he feared, placed "too much reliance on the people's attachment to what we were taught to believe were fundamental virtues – self-discipline, hard work, individual saving … in other words the practice of those stern Presbyterian principles to which you are so much attached." Like it or not, Canada had changed. "This is a more materialistic age and the people are not so much interested in the homely virtues as in security and reasonably comfortable living, at someone else's expense if possible."[7]

Power was right. In area after area, Canadians in the 1950s were slowly and tentatively stepping away from the Victorian Christian moralism that had so long dominated middle-class culture. The Baby Boomers might not often think of their parents as hedonists (and many certainly were not), but throughout Canadian culture we can see many ways in which Canada was becoming a nation much more open to pleasures previously considered sinful. Part of the turn inward, to wanting a franker and more open look at what individuals really did (*pace* Freud), was based on the fact that increasingly Canadians were loosening up about a series of habits that had previously been viewed as the kinds of activities that one would want to hide.[8]

Drinking had long divided Canadian families and communities. In the midst of the call for sacrifice in the Great War, temperance campaigners had even convinced all governments across the country to impose prohibition. This fell apart after the war, quite soon in Quebec and much later in the Maritimes. But in its place, provincial governments instituted a series of restrictive drinking laws whose main purpose was to make drinking as difficult and unpleasurable as possible. These restrictions decisively lost their popular support throughout most of Canada in the 1950s. Canadians began to consume a great deal more alcohol of all types – beer, wine, and spirits. Governments loosened up regulations, allowing things like jukeboxes and snack foods into what had been staid beer parlours. Soon, they were allowing the public sale not just of beer but also of wine and spirits. The most egregious restriction, the ban on selling alcohol to Aboriginal peoples, had ended by the mid-1950s. And the breweries and distilleries, swelling in size from sales and corporate consolidation, and presenting themselves as supporters of moderation and good citizenship, supported community and sports events with their advertising dollars.[9]

What happened in drink spread to other areas. Gambling, too, had long been considered a vice by many moralists. The views on this had perhaps been more divided than on alcohol. There had always been exceptions to government bans on gambling – betting at racetracks, for instance. But the laws against gambling arose out of a Christian moral sensibility. Gamblers irresponsibly risked their money. And even if they won the profits were seen as sinful because they weren't earned. In the 1950s, there were still Christian ministers who could be called upon to make the old moral arguments, but they increasingly found themselves with less support. As with drinking, the public came to see the problems of gambling as relating to specific individuals. This might be gamblers who couldn't control themselves, or it might also be the criminal syndicates who controlled and profited from the illegal gambling that happened in every Canadian community. For every small town in Canada had its local bookie who arranged bets, or the house or houses where you could find a game of chance on a certain night of the week. The laws wouldn't change until 1969 when the Trudeau government's Omnibus Bill opened the door to government-controlled lotteries, but even in the 1950s the moral consensus against gambling was crumbling.[10]

The same could be said for attitudes toward money and debt. In retrospect, Canadians of the 1950s seem like pillars of financial rectitude. Consumer debt was barely a concern at all. And yet the tide was already turning, washing out old ideas about the evils and sinfulness of owing money. The consumer culture of the 1950s brought many new expensive luxuries that soon came to be seen as necessities – refrigerators, electric stoves, and automobiles. Many Canadian families remained cautious about purchases, paying with cash or with only very short-term loans. Yet the federal government had committed to expanding home ownership across the country. It established programs to insure mortgages, making it more lucrative and safe for banks and other lenders to extend mortgages to potential homebuyers. The government was encouraging Canadians to go into debt, if only to fuel the economy and expand middle-class economic well-being and security. Many middle-class families in the era of Mackenzie King – indeed even King's own family – rented their homes. In post-war Canada this would increasingly come to be seen as a hallmark of the past. Home ownership, even if it meant large debt, had become the ideal.

Other kinds of credit began to appear as well. The first credit card appeared in 1950, although this kind of credit would begin to expand only by the end of the decade and in the 1960s. Purchasing items by instalments had a long history in Canada, and so did store credit. But these practices had typically been small scale, at the local level between those who knew one another, and often credit had been extended reluctantly by the lender. The post-war years, however, saw the expansion of instalment purchases for many new consumer items. None of this changed attitudes overnight, and in retrospect the views of most Canadians in the 1950s toward credit and debt remained cautious if not condemning. As Margaret Atwood said in her book *Payback: Debt and the Shadow Side of Wealth*, she grew up in a society where "there were three things you were never supposed to ask questions about": sex, religion, and money. Yet, on each of these fronts, Canadians were becoming less silent.[11]

A common joke about 1950s television and films is that you never got to see people's bedrooms. Or, if you did, they showed parents sleeping in two separate beds. Yet, in fact, this kind of artistic representation was already crumbling. Hollywood had been under a system of self-imposed censorship since the 1930 Production Code. Under the code, films were to avoid portraying everything from profanity to miscegenation. They were to be careful when showing violence and crime and especially sex and anything to do with bodily functions. Yet, by the late 1950s, the code was falling apart under the influence of foreign films, the competition from television, and liberalizing social norms. The 1959 film *Some Like It Hot* didn't receive approval from the censors and yet went on to become a money-making success. A film like *Psycho* in 1960 ran into difficulty with the censors not just because of the violent shower scene but because one of the characters was shown flushing paper down a toilet – all in full view of the camera.[12]

All of these developments showed the ways in which basic features of human existence – human desire, alcohol, gambling, money, or bodily functions – were coming out into the open in the public culture of the late 1950s. In 1976 the historian Donald Creighton wrote about this shift in the immediate post-war years. Creighton was a Tory and unsympathetic to the changes around him. Yet his dismay is useful in signalling the direction of change. The hardship of the Depression and the Second World War had been similar to the conditions of Victorian and Edwardian Canada. "Colonial and rural origins" had bequeathed to Canadians an "acceptance of hard work, the belief in personal responsibility, the habits of thrift, simplicity and order" yet "their children and grandchildren were to be creatures of affluence and uneasy peace."[13] Creighton paints the 1940s and early 1950s as years of ordered simplicity and tempered pleasure, yet still there were signs of change. While tame by later standards, they represented a kind of "coming out" every bit as significant as, and similar to, the way some wanted to expose Mackenzie King's own secrets.

If one accepted the Boomers' view of the '50s, it would be impossible to understand one of the greatest Canadian novels of that decade, Hugh MacLennan's *The Watch That Ends the Night* from 1959. MacLennan is now better remembered for his book *Two Solitudes*, which gave a poetic title to the tension between French and English in Canada. Yet *The Watch That Ends the Night* beautifully showed the moral loosening already at work in 1950s Canada. "Morality? Duty?" says one character. "It was easy to talk of these things once, but surely it is no accident that in our time the best of men hesitate inwardly before they utter these words?" In the novel, MacLennan is not entirely comfortable with the changes he sees around him. But he is an even better witness because of his discomfort.

10.2 Hugh MacLennan

The novel makes clear that the great quest in contemporary Canada was to look unflinchingly within the self. "We're like the man who tore down all the walls of his house in November and then had to face the winter naked," another character says. "Now I suppose we've got to make up the rules as we go along and one gets so tired doing that. It would have been so much simpler and safer to have kept the old rules." And what had replaced the old moral language, the old certainties? It was psychology. "Was neurosis the new word for sin?" MacLennan has a character say. That is exactly what it was. As the book ends, the narrator comes to the conclusion: "Here, I found at last, is the nature of the final human struggle. Within, not without."[14]

MacLennan's friend and fellow writer F.R. Scott agreed. Scott, whose poem "WLMK" so exemplified the desire for change at the end of the 1950s, also strove to create a less shameful, more open Canada in his other job, as law professor and lawyer. Scott acted as legal counsel in the court case that best illuminated the ways in which older standards of decorum were being cast aside at the end of the 1950s – the censorship trial over *Lady Chatterley's Lover*. The case resulted from the attempt to censor an unexpurgated version of D.H. Lawrence's famous novel. The British and American trials are better known but in fact the Canadian case went to the courts first. Moreover, the British defence attorney was an old Oxford friend of Scott's and he looked to the Canadian trial for guidance on how to proceed.

Lawrence's novel about an affair between an English woman and her gamekeeper offended sensibilities in myriad ways – in its portrayal of adultery, in its frank use of language including "fuck" and "cunt," and in its blunt eroticism, especially the scene where the lovers braid each other's pubic hair. The case was made for someone like Scott, with his unique background as a poet and lawyer. He brought in expert literary witnesses, including the novelists Hugh MacLennan and Morley Callaghan, to speak to the literary merit of the novel. Scott had to make the case that the sexual passages of the novel were only parts of it and he tried to push the court to consider the effect of the book not on a young person (as had previously been the test in censorship cases) but on the community at large. Both the lower court in Quebec and the Quebec Court of Appeal found against the publisher. Scott had expected this given the conservative judicial culture in Quebec. But he had taken on the case only on the assurance that the publisher would see it through to the Supreme Court of Canada.

By the time the case reached this stage, the famous British trial had already reached its conclusion, vindicating the publisher. The British trial became a sensation and the crown prosecutor was turned into a symbol of old-style morality to be mocked, with much of the commentary focusing on the moment when he naively asked the jury of mostly working-class men whether this was the "kind of book you would wish your wife or servants to read." The publisher, Penguin, quickly published a verbatim transcript of the trial which itself became a bestseller.[15] The trial came to encapsulate the sea change in values that led to the sexual revolution. As the British poet Philip Larkin put it, "Sexual intercourse began / In nineteen sixty-three / (which was rather late for me) – / Between the end of the Chatterley ban / And the Beatles' first LP."[16]

In Canada, Scott appeared before the Supreme Court, which decided in his favour in a split decision, with the Catholic judges dissenting from the majority opinion. Scott turned the whole experience into a poem. He felt that the desire to censor matters of human sexuality went against humanity itself. Sexuality, he wrote in his poem about the trial and in private letters, was simply part of the human experience. "It's all part of our universe," he wrote, "and I don't think we should hide a fraction of it."[17]

Here, Scott and MacLennan reflected their times. Like others at the end of the 1950s, they wrote of a Canadian culture that was tearing down older traditions in the name of being more honest and open about what was truly human – the kinds of desires and truths that an earlier morality had hidden or repressed. In the next decade, younger people who urged a more radical openness and authenticity and who were willing to tear down more of what had been traditional would take these ideas further. But on the edge of the 1960s, the direction of change was already clear.

Close-Up

A single tear, quickly wiped away, ended the most important show on Canadian television in the 1960s. A fourteen-year-old boy, Stephen Truscott, had been found guilty of murdering a classmate and sentenced to death, the youngest ever person to receive that judicial fate in Canada. The TV program *This Hour Has Seven Days* sent a reporter to interview Truscott's mother. The interview showed why so many Canadians found *This Hour* to be compelling and controversial television. The camera stays on Doris Truscott as she is asked about visiting her young son in prison. An off-camera voice asks softly if she is ever alone with him, if she embraces him, if she tells him that she loves him. Doris Truscott is quiet and composed. She taps her hands in an odd way and the camera zooms in on the physical tic – as if to signal that this is a hint of all the emotion she is keeping in check. "Do you tell him you love him?" the interviewer asks. The camera zooms upward to the mother's face. It fills the entire screen. Nothing can escape the camera at this vantage. "Is it hard not to cry when you visit him?" There is a silence, a pause as the interviewer waits to see if she will cry.[1]

The show returns to its host, Laurier Lapierre. He is clearly affected. He explains that Truscott's sentence has been commuted. A tear forms under one eye and he quickly wipes it away. It was very little, but it was enough to infuriate the CBC executives. Within a matter of weeks, they cancelled the show.

Of course, it was never just this single tear. From the beginning, there had been a continual battle between the show's creators and executives at the CBC.[2] The executives would issue directives, calling for more objectivity, less controversy. Then the journalists and producers at *This Hour* would invariably ignore the instructions. The final tear symbolized a kind of journalism that the show had practised since its first episode – and, in fact, the kind of journalism that the producers had promised when they pitched the show to those in charge at the CBC. In their proposal for *This Hour*, they argued for a program that would "draw attention to public wrongs and encourage remedial action."[3] It wouldn't simply be neutral, pretending that objectivity consisted of always withholding opinions. Two years into the show, the CBC executives had seen enough. Despite a large public campaign of protest, the show remained cancelled and its employees went on to other programs and other parts of their careers. Yet, for those in charge at the CBC, it was a hollow victory. The show had ended but the idea of television it embodied had won and would go on to inform other programs, changing the public landscape of television.

Although the story of Canadian television often highlights the cancellation of *This Hour* as a pivotal moment, in truth, the kinds of changes that the show represented had been slowly changing television even at the end of the 1950s. The show was created by two men, Patrick Watson and Douglas Leiterman, who had, since the mid-1950s, been discussing ways to create meaningful public-affairs television in Canada. Reality was inherently interesting – even more interesting, they thought, than the kind of fairy-tale shows like *Bonanza* that the public liked so much on television. The trick was to figure out ways of telling real stories that were just as compelling.

Several years before working on *This Hour*, the two men had collaborated on the documentary series *Close-Up*. It was there that Leiterman turned his attention to Mackenzie King. The medium of television through which Canadians were coming to see their political leaders was changing priorities, shifting the ground under public figures, reorienting priorities and obliging politicians to interact differently with the public. Television seemed to demand an authenticity and an emotional connection even when so much of what was presented could be staged and inauthentic. Mackenzie King would find out that this applied to dead politicians too.

In 1957 Patrick Watson went to work in the public-affairs division of CBC, his first project being the new program *Close-Up*. Television was still a novel and strange technology. Watson had planned to do a PhD and had only by chance been convinced to change plans and join the national broadcaster. He simply did not know, nor did many people, what television could do. It didn't take long before Watson was converted to its possibilities.

Close-Up's creators tried to get the established and dignified Blair Fraser of *Maclean's* to work on the show. When he declined, they turned to a young reporter in the parliamentary press gallery named Douglas Leiterman. He stood out among the Ottawa reporters in the mid-1950s. At this time, the parliamentary press gallery, consisting of only two or three dozen reporters from newspapers across the country, denied access to radio or television journalists, who were seen as a threat. As the journalist Peter Dempson recalled, the press gallery on the third floor of the Centre Block was a dingy, brightly lit room, littered with beer bottles and half-empty whisky glasses. Everyone knew everyone else, including all of the politicians and the top bureaucrats. The partisan nature of the press lingered in connections between journalists and the political parties with which they were identified. The *Toronto Star* was Liberal and the *Ottawa Journal* was Tory. But this group of journalists, including Fraser, wanted to present themselves as professionals and different from their partisan predecessors in a different age of journalism. Their professionalism, though, also meant that they treated politicians with deference.[4]

Bruce Hutchison recalled being called up short in an interview by Louis St Laurent. Hutchison asked the prime minister about his time as minister of justice in King's government and about the controversial decision to arrest and detain the suspects in the Gouzenko spy scandal. The detention abrogated the ancient rights of habeus corpus and Hutchison wanted to know what St Laurent, who had been minister of justice at the time, now had to say about it. St Laurent was known to have a temper, though journalists did not report on this. Hutchison later described how St Laurent's "smiling face hardened in a scowl. The kindly eyes seemed to congeal in black opacity." St Laurent simply said, "I don't care to answer that question." It was enough. Hutchison thought he had nearly been "decapitated." He had learned his lesson.[5]

11.1 Douglas Leiterman

Douglas Leiterman was different. His friend Patrick Watson later recalled how, "in his quietly persistent way, [Leiterman] would seize on obfuscation or dishonesty like a ferret. 'But Minister,' he would say, 'last week you said the exact opposite; here's the quote. How do you account for the contradiction?' He was courteous but relentless."[6] This is the breed of journalist that Watson wanted to have working with him on *Close-Up*. He was just the kind of probing, demanding reporter who would rise to prominence in the 1960s and

1970s. Although we often associate the rise of that more critical journalism with those later years, especially in the response to the Vietnam War and the Watergate scandal, in fact journalists like Leiterman were already at work in the 1950s, and they were developing those more probing techniques even then.[7]

The *Close-Up* team took on any number of issues that in previous decades might have been considered taboo. They sent a camera crew to Sweden to do a show on what were the allegedly more open and liberal sexual practices in that country. In another episode, they profiled a Toronto woman, whose name was not revealed, who advertised her services as a "professional divorce correspondent." At a time when divorce law in Canada restricted marriage break-up to only a few very narrow conditions, one way out of wedlock was a finding of adultery. The woman featured in the *Close-Up* episode would, for a fee, arrange to be "discovered" in a hotel room in the initial stages of an affair, and allow photographs to be taken. The show exposed the way the actual behaviour of many Canadians did not live up to the moral code that was still enshrined in the law.[8]

This particular episode upset the top brass at the *Toronto Telegraph*, who later sought out and found the "divorce correspondent" and wrote a story about the so-called Shady Lady in which she said that she did not offer these services. Patrick Watson claimed that they later discovered that the *Telegraph* had paid the Shady Lady $2,000 to change her story.[9] Such were the costs of maintaining the illusion of a society of marital harmony in the late 1950s.

In 1958, with news of the upcoming release of MacGregor Dawson's first volume of the official King biography, Leiterman had written to the literary executors asking if they would cooperate in producing a television documentary that could coincide with the book's release. Fred McGregor thought it would be an excellent idea, though his views about what the show would look like probably differed from Leiterman's. He thought that the crew could film at Laurier House and Kingsmere and suggested a list of King's friends and colleagues who could speak on camera. The list included only Liberals, all of whom would likely give a rather friendly interpretation of the old chief.[10]

Leiterman was delayed in putting together the show but he finally began interviewing subjects in the late summer and spring of 1959. The two-part *Close-Up* special on Mackenzie King aired on 10 and

17 March 1960. It was a perfect example of the way the show was an in-between experiment between the neutral and deferential television of the 1950s and the irreverent and pointed television that would eventually emerge with *This Hour* in the mid-1960s.[11]

The program begins in an expected fashion. The camera pans over King's fake ruins at Kingsmere before the host, Frank Willis, comes on screen to speak of how we could say of King, as Voltaire said of God, that "if he had not existed, we would have had to invent him." Willis gave the two common views of King, how he had been prime minister "for twenty-one of the most crucial years of our history" and how he "must someday rank among the world's great nation-builders." Yet, even so, "he was not loved. Indeed, few leaders have been so enthusiastically disliked by so many of the people who showered them with votes." This was the standard way to speak of King – his success and importance alongside his lack of personal appeal. It was Hutchison redux.

But then *Close-Up* took its cameras to the streets of Ottawa, and the statesman came off his pedestal in an entirely new fashion. "Who was Mackenzie King?" the reporter asks a young woman walking down the street. She pauses before saying she thinks he was an explorer. "We talked about him in social studies," she says. This less than a decade after King's death, and not twelve years since his retirement. The journalist goes to several more young women and an older woman. None have any idea who Mackenzie King was.

Eventually *Close-Up* finds many people who remember King and their opinions vary from the man who thinks he was "an outstanding statesman" to a woman who simply says, "Don't ask me, I'm a Conservative." An old man complains that King wanted "conscription without conscription," that he was afraid of Quebec. "A Frenchman should fight for his country just like any Canadian," he says. A taxi driver says he liked King and voted for him, though he couldn't recall anything that King had done for the country. Someone else says that at least King was "better than Diefenbaker," while a group of young kids eager to be on camera ask if King was someone from TV.

This took King entirely out of the realm of pro- and con- debate and plunked him into the democratic levelling of street opinion where the question wasn't about whether you agreed or disagreed with King's politics; rather, it was about whether he mattered at all. Leiterman later defended the decision to begin this way. He wrote that he had descended on a busy street corner in Ottawa to get the average Canadian's opinion. Leiterman "noticed some puzzled expressions as I mentioned Mackenzie King but the truth didn't dawn on me until [the cameraman] dropped his earphones and exclaimed, 'You know, I think half of these people don't know who King was!'"[12]

Close-Up offered viewers a "personal portrait" of King. This choice shaped the show in particular ways. The producers told of King's earlier years in a conventional enough fashion, though with an emphasis on King's personality, on him as a private man, much as the journalists focused on this new information in Dawson's biography. They paid particular attention to his failed romance with Mathilde Grossert. They also interviewed Princess Cantacuzene, a lady who had known King during his time at Harvard and after. She was the granddaughter of Civil War general and American president Ulysses S. Grant. She speaks on camera of King as a "gay" young man, though one who was, in the super-wealthy social circles he frequented at Harvard, considered from a "poor" background. She was amazed that he had not tasted champagne until his arrival at Harvard. When the journalist asks her if King had any love interest, she coyly answers that he had loved someone once, and again later in life. That's all she says. It's unclear if the journalists know that she is probably referring to her own short romantic dalliance with King and how it resumed in subsequent years, though again only briefly and not completely.

The camera moves on and we are faced again and again with prominent Canadian politicians and journalists who knew King and now reflected on what kind of man he had been. The personalities don't just include those the literary executors would have asked. Certainly, we get Bruce Hutchison and King's cabinet colleague C.D. Howe as well as Lester Pearson and John Diefenbaker. But we also get Eugene Forsey and the journalist John Stevenson, who disliked King intensely and speaks here about King as someone you couldn't take to the club with other men, someone who was better with women. The show gives the Liberal view of King as nation builder, but the emphasis on the private King serves mostly to bring King down. As the Liberal Bruce Hutchison had been obliged to admit earlier, King the man was an unimpressive and often an unpleasant figure.

The second episode created the most controversy because it was there that *Close-Up* played the reels of its visits to two of King's spiritualist mediums in Britain. We meet on camera both Geraldine Cummins and the Scottish medium Helen Hughes. Even though *Close-Up* gives voice to King's friends who claim that his interest in spiritualism was just a hobby, like Franklin Roosevelt's stamp collecting, viewers meet the spiritualists face-to-face and can judge for themselves how serious or ludicrous were the practices King participated in.

As much as the conservative, deferential culture of 1950s Canada was showing signs of fracture by the end of the decade, there were still many who found a show like *Close-Up*'s feature on King to be an abomination. One could expect certain Liberals to be upset and they were. Brooke Claxton, who had been too ill to be interviewed for the program, wrote to C.D. Howe of how he thought Howe's performance as well as those of Bruce Hutchison, former Liberal minister Jimmie Sinclair, and Jack Pickersgill had been the documentary's "saving grace." Otherwise, he considered it an exercise in "character assassination." Howe agreed, writing how he felt it was "a great pity that sensible people will allow comparatively minor episodes, with which they do not agree, to divert their mind from the great qualities of Mackenzie King." Chubby Power reverted to what had been the reliable logic of "no one could fool the people for so long." When the political scientist Paul Fox had told him that the program was "badly out of balance, [with] too much on his spiritualism and almost nothing on his policies, aims, accomplishments, and failures in the political realm at large," Power agreed. He reported that all of those he talked to had said the same thing. "Mr. King was Prime Minister of this country for over twenty-one years," Power wrote, "and he must have to his credit certain accomplishments, both in policy and administration, and to stress, as was done in these broadcasts, the private eccentricities of the man, was not fair either to Mr. King or to the television audience."[13]

The establishment magazine *Saturday Night* felt aggrieved enough by *Close-Up*'s portrayal of Mackenzie King to publish an article by Edwin Copps entitled "A Distorted Image of Mackenzie King" in its next issue. Copps reported that even Conservatives had been upset by the program. "Being politicians and aspiring statesmen," Copps wrote, "they were shocked that an erstwhile colleague, a man who accomplished more in our public life than most of them can ever hope to achieve, should be posthumously ridiculed by an agency of the Canadian Government for no other purpose than to provide suitably light entertainment." *Close-Up* had attacked one of the fraternity. It just wasn't done.[14]

There was a real sense in Copps's article that those who didn't truly understand the respectable world of politics were pushing in where they didn't belong. Politics wasn't about entertainment, it was about statesmanship. The idea of a program on King was a good one, he thought. At least it was better than the way the CBC's money was usually "wasted on stuff that promotes only national moronism: canned U.S. cowboy shows, 'celebrity' parlor games, and outdated Victorian dramas staged for no other apparent reason than to provide employment for immigrant British actors." Copps simply couldn't give credence to what he saw as the show's depiction of King as a "crackpot [and] an evil genius who somehow managed to trick the Canadian voters into installing him in the country's highest elective office for nearly a quarter of a century."[15]

Saturday Night gave Leiterman space to defend himself and the program. He claimed that the documentary had been balanced and that, if its emphasis on King's spiritualism had been out of proportion, this was merely because no one had yet interviewed Cummins and Hughes. As a "personal portrait" the show was bound to pay less attention to King's statesmanship, and given that King's successes had come in his public life and his personal life had been less than impressive, he inevitably would not come across as well as some might hope.[16]

Letters to the magazine rebutted past Leiterman's defence. One man, a rear-admiral in the US Navy, thought the program had been the "nadir of bad taste" and that it would have been "better left undone and ... soon forgotten." Another man, from London, England, defended King, saying that anyone "who could be the leader of any national party for a lifetime, Prime Minister for most of it, *and* Prime Minister moreover, during Canada's greatest and proudest years, is entitled to respect." A reader in Vancouver claimed to "have never known of such an attack on a national leader." He suspected that the initiative might have come from within the Diefenbaker government but felt "it will not help those in power at Ottawa. It was too small stuff."[17]

Similarly, a writer in the *Canadian Annual Review* thought that *Close-Up* was an important show which, unfortunately, was "alternatively brilliantly triumphant and sadly disappointing." Its biography of Mackenzie King was "probably the biggest disappointment of the year." The problem was that the show failed "almost entirely to come to grips, or even attempt to come to grips, with the strong core of an obviously quite extraordinary man who had been prime minister for 21 years," concentrating instead "on the more bizarre elements of his personal idiosyncracies."[18]

Clearly, there were still those who subscribed to the view that a prime minister deserved respect and a certain amount of deference simply by virtue of his position: *Close-Up* had hit a nerve. Yet, over the course of the 1960s, the defenders of the status quo found themselves under siege. When Patrick Watson and Douglas Leiterman went from *Close-Up* to the controversial show *This Hour Has Seven Days*, they created a special place in which to put prominent figures who appeared on the show. They called it the "hot seat." An uncomfortable chair in the middle of the room, without the protection of armrests, bright under the glare of the lights and in full view of several cameras that could zoom in to catch the slightest twitch of discomfort, the "hot seat" was a metaphor for the changed attitude toward authority in the 1960s. By the end of the decade, the way Canadians talked about politics had become radically less deferential and more irreverent. There were quite a few people under close-up scrutiny in the hot seat.

Ravenous for the Remaining Courses

With the publication in 1960 of *The Mackenzie King Record*, the literary executors pretended that the culture of deference in politics was not unravelling. They were mistaken.

Jack Pickersgill was at loose ends when the Liberals lost power in 1957. He had retained his seat in Parliament but this man who had been at the heart of Canadian government for his entire career found that his "duties as a Member of Parliament in Opposition did not occupy [his] full time and that [he] must find some means of supplementing [his] income."[1] With the death of Dawson, King's official biographer, Pickersgill stepped in to write part of the official biography for the years after 1939. Jack Pickersgill, the historian turned civil servant turned politician, became historian and writer again. This time, though, he would write about the prime minister he had served during one of the most pivotal moments in Canadian history, the Second World War.

It's not clear if he ever seriously thought of writing a proper biography. Another idea soon came to him. Pickersgill had access to the entirety of King's diary, and as he sat down to sift through what that huge document could tell him about King's life, he began to mull over the possibility of writing a biography that used King's own words – the material right in King's extensive diary. Perhaps all that was needed was a bit of cut and paste to tell the whole of King's story. As King had always said, the full story was in the diary. For the war years, when King dictated the diary and Handy typed it up daily, this was certainly true. If Pickersgill simply took out the important bits and pieced them together, he could be done with the whole job. At the same time, the controversy created by the mention of the diary's destruction on the dust jacket of the Dawson volume could perhaps be allayed by a halfway measure. If the extracts in that biography weren't enough, perhaps a much larger expurgated version of the diary would satisfy the critics who thought that the executors were hiding something.

On this Pickersgill was wrong, but that would only become clear over time. He set to work cutting and pasting portions of King's diary into the shape of history. By 1960, he had compiled a large manuscript covering the years from 1939 until just before the D-Day landings of June 1944. With the project's funders at *Weekend* magazine clamouring for some results, they decided to publish this as a first volume of what they called the *Mackenzie King Record* and to pre-publish extracts in *Weekend* beginning in October 1960. The University of Toronto Press still sought to go after those who wanted official publications on the statesman as monuments for their bookshelves. One could buy the regular hardback version of the *Record* or, for the extravagant price of $50, the Press offered the "De Luxe Gift Edition ... Hand Bound in Red Morocco Leather, with 14-Karat Gold Stamping."[2]

Some appreciated the unprecedented behind-the-scenes account of the war from Canada's highest figure. The reviewer in *Saturday Night* recognized that Pickersgill, as a Liberal, "may have found it congenial to leave in especially those portions reflecting credit upon his leader and party." Still, the journalist couldn't resist what he thought of as the "red-hot privacies of King's story of the war." Even though Pickersgill's *Mackenzie King Record* was incomplete, it still represented something fresh and new in Canadian political history. "It is misleading," he wrote "to call it a history book if that conveys the dullness and pedestrianism so often attached to that term in Canada's records. It is rather a 'who-dunit,' a bit of a scandal-sheet, a war mystery, a romance of great accomplishments in the high places of a world war, a juicy exposé of what went on behind the baize doors of cabinet, caucus and conference." Then he turned to the metaphor that many were using in these years to imagine the healthy exposing of secrets. Reading the *Mackenzie King Record*, he said, "gives the reader the eerie feeling that he has been sitting at the couchside while one of the strangest and greatest Canadians has 'told all' to his psychiatrist."[3]

No book like this could escape controversy. The executors had mischievously sent a copy to John Diefenbaker and he responded by giving them what they wanted – publicity. Diefenbaker claimed that the book could win an award for fiction, aiming his barbs more at Pickersgill than King. Pickersgill privately thought that Diefenbaker's criticism was "splendid advertisement" but publicly responded by professing his "surprise" at the prime minister's assessment. He said that there were only a few "references in the book to Mr. Diefenbaker because in those days he didn't count for much."[4] Petty partisan bickering was only to be expected, though even more jaded Liberals privately admitted that Diefenbaker had a point. Chubby Power sent to Pickersgill the comments of a friend, whom he did not name, saying, "I am sure you will agree with this criticism."[5] The anonymous letter (likely written by T.A. Crerar) claimed that "the diary itself is an incredible document, which will no doubt rank in time with such works as the confessions of Rousseau (or even St. Augustine) – but not those of Don Juan." Yet it was King's earnest belief in his own good intentions, even when he acted out of self-interest, that the writer couldn't help mocking. "King's wonderful dexterity in interpreting everything the way he wanted to see it, purely as a literary *tour de force*, is most impressive ... the diary reads like a grand allegorical fairy tale, full of wicked witches on one side, and King and Providence (who is apparently a Liberal) on the other."[6]

In the *Canadian Annual Review*, Ramsay Cook noted that the *Mackenzie King Record* "was obviously an extremely important book" but he did point out that "only those who have seen the entire diary (and these are few) can possibly judge whether Mr. Pickersgill has made a fair selection." To the idea that this book might sate readers' appetites, Cook's assessment was dismissive. "Like any savoury appetizer," he wrote, 'it makes one ravenous for the remaining courses.'"[7]

Revolutions always depend as much on those at the top wanting change as on those at the bottom demanding something different. So it was for the culture of deference and secrecy in Canadian politics in general and for Mackenzie King's literary executors in particular.

12.1 H. Blair Neatby

When the literary executors hired Blair Neatby to take over as official biographer, they made a safe choice. He was a Liberal with a solid intellectual pedigree. His aunt, Hilda Neatby, was a distinguished historian as well as one of the better-known public intellectuals of the 1950s, having served on the Massey Commission and then written a famous book about the state of education in contemporary Canada. When her nephew Blair completed his PhD dissertation on the Wilfrid Laurier era in Canada, a few prominent Canadian politicians asked to read it.[8] They approved. Word reached the ears of the literary executors, and eventually Neatby found himself being invited to assist MacGregor Dawson on the King biography. With Dawson's death in the summer of 1958, Neatby replaced him as official biographer, covering the years up to 1939 at which point Pickersgill took over with his *Mackenzie King Record*.

Neatby was a junior selection – almost certain not to have the kind of health problems faced by Dawson and probably, the executors must have thought, biddable. At the very least, he could be counted on to be, as had been Dawson, sympathetic to his subject. Neatby would later marry Jacqueline Côté, an archivist who had been organizing Mackenzie King's papers since before the former prime minister's death.

For all of Neatby's reliability, however, he also subtly represented change. Neatby brought new ideas about the writing of history with him – ideas that were more psychological, and more attuned to the new kinds of subjects that historians were beginning to take seriously, those that involved the private areas of life outside of politics. After the 1960s, historians in Canada and elsewhere would shatter old ideas of the discipline of history. If at mid-century it had been the preserve of those who wrote the economic and political history of great men, it soon came to be a great deal more. Historians took up the history of the working class, of women and immigrants, of Native people, and of those who lived all along the margins of Canadian society, sometimes understood as the social margins, but sometimes, too, the different regions away from Ottawa, Montreal, and Toronto.[9] These later historians would sometimes look back and scoff at the backward times when Canadian history seemed to consist of the biographies of great men.

Yet in some respects the biographers of the 1950s and 1960s actually set the stage for the changed ideas of what Canadian history could become. For as they delved into the lives of their subjects, the biographers of these years met people who were more than just politicians. They found themselves face to face with complex emotional, social, and psychological figures. If some biographers were content to stick to the public life, there were others who also pushed into the realms of personality and private life, if only in part. Neatby, in a small way, was one of these.

He would go on to write two volumes of King's official biography. The first, taking King's life from 1923 up to 1932, was published in 1964. The final volume, covering King's life from 1933 until 1939, wouldn't come out until 1976 – a very different world into which to publish on Mackenzie King.[10] Each of Neatby's volumes would follow in the style of Dawson and earlier biographers in that they mostly recounted the actions of Mackenzie King as prime minister. They devoted a good deal of space to speeches in Parliament and the extensive behind-the-scenes jockeying that went into the formation of cabinets. Neatby used King's diary to find out what had happened in discussions between King and his cabinet colleagues and at key moments in King's political life. Yet, at several key moments in his books, Neatby also sought to make a psychological assessment of King the man.

Each of the books contained detailed sections on what might in earlier days have perhaps been called King's character but which, by this point of the twentieth century, was instead thought of as King's personality. Neatby knew that King's personality shaped how he acted in public, that his psychological foibles could factor into the way he treated political colleagues for better or worse. It all depended on the diary. Even though Neatby was largely sympathetic to the Liberal version of Canadian history, he still wanted to tell the past as it really was. The diary helped enormously but also presented its own troubles. As useful as the diary was for documenting meetings that would not otherwise be the subject of written records (or at least not nearly in the detail provided by the diary), the diary also gave King's interpretation of events. And of King's own explanation for his actions, Neatby grew wary.

King didn't know himself. He was, as Neatby says several times throughout the biographies, "naïve." It is a striking assessment. What Neatby was doing was taking the kinds of judgments that Eugene Forsey made of King and putting them through the psychological factory of mid-century thought. Forsey pointed out again and again how King's actions didn't match his words. King professed to believe one thing (all good intentions) and then acted in an entirely different manner (that negated these intentions). For Forsey, this was hypocrisy, a character defect. Neatby essentially agreed with Forsey but found a different explanation. Where Forsey saw King through a moralistic language of character and hypocrisy, Neatby came to King via the language of personality and psychology.

In the diary, Neatby had a record of a man who had poured himself out on the page day after day for more than half a century. It was an unparalleled historical document, as the literary executors had been saying. But, unlike the executors, who struggled with their consciences and their need to distinguish between what King would have wanted preserved and what he would have destroyed, Neatby could simply see it as an entry point into King's personality. For this task, Neatby essentially treated King's diary as the written records of a psychotherapy session. Here was the transcript of a half-century-long quest for the "talking cure." Neatby didn't want simply to psycho-analyze King, certainly not using the techniques or jargon of a psychother-apist. Yet he approached King in much the same way – looking for repetitions and themes, silences and obsessions, the things King did and didn't say, what he spoke of again and again, and the places where King denied to himself the truth of what he was doing – a truth clearly observable to someone who was reading the entire doc-ument in its totality and years after the fact.

The King that emerged under Neatby's hand was a man who was utterly naive about his own intentions. Here was a man who was in self-denial. He professed to believe one thing, even to himself, even while it was patently obvious to someone reading his diary that he actually felt quite another way altogether. In his relations with Gov-ernor General Byng, for example, Neatby saw King at his worst and most typical. After waging a campaign against Byng's actions in the 1926 election, pushing Byng's decision not to grant him a dissolution into the spotlight, and then winning re-election, King nonetheless continued to act toward Byng in a way that suggested their friend-ship had not changed. He sent him birthday wishes in the midst of the election campaign, and right up until the time the Byngs left Canada, he continued to pretend that there could not be the slightest animosity between them. "Although Mackenzie King never admit-ted it," Neatby argued, "he derived some satisfaction from Lord Byng's embarrassing position." As Neatby says: "Without his realiz-ing it – he would have been affronted by the suggestion – King's for-mal good manners were not so much thoughtfulness for others as a proof of his own virtuousness."[11] King was keeping up appearances, pretending to be respectable when all the while his real motives were much more selfish. This is exactly the kind of psychological quirk that popular psychology was teaching North Americans to look for in themselves and others. Here Neatby played the role of historical psychotherapist even though he avoids the jargon: pointing out the unconsciously different and more base reasons behind public actions which seemed to be respectable.

King's critics had always seen him as a narrow pragmatist. He was constantly willing to compromise, to concede his supposed beliefs, in order to survive politically. The Conservatives and many old-school British Canadians thought that he sold out Canada's British traditions to appease his French-Catholic base in Quebec. The CCF and others on the left thought King sold out the civil rights and social welfare of the country to win the same base, as well as the support of corporate Canada. Yet the King that we find in Neatby is actually an idealist.

When Neatby goes looking for what King himself thought of his actions, what he finds is a man who never doubted his own good intentions. He could explain away any nefarious act of his own, any double-crossing or backtracking. Why could he do this? The answer was psychological – though with roots in that area of life that psychologists were conquering, the old certainties of Christian morality. Neatby claims that King could twist and turn and bend over backward because he never doubted his own innate goodness. As Neatby argued, "King's belief in his selfless devotion to his party and his country is an example of his fundamental naivety." This wasn't just an example of hypocrisy, as critics like Forsey put it. "He was not a hypocrite," Neatby argued, "because he deceived himself."[12]

It wasn't as if King hadn't tried to look inside himself. "Few men have made more prolonged efforts to understand themselves," Neatby wrote. "His diary was in part his conscience. In it he constantly criticized himself for wasting time with social frivolities, deplored his weakness in taking a glass of whisky, or regretted that a speech had been too hastily prepared. These criticisms were always coupled with resolutions to exert more will-power in the future and to devote himself more unsparingly to his work. But he saw in himself only minor shortcomings ... Even in his diary he never questions his motives."[13]

Neatby connected this to King's Christian faith. King could be this naive and self-deceiving because his religious faith was no different. "Like a child," Neatby wrote, "he never questioned the eternal validity of his Christian faith; like a child's, this faith was identified with a rigid moral code, immutable and uncompromising, with categorical rights and wrongs."[14] It's hard to imagine this being written in Canada in the official biography of any prime minister before the 1960s. But, by the early 1960s, it was becoming acceptable to see a certain kind of religiosity, certainly the confident assertive religiosity of the Victorian age in which King had been raised, as out of date. Even the churches themselves were in the midst of a series of modernization initiatives. By the end of the decade, the idea that secularization was a slow but unstoppable process seemed almost as certain as had earlier claims about the slow death of the "noble savage" Indians in North America.[15] This idea has not (at least not yet) turned out to be true, but it did mark a major change in the public culture of Canada that would grow more pronounced over the twentieth century.

On the question of what to do with King's diary, Neatby pushed not just to keep Pickersgill's extracts but to preserve and eventually open up the diary in its entirety. For Neatby, it would be a travesty if the executors destroyed the original diary. For several years after Dawson's death, Neatby had worked full-time on the biography. But in the summer of 1961, as he prepared to head back to full-time teaching, he wrote a final memorandum to the literary executors explaining why he felt they should not destroy the diary.

"Everything in the diaries is relevant to the political history of Canada," Neatby wrote. "[King's] comments on political problems are the central feature of the diaries but these are coloured by everything in his daily life – his health, his domestic problems, his personal antipathies. Even his dreams can be revealing." Admittedly, the diaries "reveal the foibles and eccentricities." But Neatby argued that these were "already common gossip." Moreover, "these are human qualities which give texture to the life of a man who was almost completely a political animal. His fears and his doubts only heighten his achievements."[16]

Neatby went on: "The diaries should also be preserved in their entirety, in my opinion, because I cannot see that there is any alternative. Any attempt to expurgate them after the publication of *The Mackenzie King Record* would be far more damaging than any revelations in the diaries themselves." Neatby pointed to the criticism in the *Canadian Annual Review* and claimed that the literary executors could expect only more of the same. "If any sections of the diary are destroyed," Neatby wrote, "people will imagine and believe the worst ... it would also be impossible to convince people that something too shameful to admit had not been suppressed." Ultimately, Neatby was saying, "Better out than in." Suppression and repression brought their own damage.

In Neatby's writing we see the way a certain kind of thinking about psychology and secularization seeped into the mainstream thought in early 1960s Canada. Neatby was no radical. He was a safe Liberal choice as official biographer. But, by virtue of his youth and the ideas he brought with him, he represented the changes that were already under way, that had been hinted at in Bruce Hutchison's book, and that were now what might be called the "new normal." The line between public and private could not be easily maintained. Feminists would make the same argument and to often quite radical ends later in the 1970s and 1980s. They would demand that issues previously hidden – violence against women on the streets and in marriages – be opened up and talked about. They would claim that the personal is political. The way they made the argument sounded radically new, yet the kind of logic they relied upon had already become part of the mainstream. And it is perfectly visible in what might have been considered the most staid place of all: the official biography of a dead prime minister.

13

Final Spasm of Hypocrisy

The world changes even when we do not. The truth of this ought to have become clear to Jack Pickersgill over the course of the 1960s. He and the academic political scientist Donald Forster published several more volumes of *The Mackenzie King Record*, one in 1968 and two more in 1970. If Pickersgill still believed implicitly in the doctrine of "no one could fool the people for so long," he nonetheless grew impatient with the fact that so many others publicly doubted the *Record*'s veracity.

⚅

Over the course of the 1960s, two interrelated cultural developments would increasingly transform how Canadians saw authority figures like Mackenzie King and the secrets they kept. First, the 1960s witnessed the rise of a broadly anti-authoritarian impulse across a host of spheres – from social movements calling for an end to the Vietnam War or criticizing the military-industrial complex to those demanding that the state respect the rights of a range of different Canadians; from student movements challenging the authority of university administrations to young radical workers setting themselves in opposition both to employers and to more tentative and conservative older workers. Those who operated within the system found themselves under attack. The counter-culture of the era urged withdrawal from systems of authority. To work within the system was only to be managed and co-opted. The range of anti-authoritarian movements was diverse and there were varying levels of criticism. Yet the broad shift was clear. In this context, prime ministers, even dead prime ministers, would come under more intense scrutiny.[1]

This anti-authoritarianism was inspired in part by a second major cultural shift in these years, the rise of an individualistic and emotivist version of truth. Increasingly, truth was personal. It originated not in any traditional source of authority or political and social institutions like families or churches or the state but in the individual self. The kinds of arguments that Hugh MacLennan and F.R. Scott had made at the end of the 1950s – about the intrinsic value of what was human, and the need to be open about it and not to censor it – spread more radically and fully into ever more areas of life.

As the Canadian philosopher Charles Taylor has reminded us, this individualistic ethos had been a key feature of Western culture for hundreds of years, with roots both in Christian culture and in the Enlightenment. Yet the years after the Second World War, and especially the 1960s, saw a radical speeding up of this individualistic ethos in which authenticity, being true to oneself, became the source of a powerful idea about what was both good and true.[2]

For Mackenzie King's secret life, this mattered in doubled fashion. On the one hand, the anti-authoritarian impulses of the era diminished the kind of deference that had been granted to prime ministers in the past. On top of this came the idea that ultimate truth had to be found within the self. The very parts of one's life that had been considered shameful – the secret desires or actions, the unrespectable urges and whims – these were now indications of who we really were. Not only was there no need to hide the previously shameful parts of our lives, those who did so could be criticized as concealing their true identity. If there was no need for shame, what were you hiding?

This individualistic anti-authoritarianism spanned the political spectrum. Increasingly, many on both left and right would come to frame their politics around individual truths and the need for individual choice. In this context, a figure like Mackenzie King became a useful symbol of the not-too-distant past by which Canadians of the 1960s could distinguish their age from preceding ones.

⚅

A cursory glance at the editorial pages the *Globe and Mail* newspaper in the mid-1960s shows the direction of change. Beginning in 1964, Richard Needham, then in his early fifties, began writing humorous columns that would never have appeared in that or any other mainstream paper in Canada only a few years earlier.[3] He was a conservative, albeit one who was hard to recognize because his writing showed so little respect for social convention or morality. Indeed, for much of the 1960s, he wrote columns castigating what many were coming to call "the Establishment." He dismissively called his own newspaper *The Mop & Pail* or *The Groan & Wail*, repeatedly engaging in made-up banter between his alter-ego Rudolph J. Needleberry or Rasputin J. Novgorod and the *Globe*'s editors. The young Margaret Wente and her friends used to gather with Needham in the old Lord Simcoe Hotel in Toronto to drink coffee and smoke. She recalls that he "did not believe in convention, and encouraged us to suspect the school system, the well-meaning advice of our parents and institutions of all kinds." We could now recognize Needham as an earlier kind of libertarian conservative, a kind of figure given little attention so far in accounts of how values changed in the 1960s in Canada.

Needham took on, again and again, what he saw as the puritanism of Canada's laws. He pointed out the hypocrisy of laws banning such things as lotteries, prostitution, and drugs. These laws were "designed to transform human beings into plaster saints" but he wondered if "the efforts to legislate men into virtue simply drive them into vice?" In Canada, he noted, "we do a lot of fining and otherwise punishing for what I'd call non-crimes – actions which are human and normal, actions which in other societies are tolerated, but which in our puritanical one are regarded with fear and horror." I always know I'm in Canada, Needham wrote, "when the word 'wine' produces a nervous snicker, a furtive look around."[4]

He gave space in his columns to readers who wrote to him, including the young man from Peterborough, Ontario, who pointed out the hypocrisy of drugstores that advertised pregnancy tests prominently in their front windows but weren't allowed to advertise birth control. On Valentine's day 1966, the *Globe* ran a Needham column on "Unspeakable Love" in Canada. Needham didn't mean some kind of out-of-the-ordinary sexual attraction – simply heterosexual sex. "If grand passions have helped shape our history," Needham wrote, "our historians have conspired to hide them; if Wild Raptures have inspired our statesmen, their biographers have connived to ignore them." It was as if he was anticipating C.P. Stacey by a decade. Certainly, he anticipated the phenomenon that would surround Pierre Trudeau when he ran for the Liberal Party leadership and then in the general election of 1968.[5]

The column quoted a Montreal psychiatrist on how "Canadians are still very much influenced by the ancient neurotic idea that sex itself is somehow base and dirty." In a country governed for more than a quarter of its history by bachelor prime ministers, what explained the lack of attention to their sex lives? Did they not have sex? Needham pointed out that some time ago a young playwright had tried to write a play about Mackenzie King's relations with a nurse. "Before it was produced and after the writer had withdrawn from the project," Needham wrote, "the role of the nurse was all but eliminated and the play was turned into a warm story of the future prime minister's family life, complete with a dialogue between King and his mother." The television critic Dennis Braithwaite, according to Needham, remembered it "as being absolutely without romance; let alone sex." "Isn't it all part of Canadian hypocrisy?" Needham asked.[6]

Mackenzie King stood in the role of old Victorian Canada. As the prime minister who had governed for so much of the first half of the twentieth century, as someone who was increasingly only dimly remembered, and not "remembered" at all by the young, King was a useful figure to pillory all that had come before. The worse punishment Needham could imagine was to sentence someone to reading the collected speeches of Mackenzie King. It was King, after all, who boasted that governments often did the most, not by doing anything at all, but by preventing something bad from happening. He was the prophylactic prime minister of the status quo.

In this, "Mackenzie King wasn't the greatest of our Prime Ministers, but he was probably the most typical." In 1967 Needham wrote that he had "spent the last 12 months travelling from one end of Canada to the other. I am happy to report that Mackenzie King is not only still alive, but is running just about everything in Canada save Expo 67 ... It is true he sometimes masquerades as Mackenzie Pearson or Mackenzie Douglas or Mackenzie Diefenbaker, but it's him just the same," Needham argued. "I have reached the conclusion that whenever a group of Canadians come together for any purpose, they choose Mackenzie King as their leader."[7]

If the defeat of St Laurent in 1957 had been the end of the political reign of Mackenzie King's Liberals (for a time at least), by the end of the 1960s, many wanted also to turn the page on the cultural values of King's era too. The need for both cultural and political revolution was obvious, and not just to the young revolutionaries. In speaking to the youth wing of the Progressive Conservative Party in 1966, Dalton Camp told them, "You represent the profound hope that we are now nearing the end of the Mackenzie King era of politics." A Canadian politics "still rooted in the age of Mackenzie King" had failed "to take account of the new society of Canadians under 40 who were not raised in a pioneer era and do not remember the depression." Looking at the federal scene, Camp saw signs of hope even if, at the moment, "we're having a final spasm of hypocrisy."[8]

Camp couldn't have been happy that the new era came to be associated with the new Liberal prime minister Pierre Trudeau, but surely Trudeau represented exactly the kind of symbolic cultural change that he had predicted and called for. In fact, the team of organizers around Trudeau, who orchestrated the throngs of young attractive women who chased the athletic young bachelor prime minister across Parliament Hill, seeking a smile and a kiss, did so knowing that they were feeding this more general cultural change. A bachelor prime minister at the end of the 1960s was not going to be like the bachelor prime ministers who had come before. Mike Pearson, Trudeau's predecessor, had been born in the Victorian era to a Methodist preacher. He had shed his teetotal ways only as he grew up and moved in more international circles. Trudeau, the sexually available, sports-car-driving bachelor, was the first prime minister born in the twentieth century, and the first one who was truly non-Victorian.[9]

The two remaining official biographers – Blair Neatby and Jack Pickersgill – responded to the growing irreverence in different ways. In 1968 Blair Neatby could be found taking a stand for the right of historians to examine private historical documents without interference or censorship. When the Quebec historian Fernand Ouellet found himself in legal trouble over his use of the papers of the French Canadian nationalist hero Louis-Joseph Papineau, Neatby stepped up to defend the principle that historians could and should delve into the personal lives of their subjects to make historical assessments. Historians – and not protective, worried descendants – should decide what counted as history.[10]

In Ouellet's case, he, too, attempted to borrow from the realm of psychology to write history, though in a more overt fashion than Neatby. By the late 1950s, Ouellet had written several articles about the Papineau family and in particular about Julie Papineau, the wife of the revolutionary *canadien* leader. Clearly influenced by Freudianism, Ouellet argued that she was mentally unbalanced and dominated her children in ways that caused lasting intergenerational damage. Whereas King had literary executors who were concerned with his reputation but not intimately connected to the man himself, the Papineau case was different. Surviving family members, no doubt feeling that Ouellet's analysis went too far and cast aspersions on their own lives, decided that enough was enough. When Ouellet turned his work into a book, *Julie Papineau, un cas de mélancolie et d'éducation janseniste*, Les Presses de l'Université Laval initially accepted the book and planned to publish it in 1961 – around the same time that Neatby was making his case to the literary executors for the preservation of the King diary. But the Papineaus threatened legal action. The press feared the consequences and refused to publish the book. Historians in Quebec did not come out to speak on Ouellet's behalf. It may be that they didn't sympathize with Ouellet, whose views on Quebec and its history they disagreed with (he was an outspoken federalist and critic of Quebec nationalism). Regardless, Ouellet found himself with few friends.

This is where Blair Neatby intervened. In 1968 Neatby wrote to other historians arguing that all "historians will be concerned because of the nature of the charges." The Papineaus claimed, despite the contrary witness testimony of the former provincial archivist, that the papers had been deposited to the archives under strict conditions and that the family still retained control. They also claimed to enjoy copyright for the documents, an interpretation of that law which would mean, Neatby pointed out, that "most historians have committed a breach of the copyright law."[11]

Neatby especially challenged the Papineaus' assertion that "intimate details of the health and character of Julie Papineau ... had nothing to do with history." These details could only "damage the reputation of the great grandchildren" and they therefore denied Ouellet the right to mention them publicly. Neatby saw the issue in stark terms. "They do not deny the facts," he claimed, "but they deny the historian's right to refer to these facts and his right to draw conclusions from them." If this were allowed to stand, "Canadian historical writing will be emasculated." Neatby called on other Canadian historians to help in Ouellet's legal defence. As he put it: "M. Ouellet is not only defending his own rights but is also defending the interests of all Canadian historians."[12] The Canadian Historical Association responded positively to this appeal.

At the same time, Neatby's King-biographer colleague, Jack Pickersgill, kept repeating with each volume of *The Mackenzie King Record* that he was not interested in King's personal life and so did not write about it. Pickersgill also insisted that his version of the King diary included all the relevant material related to King's politics. He arranged for the publication of a small volume on the conscription crisis of the Second World War that had been written by MacGregor Dawson before his death. This was to have been part of the official biography, but now that Pickersgill was covering the war years with the excerpted diary as biographical formula, there was no space for Dawson's work. "I insisted on having this published," he wrote to the historian Arthur Lower, "because I shall be traversing a similar field when my own second volume appears and I felt it was important to have Dawson's account [so as] ... to remove any lingering suspicion ... that I was not seeking to produce an objective and faithful record."[13]

A feeble hope. Some reporters still accepted the idea that, in selecting diary excerpts for the *Record*, Pickersgill thought simply of shortening the material. But by the time of the 1968 volume, Pickersgill also faced more strenuous criticism. Tim Reid in the *Globe and Mail* admitted that the *Record* made for "absorbing" reading but it certainly was not "complete." Reid looked to new subjects that Pickersgill glossed over, new areas of social life where King had played an important role but which hadn't, until recently, been considered serious matters of political concern for many, such as King's part in the suppression of civil rights. In the late 1960s, civil rights had become a powerful issue in Canada – both because of the African-American struggle for equality and because many Canadian groups were taking up the same issue here. Looking back to the King government's treatment of Japanese Canadians during and after the Second World War, Reid saw a policy that was every bit as racist as the American one – notwithstanding the tendency of many Canadians to see themselves as superior to those south of the border. Reid wondered why the Canadian experience in this regard didn't show up in any significant way in the *Record*. "To call the book *The Record*," he wrote, "is weird and wonderful (and flagrantly partisan) reasoning."[14]

When the former official military historian C.P. Stacey wrote a letter to the editor defending Pickersgill and the *Record*, Reid questioned the willingness of so many academic historians to accept official histories and the diaries of great men. Stacey had claimed that the reason civil rights hadn't bulked large in the *Record* is simply because they hadn't mattered a great deal in that era. Reid wondered about the version of the truth offered in the expurgated version of King's diary, especially when there was no other way of "cross-checking its accuracy or of testing its validity." Even the historian Ramsay Cook had raised many of the same concerns, noting that historians ought to have "serious questions about the principles of selection. Why are passages left out? And what else has been left out?" Reid pushed the matter one step further, asking, "What is the history of King's diaries between the time he dictated them in 1944 and 1945 and the date they finally came to rest in the National Archives?"

Essentially, Reid wondered whether you could trust the literary executors, the professionals at the heart of the Liberal government party. Pickersgill could dismiss the whole matter as simply that "silly review by Tim Reid," but the issue pricked him because it reflected a growing tendency to question the expertise of the great and the good in Ottawa. That tendency was evident even in the academic establishment, which had long been solidly behind the Liberal interpretation of history.[15]

14

To Open or Not to Open

Although the literary executors had passed ownership of King's papers to the Public Archives of Canada in 1964, they nonetheless maintained control over access to certain papers until 1975 (twenty-five years after King's death). It was only in the mid-1970s that all control over King's papers would pass to the archives. Further, in setting up the regulations for the 1964 handover, the executors decided to keep back both the diary and the special spiritualism notebooks. They retained complete control over what would happen with them. Also, anyone who wanted to consult other King documents, including those items less than twenty-five years old, or the family papers, needed to write to the literary executors and request special permission.

Yet, as Mackenzie King and the King era faded into history, historians, political scientists, and others increasingly wanted to write on the topic. They had heard about King's voluminous papers and about his extensive diary. As more volumes of Pickersgill's *Mackenzie King Record* came out in the 1960s, academics wanted to see first-hand the valuable material in the diary. They heard through word of mouth that some scholars did have access to the original diary and they wrote to the literary executors asking for the same treatment. It was largely Pickersgill who was the contact man. It didn't help that the literary executors made arbitrary decisions about who could and could not receive special access, all the while pretending that they were being fair, open, and equal to all. When the executors denied access to one young academic who had studied under the military historian C.P. Stacey, the student wrote back with polite indignation: "It is public knowledge that access has been granted to historians not working on the official biography or the Record." The executors could claim that Stacey had been granted access in his capacity as official military historian. But they stretched this boundary on several occasions, essentially opening up the diaries to those scholars whom they deemed to be safely Liberal and denying access to those they could not be sure about – such as the young academic writing on the history of Canadian-Soviet relations or a young Peter Ward who was researching the King government's actions toward Japanese Canadians during the Second World War.[1]

The research assistants who had worked on the official biography became impatient too. They had been allowed to take notes on the King papers as part of their work, and an implicit part of the agreement was that they could use this material for their own work – but not until after the official biography was published. Yet the death of one biographer after seven years on the job and the long delays in publishing the other volumes meant that these men's careers were zooming past and they could not publish important research. James Eayrs, who had been hired as an external-relations expert, and who was the most demanding of the assistants, simply published the material anyway.[2]

Eayrs's own work in the 1950s and 1960s helped to expose the behind-the-scenes functioning of Canada's international diplomacy. When the historian Kenneth McNaught reviewed Eayrs's volume on Canada's entry into the Second World War (published in 1966), he noted that "what's new in the Eayrs account comes largely from the King papers." What it revealed was not complimentary to those at the top. The story Eayrs told, with access to these documents, "is one of timidity, wishful thinking and downright misconceptions." There were important lessons for "the present generation. No one today doubts that a democracy obtains something less than the whole truth about the principles on which its foreign policy is conducted. It's worth learning just how little the ordinary citizen knows about confusion at the top."[3]

By the early 1970s, the pressure was mounting to make a final decision about the last of King's papers. The passage of time helped. More and more of those mentioned in the diary were now dead. The events the diary recounted were becoming history. Although in the early 1970s the Canadian government was still holding to the "thirty-year rule" in deciding which government documents to release, that rule was increasingly anachronistic. Both the British and American governments had already released key government documents dealing with the war years. So the excuse that King's papers contained state secrets that might impinge upon the secrecy of other countries was itself a less tenable position, and a less real concern. The reasons for secrecy were diminishing.

Although nothing changed immediately, Norman Robertson's death in 1968 was a decisive moment in deciding the fate of King's papers. Robertson had been the strongest voice among the literary executors favouring destruction. While an archivist like W. Kaye Lamb would implicitly have valued Neatby's arguments about openness,[4] and while Fred McGregor had long seen the significance of the diary, their arguments had always come up against Robertson's sense of duty. It might be that the legal advice from the Department of Justice had opened the way to using King's diary for the official biography, but the executors still needed to keep King's obvious wishes for privacy in mind. With Robertson's death, these arguments lost their most compelling advocate. The other executors would continuously invoke Robertson's views, feeling a duty to him as much as to King, but Robertson himself would not be there to make his case.

As early as 1970, Pickersgill wrote to a scholar hinting that there might be a change in the literary executors' position on the diary. He couldn't promise anything, but some more open policy could be in the offing. The fateful meeting occurred on Christmas Eve, 1971. It was the one time when all of the literary executors could be in Ottawa at the same time. Lamb was flying in from British Columbia where he was living in retirement. He wrote to Pickersgill, saying, "My feelings about the chief matter we must discuss have firmed up, just as yours have done. Let us hope that they will more or less coincide!" There is no direct record of what happened that night but it seems that their views did coincide. A few days later, Lamb and Pickersgill wrote to confirm the details. The diary would be opened in full.[5]

In the first instance, the literary executors had decided to allow access to Mackenzie King's diary until the end of 1931. Use of the diary would be unrestricted for those engaged in historical or other research. This covered the diary up to the end of the period dealt with in Neatby's most recently published volume. Once Neatby finished his part of the official biography (taking King's life to 1939), the executors would open access to the rest of the diary at that point, following the thirty-year rule. That is, researchers would be able to view volumes of the diary thirty years after King had penned them. So everything up to the 1945 diary would be opened up on 1 January 1976, and so on. In anticipation of possible criticism that they were neglecting their duty toward King, to those who might recall that King's will had seemed clear that the diary was to be destroyed, Pickersgill explained: "In making this presentation, the Literary Executors have taken careful account of the terms of Mackenzie King's Will, but have reached the conclusion that, they are acting in a manner which will best serve Mackenzie King's memory and the cause of historical truth."[6]

This was true but incomplete. In fact, they also decided to open up the diary in part out of fear of what would happen if they did not. The man who created this fear was Jean-Louis Daviault – the man who had photographed the diary years earlier and who still claimed to have bootleg copies. Daviault was still very much on the minds of the literary executors.[7] As late as 1968, Lamb received a phone call from a Canadian Press journalist telling him that "his friend" had again offered to sell copies of the Mackenzie King diary to some journalists.[8] In writing to his fellow literary executor about the decision of whether to open up to the public or destroy the original diary, Lamb reasoned: "The existence of the bootleg microfilm copy is a further complication; I don't see how we can destroy the original and thereby give the copy an immensely greater value."[9] So the little-known stolen-diary incident from the mid-1950s now played its own role in swaying the executors to openness.

This didn't mean that they had neglected their duty to King in total, or that they had forgotten Norman Robertson's concerns. They decided that the series of spiritualism binders containing King's hand-written notes of his meetings with spiritualist mediums would be destroyed – though they wouldn't destroy them until after Neatby had finished his volume. Lamb urged Pickersgill to be firm with Wilfrid Smith of the archives on the binders. They "have never been considered to be part of either the Mackenzie King Papers or the personal diaries ... We gave Norman Robertson a definite promise that they would be destroyed, at the latest when the third volume of the biography is completed. Meanwhile they should be sealed, and no one should have access to them."[10]

When Neatby had published his first volume back in 1963, Lamb had written to him requesting one change – the only change the literary executors ever directly asked that he make to the biography. Neatby had referenced the spiritualism binders in a footnote. Lamb asked that the reference be deleted. "My three fellow Literary Executors are firm in their resolve that these notes are to be destroyed," he had written in 1963.[11] Almost a decade later, they held to this resolve. They had promised Norman Robertson to destroy at least these parts of the King diary, and they would keep their promise – even when everything else was to go onto the free market of historical inquiry.

Once they made their decision, they moved quickly to implement it. Early in the new year, the archives sent out a press release, which repeated a statement made in Pickersgill's letter to Smith about the literary executors being motivated by a desire to keep King's wishes in mind and by a determination to act "in a manner which will best serve Mackenzie King's memory and the cause of historical truth."[12]

In the winter of 1971, one of the coldest and snowiest on record, it became open season on Mackenzie King's past, at least until 1931. The University of Toronto Press quickly pressed the literary executors to be even more open and to publish a copy of the diary on microfiche. Lamb had some doubts about the wisdom of this move. "Making it available anywhere to anybody does go a little beyond my intention," he wrote, "but I suppose the Archives would wish to microfilm it anyway, to save wear and tear on the original, and the end result would be much the same."[13]

The requests kept trickling in for access to the diary after 1931 and Pickersgill stuck to the same arbitrary policy of who could and could not see it. But, on the whole, the literary executors were content with their decision. They stipulated the final conditions on King's other papers, setting dates into the next century for access to King's financial and spiritualism papers. There had been no major media controversy about their decision – no dramatic series of stories on King's secret life. The deadline for the final transfer of King's papers had always been 1 January 1975 and late in 1974, as this deadline approached, Pickersgill felt that there had been no adverse repercussions to the earlier release of the diary and he was inclined to be generous. He wrote to Wilfrid Smith of the archives (who was now a literary executor himself, having replaced Fred McGregor after the latter's death in 1972), saying that he personally would be agreeable to opening up King's diary to researchers after 1931 on a thirty-year basis starting in the new year. The other literary executors agreed. Neatby still had not published his final volume but he did not want to stand in the way of opening up access to the papers to other researchers.[14] With this decision made, the archives set in motion the usual press release making the announcement. It was the second time they had opened up a large trove of King's diaries. The floodgates had already opened, and to little effect. What could go wrong?

Part Five

The People Unfooled

15

Weird Willie

The release of King's diary in 1975 unleashed a torrent of news stories and speculation. From the start, journalists dove into the diaries to find stories of "Weird Willie" Mackenzie King. The *Globe*'s Geoffrey Stevens tried to keep a dignified tone, explaining the broad story of how the archives preserved prime ministers' papers, and the general approach taken by literary executors like those of King. But even Stevens had to admit that it was "something of a special day for everyone who likes to rummage around in other people's attics."[1]

The same would follow each January with the release of another new volume of King's diary, lasting until 1981 when the final 1950 volume was released following the thirty-year rule. Almost all of the stories would focus on the weird and the wonderful about Mackenzie King, about what Canadians hadn't known, about what he had hidden or kept secret.[2]

As *Time* magazine put it, "King's keen interest in spiritualism has long been one of the more celebrated sidelights of Canadian history" but never had it been "revealed in the intimate detail" as it was with the latest batch of diaries. Here, in King's own words, were accounts of exactly whom he thought he was speaking to in the spirit world. The *Time* story opened with one seance in which King spoke to his dead mother. He asked her if he would sleep well that night but she gave much more in reply, glowingly talking of how God had a plan for him. So many important people came to talk, how could King not believe her? There were visits from King George V, Wilfrid Laurier (to thank King for all he had done), Robert Borden (to apologize for wrongly suggesting that King had flirted with joining the Union government in the First World War), and so many more. Here was King talking about the mysticism of the number "7" and the "completeness" of the number "10."[3]

It wasn't only the spirits. A *Toronto Star* reporter wrote that, although the diary did not contain any major revelations about political events (although how the journalist could know this about the thousands of pages of diary in a story published on 2 January is unclear), "they disclose much about King's curious private life."[4] And this is where most journalists lingered – wondering at the odd and often petty behaviour behind the scenes of great and grand events. When the king and queen visited Canada in 1939, the diary showed Mackenzie King pedantically battling with the governor general about who would greet "His Majesties" first, with King invoking the legacy of his grandfather, constitutional precedent, and much else besides to make the case that it should be himself, the representative of the Canadian people. In the midst of the Second World War, King devoted considerable amounts of time and energy caring for his sick terrier, Pat. The stories were private and intimate, petty and small, showing King to be a man with all of the most base and egotistical of human emotions. It was the juxtaposition of these actions and feelings with King's dignified position – the mix of high and low, of the grand and the niggling – that took up most of the space in the news articles. Here was Mackenzie King, the prime minister of Canada, in all his great, narrow, and significant smallness.

The literary executors were taken aback by the media furor. Early in January 1975, Pickersgill wrote to Lamb to remind him that they still needed to destroy the special spiritualism notebooks. Pickersgill claimed to be "a little surprised at the amount of interest that is being taken in the spooky parts of the diary." He was most concerned about any criticism that the executors might not have followed King's wishes or broken their legal obligations. Lamb agreed, though he remained hopeful. "In spite of all the fuss and some fury about spiritualism and whatnot," he wrote, "I think we did the right thing." Perhaps they believed it when Pickersgill wrote, "I suspect it will not last very long – at least in a sensational way."[5]

§

Charles Perry Stacey had a lot in common with Mackenzie King. Although he was thirty years King's junior, they both grew up amidst the Anglo-Protestant middle class of Ontario. It was a world that re-

15.1 C.P. Stacey

mained culturally Victorian in its respectable guises well into the middle years of the twentieth century. Stacey took his religion a good deal less earnestly than King but he, too, knew the world where one bore pain and misfortune quietly and privately, and where cleanliness was next to godliness. Stacey's niece, also a Canadian historian, recalled her uncle's "restraint, decorum, and gentlemanly ways" as well as his "civility and circumspection" – though, unlike King, Stacey had a witty sense of humour that he didn't keep to himself. Stacey didn't marry until middle age and when he did so it was a "measured step" and, "in fact, he consulted his older sister about the suitable candidates." He did not have children and remained a dutiful son, the apple of his mother's eye and someone who cared for her until the end. There was plenty here to allow Stacey to identify with the bachelor, mother-loving Mackenzie King. But there were differences too.[6]

C.P. Stacey didn't especially like Mackenzie King. Few military men did. And, although Stacey was a historian, he was a soldier to the core. He joined the Canadian Corps of Signals as an eighteen-year-old and served in the Reserves all through his university training and early career, first at the University of Toronto, then Oxford, and finally in his PhD studies at Princeton. He joined the history department at Princeton and didn't leave there until 1940 when he travelled to London to take up a job in the Canadian Army historical headquarters. In 1945 he would become the chief Army historian and his major publications would tell the history of Canada's Army during the Second World War. It was as an Army historian that he met Mackenzie King, and although he remained respectful during his life, it's clear he didn't particularly like what he saw. Part of this was the resentment of many Army men at King's policies, his reluctance to embrace conscription and thus support the troops. This feeling only strengthened later when Stacey realized just what a limited role King accepted in steering Canada's role in the Allied military campaign.

Stacey could tell that King was no military man. In his later years he often dined out on one particular King story. In the summer of 1946, Stacey, as the official military historian, escorted the prime minister on a tour of the Normandy battle sites. The two Canadians journeyed by train from site to site with the aging King clearly tired and not especially interested. At most stops, King wouldn't even bother to get out of the car. One day, as the train pulled to a stop and just as King was about to hunker down into his suit and wait this one out too, he caught sight of a group of journalists. With a youthful spring in his step, out King marched to do his duty, suddenly understanding the spirit of national significance that this trip and this particular battlefield represented.[7] The story always got a laugh.

As Canada's official Army historian, Stacey was given preferential access to King's papers, including access to portions of King's diary. He was one of those – like the biographers of King George V and C.D. Howe – whose work the literary executors labelled as being either part of, or an extension of, the official King biography. It was a roundabout way of saying that they trusted this quasi-official historian to follow the rules, not to let anything slip, or to quote from King's papers without permission. Stacey may have dipped into the diary for official purposes, but over the years he let his gaze wander. He went looking for King's views on external affairs in the years after he became leader. He found some of this, but he also discovered a "great deal on King's relations with women." This came as a surprise. Mackenzie King had women friends. Impossible, thought Stacey. "I was drawn, as they say, to read on."[8]

When the literary executors loosened restrictions on the diary in the early 1970s, Stacey could read on with impunity and also publish what he had found. So, although the initial response to the release of the early years of King's diary was muted, Stacey was one of those scholars who were quietly dipping into that sprawling document and becoming even more shocked the farther they read. In the mid-1970s Stacey was approaching retirement, and in the odd and bizarre King diary entries about women, mediums, and spirits Stacey thought he found a book project which might nicely supplement what he called his "meagre" pension. The official biography in all its various guises had more than adequately covered King's public life. It hadn't, though, thoroughly exposed King's odd private life. Stacey gave several talks on Mackenzie King's private life in 1974 and 1975 and had, by early 1975, signed a contract with Macmillan to publish a book on the private world of Mackenzie King.[9] The book would eventually be published in the spring of 1976 as *A Very Double Life: The Private World of Mackenzie King*. The posthumous life of Mackenzie King would never be the same.

Even before its publication, *A Very Double Life* created a controversy in the pages of the *Globe and Mail* over the kind of revelations it was said to be making about the hidden life of Mackenzie King. Peter Newman, the editor of *Maclean's*, fired the first salvo, claiming that he was looking forward to Stacey's book, which would be the "first impartial examination of the [King] diaries." By this he meant that it would be the first book based on the diary not to come directly from the official team at Laurier House and not directly or indirectly under the control of the literary executors and especially Jack Pickersgill. Newman wrote of how "Pickersgill can look back on nearly four decades in the service of himself and his country." As the literary executor not only of King but also of St Laurent and Pearson, "he finds himself in position to rewrite or at least re-interpret much of the Canadian history that was being made between 1919 and 1968. And he's been doing just that."[10]

The historian Ramsay Cook couldn't let this stand, and came to the defence of his historian colleagues associated with the official biography project. Cook played the part of historian pedant, the man who knew his sources and stuck to the letter of the law. "Presumably, before making his judgment, Mr. Newman read Charles Stacey's forthcoming book and also enough of W.L.M. King's unpublished diary to satisfy himself that previous authors had been partial. Otherwise his charge is without foundation."[11]

Blair Neatby also wrote to defend himself against what he called a puzzling and "extravagantly partisan" attack. Neatby claimed that the literary executors had given him and others on the official biography "free access to the King papers and diaries. Mr. Pickersgill did not interfere with our research and did not exercise any control over our manuscripts. If the volumes we have produced are Liberal propaganda the responsibility is ours and not Mr. Pickersgill's." By this point, Neatby could point out that the literary executors had not only not hidden King's records, they had opened up the full texts of King's diary to the public. Anyone could check the record themselves. This was a slightly legalistic argument for the executors had made this decision only after quite a bit of coaxing and decades of indecision, only after they had long considered destruction, and only after Pickersgill's much-edited version of the diary, *The Mackenzie King Record*, had been criticized for what it might or might not have hidden. Yet Neatby was certainly right that, in the end, the literary executors had opted for openness.[12]

There followed a back-and-forth exchange of letters between Newman and Cook, with Cook saying, essentially, that we'll have to wait to see what is in Stacey's book, and how it will cover King's relations with prostitutes, certainly not something that was in Pickersgill's volumes. Cook pointed out that this didn't fall within the years of Pickersgill's *Record*. By this point, the disputants had probably lost most readers, but Newman brought it back to an issue that would come up again and again in the 1970s, and especially when Stacey's book came out later in the spring: the question of trust. "I find it bizarre that a historian with Prof. Cook's reputation for the defence of liberal ideas," Newman argued, "should engage in this absurd posturing in the indirect defence of the greatest monopoly and control of historical sources this country has ever seen."[13]

Only a few books each year receive the kind of attention given to C.P. Stacey's *A Very Double Life* when it was published in the spring of 1976. Newspapers across the country including the *Toronto Star* and the *Ottawa Journal* published extracts in early March. When the book was eventually officially published later in the month, it went straight to the best-seller lists, where it stayed for much of the summer. By early May, Stacey had signed a lucrative deal to make a television program based on the book. It was a Book of the Month selection in August. Eventually it would be translated into French and more than a decade later it would be republished again. Stacey later estimated that he made more than $17,000 not including royalties from the television program.[14] This didn't put him in the ranks of a Pierre Berton but it certainly meant that the book was wildly successful for something written by an academic historian.

For a brief time, Stacey was everywhere – on the television, on the radio, and in the newspapers. He was opening a public library in Toronto and speaking at Canadian Club lunches across Ontario. You could listen to him on *As It Happens* on the CBC or watch him on CFTO news at night or the CHCH midday program. All of this kept the just retired Stacey busy that summer. It also meant that his version of Mackenzie King was the one that saturated most into the popular culture of the year. Because of the kind of revelations Stacey made, and the way these matched the preoccupations of the age, it was also a version of Mackenzie King that endured. The media handed Stacey a loud megaphone, and his message was exactly what many wanted to hear.

Stacey confirmed, and then elaborated upon, the idea that Mackenzie King was not who he had pretended to be. Canadians were already familiar with King as the man of secrets. The stodgy and dull prime minister had all along hidden a much more fascinating private life in which he communed with spirits. Ever since the early news stories in 1950, and especially after Blair Fraser's *Maclean's* article, some Canadians again and again seemed to enjoy expressing surprise that their most successful prime minister had really done this kind of thing. Certainly, the project of "outing" King as a spiritualist kept its lustre of excitement even when there were few new details. Stacey took this idea of King's double life and pushed it into the 1970s, mixing it with the language and assumptions of Watergate, Woody Allen, and the sexual revolution.

Mackenzie King, Stacey wrote, was "an inhabitant of two worlds ... One was the very practical world of politics and public affairs ... The other was his private world." This was the inner "dark side" of King that Stacey would expose in *A Very Double Life*. During King's life, the former prime minister had "contrived with striking success to keep this emotional and frequently irrational private life separate from his rational public world." In fact, Stacey went on to say, "in his lifetime very little knowledge of it reached his countrymen."[15] Until now.

It was a good opening to a book, this promise to unravel the secret story behind something Canadians thought they understood. It also matched well the ethos of the times. For Stacey had something new to add to this well-trod path of King the man of secrets. King hadn't just spoken to the spirits, though he did that too. He also had another kind of secret life. King was a "ladies' man."

To some the idea might have seemed preposterous. Hadn't Bruce Hutchison, in 1952, remarked how the only woman in King's life had been his mother? The large group of King haters, Hutchison had written, who had spent so much time "sleuthing the secrets of [King's] life can find no other woman in it, only a few clumsy and boyish flirtations."[16] This view had been modified somewhat. Dawson's version of the official biography recounted some innocent stories of King's youthful dalliances. Moreover, the literary executor Fred McGregor published his own book in 1964 covering King's years between leaving Laurier's government in 1911 and his return to politics as Liberal leader in 1919. This volume briefly and respectfully told a few anecdotes about King's quest for a wife, but always in a rather deferential fashion. Neatby's 1963 second volume of the official biography had given a few more details.[17] Yet the version of Mackenzie King as "ladies' man" from *A Very Double Life* differed decidedly from these earlier accounts.

Stacey outlined King's relations with various kinds of women, starting with the "respectable" girls whom he wooed as a young man. There were many. "Collectively," Stacey argued, "they are the subject matter of a tremendous proportion of the diary. Only one of those up-to-date historians who have called the computer to their aid could do full justice to this theme; for Mackenzie King's lady friends were as the sands of the sea for multitude." King's efforts to court the young ladies are sketched out in the book in painful detail. For, although Stacey conceded that King had "colossal physical energy" in his ability to carry on with all the socializing that romance required as well as keep up his work and studies, he was also unsparing in his assessment of King's earnest and fumbling romantic methods.[18]

We learn of King's brief infatuation with a Kitty Riordan on a holiday to the Muskokas. "She ... must have been attracted by the young man," Stacey suggested. "At any rate, she apparently made no complaint when he sought to entertain her, day after day, by reading aloud long, long passages of Gibbon's *Decline and Fall of the Roman Empire*." When King called off the budding affair, he complained in his diary about how she had been "very unpleasant all day." Still, this "did not prevent him from continuing to read Gibbon to her on the days that followed." As Stacey says later of King and his good friend Bert Harper, the young men were "utterly earnest, wholly humourless, and ineffably pompous."[19]

It was all part of Stacey's portrayal of King's oddly serious and morally troubled idea of romance. He had a "religious obsession" which meant that he was infatuated with nurses and with women in general who reminded him of his mother. Again and again Stacey shows us a King who would court a young lady only to back away when she somehow failed to live up to his high moral ideals. He seemed repulsed by his own physical urgings. This was what happened in the case of his wooing of Mathilde Grossert, the Chicago nurse to whom he had briefly been engaged. Stacey goes much deeper into this affair than had Dawson twenty years earlier. Moreover, he points out King's hypocritical and less than honourable behaviour, including how King told Mathilde that he had burned her letters as requested but neglected to admit that he had already copied these out in his diary.[20]

Yet Stacey's most dramatic revelations dealt not with the wooing of a potential wife but with women who sold their sexual services. MacGregor Dawson had already briefly mentioned King's attempt to reform prostitutes in the official biography, noting it alongside the earnest moral religiosity of his youth. Stacey found something a good deal more salacious than uplift. Stacey saw hypocrisy, lust, and sin.

It all depended on what King meant by a "wasted" evening. In only the second entry of his diary, when he was still a student at the University of Toronto in the 1890s, King is complaining of a night having been "practically wasted" and how he had seen "a little … of the wickedness of the world." Stacey finds more and more of these kinds of entries as the diary goes on, not only in Toronto but also when King moved to Chicago and then Harvard. Similar entries show up in King's record of his financial outgoings – how money was "wasted," how he had committed a "sin" and earnestly vows to do better. He speaks of his "weakness" and gets down on his knees, praying to avoid temptation in the future. These entries always come after King has gone out in the evening on a "stroll." He talks of how he is "ashamed to record" what he did. He cries, and repents. These kinds of entries did not make it into the official biography. These were genuinely new. But what did they signify?[21]

"The precise nature of his sins he does not tell us," Stacey notes. "But it can hardly be doubted that these 'strolls' were visits to prostitutes." *A Very Double Life* retells the story of King's attempts to rehabilitate prostitutes but the meaning is entirely different. In Stacey's version, King is an "amateur libertine" who concocts the sociological scheme at salvation to salve his conscience. Stacey is in no doubt that King succumbs to temptation and his urges. It is King who sins in these encounters, which don't, in any case, succeed in lifting the women in question out of their conditions or their method of employment. But his dejection is more than just sociological. He deeply feels his own personal failure to live up to his Christian ideals and rein in his bodily desires. This story of King the "ladies' man" was wholly new. Mackenzie King, it seemed, really did lead a "double life."[22]

If King's carnal appetites and post-coital guilt provided the most excitement, the rest of *A Very Double Life* went on to confirm the completeness of King's oddity. Stacey devoted chapters to King's three closest friends. Each friendship was unconventional, and in each case King reaped more than he sowed. With the young man Bert Harper, King sat up late at night in front of the fire in their shared apartment as they read Tennyson aloud and devoted themselves to idealistic truths and ideals. The attraction wasn't, so Stacey says, homosexuality but simply the "consciously romantic and affectionate friendship" of the era taken to extremes. The two men kept each other on the right path. With Harper in the picture, King could avoid his late-night strolls and pledge himself to lead a better life.[23]

With Marjorie Herridge and Joan Patteson, the other two most important women in King's life, the situation was tricky. These were love triangles, though it seems Platonic ones. Each was a married woman, and yet in each instance King inserted himself into the family circle, capturing the woman's attention. In Patteson's case, this lasted for the better part of her adult life. She became King's social convenor, hosting parties at Laurier House, acting the part of King's missing wife. We don't know how her husband, Godfroy, felt about the relationship, though it is clear that Marjorie Herridge's husband was not pleased. At one point, the man slammed the door in King's face when King and Mrs Herridge returned from an outing after midnight.

As he would with so many delicate situations in his life, King showed no shame, arranging to meet with Dr Herridge and professing his innocence and good intentions – so much so that the husband conceded that he was thinking only of "what the neighbours might say." After King's explanation, King escorted Mrs Herridge to the theatre with his mother. She even spent the night in King's apartment with his mother. If this wasn't as sensational as sex with streetwalkers, it was equally odd behaviour.

Stacey didn't expose King's spiritualism to Canadians, but he did give the subject much more detail, and he wrote about it in terms that were more frank, exhaustive, and less deferential than any before. The craziness, indeed, was in the details. It's through Stacey that we get the salacious stories of King's over-the-top devotion to his dog, Pat, the way he interpreted a wagging tail or a friendly canine rub against his shins as signs that his mother was watching over him and was communicating to him through his dog. When Pat died in 1941, King's reaction was just too much for Stacey. King had arrived back in Ottawa to find Pat very ill and instantly began berating himself for having been away. As the poor dog neared death, King put off a meeting of the cabinet's War Committee so that he could be with Pat until the end. King devotes page after page in the diary to Pat's last moments on earth, and Stacey finds the whole thing "maudlin" and "repulsive."[24] The "most extraordinary thing" about this entry, Stacey wrote, "is that it was set down by the Prime Minister of a country engaged in a desperate war. Here, surely, we have a prime example of King's double life, his capacity for keeping his curious private affairs separate from his public career."[25]

Stacey then goes on to talk about King's devotion to his family, his mother, and his grandfather. He recounts a particularly odd celebration for King's mother's seventy-fourth birthday in which King kisses her seventy-four times, and then more for the years to come. King writes of the significance of the number of candles on the cake, and the destiny that God has in mind for him and his family. This bleeds into Stacey's explanation for King's growing interest in spiritualism. "The line between spiritualism and religion is hard to draw,"[26] Stacey confesses. King very early on saw significance in coincidences and numbers. Later, and only gradually, he was drawn into the world of outright spiritualism. Stacey revealed that King and Joan Patteson had themselves held seances on their own, over "the little table." The exact mechanics of how it worked is difficult to discern. At first they spelt out messages of raps on the table supposedly made by spirits. But as time went on the messages became so elaborate, developing into back-and-forth conversations, that Stacey thinks King and Patteson must have devised some simpler method, perhaps King himself becoming the medium.

"The reader is at liberty to believe, if he wishes," Stacey wrote, "that King's messages actually came from the spirit world." But Stacey himself couldn't help but think that they came out of King's own head, especially because, so often, "the 'spirits' told King why he most wanted to hear."[27] If back in 1951 Blair Fraser had contented himself with simply reporting the fact of King's spiritualistic beliefs and practices, Stacey was prepared to go much further. It was in his nature as a historian. And the cultural changes of the last two decades made it more possible, and perhaps even necessary, that he not just leave it at observation.

"One feels driven to attempt some assessment of the man's intellect," Stacey wrote after outlining King's practices at the little table. "The assessment I fear can only be unfavourable." It was not simply the fact of King's spiritualism. There had been a number of prominent individuals to have believed in the possibility of communication with the spirit world. "It is the extraordinary crudity of the manifestations of his spiritualism," Stacey concluded, "the shattering naïveté of his judgments in these matters, that leave one with the ineradicable impression of a limited intelligence. At times, it is simply impossible to take him seriously."[28]

A Very Double Life generated a tumultuous public reaction. The syndication of excerpts meant that many people across the country (many more than would ever buy the book) read or read about Stacey's account. Moreover, the parts of the book that the publisher (not Stacey) chose for syndication were the most sensational. Stacey himself later regretted not choosing the selections and apologized to W. Kaye Lamb for the mistaken impression they created. They focused, of course, mostly on King's oddities and his relations with women and the spirits. The media train sped along even faster because at the same time that excerpts of the book were being published, Stacey was giving a series of public lectures on Mackenzie King at the University of Waterloo which themselves made their way into the papers.[29]

The headlines almost wrote themselves. There was "prostitution if necessary, but not necessarily prostitution" and, on King's previously unknown hunt for a wife among the daughters of American millionaires, "marriage if necessary, but not necessarily marriage." There were references to King's "dark side," large block letters telling of how King "worshipped his mother," and leading suggestions about just what "Mackenzie King's diary reveals." The stories and pictures worked so well because they inverted the assumptions of most accounts of great statesmen and King in particular.[30]

Back in the 1950s, and ever since, if King showed up in a newspaper or magazine, he often came pictured along with either Roosevelt or Churchill. These two leaders were the wartime greats, and King was the Canadian equivalent. In the articles on A Very Double Life, the newspapers gave readers the same pictures. Here, again, was the great Canadian war leader. But this time the captions subverted the earlier meaning. Under the picture of King with Roosevelt at Ogdensburg, the caption tells of how a spirit of Roosevelt came to King in a 1947 seance telling him, "You are not clever, you are wise." Next to a picture of Churchill and King, the caption explained how

King had once given Churchill the transcript from a seance in which the dead Roosevelt was said to have praised King for having the wisdom Churchill lacked. There was no indication of Churchill's reply.[31]

Many readers couldn't help but be amazed at the story that Stacey had served up to them. This was not the King they knew. The reactions ranged from fascination to alarm, from censure to glee. "Mackenzie King isn't one of Canadian history's stuffed shirts – not any more," is how the *Hamilton Spectator* reviewer put it. One man wrote to the *Toronto Star* that he was "delighted" to learn that King had enjoyed a "lady on the side" just like Jack Kennedy and John Profumo in England. The writer had thought King to be, as he homophobically put it, a "fruitcake." But not now. "Mackenzie King, wherever [you] are, your diaries prove you to be all man." The *Globe and Mail* reviewer William French had a similar, if less obviously prejudiced, view, saying that he was "glad to read that King had a sex life. He's always seemed prissy and sexless; now we know he had hormones, like any other red-blooded Canadian boy."[32]

This talk of sex and hormones was much more open than twenty years earlier. In the 1950s, psychologists were advocating a more mature and frank admission of human sexuality, but such an approach hadn't made its way into the general run-of-the-mill news stories on former prime ministers. In the mid-1970s, things had changed. The same went for discussions of King's spiritualism. If William French was fine with the discovery that King had a libido, he dismissed King's spiritualism in even stronger terms than Stacey: "Those aspects of his character put him right back among the eccentrics on the fringe of bananaland."[33]

Not all approved of Stacey, nor of the decision of the newspapers to publish his sensational excerpts. A reader from Peterborough, Ontario, wrote personally to Stacey, complaining that surely he could "find something better to do than desecrate the dead." Even if it was legal, it was "unforgivable" "to destroy a man morally that has been dead for at least twenty-five years." A reader of the *Ottawa Journal* complained about those who found entertainment "in reading what is written of the 'sensational past' of the defenceless dead. Truly decent people deplore being presented with news and articles that belong in the sewer." She left readers with this thought: "Bees pick up honey, flies pick up dirt." Other reviewers noted that there was a little too much "glee" in the way Stacey exposed King's indiscretions and oddities. Although Blair Neatby remained friendly with Stacey publicly, he privately complained that he could "see no sign of political analysis or psychological interpretation, which seems to mean that it is little more than 'voyeurisme' [sic]." This had been the worry of the internal editor at Macmillan who wanted changes to the manuscript to remove the impression that "the author has with a certain degree of malice and mockery decided to lift the veil from the public figure of a great prime minister to show the unbalanced hypocrite beneath."[34]

The most observant critic was the literary executor W. Kaye Lamb. Stacey had written to Lamb, offering an apology of sorts for the sensationalistic excerpts and offering to send a copy of the book itself. When Lamb had read *A Very Double Life*, he responded to say that he was much happier with the book itself. He even thought he detected a strain of sympathy for King that ran throughout. The ending, he said, reminded him of the ending of Lytton Strachey's *Victoria* where Strachey imagines the final thoughts of the great queen in the moments before her death. No more apt comparison could have been made. Stacey was a Canadian Strachey, several generations later, in the midst of a culture that had taken that much more time to allow serious and respectable authors to write in the same vein. A friend had written to Strachey after reading *Victoria* about what he had achieved. "You've discovered a new style which gives the essential and all-pervading absurdity of most human and all official life without losing anything of its pathos," the man had stated. "You're so kind and so unsparing. It seems to me more nearly a true perspective than anything yet found." There could have been no truer assessment of what Stacey sought to achieve – to show in full the absurdities of official life, the real banalities and oddities of the great statesman King, all without ever taking anything away from the real public achievements already outlined in other biographies. He highlighted the disjuncture between one and the other, the public and the private, the two worlds of Mackenzie King.[35]

C.P. Stacey did more than anyone else to create the image of "Weird Willie" Mackenzie King. Yet, in the middle of the 1970s, he wrote in a cultural milieu that was ready and eager for what he had to say. Many wanted to learn that their politicians led secret lives. They also were keen to pore over the odd sexual and moral lives and values of those who used to dominate Canadian society. The moral values of King's era were coming to be diagnosed as both backward and almost as signs of mental illness. If some were amused and glad to see that the bachelor King really had a sex life, King's mawkish manner still set him apart. In taking on the odd life of Mackenzie King in an open fashion – in exposing his secrets – commentators in the 1970s were establishing the new values of frankness, authenticity, and self-worth. Mackenzie King was simply a convenient Victorian scapegoat.

16

Victorianitis

Even in the late 1940s when Mackenzie King retired, he had come to seem like a relic from a different age. Harry Ferns, who would go on to write *The Age of Mackenzie King*, wrote a series of short articles about the retired prime minister in the *Canadian Forum*, describing King as a gentleman of the old school. He was, claimed Ferns, a "respectable gentleman of no pretensions" and without any "wasting passions." This latter mattered a good deal. "In the honored tradition of the old-fashioned Protestant middle class, [King] husbands his money, husbands his energy and works hard." He didn't smoke, nor was he a drinker – though he wasn't an outright teetotaller. Ferns slyly joked that the prime minister's closest staff were part of King's image. They were also "non-smokers and non-drinkers." Indeed, "his most effective principal secretary was one who even shunned coffee and liked his tea extremely weak."[1] King was, in other words, a Victorian. It might have been an odd assessment of someone who didn't become prime minister until 1921, almost two decades after Victoria's death, were it not for the fact that the term Victorian meant much more than simply the long reign of a single monarch.

In the years immediately after King's death, Canada could still appear, at least on the surface, to conform in part to some of the respectable Victorian virtues. Sunday observance remained the norm, and even though the temperance movement was no longer active, the issue of drink continued to divide Canadian families. Further, in his book introducing Canada to outsiders, the journalist Ernest Watkins admitted that, while a majority of Canadians could not "accept without question the whole dogma of some Christian church ... there is a majority that has faith in the values of the Christian civilization of this last five hundred years, of which the core is the conviction that the individual is accountable in the sight of God for his actions, that there are absolute standards of value against which every individual, be he commissar, general, priest or salesman, is to be judged."[2] Parents of Baby Boomers raised their children according to these principles.

Over the next two decades, the old moral certainties disappeared, replaced by a much more raucous maelstrom of competing ideas of what was fit and proper. In the process, to call something Victorian increasingly came to mean not just a little old-fashioned but also repressed and repressive. While much of this social revolution centred on youth – on rock'n'roll and sex and drugs – it's also clear in retrospect that the cultural revolt was widespread and involved people of all ages. The parents of the Baby Boomers may not have always liked (may have violently objected to) the degree of change that they saw among some in the youth culture. But many older Canadians, those who were already adults at the start of the 1960s, had already been loosening up in the kinds of ways that the '60s young radicals would push to extremes.

By the early 1970s, the Victorian values that had only so recently seemed common sense and powerful were, for many, the subject of ridicule. Canadian writers made names for themselves by shocking their readers with just the right kind of daring rebellion. In Margaret Atwood's *Edible Woman*, the young female main character who breaks with convention does so while living in a rented apartment above a prim landlady simply called "the lady down below." In the novel, the landlady stands in for the socially conventional – peeking out from behind velvet curtains or listening for the sound of men's steps on the stairs. Certainly, it wouldn't be respectable to sully the backyard by anything so private as the hanging of laundry. If Atwood subtly mocked the lady down below, other writers eschewed subtlety. The 1976 Governor General Award for fiction went to Marian Engel's *Bear*, a novel that imagined an erotic and romantic relationship between a middle-aged female archivist and a bear.

It wasn't just fiction. Canadians came to appreciate a book like John Glassco's *Memoirs of Montparnasse*, his slightly fictionalized memoir that was a tale of the sexual and social anti-Victorian revolution lived by one young man in 1920s Paris. In the 1970s, literary Canada was willing to celebrate, en masse, exactly the kind of social daring and turning away from the past that Glassco presented as part of his coming of age. The Canadian diplomat Charles Ritchie became a literary sensation with the publication of his artful, witty, and anti-puritanical diaries. Ritchie's life story just happened to coincide with the recent past of international high politics – London in the middle of the Second World War, negotiations over the creation of the United Nations. But what Ritchie revealed was a world where what happened on the surface was not at all what happened underneath. We learn of his multiple sexual affairs, his drinking, and mostly his skeptical and intelligent critique of his political bosses. All was not at it seemed behind the curtains, either in Margaret Atwood's Toronto or in Charles Ritchie's diplomatic London.[3]

In 1975 Christina Newman wrote a series of articles in *Maclean's* on how the old Ottawa Establishment of the Mackenzie King and St Laurent years had been replaced in the Trudeau era. She referred particularly to the federal civil service, but she also meant the culturally closed world of the Oxbridge-educated, old-boy network that Blair Fraser and Jack Pickersgill and Bruce Hutchison and others had inhabited. The social centre of the new Ottawa under Trudeau could be found at the annual New Year's party of a dynamic middle-aged Jewish couple, both of whom were deputy ministers in the Trudeau government. They also had a unique connection to Mackenzie King. For the article presented the brilliant statistician Sylvia Ostry and her husband, Bernard, as the symbols of this new Ottawa. From his time as a slightly too risqué critic in the 1950s, Bernard Ostry had risen far. The Liberal Party ruled again in Ottawa in the 1970s. But it was not your grandfather's Liberal Party. This time, that critic of Mackenzie King who had been too controversial for the 1950s now represented the new guard.[4]

The publication of C.P. Stacey's *A Very Double Life* fitted perfectly into this context of a belated revolt against Victorianism. The public pounced on news of King's sexual exploits in the 1970s. Partly this was because Stacey had finally given them the evidence. The newly released diaries served up details of King's private life which had previously been hidden. Even though the evidence that King had sex with prostitutes was tentative and unclear, Stacey's argument was logical and convincing. King's references to nights and money being "worse than wasted," especially when buttressed by his self-flagellation and guilt, certainly sounded like evidence of a young man succumbing to his sexual desires. There had always been a keen interest in King's private life and now Stacey seemed to show that there was a great deal that had previously been concealed.

But it's one thing to be interested in King's romantic or private life, and quite another to be willing to embrace this curiosity openly and unreservedly. In the 1950s, there was still a culture of restraint (and perhaps shame) about being so avowedly voyeuristic. By the mid-1970s, in the midst of the sexual revolution, the fascination with Freudianism, and the quest for more authentic, real, frank expressions of all aspects of human desire that was being promoted throughout the culture, there were many willing to consign shame and restraint to the past. The anti-Victorian cultural revolt involved not just the young but also middle-aged professors and journalists, members of the "over thirty" crowd who only so recently weren't to be trusted. These critics saw in stories of King's secret sex life a confirmation that everything they had thought about the recent past was true. Earlier generations really had been repressed, and when they hadn't, they had covered it up. The fact of King's excessive guilt and odd self-flagellation only fit more perfectly into this sense of the inevitable progression away from the repressive Victorianism of an older Canada.

The differences between King's day and 1970s Canada were obvious and frequently emphasized. Even when a reviewer sympathized with King, it was often because of how naive King and his era seemed in retrospect. "Poor old Mackenzie King!" wrote one critic. "Here we all are, in this easy age of whooping around on water beds, snickering over his diaries because they indicate how often he was tempted as a young man to find unholy beds on King Street ... His diaries really tell us nothing. Our 1976 minds write between the lines." Allan Fotheringham earned plenty of laughs when he joked about the state of Canada in the 1970s. Here Canadians were in 1976 with the Governor General's Award going to a novel that imagined an erotic relationship between a woman and a bear "and 30 years ago we have a prime minister who was getting it on with his dog."[5] Of course, Stacey's book said no such thing about King and his dog, but the details didn't matter. The laughter that greeted Fotheringham's quip underlined how Canadians could now joke openly about the bizarre desires and actions that earlier generations had hidden.

Commenting on Stacey's book, a *Toronto Star* book reviewer quoted from Marian Engel, author of *Bear*, about the secrets and hidden lives of previous generations. "The Canadian tradition was, on the whole, genteel," she argued. "Any evidence that an ancestor had performed any acts other than working and praying was usually destroyed." The *Ottawa Journal* devoted its main editorial to the issue, arguing that "part of the shock of the revelations about King comes from a peculiar Canadian tradition that a prime minister – especially a prime minister such as King – is an office, not a person. The country now knows that public men do have private lives." With these new revelations the public could see what resulted from "the pressures of Victorian morality."[6]

Not all celebrated this outing of what had previously been hidden. But in writing to decry Stacey's book and the publicity journalists gave it, they only reinforced the notion that society was changing – away from the values they held dear. One critic complained that the outing of secrets was something that American and not Canadian journalists did. It was Americans who wanted to "hang their dirty linen on the line." "Is nothing sacred anymore?" he asked. Though, of course, that was just it. Dirty linen, including undergarments soiled with bodily secretions or the stains of sexual intercourse, is exactly what those who were overturning Victorian notions of privacy were so keen to expose. Perhaps these parts of normal human existence could simply be spoken about openly.[7]

Some critics saw that C.P. Stacey was himself a product of an earlier age. Even though Stacey exposed King's private life in ways that he wouldn't have done twenty years earlier, his views were decidedly old-fashioned. How else could he see in the diary evidence that King was a "ladies' man"? In *Saturday Night* James Eayrs gave a more worldly reading of the evidence. King was no "victim of satyriasis," Eayrs wrote. Indeed, the diary is full of entries of King returning home, having defeated "temptation" and having not "fallen." For a real account of a "voluptuary," one could peruse the diaries of the "American composer Ned Rorem, with its bodycounts of buggery, its checklists of orgasm, its tales of nights of orgy at the Continental Baths." Surely, thought Eayrs, "King's libido, so far from flaring like an oil-well, flickered rather briefly."[8]

Reg Whitaker, perhaps the most observant critic of all things Mackenzie King in these years, agreed. For those living in the "jadedly permissive age" of 1970s North America, especially if "one's tastes run to *Deep Throat* and *Penthouse*," Whitaker wrote, there wasn't much in *A Very Double Life* to titillate. Instead, "the question of sex and the Canadian Prime Minister recalls Dr. Johnson's quip about the dog walking on his hind legs: it is not that the thing is done well, but that it is done at all."[9]

※

The assuredness with which some critics labelled King's Victorianism as backward came from a switch in moral language in the 1970s. The Freudian-infused age of psychology from the 1950s had spread outward in various directions but with the ultimate effect of locating claims for truth in the self. Even though psychoanalysis itself became largely discredited within official psychiatry in the 1970s, its influence in the wider culture continued. But even more so, a hodgepodge of psychological ideas, often mixed together in confusing and contradictory ways, pushed forward a therapeutic culture of self-fulfillment and authenticity. These ranged from the spread of self-affirming psychotherapeutic methods to the widely discussed Esalen Institute and the human-potentiality movement. Even the anti-psychiatry movement was itself rooted in a wider trend to find truths in the self. Anti-psychiatry intellectuals – from Michel Foucault to R.D. Laing – argued that it was society itself that was sick, not the mentally ill. They criticized the treatment of those in mental institutions and the very idea of sanity itself. Ken Kesey's novel *One Flew Over the Cuckoo's Nest* became a popular movie of the same name. Ironically, although the movement railed against uncaring psychiatrists, its own ideas could be traced back to many of the key themes of post-war psychoanalysis, rooted as they were in the view of mental health as existing on a spectrum. For different reasons, and with different intentions, the popular culture of 1970s North America was suffused with references to the need to find truth in authenticity and the self. When Canadians looked back on an earlier era, these therapeutic insights helped them to label entire historical periods as being not only backward but almost deranged.[10]

Writing in *Maclean's* magazine, the political scientist Paul Fox borrowed Freudian language to diagnose the image of Mackenzie King that Stacey revealed in *A Very Double Life*. The book showed King to be "a genuine neurotic whose anxieties were produced by the double standard of Victorian puritanism and the muddy sentimentality of the Sir Galahad complex." The difference between King and others of his age was only, wrote Fox, the "severity of his Victorianitis." Others made the same diagnosis. The *Vancouver Province* reviewer labelled King "the troubled product of the senseless sensibilities, prudery, morals and attitudes of the Victorian Age as it prevailed in Canada." Victorian-era morality had become a mental illness. The therapeutic shift in the wider culture had invited Canadians to consider openly what was more naturally human and by the 1970s it was a mix of psychological notions that provided the language by which they could distance themselves from earlier generations.[11]

Many people in the 1950s raised the issue of Mackenzie King's psychological particularities but the comments had remained tentative. When Bruce Hutchison had interviewed Liberal Party grandee Norman Lambert, Lambert let loose a long stream of anecdotes "on the machinations and the Freudian mysteries of King." While Hutchison found this "very interesting and impassioned," he concluded that it was of "no use for publication." By the early 1970s, what had once been only brief references to new exotic terms like "complexes" and "Oedipus" and "mother cult" had morphed into a much more mainstream, widespread, and serious way of thinking.[12]

The power of this language is perhaps best found in the novels of one of the most influential Canadian novelists of the decade, Robertson Davies. In his Deptford trilogy, Davies poked and prodded the dark and hidden underside of Canadian life, the kinds of people who in the United States would have been called WASPs. This is nowhere more obvious than in *The Manticore*, the second volume in the trilogy, all of which is devoted to the extensive session of Jungian therapy undergone by the main character, David Staunton. The readers

16.1 Robertson Davies

follow Staunton's investigation of his own personality, unravelling his idiosyncracies as well as those of Canadian culture and the recent Canadian past, both fictional and real.

Davies assumes that readers will be as interested as he is in the inner workings or shadow side of life. Individuals need to know themselves – what they want others to see, what they themselves want to see, and even what they might prefer to hide. Staunton's therapist explains that one's "Shadow" is "that side of oneself to which so many real but rarely admitted parts of one's personality must be assigned." Even if the "Shadow" was dark and unpleasant, still it must be known and acknowledged. "Can you imagine a man without a Shadow?" she asks. "No ... But you must recognize him, you know, your Shadow ... accepting this ugly creature is needful if you are really looking for psychological wholeness."[13]

It isn't long before Davies turns to Mackenzie King. As elsewhere, in the novel King stood for an older Canada. Staunton recalls that "there was something terribly stuffy about Canada in my boyhood – a want of daring and great dimension, a second-handedness in cultural matters, a frowsy old-woman quality." For Staunton's father, the reason was obvious: "It was the Prime Minister." Davies goes on at length about King's oddities, his hypocrisy, and his "conjuror-like ability to do something distracting with his right hand while preparing the denouement of his trick unobtrusively with his left hand." But still Davies ultimately thinks that there was more to King than simple trickery or hypocrisy. "Mackenzie King rules Canada," another character announces, "because he himself is the embodiment of Canada – cold and cautious on the outside, dowdy and pussy in every overt action, but inside a mass of intuition and dark intimations." In this novel, and increasingly in the Canada of the 1970s, it is the dark intimations that matter. Others would later gleefully quote Davies's statement that Canadians were secretly a "bizarre and passionate people." "Accept the bland, quiet, rather dull Canadian for what he seems to be," Davies warned, "[and] it's just like putting your hand into a circular saw."[14]

By the mid-1960s, a group of Canadian psychiatrists, led by one at the University of Toronto, urged that all acting politicians undergo psychiatric evaluation. An editorial in the *Globe and Mail* explained that "candidates would not only have to appear to be suitable, they would have to be suitable right to the very bottom of their psyches." The idea matched the growing concern about what was being hidden in politics and in the individual psyche. Still, the proposal did raise skepticism. The paper wondered "how many statesmen of the past would have gotten past the examiner's couch?"[15] But this was just the point. The psychiatrists met with Blair Neatby, King's official biographer, to speak to him on the subject. They saw King as the perfect test case, someone who clearly had been hiding a good deal of his life from the public, and perhaps an instance of just the kind of psychologically damaged leader that could be avoided in the future. Of course, the fact that King also was the most successful Canadian prime minister raised the issue of whether it took mental instability to succeed in politics.[16] In any event, no politicians are on record as accepting the psychiatrists' advice.

By the end of the 1960s and moving into the 1970s, a number of scholars came to start thinking about King from a psychological and psychoanalytic perspective. Some of them were historians and political scientists who were taking up this increasingly respectable science to see what its uses could be in the social sciences. Dawson had toyed with the ideas very loosely. But others wanted to apply the new concepts methodically. A young scholar, Joy Esberey, requested and was granted access to King's family papers and correspondence in 1970. She wanted to explore whether a study of King's childhood and family relations could explain his later political leadership. If psychiatrists told us that people's personalities were formed at such an early age, why would this not be true of politicians? Esberey wasn't alone. Another young graduate student wanted to study the same kind of thing – applying a psychological model outlined in studies of American foreign policy to the idiosyncratic Canadian prime minister. By the mid-1970s, Esberey was waging an academic debate with the political scientist John Courtney on the question of prime ministerial self-image and personality type and how these shaped decision making.[17]

Even Blair Neatby argued that biographers could no longer simply write a story of the political life while "drawing a decorous veil over [the subject's] private idiosyncrasies." As Neatby put it, "Sigmund Freud destroyed this convenient dichotomy between public and private life." Given all that Freud had explained about the impact of early childhood experience and sexual repression on personality type, "it seems almost unscholarly not to look to a man's relationship with his parents and siblings for enlightenment." Yet Neatby had to admit that, as of yet, there was no good model of exactly how this should be done.[18]

Erik Erikson had written psychobiographies of Martin Luther and Mahatma Gandhi, yet, for historians, these works weren't useful, revealing almost nothing about the wider historical context. Still, the psychological quirks of the individual had to be accounted for, especially in the case of Mackenzie King, where the evidence was so abundant. Even if King's diary was often nothing more than "naïve rationalizations" of his behaviour, that still could be valuable. After all, "few exercises can be more revealing than daily self-justification over a period of fifty years. It might even be as informative as adult revelations during hourly sessions on a psychiatrist's couch." King described his dreams in great detail, "in a simple non-Freudian way." Neatby pointed out that, when King saw "his mother in a red dress, it is enough for him that she is making her presence known; when he dreams of smashing busts of Laurier, he interprets this as a reminder that he should learn French." Yet those coming later cannot accept King's interpretation as sufficient: "A psychiatrist would surely arrive at a different interpretation."[19]

Even if the proper way forward wasn't clear, it seemed necessary to go deeper and deeper inside the psyche of political leaders. This is one of the things that the revelations about King did: they provided the best case study to confirm that successful politicians needed scrutiny. Several months before the publication of *A Very Double Life*, the political scientist Reg Whitaker was already giving readers of *Canadian Forum* an account of the revelations in King's diary, calling King the "dingbat in the Canadian belfry" but also citing the anti-psychiatry icon R.D. Laing and arguing that there could be "method in madness, and lessons in lunacy." For Laing (and for Whitaker here), the seemingly mad had stories to tell – insights to offer.

Whitaker took readers with him as he sat down to read the Mackenzie King diary in the reading room of the Public Archives in Ottawa. At first, he claimed that it seemed like "strange territory, not like other matter-of-fact diaries I have read before." King appeared "an odd gentleman." He believed that his dead loved ones, his ancestors, literally hovered around him. A small bump or rub from his dog could be a message from beyond. Any coincidence – the hands on a clock, the design in shaving foam – could be a sign of divine providence, a confirmation that King was destined for greatness. The more Whitaker read, the odder King seemed: "I read on and then realize that I am losing my moorings," Whitaker wrote. "The man is quite crazy. The contradictions become noticeable, then significant, then insurmountable. The inner world of the public man begins in incongruity and ends in hallucination. The stream runs faster and wilder, the light darkens, and the shore is lost from sight."[20]

Still, Whitaker felt compelled to go onward. If King were alive in the 1970s, Whitaker thought, he might be found "browsing happily in the occult section of the paperback racks among the Lapsang Ramas and Tarot primers." Yet this was a prime minister of Canada in the first half of the twentieth century. King's love of his mother was almost too obvious. "A crude Freudian could have an endless picnic in the King diaries," Whitaker exclaimed. "The Oedipal evidence abounds." It is fitting that Whitaker ends the article on a note of pride. When Canadians bravely went inside themselves or inside the diary and the psyche of their most successful prime minister, they ultimately found something fascinating. Here the psychological journey inward matched the quest to do away with Victorian restraints, with respectability's insistence on the surface of things. King may have been odd. But he also confirmed that Canadian politics, and Canada itself, wasn't as dull as many had previously thought. "A strange man, a strange age, a strange country," is how Whitaker put it: "There is more to Mackenzie King, and to Canada, than meets the eye."[21]

The "Weird Willie" phenomenon that exploded in the mid-1970s, and especially around publication of C.P. Stacey's *A Very Double Life*, partly grew out of the mainstreaming of a kind of "loose Freudianism" that, by the 1970s, was very loose indeed. Stacey benefited from the increasing acceptance of poking at the dark innards of private life. This is one reason why Stacey could publish this book in the mid-1970s when, as he admitted, he couldn't have imagined doing so twenty years earlier. Yet Stacey, a septuagenarian and a retired historian by the time his book came out, was prepared to go only so far. He referred to psychiatrists and to psychological concepts many times in the book. He explained King's keeping of a diary by saying it was a form of "psychological relief." He wrote of King's "tendencies and susceptibilities." He attributed his "obsession" with the Chicago nurse Mathilde Grossert to the fact that he saw her as a "mother figure," and he noted the "element of fantasy in the attachment." All of this shows that old historians can learn new tricks. But Stacey remained content mostly to point out the oddities. Other scholars could investigate King's intentions more systematically. Stacey concluded: "I am content to let the psychologists and psychiatrists resolve these riddles, if they can."[22]

In fact, others did want to solve these riddles. One of the criticisms of Stacey's book was that it wasn't rigorous enough in the way it investigated King's inner life. If one was really going to go down the rabbit hole, then it needed to be done professionally. David Lewis of the New Democratic Party complained that he finished the book wanting "some intellectual probing into the character that the diaries revealed." Still, he had to admit that Stacey was "a historian, not a psychiatrist or psychologist." The *Financial Post* reviewer admired the book but concluded that "the deeper psychological bases of both his public and private life ... remain to be explored." This was, perhaps not surprisingly, also Joy Esberey's conclusion. "All historical biography need not be psychobiography," she wrote, "but surely any study that purports to deal with the personality of the political actor, rather than the political office, must have a base more scientific than the personal opinion, no matter how perceptive, of the author."[23]

After reading *A Very Double Life*, a University of Toronto medical student wrote a psychobiography of King that she published with her professor. What is striking is that, although they used a more scientific language, their overall assessment of King followed the same general direction set by Stacey. They spoke of how he led a "double life," divided between his carnal lusts about which he felt abnormally guilty and the opposing sense of nobility and idealism rooted in a "childlike" moral code. There was no doubt that "King's idealization of his mother is a classical case of the Freudian Oedipus complex – that is, failure to resolve the Oedipal conflict which psychoanalysts have associated with heterosexual loss of libido and in King's case, impotence, except with debased women."[24]

The psychobiography essentially found that King took too seriously the ideals of his own age. He was born in what it called the "hypocritical Victorian era" and was "crippled by guilt," especially after he yielded to his sexual desires with prostitutes. Still, the study concluded that this guilt, and therefore King's psychological state and formation, directly shaped his career choice. He "sublimated" his sexual urges, turning his energies instead into a passion for social reform. So to those who might say that the story of King and the prostitutes was nothing more than a private matter, the psychoanalytic answer was to show how profoundly these private urges and psychopathologies ultimately shaped King's public decisions. The public and the private could not be so easily separated.

Joy Esberey's book similarly took the language of morality and turned it into science. Where others – including the old-fashioned Stacey – saw King's hypocrisy, Esberey pointed out the signs of neurosis. Esberey insisted that to speak of the importance of King's "neurotic tendencies" did not imply condemnation or judgment:

"The clinical label is useful only in so far as it is a key to identifying complex and interrelated set of interactions and defences, which had political as well as personal repercussions." Again, she claims that King was "essentially a Victorian," suffering from the Victorian need to catalogue his own sins. In this, his mother shaped King for the future. Esberey's assessment of the mother-son relationship mirrored what many said about the Victorians in general. His mother's love was "characterized by form rather than substance ... Church going was more important than Christian service to others; people who could be helpful should be assiduously cultivated and companions selected from among their offspring; attainments should be pursued for financial rewards and enhanced status rather than for their own sake." In this kind of assessment, King was the victim of a kind of society – its privileging of surface respectability and not authenticity.[25]

Only a few serious attempts were made to psychoanalyze King retroactively.[26] The task demanded a kind of scientific rigour that was difficult to achieve. And it wasn't always necessary in order to gain wider insights. Yet, even if psychobiography ultimately did not become a dominant form of writing, the general thrust of scholarly study, especially in the historical profession, pushed ever more toward the complexities of identity. Beginning in the 1970s, historians came to complicate the nation's past by emphasizing the many different kinds of Canadians whose stories were supposed to be told (but often weren't) – highlighting the role of class, region, gender, sexuality, race, and religion in the process. The psychologizing of King was an early example of this trend: insisting on the need to explore rigorously the previously hidden and shameful parts of private life, and doing so out of a certainty that real answers could be found.

Canadians in the post-war decades, and especially in the 1970s, looked back increasingly derisively on the repressive moral codes of an earlier era, labelling them Victorian and out of date. A loose mix of psychological ideas, with their insistence on poking into the private, on using science to overturn taboo, provided one of the main justifications for this view. Critics could draw on a range of somewhat contradictory psychiatric languages – picking up Freudian terms one moment and then mixing them with the arguments of the anti-psychiatry movement. The consistency of the approach was not the issue. Instead, the general thrust was to allow Canadians to reflect on an earlier era and a leader like King and see how the values of that time had created a kind of mental illness. What better way to do away with old moral codes and ways of behaving and thinking? To talk openly about King's secret life wasn't prurience, it was mature frankness. And, once one looked openly and clearly, the conclusion was obvious: these earlier generations of Canadians and their leaders had been hiding something all along.

The Cover-Up Is *the Story*

The Security Service came to tea in August 1972. It wasn't the first espionage-related social call for W. Kaye Lamb. Over the years, the former head of Canada's Public Archives and Mackenzie King literary executor had entertained RCMP Security Service officers from time to time. Usually he offered his advice as best he could. This time, though, they brought him some information: Jean-Louis Daviault was dead.[1] Lamb called it a "sad end to a sad story" – only it wasn't quite an ending. For the Security Service was still very much interested in Daviault and the Mackenzie King diaries and the secrets they might reveal.

In the 1970s, the public pounced on authority figures who were suspected of covering up secret scandals and withholding information. The fixation on cover-ups ranged from the real-life scandals of Richard Nixon to the Hollywood fantasies of films like Steven Spielberg's *Jaws*, where the danger lurks below the surface of the ocean and the local authorities try to prevent the news from spreading and scaring off tourists. To read the newspapers of the 1970s is to immerse yourself in a world of suspicion and intrigue where constituted authority ought not to be trusted.

The story of Mackenzie King and his diary wound its chameleon-like way through these cultural trends. King could easily stand in, as we have seen, for a public authority figure that hadn't been the man he had publicly professed to be. Yet it went slightly deeper than that – and along a more convoluted route. There were secrets within secrets and the RCMP Security Service seemed to think that Jean-Louis Daviault and the King diary could help them make sense of it all.

For years, the RCMP had been checking the loyalty of high-level civil servants in an operation they code-named "Operation Featherbed." Over the years the top-secret files of the same name grew to include the names of many individuals, even men who held the highest office in the land, such as Lester Pearson and Pierre Trudeau. The premise behind Operation Featherbed rested on solid foundations. Soviet moles working secretly and undetected had risen to prominent positions in the governments of Canada's allies, the United States and Great Britain. In fact, the moles infiltrated not only government agencies but the security establishments of those countries – the very entities meant to ferret out such spies. The names became synonymous with intrigue and Cold War deception – those like Kim Philby, Guy Burgess, and Anthony Blunt in Britain and Julius and Ethel Rosenberg in the United States. If it happened in the United States and Britain, why not Canada?[2]

When the Canadian diplomat Herbert Norman committed suicide by throwing himself off the top of a Cairo building in 1957, the RCMP was convinced that he did so out of guilt. Norman had long been considered by the Security Service to be a possible Soviet mole within External Affairs but he had been cleared by his civilian bosses in earlier investigations. The FBI and sympathetic anti-communist American politicians repeatedly questioned Norman's loyalty and, for them, this is what had precipitated his suicide. Opinion within Canada was divided, with many criticizing the way American hysteria had brought down an innocent Canadian. The Mounties, for their part, responded to the Norman case by creating Operation Featherbed to keep track of other possible Soviet sympathizers who were working at the highest levels of the Canadian government.

In the end, the Mounties' Cold War logic would be proven wrong. The most prominent Canadian spies often weren't ideologically motivated. They did it for money, something that the Mounties did not overlook but that they did not fully appreciate either. Operation Featherbed never uncovered a top mole in the Canadian establishment. But over the next fifteen years the operation's files stayed open and were occasionally the basis of a number of investigations. The files grew, as security files did, and took on a life of their own. Names were added to "indices," backgrounds were checked, and leads followed up. One trail of evidence led to Mackenzie King's literary executors.

In the summer of 1969, two RCMP agents asked to meet with two of King's literary executors, W. Kaye Lamb and Jack Pickersgill. They had read parts of Pickersgill's *Mackenzie King Record*, the published version of excerpts of King's diary. They sat down in Pickersgill's office at the Canadian Transport Commission and laid out their case for why he should help them in their search for spies in the top echelons of the Canadian government. The RCMP thought that Pickersgill could assist them given "his long association with the country's political elite" and "his actual presence in the Prime Minister's office during the war years." They wanted to develop Pickersgill as a source. They also wanted access to the Mackenzie King diary, which was not at that point open to the public.[3]

The agents were taking up an old idea within the Service – that there had been a cover-up following the Gouzenko investigation. When the Soviet embassy cipher clerk Igor Gouzenko had defected in September 1945, bringing with him evidence of Soviet spy networks in Canada, the Canadian government initially kept the defection secret. Mackenzie King busied himself meeting with his British and American allies while, behind the scenes, the RCMP investigated the documents and the names they contained. It was only in the spring of 1946, after an American radio program leaked news of Gouzenko's defection, that the Canadian government admitted to the scandal and quickly rounded up suspects. What if a Soviet mole had known about the defection before it became public? What if they had taken action to tidy up their own connections, hiding them from later discovery? This was the suspicion that had lingered on among the RCMP Security Service.

Their meeting with Pickersgill and Lamb gave some support for this theory. It was then that the agents learned that a portion of the diary was missing. It wasn't just any portion. It was King's diary for the final part of 1945, from 10 November until the end of December, the exact period when King held high-level meetings to decide what to do about the spy ring. This seemed especially suspicious. If that portion of the diary contained sensitive information about Soviet moles within the Canadian government, what better way to cover it up than to steal the diary? Alternatively, what if someone had stolen the diary to learn about King's secret meetings? In either case, the Security Service decided that the matter had to be investigated.

The agents left pleased with their meeting. They found Pickersgill to be cordial and helpful, even if he confessed to being "of the school which may hold some skepticism as to what secrets Canada may hold." He agreed to help them again in the future. The agents clearly liked that Pickersgill confessed to always feeling a bit dubious about the National Film Board, long a dumping-boy of the RCMP. Both Lamb and Pickersgill "felt that the c.b.c. policy which is so blatantly anti-American cannot be a mere accident." As ever, the cultural departments of government elicited the most skepticism among Cold Warriors.[4]

Several years later, the Security Service returned to the King diary when an agent seems to have read the journalist Peter Dempson's memoir *Assignment Ottawa*, his account of his time as a reporter in the parliamentary press gallery. Dempson recounted an anecdote about how someone had stolen copies of Mackenzie King's diary and offered them for sale to the *Toronto Telegram*. The book was published in 1968 but it was four years later, early in 1972, that a Security Service officer visited the Public Archives to inquire about Dempson's revelations.[5]

The Mounties seemed to have thought Dempson was referring to the same issue of the missing King diary covering the Gouzenko years. But in meeting with Lamb they realized that this episode referred to the separate situation in which it was believed that Jean-Louis Daviault had stolen copies of the diary. Lamb recounted the Daviault story to them. He explained that no one else in the archives, aside from himself, knew about the incident at the time and that the RCMP had investigated but could not find enough information to charge Daviault. Lamb also told them about the incident only a few years earlier, in 1968, when a reporter had said that Daviault was again offering the diary for sale. The fact that Daviault also had access as part of his job to minutes of cabinet meetings and other Privy Council materials struck the Mounties as significant.[6] Over the next year, Daviault became a priority for Operation Featherbed.

Unfortunately, at this point, the operation's files become frustratingly unclear. Many portions of text have been covered over to omit the names of individuals and, in some cases, whole pages of information are missing. All we can see is a blank page. What is clear is that the Security Service thought that Daviault might have had links to other moles and to someone in the Russian intelligence service either directly or via a go-between.

The Mounties couldn't speak to Daviault in person. In May 1971 Daviault had checked into the Holiday Inn on Dalhousie Street in Ottawa and never checked out. Hotel staff later found Daviault in his room, dead of an overdose of barbiturates. It seemed to be a suicide but the Mounties suspected something more. An agent recorded that Daviault's shoes and tie were missing when his body was found. Perhaps this was "important," they mused.[7] They wondered if anything might have driven him to emotional desperation and instability. They checked their records to see which Russian Intelligence Service (RIS) agents had been in Ottawa and especially around the Dalhousie Street area in 1971. They were in touch with other parts of the RCMP in an attempt to track down the copies of the King diary that Daviault might have had in his possession. They interviewed his former friends and acquaintances, obtained his employment files and his death certificate. They even discovered information about his recent medical history, including the doctors he had been seeing, and why.[8]

Although the many blanked-out sections of the files don't allow us to know why this mattered so much to the Security Service, it's clear that, for a time, they considered the matter of great importance. On the recovery of the diary, they wrote that there was a "degree of urgency" to the process. By September 1972, A.M. Barr of the Service thought that "there is a very good possibility that Jean DAVIAULT was the agent, or at least the source of the information for the agent, [blank]." Daviault had "access" and "motive." Some unidentified person, Barr said, was "on the scene and no doubt, [blank] knew that DAVIAULT was desperately trying to find a buyer for the documents which he had in his possession." They needed to do more homework and establish what connections there were between Daviault and this unnamed agent. "My personal feelings are," wrote Barr, "that DAVIAULT was somehow involved in this matter and is in some way the key to the puzzle." Ultimately, the Mounties could prove nothing. Corporal D.L. McKinnon agreed with Barr that Daviault was likely key to the whole puzzle but, he pointed out, "there is already a great deal of circumstantial evidence but not conclusive unrefutable [sic] evidence." The Featherbed files become more sparse at this point, though an unnamed Mountie remarks regarding another investigation in 1974 that "I would not want us to loose [sic] sight of DAVIAULT, as I feel that he is the original source of the info."[9]

The Mounties might not have lost sight of Daviault, but it's difficult to tell. There is no additional information in the files indicating that they discovered that Daviault had been an agent or a go-between selling information to the Soviets. Yet the King diary itself would pop up in public discussion of the RCMP at several points over the 1970s and early 1980s. It emerged, though, in reference not to King's secrets but to the secrets of the RCMP and the government itself. For in the mid-1970s, even as the RCMP Security Service continued its Cold War investigations, the force came under scrutiny. This suspicion about the RCMP was one manifestation of a wider trend, as Canadians came to ask hard questions about their government and its secrets.

The Canadian political tradition was supposed to be deferential. In the post-war decades, commentators frequently said that what distinguished Canada from the United States was Canada's Tory tradition, particularly its British heritage and its respect for authority. This was supposed to be as much a mark of French Canada as of English Canada. Canadian heroes were not revolutionaries or rebels. The great line from the Canadian constitution (the British North America Act until 1982) was "Peace, order and good government." Canadians were more lawful than Americans; they had settled the West with the Mounties and law and order and not with warfare; Canadians were more open to government interference in the economy and less critical of elites. Yet, even as political scientists, historians, and writers mythologized this more deferential Canada, others were busy undermining the semi-solid foundations of this myth.[10]

The usual way of explaining the growing distrust of politicians in the 1960s and 1970s is to blame two American phenomena: Watergate and the Vietnam War, both of which Canadians followed avidly. The revelations of wrongdoing in connection with these two events were clear proof of the manner in which politicians at the highest level lied to the public and engaged in base and illegal acts. They weren't who they said they were. Even if one didn't disagree with the bombing of Cambodia, the mere fact that the Nixon administration had tried to keep this major act of war a secret from its own people demonstrated what the public might not know of the most basic facts of the current political situation. And so it was with the dirty tricks of the Nixon administration that were unravelled in the Watergate scandal. A burglary at the head offices of the national Democratic Party went from being a minor local story to a national crisis as it became increasingly plain that the smell of corruption emanated from the Oval Office itself. At the centre of it were two investigative journalists determined to ferret out the secret truth that was being denied them. Ultimately, Nixon was forced to release secret transcripts of conversations in the Oval Office, the infamous White House tapes, that not only showed that he had ordered the burglary but also revealed Nixon to be much less than "presidential." Americans may have expected something high and noble in their presidents, but the White House tapes revealed Nixon to be foul-mouthed, petty, and corrupt. In the standard accounts of these years in American politics, the Watergate scandal encapsulated all that was wrong with the political system at the tail end of what had promised to be the idealistic decade of the '60s.[11]

Yet the decline of deference was much more than an American phenomenon. It also clearly was as much about changing cultural values as it was about specific events. Long before Watergate, Canadian commentators began to voice more strident criticism both of government secrecy and of the wrongdoings of that vaguely defined category, the "establishment." In 1965 the sociologist John Porter published what became a surprise academic best-seller, *The Vertical Mosaic*. In this dense book that was probably bought and discussed more often than read, Porter exposed the hidden and not-so-hidden hierarchies of class that pervaded Canadian society. What truly stuck with the public was Porter's argument that Canada had an establishment, an old-boys' network of power and prestige, rooted in everything from clubs and directorships to the cultural activities of wealthy children, from ballet classes to elocution lessons. Canada was not only governed by an elite class that was strikingly homogenous but the people fortunate enough to belong to it lived lives differed markedly from those of other Canadians. In *The Smug Minority*, popular journalist Pierre Berton lambasted the establishment and presented its members as a small group of individuals defending themselves against the inevitable tide of progress that would wipe away their Puritan values.[12]

Richard Needham poked fun at these people in his *Globe* column. "It's a strange world our rulers inhabit," Needham wrote. "They ride in the back seats of huge, black, chauffeur-driven cars. They make, and listen to, speeches of excruciating boredom. They hold testimonial dinners for each other, and present each other with scrolls and honorary degrees and stuffed owls ... the more powerful you become the more you move away from people; you end up resembling Mackenzie King or some other such human disaster."[13]

The Mackenzie King reference was more than a passing phrase. Over the 1960s and especially in the 1970s, the revelations about Mackenzie King fed the public's skepticism about the political establishment and what they were hiding. The most successful Canadian prime minister had been a secretive man. So much of what the public thought they knew about him was proving to have been untrue. What else had he kept hidden? If King had fooled everyone so thoroughly, what were contemporary politicians hiding? Revelations about the past confirmed current fears and assumptions.

In 1971 the United States Supreme Court rejected a bid to ban the publication of the Pentagon Papers – those secret documents that exposed how American governments had consistently and systematically lied both to the American people and to Congress. The public would get to see what really went on in the war rooms of government. The *Globe and Mail* pointed out that Canadians should not assume that this government secrecy and malfeasance was confined to United States. "Government in Canada has always functioned on the basis that the people need know only its decisions, not the facts and opinions on which those decisions are based," the *Globe* warned. Many important government papers simply disappeared. They became the property of "the men who chance at the time to be governing." The best example to hand was the case of Mackenzie King and his voluminous papers, which became the property of his literary executors. It was only the arbitrary decision of these men that determined if Canadians could see some of the most important documents about their government's history.[14]

The Canadian political scientist Donald C. Rowat argued in 1965 that "any large measure of government secrecy is incompatible with democracy." He wondered about the existence of an "establishment" or "inner circle" in Canadian government and how this contributed to secrecy. "Does there exist, for example, an 'inner circle' of politicians and perhaps certain members of the press who share knowledge about the inner working of party politics and the sources of election expenses? Is there a gentleman's agreement within the circle that certain embarrassing subjects should not be revealed or discussed publicly?" As an example, Rowat turned to Mackenzie King. "It would be interesting to know for how long reporters knew about Mackenzie King's spiritualism before it was finally revealed."[15]

When King's diary was released to the public, and especially after Stacey's book made the diary such a sensation, commentators couldn't help but connect King's secrets with the secrets of Richard Nixon. The connection seemed too obvious, too clear – especially the way in which both men proved to be their own worst enemies. In Nixon's case, he revealed himself on the White House tapes; in King's, his secrets were in his diary. On the release of another batch of the King diary in 1975, the Canadian edition of *Time* magazine claimed that it constituted "a document as revealing as the White House tape transcripts." The *London Free Press* talked about the "diarist's dilemma," the desire both to confess in the diary and to use the diary as some kind of memorial. "Often the two prove mutually destructive," the paper noted, "as when Richard M. Nixon refused to destroy the telltale tapes which eventually destroyed him, because they would, he believed, assure him a place in history. They did, but not the place he expected." And so it was with King. The diary and the tapes showed that both men had led a "double life."[16]

Although Nixon had resigned in 1974, the story of Watergate lived on in books and cinema. The two journalists who had doggedly broke the story published not one but two best-selling accounts of their activities. One of these books sat atop the best-seller list at the same time as *A Very Double Life* earned Stacey his extra retirement income. The Americans had Nixon and corruption. Canadians had King and the prostitutes. Hollywood saw a winner and turned Woodward and Bernstein's *All the President's Men* into a film of the same name starring Robert Redford and Dustin Hoffman. The film was wildly successful and won many Oscars at the 1976 Academy Awards.

Harry Ferns went to see *All the President's Men* in May 1976 and he immediately wrote to his former co-author, Bernard Ostry.[17] The two men had finally contacted each other again after more than two decades, this time at the behest of a publisher who wanted to take advantage of the fresh interest in Mackenzie King. James Lorimer had started an independent publishing house to publish radical books that were critical of the Canadian establishment. It was exactly the kind of press that hadn't existed in Canada two decades earlier. Lorimer saw a forgotten gem in *The Age of Mackenzie King*. The fact that the book had ostensibly been censored and had been just too radical for the 1950s made it all the more attractive.[18]

By the mid-1970s, Harry Ferns both was and wasn't the same man. He still had an amazing and insightful intelligence, and the ability to cut through so much nonsense to get to the heart of an issue. He remained as prickly as ever, still wary of his reputation and Canada, and resentful at how he had been treated by the Liberal establishment. But Ferns had moved far to the right politically. He would title his memoirs *Reading from Left to Right* and it certainly matched his own trajectory. By the 1970s, he had become a libertarian critic of what he saw as Western democracies and their devotion to bureaucratically controlled socialism. He advocated free-market approaches to all kinds of social issues, and in his own world of the university he helped to create Britain's first for-profit free-enterprise institution of higher learning, the University of Buckingham. In other words, Ferns went from being a Marxist to being one of those free-market laissez-faire liberal thinkers who preceded Margaret Thatcher's rise to power.

He still valued, though, the work he had done in exposing the hypocrisy of Mackenzie King and the Liberal Party in Canada. He agreed to republish the book with Lorimer, and when he saw *All the President's Men* he wrote to Ostry saying that he had to see the film. Just as had happened to Ostry in Ottawa, Woodward and Bernstein were shut out of the Library of Congress when they went looking for documents to prove their case. Ostry saw the parallel immediately. He wrote to Lorimer and urged the press to dramatize how his own experiences matched those of Woodward and Bernstein. Ultimately, Nixon was found out by his tapes, but the initial work to bring the White House under suspicion came from two journalists doing the legwork and building up a case based on what evidence they could find. So it was with Ostry. He didn't have access to the diary but he "was able to arrive at reasonable conclusions by employing all the materials that were in the public domain but had not been used by historians or political scientists up to that time." He continued: "At a time when there is so much concern about access to information," Ostry wrote, "the need [is] for young people to employ every resource in gaining access to information. You do not need to know 100% of the facts or have every scrap of information on a subject to make fundamental judgements."[19]

With Ostry's connections, he arranged for promotional quotes and reviews by some of the leading journalists and academics in the country: Peter Newman, George Grant, Larry Zolf, John Gray, Dalton Camp, Donald Creighton, W.L. Morton, Kildare Dobbs, and others. Ostry wrote to his good friend Mordecai Richler to get him to work on his friends at the Book of the Month Club. The scandal of their book, the fact that there were rumours of it having been censored, made it an attractive and even "sexy" sell in the mid-1970s. This was a far cry from the world of respectable Canadian politics in the mid-1950s where controversy was to be avoided at all costs; this time the controversy is what the press used to sell the book. Reviewers revelled in exposing how the times had changed and how this book, which had been smothered and hushed up in the repressive climate of the 1950s, could now be published.[20]

Dalton Camp's comments were indicative. He talked about there having been "a conspiracy to keep the truth about Mackenzie King from the Canadian people." The official biographers, he wrote, "were in on the cover-up." Laurier House, where they worked on the official biography, "was not so much the prime resource for King scholars … as it was a fudge factory." It mattered to this generation of journalists, writers, and thinkers that the Canada of the 1970s was different from the Canada of their youth. In his introduction to the new edition, John Meisel wrote that it "is difficult to now recollect … what things were like in 1955." He wrote of how, at that time, the official biographers were like many Canadians in that they "shared King's commitment to the bland politics of non-doctrinaire, compromising, pluralist democracy." The academic establishment in the mid-1950s "was essentially liberal democratic, bourgeois and genteel. Harmony at all cost, rather than conflict, was indisputably deemed by virtually everyone to be the most desirable form of inter-action." This is what needed to be kept to the forefront of one's mind in reading the book, Meisel wrote, for Ferns and Ostry's creation "splashed onto this benign scene and mightily disturbed the smooth academic calm."[21]

This wasn't exactly true. But it mattered to commentators in the mid-1970s that they were resurrecting a book that an earlier genera-tion had deemed too risqué. It also mattered that it might have been censored – that the establishment might have tried to hide something from the public. Peter Newman wrote of how *The Age of Mackenzie King* had been "condemned at the time of its initial publication by Canada's academic establishment (who have always shown a penchant for gentility over honesty)." One 1976 letter to the editor announced that he assumed "Liberal (cap L) historians, professional and amateur, would have gone underground at least temporarily after their long-standing Mackenzie King cover-up had been exposed by Col. C.P. Stacey and a few others." A review in *The Liberal* magazine, of all places, wrote of how the new vision of King was so surprising in large part because of the "unimaginative narrowness of ... historians who have long guarded their readers from anything that might suggest hu-manity in their national leaders." Lorimer played up this idea in its own publicity, talking of how the "history establishment" had tried to suppress the *Age of Mackenzie King* when it was first published.[22]

The journalist Heather Robertson wrote a scathing review of Neatby's final volume of the official biography in *Maclean's*. "The contrast between the official biographies of King and C.P. Stacey's lurid revelations in *A Very Double Life* is so startling," she com-plained, "that it's hard to believe they're all writing about the same man." This despite the fact that King's diary had quickly become like a "bible of Canadian history for the period." But it needed good his-torians, unafraid to look straight at the real Mackenzie King, to make it come alive. This just wasn't the case. "No wonder Canadian history is such a bore," she complained. "All the good parts have been left out."[23]

If you're going to blame someone for a cover-up, it helps if you have a small group of conspirators who can easily be singled out. In the case of Mackenzie King's secret life, the culprits were obvious: his literary executors. Their prominent place in the political establishment of post-war Canada made them likely targets. This was especially true of Jack Pickersgill, who was the most publicly visible as a former cabinet minister and someone who was also the literary executor of three Liberal prime ministers. More than anyone, Pickersgill controlled what Canadians could learn about the private lives of leading politicians and the behind-the-scene events of recent politics.

This is the angle that Bernard Ostry and his publisher played up in their publicity. When Ostry appeared on television or on the radio, or when he did interviews for newspapers, he told the story – over and over again – of his encounter with King's literary executors and the Liberal establishment.[24] He recounted how documents were taken from him and then, mysteriously, given back – and how he had to pay a visit to Jack Pickersgill to plead for their return. W. Kaye Lamb, retired in Vancouver, had to defend himself. He happened to be giving a public lecture on the same day that stories appeared in the papers about how Ostry had been denied access to documents at the archives. Lamb conceded that Ostry had been denied access to certain papers, though he explained that this had been a misunderstanding, not a conspiracy. He was also put on the defensive by allegations that the literary executors had not shown MacGregor Dawson the original diary – that they had in fact tailored the diary so that Dawson (and hence the public) saw only doctored parts of it. "That is quite untrue," Lamb said. "The truth is that Dr. Dawson had not the patience to read the whole diary." By this Lamb meant that Dawson had asked to see only "the part [of the diary] that related to public affairs." The news story replayed the funny account of the literary executors' attempt to hush up the spiritualist medium Geraldine Cummins's memoir. Lamb admitted to this, though, on the more recent sensationalistic account of King having solicited the sexual services of prostitutes, he said that the evidence in King's diary did not back it up.[25]

Still, there was only so much that Lamb and the literary executors could do to challenge Ostry's account. On many points, what Ostry said was factually accurate. But the spin that Ostry put on these facts made it look as if the literary executors had been more conniving than they had been – certainly than they had considered themselves. What had changed was the public context in which these stories were recounted. Gone was the deference that Lamb could expect to receive from the press.

Ostry had more than just old stories. He had a whole new scandal to hit the headlines – or, rather, he had new evidence on an explosive old scandal. Late in 1976, after his book came out and after Ostry had been in the headlines, someone approached him – a "deep throat," he called him – and "dropped onto my lap the most compromising material on King yet." In the early 1930s, King went through what he called his "valley of humiliation." It all had to do with his involvement in a corruption scandal concerning the Beauharnois Light, Heat and Power company's bid to develop hydro-electricity along the St Lawrence River. The company had lobbied the government for permission to go ahead and it was clear that much of this lobbying happened unofficially. On such a high-stakes investment, the company was not inclined to take chances and offered a $700,000 donation to the Liberal Party (and, it seemed, to the Conservative Party as well). Liberal Senators Wilfrid McDougald and Andrew Haydon also reportedly enriched themselves personally out of the deal for their help in ensuring the Liberal government's approval of the process. The scandal came to light only in 1931, at a time when King was out of office. It was made more difficult for King personally when it became public that McDougald had paid for part of King's holiday to Bermuda. This wasn't direct evidence that the prime minister had been bribed, but it certainly did not look good.[26]

In 1977 McDougald's niece, Nan Pollitt, gave documents to the Public Archives that included financial records further implicating King in the scandal. She had cheque stubs showing that McDougald had deposited into King's Boston bank account $25,000 in two instalments, one in 1927 and another in 1928. This was at the exact same time that McDougald was helping the company lobby the government for approval of the power development. McDougald's niece reported that her uncle had always claimed he had been a scapegoat, blamed to hide King's involvement in the scandal.[27]

When reporters turned to Ostry for comment, he had a good deal to add. He pointed out that he had been aware of the transactions many years earlier. Another former Liberal senator and fundraiser, Charles Murphy, had written a letter to the editor of the *Ottawa Journal*, Grattan O'Leary, claiming that he had personally delivered money from McDougald to King.[28] Historians like Ramsay Cook and J.L. Granatstein disputed Ostry's claims. They referred to other funds created for political leaders, such as those for Lester Pearson, and argued that in King's case there was no proof of any direct link between the funds and any specific King action. Moreover, as Granatstein put it, "none of this smells very sweet but clearly Mr. King was no better or worse than his successors." To this Ostry responded by saying how dismayed he was "at the unprofessional approach of a historian [like Granatstein] who is capable of equating a fund publicly established toward the end of Lester Pearson's distinguished career ... with the *fact* of laundered funds deposited secretly in a foreign bank to a personal account of a prime minister the details of which are still locked behind closed doors, controlled by his literary executors."[29]

But for Ostry the issue was bigger than a single bribe. King "was on the take until the day he died," is how he put it to one journalist. All one had to do was to think about the whole story of King's life. King went into politics at a young age and as a man of modest means. He spent several years as a deputy minister and then cabinet minister. After several years in private employ, he again re-entered government and spent the rest of his life as prime minister or leader of the Official Opposition. He "died a millionaire." "His estate in Kingsmere, which began as a small cottage, expanded throughout his career in quality and quantity, most often financed by those who heard of his 'needs' and 'interests' and 'difficulties.' His house was filled with expensive gifts while his travels, when not paid for by the public, were financed by his wealthy friends like P.C. Larkin ... So assiduously devoted to his financial 'problems' were his patrons that, clearly, his personal expenses were ever minimal ... Indeed when one considers all the time he spent writing and re-writing his diaries and is witness to the incredible number of personal notes to rich friends thanking them profusely for their generosity, one marvels that he found the time for the politics he carried out with such skill.".30

How could historians like Granatstein turn to King's diary to explain his actions? Why trust King's word over the word of someone still living, or the research of historians like Reg Whitaker who were showing some of the more corrupt fundraising practices of the Liberal Party? More importantly, Ostry wrote, given all of this information about King that had for so long been in the public domain, "serious historians, one would have thought, would try in their analysis to distinguish between what King told himself he was doing, what he did and what he told (or kept secret from) the public about what he was doing. When you do this, you soon recognize that Mackenzie King not only took money but he 'took' the Canadian public."31

That last line appeared in the respectable *Globe and Mail*. In an interview with Vancouver's counter-culture paper the *Georgia Straight*, Ostry was blunter: "It's interesting to know whether King was running out late at night looking for ways of screwing prostitutes," he said, "but I must say that it strikes me ... as far more important for students and the general public to understand the screwing he gave the Canadian people."32

Ostry certainly wrote like this privately back in the 1950s, but the media landscape had changed considerably by the mid-1970s and his language now made for a good story, and good copy. Pickersgill professed ignorance. He defended King by claiming that he had always lived well within his means, rarely spending even his own salary. What use did he have for these funds? Blair Neatby suggested that the money from McDougald seems to have been part of the anonymous fund established by Peter Larkin to help refurbish and maintain Laurier House when Lady Laurier willed it to the leader of the Liberal Party shortly after King became leader.33 But, as even Granatstein admitted, it didn't "smell very sweet."

It all fit into a wider way of thinking about politics in which it increasingly became common to assume that politicians were hiding something about their real selves. This might be evidence of corruption or personal idiosyncrasies and oddities, or the real way in which power worked. By the end of the 1970s, Mackenzie King stood in the public mind – for all of the above reasons – as the prime Canadian historical example of the truth that politicians weren't who they said they were.

A few years later, in the spring of 1981, the Mackenzie King diary yet again made the news, though this time in the context of government secrecy more generally. The Trudeau government was being asked to explain why it had not yet released the government documents concerning the Gouzenko spy trials from 1946. In 1976 the government had refused to open up the documents after the usual thirty-year period had elapsed, and had kept the files secret for ten more years. Under pressure, the Trudeau government agreed to review the files after five years, in 1981. Critics wondered what it was trying to hide. The comments of historian J.L. Granatstein (in his biography of top civil servant and King literary executor Norman Robertson) had made the news in garbled form, with a suggestion that some of the documents were missing. Journalists mixed this up with tales of the missing copy of the Mackenzie King diary that covered the latter months of 1945 and so included some of the Gouzenko period. Would the government release the files? Were some of these documents, including the King diary, missing and why?

The news stories came just as the McDonald Commission into the RCMP Security Service was about to release its final report in May 1981. The federal government had been pushed into creating the commission in 1977 in the maelstrom of controversy over illegal activities conducted by the Security Service that had come out in the Quebec government's Keable Inquiry. The Parti Québécois government of René Lévesque had gleefully helped to expose the RCMP's surveillance of separatist and left-leaning organizations in Quebec. In the national inquiry, from 1977 to 1981, still more attention was focused on the many shady activities that the government's spies had been performing in the name of protecting Canadians from threats to national security. Ultimately, the Commission recommended that the Security Service components of the RCMP be removed from that organization and a separate Canadian Security Intelligence Service (CSIS) be created.

The attack on government secrecy came from critics on both the left and the right. One of the most vociferous was Tom Cossitt, a Conservative MP who had once been a Liberal and who bore a grudge against Pierre Trudeau. Even though he had been a Liberal, Cossitt soon became one of the more right-wing Progressive Conservative MPs, increasingly dissatisfied with the centrist turn of the party under Robert Stanfield and then Joe Clark. Cossitt was one of a new breed of MPs who challenged the typical deference of those in Ottawa for the way the regular game of statesmanship was played. He took the lead in attacking things like the public cost of the prime minister's liquor cabinet and the fund created to build a swimming pool for Trudeau at his home on Sussex Drive. All matters, big and small, deserved and received Cossitt's attention.

It was Cossitt who had helped to publicize Operation Featherbed and the hunt for Soviet moles within the Canadian government. In December 1975 he put a question on the parliamentary order paper about the existence of RCMP files "commonly referred to as 'Featherbed.'" Where were these files? Had the RCMP shown their contents to the CIA or the FBI, and what was the name of the person referred to there?[34] It's not clear who tipped off Cossitt about the existence of Featherbed but he didn't forget it. Over the next decade he would return again and again to questions of national security and what the government and possibly the RCMP were hiding.

Two years later, in November 1977, just as the McDonald Commission on national security was starting its deliberations, Cossitt came back to the question of Featherbed. This time he had allegations to go with the questions. Cossitt alleged that the Featherbed files contained information on prominent members of the press gallery and even top members of the cabinet. Within days, the *Globe and Mail* was reporting that a copy of the Featherbed files had been offered for sale to some media in Toronto for the whopping price tag of $100,000.[35]

The public debate crashed into the RCMP with serious but hard-to-decipher consequences. Internally, one officer was obliged to defend himself against allegations that he had briefed a journalist about Operation Featherbed. On Cossitt, the RCMP thought they knew what they were dealing with. They claimed that, ever since a controversy over his run for the Liberal nomination in his constituency in 1971, Cossitt had borne a deep grudge against Trudeau. Cossitt believed that Trudeau's was one of the names in the Featherbed files. Moreover, he thought the files would reveal facts about Trudeau's alleged homosexual activities. This had been a slow-burning obsession for some

Conservatives despite Trudeau's many public flirtations with women. Even Richard Nixon had thought Trudeau was a homosexual, "all evidence to the contrary," as Henry Kissinger had put it. Cossitt clearly hoped to get any "proof" out into the open.[36]

The issue emerged once again in 1981, and again in connection with questions by Cossitt in the House and revelations made in yet another book. In *Their Trade Is Treachery*, Chapman Pincher made a number of allegations, including that the British spy Roger Hollis had been a double agent, the so-called Fifth Man among the many prominent Soviet moles who had infiltrated the British spy agency MI5. The Canadian connection came in because Hollis had visited Canada in 1945 to interview the defector Igor Gouzenko. Allegedly, Gouzenko had been suspicious of the man, and the suggestion was that Hollis had even then been working for the Soviets. Cossitt used this latest revelation to bring up again the question of the secret documents that the government was keeping from the public. Under pressure, the government once more instructed the RCMP to review the Gouzenko files and then ordered them opened late in 1981. This happened at the same time that Cossitt again demanded to know about the Featherbed files and what the government was hiding. Did the files include revelations about senior government ministers and public servants?[37]

This is when attention turned to the missing volume of Mackenzie King's diary. Journalists wondered why it had gone missing. Charlie Greenwell from CJOH News raised the question that the RCMP had also been asking: "Is there something in the missing entries someone still living doesn't want the rest of us to know about?" Greenwell quoted unnamed "espionage specialists" who claimed that, with "so many people close to KING ... involved with the RUSSIANS," it would "indeed have been advantagous [sic] for those individuals to remove potentially embarrassing documents from public view. One way to do that would be to have portions of the diary mysteriously disappear before it reached the archives." This left the government and the archives with the duty of explaining away the gaps.[38]

The national archivist (and King literary executor), Wilfrid Smith, explained to the press that the missing volume of the diary was never received by the archives – though in truth he couldn't have been certain about this. Within the government, the solicitor general asked

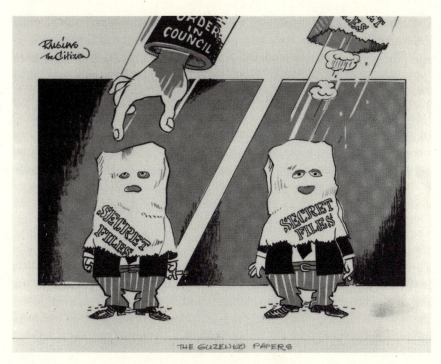

17.1 Gouzenko Papers Cartoon

the RCMP for an explanation.[39] Eventually, he reported the same thing as the archivist, and also claimed that there had been a special copy of the King diary dealing with the Gouzenko case and that it was still in the archives' possession. Meanwhile, the Security Service agents were forced to learn again what they did and didn't know. Institutional memory seemed short-lived and the agents tried to figure out which documents the press could be referring to and which volumes of the King diary were and weren't missing.

In this confused mishmash of documents that were or weren't missing, or secrets kept or lost or stolen, Mackenzie King and his diary were bit players, symbols of secrecy writ large. Yet behind all of the back and forth could be felt a general sense of government secrecy as both an expectation and a problem. They were hiding something. The idea of an excerpted version of the Mackenzie King diary that could count as the official "record" now seemed both quaint and preposterous. Official histories were little more than attempts to brainwash the public into believing an acceptable version of events. The controversy that had quashed Ferns and Ostry's book back in the 1950s was the new normal. In the midst of the annual release of new versions of the King diary (what *Maclean's* magazine called "Mackenzie King's annual, posthumous striptease"), and with the backdrop of Watergate and the McDonald Commission's revelations of RCMP dirty tactics, journalists could easily write about the "laundered version of the diaries," about King's "double life," and especially about the petty things done by someone who was ostensibly supposed to be a great public figure.[40]

There were still some who could argue that no one could fool the people for so long. But this old chestnut now vied for supremacy with a new common sense – certainly an idea that had gained a greater respectability in the way in which people talked about politics – that politicians were always trying to fool the people. And one thing was clear: the people would be fooled no longer.

In the end, Mackenzie King kept a few secrets. In releasing his diary to the public, King's literary executors believed they were doing what was best. After the passage of time, after the other revelations of King's private life that had already come out, and after the nightmare of the stolen copies of the diary, it seemed to them that ensuring the public could see the whole of King's diary was the best way of to preserve his memory.

This didn't mean that they would let the public see everything. Some documents, including the papers outlining in greater detail his interest in spiritualism, and his financial records, they kept restricted for several more decades into the next century. One set of documents, though, they destroyed. These were the set of binders that contained King's extensive personal notes about his spiritualistic activities, including handwritten transcriptions of some seances. Some of this material, but not all, had already showed up in the released portions of the diary. Other material could be found in his correspondence with mediums that would be opened in later years. But, when the literary executors met on Christmas Eve in 1971 and decided to open up the diary, they promised themselves that they would destroy these binders.

They would wait until Blair Neatby finished with his final volume of the official biography. And then they would be destroyed.

In March 1977 that is exactly what happened. Two of the literary executors, Gordon Robertson and Jack Pickersgill, made themselves a fire. It had been twenty-seven years since the literary executors had taken on their duties. Two of the original literary executors – Fred McGregor and Norman Robertson – had died in the intervening period and been replaced. No one had expected to carry out their duties to King for so long. But, on that day, they carried out one final obligation. The myths and mystifications of Weird Willie King were everywhere about them. Each year saw a new batch of Weird Willie stories with the release of yet another volume of the King diary. Novelists and poets, to say nothing of bemused history professors and journalists, had turned King into a subject of amusing asides and anecdotes. Even so, and perhaps partly as a result, Robertson and Pickersgill dropped the spiritualism binders into the fire. These, at least, would not be fodder for public controversy. In some small way, they had kept their promise to the old chief.[41]

The Greatest Prime Minister?

By the early 1980s, Mackenzie King lived the afterlife of a palimpsest, those ancient documents whose original words had been erased so that something new could be rewritten over the top. Yet the original wording still revealed itself, ghostly scratchings under the surface, a text that was always double. So it was with King's afterlife – Weird Willie and the statesman, a double life seen together and not separately. What had changed was that, by the end of the 1970s, Canadians had become fascinated with the hidden stories of official life, the truths previously hidden. For Mackenzie King, this meant that Weird Willie was every bit as much a part of the meaning of Mackenzie King as his public record. The real Mackenzie King was there, exposed, if difficult to render comprehensible with all his complexity and contradictions.

The figure of Weird Willie King popped up across the Canadian cultural landscape in novels and poetry and film. In Mordecai Richler's 1980 novel *Joshua Then and Now*, there is the "Mackenzie King Memorial Society," an organization founded by the main character and his Jewish friends as a send-up of the hypocrisy and bunk of official life. Allan Stratton's play *Rexy!* premiered in 1981, winning many awards. Most of the humour in *Rexy!* arises from the irreverent portrayal of King's pettiness, massive ego, eccentricities, and self-serving delusions. It still has King at the height of his power in the Second World War and making tough decisions, but there is always the striking contrast between the petty man and his large role.

In 1983 the journalist Heather Robertson gave Canadians perhaps the wackiest version of Mackenzie King when she published *Willie*, the first of a trilogy of novels about the King years. The book was inspired by the fantastic fictionalization of real historic figures in

E.L. Doctorow's *Ragtime*. In *Willie* Robertson has Mackenzie King marking his place in his Bible with a pair of women's panties and even raping the book's main female character. Reviewers revelled in what they repeatedly called the book's "irreverence." *Willie* became a best-seller and award-winning novel, even beating out works by literary giants like Morley Callaghan and Margaret Atwood. Robertson herself talked about how cathartic the writing process had been – to get out fully what she wanted to say. At first, the writing proved difficult, but eventually Robertson let herself go. "My moment of liberation as a fiction writer came," she recalled, "when I sat down at my typewriter and wrote 'The Red Cross sucks cock.'" Apparently that was enough. "To get that out of my Wasp Presbyterian subconscious was totally liberating," Robertson recalled. "After that the novel took off."[1]

There were other appearances of Weird Willie King, including in his very own CBC television mini-series directed by the Canadian cinematic great Donald Brittain. And then there was, of course, Dennis Lee's subtly small entry in his famous book of children's poems, *Alligator Pie*, where Lee writes of how the former prime minister "Sat in the middle and played with string" and "Loved his mother like anything." Brief and to the point. It encapsulated the way King had become a cultural metaphor in himself. He stood for a way of looking at prime ministers and public figures on an ever more level field, and in a less deferential fashion.[2]

A funny thing happened on the way to the 1990s: Mackenzie King's reputation was resuscitated. Commentators began speaking again of Mackenzie King as one of Canada's greatest prime ministers, as if the whole fuss over his private life had been a bad dream. In 1997 *Maclean's* magazine ranked William Lyon Mackenzie King as Canada's "greatest prime minister." Two senior political historians, Norman Hillmer and J.L. Granatstein, had asked experts to rank all the prime ministers on a scale of 0 to 10 – "from utter failure to greatness." It was no surprise that John A. Macdonald and Wilfrid Laurier ranked among the "greats" in the top three. But the fact that King took top spot might have raised eyebrows. Hillmer and Granatstein acknowledged that "this [ranking] might surprise those who know nothing of King beyond Dennis Lee's little poem," yet they went on to say that "the historians ... were more impressed by King's great political skills, his devotion to unity, his establishment of Canada's international persona, his crucial steps towards establishment of the social welfare safety net, and the brilliant way he ran Canada's enormous war effort. No historians admired King as a man ... but few denied his brilliance as a political leader."[3] It was as if Bruce Hutchison had been resurrected and made a professor of political history.

Weird Willie and all his antics didn't disappear. Commentators simply turned down the volume, and different voices rose up to offer once again a version of Mackenzie King as a political actor and prime minister. Hillmer and Granatstein argued that "the trick in politics is to survive. Without that, there can be nothing, no argument the people are on side, no scope for action, and no lasting impression." And, as his twenty-two years in power demonstrated, "King was the master survivor of Canadian politics."[4] Like the King-friendly writers of the 1950s, they admitted King's personal inadequacy. "Up close, King's actions – and King himself – were often unimpressive," wrote Hillmer and Granatstein. "With perspective and time, however, the grand pattern emerges: Mackenzie King was Canada's greatest prime minister, party leader, and politician." They celebrated the fact that the pendulum of opinion had now swung back in King's favour. After all, they wrote: "No one can rule a nation as disparate as Canada for so long without talents of a high order, and King's place at last is being properly recognized."[5] It wasn't quite the same wording as Grant Dexter's "No one could fool the people so long," but it was pretty close.

This wasn't, though, a return to the 1950s. Context matters. In the 1990s, the King legacy looked better and better. French–English relations had reached an all-time low with the rise of the Bloc Québécois and the failure of Meech Lake and Charlottetown accords. There was also the national hangover from decades of what some had come to see as too-ambitious prime ministers, Pierre Trudeau and Brian Mulroney. In ranking the prime ministers and assessing leadership, Hillmer and Granatsein and their experts warned of the dangers of being too decisive. For decisiveness was "not always its own reward, nor suited to a cautious and conservative people." They asked instead if it wasn't "better to govern as Mackenzie King did, piling compromise on hesitation in this all too easily divided country." It seemed, with Jean Chrétien as prime minister in the 1990s, that the country had returned to more successful, older ways. "Cautious and conservative by temperament and experience," they wrote, "Chrétien embraced the King philosophy of governing from the middle, day by day, avoiding the hard choices whenever possible, making the deals when necessary."[6]

A few years earlier, the historian Michael Bliss had taken his turn to debunk the myth of Weird Willie. In his best-selling book on Canada's prime ministers, *Right Honourable Men*, Bliss complained that "my late colleague Colonel C.P. Stacey did a shabby thing to Mackenzie King, the greatest and most interesting of Canada's prime ministers." The image of Weird Willie that Stacey had propagated in *A Very Double Life* had corrupted Canadians views. "For years," Bliss wrote, "it was the first book about King that curious Canadians were apt to pick up. It had immense impact in further vulgarizing" King's image.[7] This simply wasn't deserved.

"So what if [King] had been lecherous, silly, or immature in private?" Bliss asked. "No one, including Stacey, had shown that these activities had the slightest effect on King's conduct of government." And, as for King's sexual proclivities, "So what if he sowed wild oats in his youth (if he actually did), had lady friends in old age, and became superstitious, self-absorbed, and maudlin about his dogs? Does not our tolerant age understand the normality of a little harmless deviance?" King's spiritualism may have been odd – "there was always a silly, fraudulent side to organized spiritualism" – but "there was also a serious interest in life after death, psychic powers, and the possibility of spiritual communications."[8] Bliss quoted Harry Ferns, who himself had been a King critic, but not of his personal life: "It will take a long time to rescue the reputation of Mackenzie King from the psychologists and the pornographers." Much of the speculation about King's oddities "is at best half true," Bliss argued. Directly taking on the double-life argument, Bliss claimed that "the King diaries are not the record of a public success and a private failure. King's life is not a Jekyll-and-Hyde epic. Carefully read, his public and private records portray an extraordinarily gifted and sensitive man, the product of a certain moment in cultural history, who dedicated his life to public service and succeeded beyond even his own ambitious dreams. Willie King did a good job both as a politician and as a human being."[9]

The psychologists and the pornographers: it's not a coincidence that these were the terms of Ferns and Bliss. For who better to represent the cultural opening up of previous secrets that had been so much at the centre of cultural change over the 1960s and 1970s than those who delved into the minds and sex lives of Canadians? The difference was that, in the mid-1990s, Bliss lived in a world that was no longer as easily titillated by King's secrets. The very fact of a politician's double life – and to write about it in mainstream publications – no longer seemed so novel. In fact, a more cynical public culture would take a politician's duplicity for granted.

Mackenzie King had served his purpose. When he again excited public discussion it came in new areas – in the role he had played in denying entry to Jewish refugees at the end of the 1930s or in the treatment of Japanese Canadians in the Second World War. When *Maclean's* published another ranking of prime ministers in 2016, William Lyon Mackenzie King once again earned the top spot. This time, it was John A. Macdonald who had fallen several spots because of controversy over his treatment of indigenous peoples.[10] History is never finished with its main characters – it is only the questions and passions that change from one generation to the next.[11]

But for over thirty years, from the 1950s to the 1980s, Mackenzie King had symbolized an older kind of Canada. He played a role in helping later generations of Canadians reorient themselves away from the values of their Victorian forebears and to create a new culture of the self and individual rights. Partly this had been about private actions and cultural values. But these transformations also impinged on the way politicians were talked about. At the height of the Weird Willie craze in the mid-1970s, it had seemed almost utopian and certainly liberating to expose the dark secrets of figures like King and of the inner workings of official institutions and "The Establishment." King became a symbol of an older Canada and of a kind of culture and politics that had secrets. And he did so just as the culture at large – in Canada but not only in Canada – became obsessed with turning the inside out, with exposing secrets, with overturning standards of decency and respectability, with making open and obvious what had previously been considered private and secret.

Two decades later, the utopian hopes had faded. The genie was not being put back into the bottle. It was much harder to write, as some had in the 1950s, about the greatness of political leaders.[12] The idea of the statesman (or stateswoman) seemed an ever more elusive ideal. The democratic levelling continued apace. On Canadian television screens, the *Royal Canadian Air Farce* launched a "chicken cannon" that shot a gross mixture of concoctions at the images of prominent figures. No one could get so high that they couldn't be taken down a notch. But few cared. Revelations had become so standard and routine, especially in the much-watched world of American politics. The 1990s saw another American president's secret activities become fodder for a continuous news cycle – this time concerning Bill Clinton's relations with a female intern. Once again sexual secrets and political secrets – the personal and the political – tumbled together on news channels across the world.

All of this had simply become common gossip – fascinating in detail but no longer amazing in what it said about the state of modern politics. The expectation that politics and politicians generally could be something else had diminished. For good and ill, Canadians lived in an irreverent democracy.

Conclusion

We don't much admire politicians these days. In lists of professions Canadians trust the most and least, politicians scrape the bottom, only barely above used-car salespeople.[1] The talking heads on our television screens regularly provide certain kinds of explanations for these problems with our democracy. If only the Senate wasn't such an affront to democratic sensibilities. If only our parliamentarians could debate seriously and effectively the issues in Question Period. If only the Prime Minister's Office wasn't so secretive and all-controlling. All of these criticisms have merit.[2] What they don't do, however, is explain how we got here. The Senate, after all, has always been an undemocratic institution. Question Period has often been a raucous affair and the laments about the lack of good debate in the House of Commons go back at least to Confederation. The Prime Minister's Office has gained power, though in other ways, especially with the advent of public-opinion polling, the popular check on the executive is still strong. There are, in other words, many faults with our current political system. But they tend to be more of a constant than a new development.

Writing in the early 1990s, the political scientist Neil Nevitte traced a decline in deference toward a host of different kinds of social institutions and sources of authority. He was writing about the 1980s and he linked this with the rise of "post-materialistic" values and tentatively connected it to what has come to be called the "democratic deficit" of modern Western polities. There is much disagreement among political scientists about how extensive the democratic deficit really is and what it means. The trajectory of the story about Mackenzie King's secret life suggests that the kinds of changes Nevitte was finding in the 1980s were part of a longer-term trend in Canada's political culture. This book has been a kind of historical case study of the decline of deference, looking not to politics as a whole but to one political figure and how Canadians came to speak in ever less deferential fashion about him in public. Unlike the political scientists who draw on the World Values Survey, the analysis here has looked farther back in time than this data allows and examined not individual-opinion data but the language of public speech.[3]

What the strange case of Weird Willie Mackenzie King has offered us is a different way of explaining the origins of this problem. If we have broken up with our politicians in recent decades, it might be worth taking seriously that clichéd break-up line from the world of romance: "It's not you, it's me." In the case of Canadians and their politicians, it would seem to have some bearing. It's not them, it's us.

Canadians looked at King differently in the 1970s and 1980s because they understood themselves differently. Between King's death in 1950 and the height of the Weird Willie phenomenon in the 1970s, a rising tide of individualism and individual rights, as well as a new notions of truth rooted in personal authenticity, revolutionized Canadian culture. The arch of this book has spanned the gulf between these two Canadas, the country of Mackenzie King and that of the late twentieth century. The argument has been that, to make sense of how King came to be so exposed as "Weird Willie" in these later decades, we must come to grips with how this culture of individual rights and the authentic self transformed the way Canadians talked not only about themselves but also about everything from traditional institutions like churches and schools to the intimate touching of men and women, and what could be publicly spoken about the secrets of each. There was, to borrow Daniel Rodgers's term, a "contagion of metaphors" wherein the language of authenticity and openness moved from one space to another – from psychiatry to family life to politics and back again.

One of the key tasks of this book has been to note where the contagion spread – showing up the parallels between the rise of this more open culture of the self and the rise of a less deferential attitude toward political authority more generally. Historians can rarely offer certainties. We are better with correlations than causation. We can detect the patterns and similarities across different contexts that seem clearer in hindsight. So it is with this book. Its primary goal has been to reveal the shared language of the self and exposure, of authenticity and the attack on secrecy, that proliferated across Canadian culture – in discussions of traditional politics as much as in discussions of sex or sin or neuroses.

What we see over the course of the years from 1950 to the early 1980s is what could best be described as a long continuous striptease. Year by year, as the evening lengthened and inhibitions diminished, Canadians dared themselves to go further. They stripped Mackenzie King of his garments again and again, peeking to see what he had really been like, even when there was little new information or none at all. What was revealed didn't matter so much as the act of revealing itself. Broader cultural changes increasingly allowed and even demanded a closer exploration of what had been sort-of hidden.

Look at what this man had been. Our most successful prime minister was really just as petty, small, and odd as anyone else – and everyone had their secrets, about which there was no need for shame. Certainly, there were debates about the merits of gossip. Some fretted about the "airing of dirty laundry." But, as the 1950s turned into the 1960s and especially as the 1960s gave way to the 1970s, those who fretted about such things came to seem as old-fashioned as the clichés they invoked.[4] In other words, when Canadians learned that their very own Mackenzie King seemed to have visited prostitutes, it fit right into the ethos of the age. Weird Willie King may have been prime minister in the first half of the twentieth century, but he seemed to be reincarnated as a figure who very much fit into these later decades. Even a fairly safe and respected scholar like C.P. Stacey could be found writing the tell-all book about Mackenzie King's "double life." Politicians led double lives. Everyone knew this from the Watergate scandal. They also knew it because the stories about Mackenzie King confirmed what they already believed. The revelations about King did not cause these changes, but they do serve as a poignant example of the changed cultural context.

To be sure, King was not alone in facing a new level of scrutiny. Other prime ministers shared the same fate. In 1964 newly opened documents at Canada's national archives suggested that former prime minister Sir Wilfrid Laurier, the man in whose home King lived, might have had a mistress. This had not shown up in earlier biographies of the country's first French Canadian prime minister but one historian revealed a new stash of letters between Laurier and the woman who was said to be his love interest. John A. Macdonald received his own newly personal treatment. It had always been known that John A. had been a heavy drinker. During Macdonald's life George Brown's *Globe* newspaper had tried to make use of this for political gain. Yet by and large the attempt to discredit failed, in part because the attacks were considered to be in bad taste. While historians had not explicitly hidden Macdonald's drinking problem, they hadn't emphasized it either. Donald Creighton's two-volume biography of Macdonald in the 1950s artfully recreated some scenes of drunkenness but the overall effect was muted, with references to Macdonald's "lapses" and periods where he was too ill or out of sorts to be effective. Beginning in the 1970s, though, John A. as the drunk prime minister increasingly became an amusing cultural motif. And, of course, the then current Canadian prime minister, Pierre Trudeau, had his personal life splashed across front pages as never before – both his wooing of Maggie Sinclair and then their marriage and eventual divorce. There is some evidence that his personal travails actually garnered him sympathy among voters, yet the overall coverage of his personal life reflected the changed media and cultural landscape of the 1970s.[5]

The decline of deference has posed particular problems for a perennial question in democratic leadership: What does the choice of a certain kind of leader say about the people of a country? In 1952 a reviewer of Bruce Hutchison's *Incredible Canadian* candidly explained why it would be so hard for Canadians to accept that Mackenzie King really had been the feeble excuse for a man that Hutchison presented. "Maybe King was not a great man," the reviewer admitted, "yet we must believe he was, else for thirty years Canada in her greater days was led by an inferior person; this is impossible to suppose unless we admit that Canadians are inferior people."[6]

By the late twentieth century, Canadians were much less likely to give a political leader the benefit of the doubt. Moreover, in a culture in which truth is about being true to oneself and yet there are so many different selves, so many different citizens, how could any political leader really represent the people? And when politicians need to represent so many people at the same time, how can they seem anything other than inauthentic? The problem is more broadly about a crisis in representative democracies in countries where an individualized culture of rights and the authentic self has become predominant. The story of Mackenzie King's secret life doesn't tell us what to do in the future. It does, though, suggest how we came to be where we are.

There are many examples where this question has reappeared in pressing circumstances in the ensuring years. This includes the embarrassing case of Toronto mayor Rob Ford, whose crack-smoking habit and problem-drinking – as well as his befuddled attempts to minimize the issue – became rich material for comedians around the world in 2013 and 2014. Many Torontonians and Canadians were left to puzzle how Ford could have been elected. Similarly, in 2016 the business tycoon and reality TV star Donald Trump was elected president of the United States. While Trump's unfiltered rants and attacks attracted many people who clearly saw a leader unlike any who had come before, his success also prompted many others to ask the same question: If we chose him, what does this say about us? The conundrum is an old one but the rise of a culture of authenticity and individual rights makes it more pressing. For these kinds of figures have come to seem compelling because they are so authentic – true to themselves if not to the standards of decency of large sections of the electorate.

Yet how can anyone really complain? When truth resides in the self – when being true to yourself is the highest standard of morality – how can we be surprised that authenticity is occasionally not very pretty? In the 1960s and 1970s, a generation of Canadians were trying to disentangle themselves from the Victorian morality of an earlier era. The arguments in favour of fully expressing the self seemed liberating. The same was true for those who pushed for protection of individual rights, regardless of the individual, against any kind of discrimination. To liberate and expose the self for what it was – and to value the authentic self for what it really was – went hand in hand with undermining the secrecy and deference that had gone along with political authority.

Yet, in the twenty-first century, the triumph of a culture of the self forces a reinterpretation of that age-old question of democracy – what does *this* leader say about us? It isn't so much now what is hidden that matters. It isn't a problem of hypocrisy that disquiets. It is, instead, that authenticity might not be so liberating after all.

Postscript

What happened to the missing volume of Mackenzie King's diary – the one covering the final months of 1945? It has never been found. As late as the mid-1980s, the Mounties were still searching. They seemed to consider the possibility that Donald Forster, the political scientist who assisted Pickersgill with *The Mackenzie King Record*, had some involvement in its disappearance. When Forster died in 1983, the Mounties kept a clipping of the obituary and underlined the section where it mentioned Forster's role in *The Mackenzie King Record*. A likely assumption is that the Mounties were at least curious about Forster, although all of the blanked-out pages in the Security Service records make this only speculation. The granddaughter of Fred McGregor, Mackenzie King's assistant and literary executor, recalls that in the mid-1980s her parents received a visit from CSIS agents, who questioned them about the diary.[1]

In 1985 someone in CSIS wrote a memo outlining three possible scenarios for what happened to the diary: (1) theft by the Russian Intelligence Service, (2) theft by someone like a chauffeur, stenographer, and so on; or (3) destruction by King himself. The agent went through each of the three scenarios, finding problems with each. If the RIS took the diary, why not also take the earlier volume that also dealt with Gouzenko? The agent also didn't think it made sense for King to have destroyed it, though this is what the political scientist Reg Whitaker had suggested in a *Toronto Star* article (which, as ever, the Security Service had clipped and put in the Featherbed files). The agent thought that this possibility didn't fit King's psychological profile or mentality. The only option the agent didn't seriously discount was theft by someone like a "cook, butler, maid, chauffeur, literary executor, secretary, CBC crew member, etc." With a list like that, it became a real-life version of the board-game Clue.[2]

It is almost impossible to say anything definitive at this point. But a few conjectures can be offered. The first odd point about the missing King diary is that it simply isn't mentioned at all in the papers of King's literary executors until a 1969 meeting with the RCMP. Publicly, it was first mentioned only when Pickersgill and Forster published (in January 1970) the third volume of *The Mackenzie King Record*, which included the 1945 diary.[3] For almost twenty years, the literary executors conversed with each other and debated what to do with the diary but without ever putting in writing anything about a missing volume.

Pickersgill claimed to have done a thorough search of Laurier House after King died, looking for the missing volume. This may very well have happened but there is no record of it. The Security Service tried to determine if the RCMP had been involved in the search for the diary, but it seemed to be mistaking this search with the Daviault investigation in 1955. When the RCMP interviewed Edouard Handy, King's assistant, he claimed that the missing volume was there when he left Laurier House in 1955. So, in other words, his story and Pickersgill's don't match. Could Jack Pickersgill have taken the volume himself? There is no record that the RCMP ever suspected that he did. But it remains one possibility. Another is that Donald Forster, who worked on the diaries so closely in the 1960s, took it.

But there is one other possibility that seems more likely. In 1955, when the literary executors discovered that someone had made copies of King's diary and sold them, they began an investigation of where all of the diary books were at that point. They drew up a list of the books that had been copied. The list begins with the 1938 diary and then moves steadily forward in chronological fashion. The last volumes on the list are the diary books up to 9 November 1945 – in other words, right up until the period where the diary is missing.[4] These were the last volumes copied before the literary executors began looking into Daviault's activities.

This could very well be a coincidence. But it is striking that the next volume to be copied by Daviault, just at the moment where the literary executors learned of his deception, is the very one that was later reported to be missing. There is no record at this point in the files of that volume going missing. But one wonders. The literary executors tried to keep the whole matter confidential. They didn't tell anyone else in the archives and only very belatedly went to the RCMP to launch an official investigation. In the climate of the 1950s, and especially around these kinds of people, controversy was to be avoided at all costs. What could be more controversial than a lost or stolen diary? If Daviault had taken it, and they and the RCMP could not prove that it was missing, perhaps they decided that it was best to keep the whole matter quiet, not to admit to the problem. Doing otherwise would add weight to the fear expressed about what Daviault might do with any copies of the diary that hadn't been recovered. If he had a copy of the diary for which the executors didn't have the original – the missing diary from late 1945 – then the possibility of what Daviault could have done with this would seem even more ominous. It would only have underlined further the need to preserve the whole diary and not destroy it, which King's will seemed to indicate is what he wanted.

Of course, this can only be speculation, guided by a few bits of evidence. But it is at least as well substantiated as any theory that the Security Service proposed. Until this missing volume of the diary is found (if it ever will be), Mackenzie King still has a few more secrets to reveal.

Notes

PREFACE

1 Of course, as E.H. Carr pointed out eloquently half a century ago in *What Is History?* the historians' "facts" are already preselected at numerous stages and the writing of any kind of history, narrative or otherwise, is really a conversation between the historian and these facts, between the historian and the many versions of the past that one wants to, but never will, know.

2 This is best noted in Jenkins, *On "What Is History?"*

3 Although it is about fiction, James Wood's defence of the realist novel seems most pertinent to a similar defence of narrative history. Wood, *How Fiction Works*. Also useful is Pyne, *Voice & Vision*.

4 Alan Gordon, *The Hero and the Historians*, 189. See also other important Canadian contributions, including Morgan, *Creating Colonial Pasts*; Coates and Morgan, *Representations of Madeleine de Verchères and Laura Secord*; and Pope, *The Many Landfalls of John Cabot*. Key international works in this field include Nora, *Les lieux de mémoires*; Lowenthal, *Possessed by the Past*; Halbwachs, *On Collective Memory*; and Glassbert, *Sense of History*. The key difference between King and the many figures given this kind of historiographical treatment in these works is that King came to be a kind of anti-hero. He was useful not so much to nationalists but to other figures who wanted to change the attitudes toward political figures. In other words, he came to be used and memorialized (just as other so-called heroes were) but he was given a different kind of treatment by those who wanted a less reverent, more egalitarian politics. While the politics of commemoration often interrogates nationalist heroes, King's memorializations in the 1970s especially show that a more irreverent anti-memorialization was also tied to the growing common sense and ethos of the age.

5 Lara Campbell and Dominique Clément, "Introduction: Time, Age, Myth: Towards a History of the Sixties," in Campbell, Clément, and Gregory S. Kealey, eds., *Debating Dissent*, 18. See also Magda Fahrni and Robert Rutherdale, "Introduction," in Fahrni and Rutherdale, eds., *Creating Postwar Canada*.

6 Gidney and Dawson, "Persistence and Inheritance," 47–74; and Mount, "The Doctrine of Unripe Time."

7 For examples of these kinds of approaches in the Canadian context, see Palmer, *Canada's 1960s*; and Kostash, *Long Way from Home*.

8 Borstelmann, *The 1970s*, 3. Bailey and Farber make a similar comment in the introduction to their edited collection *America in the 70s*, 2, arguing that "it was during the 1970s that the results of the major social movements of the previous two decades became concrete in American communities and in Americans' daily lives." See also Binkley, *Getting Loose*.

9 The "thinning out" line is from Rodgers, *Age of Fracture*, 3.

10 On the effect of neo-liberalism at the national level in Canada, John English's second volume of his Pierre Trudeau biography shows the way in which the prime minister tried to steer his own course among the intellectual debates of the time. See English, *Just Watch Me*, various pages but esp. 271–3 and 290–9.

11 Borstelman, *The 1970s*, 4. Owram's history of the Baby Boom generation covers the impact of these economic and life-cycle changes on the era's declining radicalism. Yet even Owram is alive to the "fundamental shift" that had occurred between the Second World War and the 1970s and that was not reversed – the transformed view of authority, and the idea that, when social norms or institutions conflicted with individual needs, it was the society that would increasingly be expected to change. Owram, *Born at the Right Time*, 314–15.

12 Rodgers, *Age of Fracture*, 3, 8.

13 Himmelfarb, *The De-Moralization of Society*; Collier, *The Rise of Selfishness in America*, 4; Fukuyama, *The Great Disruption*; and Nolan, *The Therapeutic State*.

14 One searches in vain, for example, to find any Canadian historians interested in the work of Brian Lee Crowley, who, in a Canadian context, offers a conservative interpretation of the rise of the welfare state. See Crowley, *Fearful Symmetry*. I am not endorsing Crowley's analysis, but the absence of these perspectives from historical debate is striking. So is the historical profession's reaction to certain moves on the part of the government of Stephen Harper to engage with history – including the new citizenship guide *Discover Canada*, the commemorations of the War of 1812, and the renaming (and repurposing) of the Museum of Civilization as the Museum of Canadian History. In a roundtable involving sixteen different historians and political scientists, not a single conservative perspective was given, with almost every scholar (aside from Adam Chapnick and Jocelyn Létourneau) denouncing the government's actions. See "Forum: History under Harper." Although one could offer many suggestions for improvement to the Harper government's citizenship guide, the alternative offered by these academics was even more partisan and unbalanced. See Jones and Perry, *The People's Citizenship Guide*. See also Chapnick, "A 'Conservative' National Story?"

15 I have written on this in greater detail elsewhere: Dummitt, "The 'Taint of Self'"; and "Mackenzie King Wasn't a Libertarian: Drug History and the Forgotten Sixties." For the examples in this paragraph, see (on drugs) Martel, *Not This Time*; (on censorship) Jochelson and Kramar, *Sex and the Supreme Court*; and (on sexuality) Kinsman and Gentile, *The Canadian War on Queers*. In his history of morality and vice in Canada, Marcel Martel reflects this general tendency to avoid giving the larger picture and to refuse to characterize overall change while instead simply speaking of shifts in regulation. See Martel, *Canada the Good*.

16 Charles Taylor, *Sources of the Self*; and Taylor, *The Malaise of Modernity*. On the culture of authenticity see also Potter, *The Authenticity Hoax*.

CHAPTER ONE

1 For views of King ahead of the "Weird Willie" phenomenon, see the various memorial pieces published at the time of his death, the best of which were Frank H. Underhill, "Concerning Mr. King," *Canadian Forum* 30 (September 1950), 121–2, 125–7; Blair Fraser, "Mackenzie King as I Knew Him," *Maclean's* (1 September 1950), 7–8, 52–4; and Arthur Lower, "Mr. King," *Canadian Banker* 57 (autumn 1950): 46–53. See also the first volume of the official biography, Dawson, *William Lyon Mackenzie King: A Political Biography*. More generally on King, the best single reference, though dated, remains Henderson, *W.L. Mackenzie King*.

2 The media hoopla of that year coalesced around the publication of Stacey, *A Very Double Life*, but there were many other manifestations, including the republication of a book that had been controversial in 1955 and now gained notoriety because of the earlier controversy: Ferns and Ostry, *The Age of Mackenzie King*. Even the volume of the official biography that was published that year devoted significant attention to making sense of King's particularities: H.B. Neatby, *William Lyon Mackenzie King, Volume III, 1932–1939*. The beginning of the year saw what was becoming an annual series of stories revolving around the revelations in King's diary. In January and February 1976, the *Globe and Mail* devoted many different letters and articles to the question of whether Mackenzie King had been bribed and whether King's literary executors had hidden key details of King's life from the public. See, for example, Peter Newman, "The Nobility of Sailor Jack's Last Career – Literary Chamberlain, History's Guardian," *Globe and Mail*, 17 January 1976; J.L. Granatstein, "Was King Really Bribed? Diaries Cast Doubt on It," *Globe and Mail*, 18 January 1976; and letters to the editor from Ramsay Cook (21 January and 13 February 1976), H.B. Neatby (29 January 1976), the national archivist W.I. Smith (9 February 1976), Peter C. Newman (10 and 14 February 1976), Robert Bothwell (17 February 1976), and Donald Creighton (28 February 1976). In the midst of the many reviews and discussion panels on television, on radio, and in the newspapers of Stacey's book and also those of

Neatby and Ferns and Ostry, the focus remained on what King had hidden from the public.

3 His niece, the historian Jennifer Brown, recalled "his restraint, decorum, and gentlemanly ways." She said, "Civility and circumspection always prevailed in him, it seemed, as did an Irish Protestant (or Anglo-Ontario) restraint." Jennifer S.H. Brown, "Some Memories of My Uncle, Charles Perry Stacey," 1 March 1990, University of Toronto Archives (hereafter UTA), B94-0014 (Stacey Family Papers), box 1, file 7. Desmond Morton also recalled that Stacey had been "firm in the Victorian tory values he had inherited as a Toronto doctor's son," though he also said that Stacey had been able to communicate well with the younger generation as he aged. Desmond Morton, "Obituary: Charles Perry Stacey, 1905–1989," *Books in Canada* (n.d.), UTA, B94-0014, box 1, file 7. See also Stacey, *A Date with History*.

4 On the culture of exposé and the way in which what had once been private was coming out into the open, see Borstelmann, *The 1970s*, chapter 1; and Jenkins, *Decade of Nightmares*, chapters 1 and 2. On changing notions of obscenity, see Collier, *The Rise of Selfishness in America*, chapter 15.

5 Stories of King's spiritualism started appearing only weeks after his death in 1950 but initially only in spiritualist papers: J.B. McIndoe, "Mackenzie King a Spiritualist," *Psychic News*, 12 August 1950, in William Lyon Mackenzie King Papers [hereafter WLMK], Papers of the Literary Executors [hereafter Lit. Execs.], MG26, J17, vol. 4, file "clippings"; and "Mackenzie King Paid a Great Tribute to Famous Medium," *Psychic World*, 21 September 1950, 2. One story was then picked up and republished in Canada by the *Ottawa Citizen*: Fred Archer, "WLMK: Spiritualist," *Ottawa Citizen*, 10 October 1950. Other publications eventually also printed details, including the *Calgary Herald*, the *Victoria Times*, and *Time* magazine.

6 Stacey made this case in his book and in several addresses. The words here are drawn from Charles Perry Stacey, "Mackenzie King and His Friends" [public address, UBC, 14 February 1975], UTA, B90-0020, box 46, 1975-02-14.

7 See the section on "Strolls in the Sub-World" in Stacey, *A Very Double Life*. It should be pointed out that other historians at the time and since have questioned Stacey's interpretation of the diary evidence as it relates to King's relations with prostitutes. Certainly, the version in the official biography did not give King's relations this interpretation: Dawson, *William Lyon Mackenzie King*, 39. Michael Bliss offered a counter-interpretation, reading the diary notations as, at most, coded references to masturbation: Bliss, *Right Honourable Men*, 131–2.

8 *A Very Double Life* was first published as extracts in leading Canadian papers across the country, guaranteeing that its readership was much higher than its book sales alone would suggest. The book itself spent sixteen weeks on the best-seller lists from April through July 1976. See clippings in UTA, B90-0020, box 56, "AVDL Letters, etc. 1976-78."

9 Indeed, the *Times* of London correspondent in Ottawa, John Stevenson, had

tried to publish a critical biography of Mackenzie King in the 1940s and the book was censored. Parts of the manuscript, as well as a note reading "Suppressed at request of the London *Times*," can be found in his papers at Library and Archives Canada [hereafter LAC]. See John Stevenson, [unfinished biography of Mackenzie King], n.d. [c. 1943], Stevenson Papers, LAC, MG30, D199, vol. 1, file 6. There were many who were critical of King but thought that there was a proper way in which this was to be done. There was also the option of self-publication, as with Grierson, *William Lyon Mackenzie King*. Robert Bothwell suggests that another biography was suppressed; all of the volumes were purchased before they could even reach a bookstore. See Bothwell, "'Let Us Now Praise Famous Men,'" 126–7. Also, see Donald Creighton's amusing send-up of the kinds of political biographies that were typically published in the first half of the twentieth century: Creighton, "Sir John A. Macdonald and Canadian Historians."

10 As if to prove Stacey's point, the story was published in a publication of the Liberal Party of Canada: "Historian Tells of Flesh-and-Blood PM," *The Liberal*, 5 May 1976.

11 On the changed psychological notion of the self that he calls the "emancipated self," see Nolan, *The Therapeutic State*, esp. 2–12. I am also drawing on the work of Charles Taylor and his explanation of changing notions of the self as lying at the heart of the modern experience. See Taylor, *Sources of the Self*; *A Secular Age*; and *The Malaise of Modernity*. I have discussed these issues more thoroughly in Dummitt, 'The 'Taint of Self.'' On the growing importance of individualized, atomized language and metaphors at the expense of socially rich, interconnected language, see Rodgers, *Age of Fracture*.

12 King's instructions to destroy the diary except those portions he indicated were to be preserved were no secret. This was directly stated in a broadcast on CBC radio at the time of the release of King's will by one of the executors of his estate: Leonard Brockington, "Broadcast over C.B.C. Network, August 8, 1950 by Mr. L.W. Brockington," LAC, Markham Papers, MG32, F6, "WLM King – Bequests 1950." See also "Copy of Last Will and Testament of the Right Honourable W.L. Mackenzie King, Embodying Amendments Contained in a Codicil Dated June 24, 1950," Gowling, MacTavish, Watt, Osborne and Henderson, Ottawa, Canada, in J.W. Pickersgill Papers [hereafter JP], MG 32, B34, vol. 278, file 5.

13 It was a Sunday, incidentally, and King and his friend Bert Harper went to the Clemows for dinner. After dinner King had a long conversation with Miss Clemow, whom he thought had "a bright intellect" and "would be a fine clever woman if she would be her best self only." Stacey might have said the same of King himself. King then returned to his apartment that he shared with Harper where they read Book II of Carlyle's *Past and Present* in front of the fire on one of those nights of manly companionship that has fired some speculation, without out real proof, about the sexual relationship between the two friends.

14 The entire diary is available for research online through LAC, though there are some discrepancies. The archives staff chose to digitize the most easily read-able form of the diary. This was a transcribed version created after King's death by his literary executors for use in the official biography project. Some material was left out of the transcription, allegedly indicated by ellipses. The literary executor in charge of the transcription, Frederick McGregor, claimed that they omitted only sections that were entirely irrelevant and of minor im-portance. So far as I know, no one has ever gone through the time-consuming process of comparing the different diary versions to verify if this is true.

15 I have noted what could be a major discrepancy. There are two versions of the 1925 diary, one handwritten and the other typed. This is before the time when King came to dictate his diary entries to a secretary who then typed them. It's unclear why there are two versions of the diary for this year, though the fact that this period overlaps with a major political controversy, that of the King-Byng affair, could be highly significant. In that controversy, the exact actions of King and his relations with the governor general came under scrutiny, espe-cially regarding exactly what arrangements had been set in place between King and the governor general after the 1925 election when King lost his seat and his party's position in Parliament was much reduced. King's decision to stay on until Parliament met to see if he could gain the confidence of the House of Commons was not supported by Byng, who turned instead to the party with the most seats in the House. It would certainly have been in King's interest to set the record straight in a clearly typed and potentially modified version of the diary. The LAC team that created the accompanying website for the diary provide a detailed explanation yet, tellingly, do not mention King's will. See the "Behind the Diary" section of LAC, "A Real Companion and Friend: The Diary of William Lyon Mackenzie King," https://www.collections canada.gc.ca/king/023011-1030.01-e.html (accessed 17 June 2015).

16 On the history of the diary itself, see Dryden, "The Mackenzie King Papers"; and LAC, "A Real Companion and Friend."

CHAPTER TWO

1 Editorial, *Ottawa Journal*, 24 July 1950, 6.

2 See Wright, *Three Nights in Havana*.

3 "Diary," 23 July 1950, Grant Dexter Fonds [hereafter Dexter Papers], Queen's University Archives (QUA), 2142, box 6, file 1.

4 Editorial, *Globe and Mail*, 24 July 1950.

5 Editorial, *Ottawa Journal*, 24 July 1950, 6.

6 "President Roosevelt Only Man Who Called Canada's Premier 'Mackenzie,'" *Globe and Mail*, 24 July 1950, 9. On the real history of King's and Canada's involvement in the wartime conferences, see Stacey, *Canada and the Age of Conflict*, 334.

7 Stacey, *Canada and the Age of Conflict*, 334.

8 Warren Baldwin, "PM Joins Long Queue to Respect Mr. King," *Globe and Mail*, 26 July 1950, 1–2.

9 Ralph Hyman, "Throngs Stand Hours in Hot Sun," *Globe and Mail*, 27 July 1950, 1.

10 "Talk by Maud Ferguson" [transcripts, CBC radio], 1 August 1951, WLMK, Lit. Execs., MG26, J14, vol. 3, file 6.

11 Warren Baldwin, "Newsmen Keep Tradition, See Ex-PM off at Station," *Globe and Mail*, 27 July 1950, 3.

12 Brooke Claxton, "Mr. King's Last Days," n.d. [unpublished manuscript], LAC, Brooke Claxton Fonds [hereafter Claxton Papers], MG32, B5, vol. 249.

13 Arthur Meighen to Eugene Forsey, 8 August 1950, LAC, Meighen Papers, MG26, I, vol. 223, "Forsey."

14 John Stevenson to [no name], n.d., [c. late July 1950], LAC, Stevenson Papers, MG30, D199, vol. 1, file 2.

15 The brief biography of King offered here is mostly meant to present a view of King as he would have seemed in 1950 at the time of this death. On many parts of his career, the perspective has changed over time and recently much more detailed work has appeared. The notes throughout the book will guide readers to other resources, but a useful start should include: Levine, *King*; Tim Cook, *Warlords*; and biographies of key civil servants with whom King worked, including Wardhaugh, *Behind the Scenes*; and Hillmer, *O.D. Skelton*.

16 Arthur Lower, "Mr. King," *Canadian Banker* 57 (autumn 1950): 52.

17 B.K. Sandwell, "How Mr. King Kept Power," *Saturday Night* 65:6 (1 August 1950), 12.

18 Laurendeau, *La crise de la conscription, 1942*, 14.

19 Granatstein and Hitsman, *Broken Promises*, 177.

20 A.R.M. Lower, "Mackenzie King and Recent Canadian Politics," Speech to St Lawrence University, Canton, NY, 9 August 1950, A.R.M. Lower Fonds [hereafter Lower Papers], QUA, Collection 5072, box 21, file 66.

21 Blair Fraser, "Mackenzie King as I Knew Him," *Maclean's* (1 September 1950), 7–8, 52–4.

22 "Close Up on Mackenzie King," Dir. Douglas Leiterman, 10 and 17 March 1961, LAC, Canadian Broadcasting Corporation, Television Fonds, Acc. no. 1986-0810, consultation copies V1 2012-09-0002.

23 Douglas How, "Mackenzie King and the Canadian People," 14 September 1950, LAC, Henry William Erskine Kidd Fonds [hereafter Kidd Papers], MG32, G9, col. 8, file 13.

24 Lower, "Mr. King," 46–53.

CHAPTER THREE

1 Fred Archer, "Mackenzie King Sought Spirit Aid in State Affairs," *Psychic News*, 19 August 1950. Although this is the story that got attention in Canada, it was actually the second story published on King's spiritualism. See

also J.B. McIndoe, "Mackenzie King a Spiritualist," *Psychic News*, 12 August 1950, WLMK, Lit. Execs., MG26, J17, vol. 4, file "clippings"; and "Mackenzie King Paid a Great Tribute to Famous Medium," *Psychic World*, 21 September 1950, 2.

2 Archer, "Mackenzie King Sought Spirit Aid," and "Fraud: Leading Spiritualist Advice Tests," *Psychic News*, 19 August 1950.

3 See, for example, Eugene Forsey to Arthur Meighen, 29 August 1950, Meighen Papers, MG26, I, vol. 223, "Forsey."

4 Fred Archer, "WLMK: Spiritualist," *Psychic News*, republished in *Ottawa Citizen*, 10 October 1950, LAC, Forsey Papers, MG 30, A25, box 10, file "King, Mackenzie 1949–1956."

5 Michael Bliss, *Right Honourable Men*, 128. More recent historians of spiritualism and King's connection to it have been keen to contextualize spiritualism in its age and diminish the oddity of the practices. See McMullen, *Anatomy of a Séance*; Margaret Elizabeth Bedore, "The Reading of Mackenzie King"; and Oppenheim, *The Other World*.

6 Brandon, *The Spiritualists*.

7 On the Austin case, see Ramsay Cook, *The Regenerators*, chapter 5.

8 On rumours of King's spiritualistic beliefs even before later revelations, see Lotta Dempsey, "Letter from Mr. King," *Globe and Mail*, 12 January 1951; "Report: Mackenzie King Practices Spiritualism," *Globe and Mail*, 11 December 1951, 5; and "Mr. King's Hobby," *B.C. Times* [Vancouver], 26 January 1952.

9 McGregor to Carruthers, 22 February 1951, LAC, Markham Papers, MG32, F6, "Correspond – F.A. McGregor."

10 J.V. McAree, "New Light on Mr. King," *Globe and Mail*, 10 November 1950, 6.

11 "Always on the Ground," *Victoria Times*, 25 October 1950; and J.V. McAree, "Salute to the Great Doctor," *Globe and Mail*, 20 December 1950, 6.

12 "Mr. King's Spiritual Beliefs," *Toronto Star*, 9 November 1950.

13 "In Quiet & Reflection," *Time* (Canada), 23 October 1950, 29.

CHAPTER FOUR

1 "What a Story He Could Write!" *Ottawa Journal*, 3 May 1949.

2 J. Edouard Handy, "Private and Confidential Memorandum re Mr. King's Diaries at Laurier House," 17 August 1950, LAC, WLMK, MG26, J17, vol. 9, file 3. George Hambleton, "The Mackenzie King Diaries," *Ottawa Citizen*, n.d., LAC, Forsey Papers, MG30, A25, box 10, file "King, Mackenzie 1944."

3 Markham, *Friendship's Harvest*, 167.

4 "Memoirs Backed: Rockefeller and McGill Aid Mr. King," *Globe and Mail*, 8 April 1949.

5 [List of Honours Conferred upon WLMK], WLMK, MG26, J17, vol. 7, file 6.

6 [WLMK], "What Originally Contemplated – a Personal Biography," n.d. [c. 1949], WLMK, Lit. Execs., MG26, J17, vol. 4, file 19.

7 As King put it himself, "in this connection, one might work out the associations and personal relationships which had helped to enable one to get a beginning in one's career ... much would relate back to my father's membership on the Senate of Toronto and those who were personal friends of his, for example, Willison of the Globe, Mulock and others." See "Copy of Mr. King's Draft no. 1, Personal Memoirs, re: Finances," 25 April 1949, WLMK, Lit. Execs., MG26, J17, vol. 4, file 20.

8 Dawson, *William Lyon Mackenzie King*.

9 The draft outline for the memoir, including a list of possible individuals who might be hired to help him with the project, can be found in "What Originally Contemplated – a Personal Biography."

10 "The Bookshelf," *Saturday Night*, 24 February 1923; and McGillicuddy, *The Making of a Premier*. For McGillicuddy's sake, you can only hope the book earned him valuable friendship for it did not sell especially well and never made him more than $100. See "Royalty Statements, the Making of a Premier, Hodder and Stoughton, various years], Owen Ernest McGillicuddy Fonds, LAC, MG30, D262, vol. 1.

11 On the real story behind the biography, see Moher, "The 'Biography' in Politics." Coincidentally, this story was picked up by the popular press in the mid-1970s at the same time as other stories of King's secrets were making the news. See Geoffrey Stevens, "The Old Ghost Writer," *Globe and Mail*, 8 January 1975.

12 Rogers, *Mackenzie King*, xi, 1.

13 John Stevenson, [unfinished biography of Mackenzie King], n.d. [c. 1943], Stevenson Papers, LAC, MG30, D199, vol. 1, file 6; and Geoffrey Stevens, "A Suppressed Biography," *Globe and Mail*, 17 January 1975.

14 Bothwell, "'Let Us Now Praise Famous Men'"; and Lapalme, *Le bruits des choses reveilles*, 323–30. Lapalme recalls a plan to publish Rumilly's volume in advance of the 1949 election. Rumilly had since become a spokesperson for Duplessis in Quebec and the idea was to embarrass the Union nationale. However, he claims that St Laurent opted for caution and to leave the book's existence a secret.

15 Memo, Reginald Hardy to King, n.d., LAC, WLMK, MG26, J2000-01436-4, vol. 3, file 2.

16 Quotations from this paragraph are from Hardy, *Mackenzie King of Canada*, 157–61.

17 Granatstein, *The Ottawa Men*.

18 McGregor spells out some of his own relations with King in the book he wrote on King's time out of office between 1911 and 1917. See McGregor, *The Fall and Rise of Mackenzie King*; and Warren Baldwin, "Helps Mr. King

on Memoirs," *Globe and Mail*, 4 January 1950. I draw, too, on my interview with McGregor's granddaughter, Lucile McGregor, 22 February 2008.

19 On Pickersgill, see his own memoir, *Seeing Canada Whole*, though he is not forthcoming there about his blurring of boundaries between his civil-servant and partisan roles. On this, see Granatstein, *Ottawa Men*, 207–25. See also Robertson, *Memoirs of a Very Civil Servant*, 39, 47.

20 Ferns, *Reading from Left to Right*, 143; and Granatstein, *Ottawa Men*, 209, 218.

21 Granatstein, *A Man of Influence*.

22 Terry Cook, "An Archival Revolution."

23 McGregor to J. Herbert Cranston, 6 November 1950, LAC, WLMK, MG26, J17, vol. 2 file 5.

24 "Mr. King's Biography," *Montreal Star*, 9 February 1951.

25 This was certainly F.R. Scott's assessment: "It is a pity his private diaries will not be fully preserved so that we might understand him better." F.R. Scott, "Mr. King and the King Makers," *Canadian Forum* 30 (December 1950), 197–9.

26 The documents consulted here come from the papers of King's literary executors that are part of the WLMK Fonds at LAC. On the initial decision not to destroy the diaries, see Handy, "Private and Confidential Memorandum re Mr. King's Diaries at Laurier House," 17 August 1950, LAC, WLMK, MG26, J17, vol. 9, file 3; J.W. Pickersgill to Stuart Garson, Minister of Justice, 19 September 1950, LAC, JP, MG32, B34, vol. 278, file 5; and McGregor to Carruthers, 2 November 1950 and 27 December 1950, LAC, Markham Papers, MG32, F6, Correspond – F.A. McGregor.

27 D.W.M., "Memorandum to the Deputy Minister re: Interpretation of Will of Right Honourable W.L. Mackenzie King," LAC, JP, MG32, B34, vol. 278, file 5; and F.P. Varcoe to Pickersgill, 14 December 1950, LAC, Norman Robertson Papers [hereafter NR], MG30, E163, vol. 3(b).

28 Patteson to Carruthers, 11 March 1951, LAC, Markham Papers, MG32, F6, Correspond – F.A. McGregor.

29 Memo from F.A. McGregor to Pickersgill and W.K. Lamb, 23 October 1952, LAC, JP, MG32, B34, vol. 278, file 7; Norman Robertson to W.K. Lamb, 13 March 1953, LAC, NR, MG30, E163, vol. 3(b); and Lamb to Pickersgill, 2 December 1973, LAC, JP, MG32, B34, vol. 279, file 1.

CHAPTER FIVE

1 McGregor, memo for file, 13 January 1951; [McGregor] to G. O'Neill Lynch, 23 January 1951; "Princess Mary Victoria" to executors of the WLMK estate, 23 October [1951]; "Mary Mackenzie King" to executors of WLMK estate, 2 January 1952; and "Mary Victoria" to executors of the WLMK estate, 26 August 1953: LAC, WLMK, MG26, J17, vol. 1, file 5.

2 Cummins to Handy, 10 August 1950, LAC, WLMK, MG26, J17, vol. 4, file 15.

3 Cummins, *Unseen Adventures*, 183.

4 WLMK to E.B. Gibbes, 27 April 1948 [copy], Cork County Archives (CCA), Ireland, Geraldine Cummins Papers [hereafter Cummins Papers], U206, box 19, file 134; and David Gray, preface to Cummins, *Unseen Adventures*, 9.

5 Cousins, "Writer, Medium, Suffragette, Spy?"

6 Ibid.

7 Cummins, *Unseen Adventures*, 112–13; and Cousins, "Writer, Medium, Suffragette, Spy?"

8 Handy to Cummins, 2 November 1950, LAC, WLMK, MG26, J17, vol. 4, file 15.

9 Cummins to Handy, 17 November 1950, ibid. Emphasis in original.

10 Ibid.

11 Handy to Cummins, 12 December 1950, ibid.

12 Handy to Cummins, 14 January 1951 [cable], ibid., file 16.

13 Geraldine Cummins to Handy, 1 March 1951, LAC, NR, MG30, E163, vol. 3(b); McGregor to MacTavish, 19 January [1951], LAC, WLMK, MG26, J17, vol. 4, file 16; and Tom Barrett, "Former Archivist Admits Denying Writer King Papers," *Vancouver Sun*, 22 November 1976.

14 McGregor to Cummins, 29 March 1951, LAC, NR, MG30, E163, vol. 3(b).

15 See cables at end of January 1951 in WLMK, MG26, J17, vol. 4, file 16.

16 The sketch of Blair Fraser here is based on Brennan, *Reporting the Nation's Business* chapter 5; Fraser and Fraser, eds., *Blair Fraser Reports: Selections, 1944–1968*; and author's interview with Graham Fraser, 31 May 2013.

17 Brennan, *Reporting the Nation's Business*, 109

18 McGregor to Carruthers, 15 October 1951, LAC, Markham Papers, MG32, F6, Correspond – F.A. McGregor.

19 John Stevenson, [unfinished biography of Mackenzie King], n.d. [c. 1943], LAC, Stevenson Papers, MG30, D199, vol. 1, file 6.

20 All the quotations in this section attributed to Fraser come from Blair Fraser, "The Secret Life of Mackenzie King, Spiritualist," *Maclean's*, 15 December 1951.

21 For example, see Sam Welles, "Statesman's Other Side," *Life*, 23 March 1953; "Tourists See Mackenzie King's Crystal Ball as 'Bit of Magic,'" *Ottawa Journal*, 24 October 1953; and Arthur Blakely, "Among the One-eyed," *Montreal Gazette*, 16 January 1954. Perhaps the best example of this whimsical humour at King's expense in the mid-1950s was the CBC broadcast of a talk by Percy Philip who claimed to have had an encounter with King's ghost while sitting on a bench at the former prime minister's Kingsmere property just outside Ottawa. Papers across the country reported on the talk and tried to get Philip to admit that it was a spoof – something he did not do. See, for example, "Ghostly Gossip on a Bench with Mackenzie King," *Globe and*

Mail, 25 September 1954, 1; Richard Jackson, "Believe It or Not!" *Ottawa Journal*, 27 September 1954; and James A. Oastler, "Shade of Prime Minister Apparently Needs No Bed," *Montreal Star*, 28 September 1954. Percy Philip reflected on the experience again in "My Conversation with Mackenzie King," *Liberty Magazine* (January 1955).

22 Denys Paré, "King, Laurier, Leur Souvenir y Reste Vivace," *La Patrie*, 16 December 1951; "Mysticism of Former Prime Minister," *Windsor Star*, 12 December 1951; and James McCook, "Spiritualist Mackenzie King Tried 'Communication' with the Dead," *Ottawa Journal*, 10 December 1951.

23 All quotations from letters in these paragraphs can be found in "Mailbag: The Private Life of a PM," *Maclean's*, 1 March 1952.

24 Betcherman, *Ernest Lapointe*, 107–19.

25 On King's apparent ghostly communication with Cummins after the *Maclean's* article, see "Communication from Mackenzie King," 16 May 1951, CCA, Cummins Papers, box 16, file 109; and [Notes on sitting, Geraldine Cummins with Kathleen, Viscountess Falmouth, in which Mackenzie King appears], 16 May 1951, ibid.

26 McGregor to Carruthers, 11 December 1951, LAC, Markham Papers, Correspond – F.A. McGregor.

CHAPTER SIX

1 R. Buchanan, letter to the editor, *Ottawa Citizen*, 8 July 1952.

2 Forsey to editor, *Ottawa Citizen*, 8 July 1952, LAC, Meighen Papers, MG26, I, vol. 223, "Forsey."

3 In fact, Forsey knew of the rumours of King's spiritualism weeks before the news was published in Canadian newspapers. See Eugene Forsey to Arthur Meighen, 29 August 1950, LAC, Meighen Papers, MG26, I, vol. 223, "Forsey."

4 King's own version of these events was published in his book *The Secret of Heroism: A Memoir of Henry Albert Harper* (Toronto: Ontario Publishing 1919 [1906]). The young King's moral earnestness was often later ridiculed, lightly in the MacGregor Dawson's official biography and then with more directness in Stacey's *A Very Double Life*.

5 King's second official biographer probably spent more time than anyone else pondering King's psychological make-up and his assessments are usually the most balanced. Neatby points to King's habit of self-deception and naivety about his own desires. See H. Blair Neatby, *The Lonely Heights*, 204.

6 The details on Forsey's life in this section are drawn especially from his own memoirs: Eugene Forsey, *A Life on the Fringe*. See also Helen Forsey, *Eugene Forsey*; Milligan, *Eugene A. Forsey*; and Hodgetts, ed., *The Sound of One Voice*.

7 Hodgetts, *The Sound of One Voice*, 19–20, 35.

8 The most detailed account of King-Byng is in Eugene Forsey, *The Royal Power of Dissolution of Parliament in the British Commonwealth*. For a briefer but still full account from all angles, Graham, *The King-Byng Affair, 1926.*

9 Eugene Forsey, letter to the editor, *Maclean's*, 29 December 1949, LAC, Meighen Papers, MG26, I, vol. 223, "Forsey."

10 Forsey, *A Life on the Fringe*, 108.

11 Eugene Forsey to Arthur Meighen, 21 July 1949, LAC, Meighen Papers, MG26, I, vol. 223, "Forsey."

12 Eugene Forsey, letter to the editor, *Maclean's*, 29 December 1949, LAC, Meighen Papers, MG26, I, vol. 223, "Forsey."

13 Eugene Forsey to Arthur Meighen, 25 July 1952, LAC, Meighen Papers, MG26, I, vol. 223, "Forsey."

14 The Google Ngram viewer tracks the appearance of terms in the large library of books digitized by Google. For English, where the library is large, it can be a suggestive guide to the rise and fall and overall usage of key terms, and when read contextually with other evidence, it can help to corroborate overall trends in usage. On some of its limitations, see Sarah Jang, "The Pitfalls of Using Google Ngram to Study Language," *Wired* (12 October 2015), http://www.wired.com/2015/10/pitfalls-of-studying-language-with-google-ngram/ (accessed 2 May 2016).

15 The peak usage of the term seems to have been early in the twentieth century, likely in the year after the end of the Great War and the signing of the Treaty of Versailles.

16 On these tensions in the campaign for universal education, see Prentice, *The School Promoters*; and Prentice and Houston, *Schooling and Scholars in Nineteenth-Century Ontario*. On the public sphere, see McNairn, *The Capacity to Judge*.

17 The discussion that follows draws on Appiah, *The Honor Code*; Welsh, *What Is Honor?*; Bowman, *Honor*; Woodruff, *Reverence*; and Krause, *Liberalism with Honor*.

18 Noel, *Patrons, Clients, Brokers*.

19 On the decline of patronage opportunities, see Ward, *Dawson's The Government of Canada*, 26, 40, 99.

20 Victorian notions of respectability would later come to be seen as hypocritical, yet, as Gertrude Himmelfarb has argued, respectability was very much about keeping up form even when (especially when) the content did not match the shape of the ideal. The move toward a more authentic notion of the self, and the expectation that social structures should move from the self outward, is one of the transitions that this book traces and one of the cultural developments that came to make these Victorian notions seem backward. Himmelfarb, *The De-Moralization of Society*, 26. On notions of courtship,

social relations, and the home in Canada, see Azoulay, *Hearts and Minds*; W. Peter Ward, *Courtship, Love and Marriage in Nineteenth-Century English Canada*; and W. Peter Ward, *A History of Domestic Space*.

21 On the transformation of the modern newspaper, see Johnston, *Selling Themselves*.

22 On patronage and the Liberal Party in these years, see Whitaker, *The Government Party*. On changes in the administration of the public service and the decline of patronage appointments, see Ken Rasmussen, "Administrative Reform and the Quest for Bureaucratic Autonomy, 1867–1919"; and Hodgetts et al., *The Biography of an Institution*.

23 Ward, *Dawson's The Government of Canada*, 32.

24 Indeed, McGregor joked about it in a postscript of a letter to the official biographer. "I started on you months ago with a Dear Sir, (or was it Sir) graduated to Dear Dr. Dawson, then had the temerity to address you as Dear MacGregor Dawson. The pleasant relations have now developed to a point where I have dropped the surname. If no rift in relations occurs I plan, cold bloodedly, to change the MacGregor to Bob eventually, but I am reserving this intimacy to some later date, probably about June the 13th, or to such time as you yourself drop this abominable English habit of Dear McGregoring me. The only man who ever got away with that without ultimate protest was Mackenzie King. Some day I am going to write a sprightly essay on the subject, under the title perhaps of 'Dear Dawson.'" McGregor to Dawson, 25 January 1951, LAC, WLMK, MG26, J17, vol. 4 file 2.

25 In *Nixon's Shadow*, David Greenberg argues that Richard Nixon became the embodiment of these shifting sensitivities to authenticity and artifice in the television age. In this Greenberg is picking up on the contemporary critic of the era, Daniel Boorstin, *The Image, or What Happened to the American Dream*.

CHAPTER SEVEN

1 [Advertisement for *The Incredible Canadian*], *Globe and Mail*, 15 November 1952, 13.

2 "Bruce Hutchison and Lawrence Earl Win Medals for Biography and Humor," *Globe and Mail*, Saturday Review of Books, 23 May 1953, 7.

3 "Loose Freudianism" is the term used by Owram in *Born at the Right Time*, 38.

4 Joel Paris, *The Fall of an Icon*, 26. Erika Dyck in *Psychedelic Psychiatry* has traced, for example, the important work of LSD researchers in Saskatchewan in these years as part of a broader move among some psychiatric researchers to develop anti-psychotic drug treatments. While LSD research would be sidelined, other anti-psychotic drugs, first developed in the 1950s, would ultimately transform psychiatry and help to overturn psychoanalytic perspectives by the 1970s. See Gerald Grob, *The Mad among Us*, 276–7.

5 Paris, *Fall of an Icon*, 17, 19.

6 Shorter, *A History of Psychiatry*, 145.

7   On the way Freudian ideas became part of new common sense; see Heath and Porter, *Rebel Sell*, chapter 2.

8   Hale, *The Rise and Crisis of Psychoanalysis in the United States*, 276–99.

9   Of course, Shorter is in fact quite critical of the psychoanalytic perspective, noting that this view of mental illness could not be true if the biological view of mental illness was also true, and that, indeed, the biological view has won out. Shorter, *A History of Psychiatry*, 178–9.

10 Robert White, *Scientific American* 201 (September 1959): 269, cited in Hale, *The Rise and Crisis of Psychoanalysis in the United States*, 289. Hale argues that Freudian psychiatry still upheld conservative social norms around sexuality, particularly with respect to ideas of homosexuality and gender ideals, and this led it to be associated with a more conservative social consensus that opened it to criticism in the radical 1960s and afterward.

11 Farley, *Brock Chisholm, the World Health Organization, and the Cold War*, 33, 40–7.

12 Heron, *Booze*, 353–6; Rotskoff, *Love on the Rocks*, chapter 3.

13 Eugene Forsey to Arthur Meighen, 21 July 1954, LAC, Meighen Papers, MG26, I, vol. 224, "Forsey."

14 Owram, *Born at the Right Time*, 128.

15 Burtch, *Jack Bush*, 47, 65.

16 Fukuyama, *The Great Disruption*, 74. See also two books with different perspectives on the same issues: Collier, *The Rise of Selfishness in America*; and Rutherford, *A World Made Sexy*, chapter 2, which discusses the uses of Freud by Marxist intellectuals.

17 "Notes of Meetings of Literary Executors," 9 November 1950, LAC, WLMK, MG26, J17, J18, file 1.

18 The sketch of Hutchison here draws on Hutchison, *The Far Side of the Street*; and William French, "Beyond Journalism, Hutchison Has a Talent for Planting Beans and Building a Solid Privy," *Globe and Mail*, 25 September 1976.

19 Hutchison was conscious of the blurry line he traversed in his friendship with Liberal insiders and tried to limit his exposure to criticism. See, for example, Bruce Hutchison to Grant Dexter, n.d. [c. 18 February 1958], Special Collections, University of Calgary (UC), Bruce Hutchison Fonds [hereafter Hutchison Papers], MSC22, box 1, file 11; and Bruce Hutchison to Grant Dexter, n.d. [c. December 1957], ibid.

20 Bruce Hutchison to C.G. Power, 30 May 1951, QUA, C.G. Power Fonds [hereafter Power Papers], Collection 2150, box 6, "Hutchison, Bruce."

21 I.N.S. [Norman Smith], "A Spade Should Be a Spade Even in a Biography," *Ottawa Journal*, 18 July 1951.

22 D.G. Creighton, "Sir John Macdonald and Canadian Historians," *Canadian Historical Review* 29:1 (1948): 4; and Berger, *The Writing of Canadian History*, 218–19. On the critique of biography at this time, see also Wright, *Donald Creighton*, 175–6.

23 Bruce Hutchison, "How Mackenzie King Won His Greatest Gamble," *Maclean's*, 1 November 1952; and Hutchison, *The Incredible Canadian*, chapter 1.

24 Eugene Forsey, "John A. Macdonald and Mackenzie King (circa 1878)," 9 December 1952 [*Ottawa Citizen*], Clara Thomas Archives, York University Archives [YUA], Bernard Ostry Fonds [hereafter Ostry Papers], F0370, 1991-030, vol. 20, file 135. Forsey had wanted Meighen to reply and wrote the *Saturday Night* article only when Meighen refused. It says something about Meighen's view of politics that, though he was disgusted with Hutchison's account of King-Byng, he did not want to be drawn into the fight, for he couldn't bear to think of Hutchison as his "last fellow gladiator." Arthur Meighen to Eugene Forsey, 6 November 1952, LAC, Meighen Papers, MG26, I, vol. 223, "Forsey."

25 Eugene Forsey to Arthur Meighen, 25 October 1952, LAC, Meighen Papers, MG26, I, vol. 223, "Forsey."

26 Eugene Forsey, "The Incredible Mr. Hutchison," *Ottawa Citizen*, 6 December 1952; Eugene Forsey, letter to the editor, *Saturday Night*, 22 January 1953, LAC, Meighen Papers, MG26, I, vol. 224, "Forsey."

27 Quotations on conscription crisis from Bruce Hutchison, "Mackenzie King and the Revolt of the Army," *Maclean's*, 15 October 1952.

28 See, for example, Stuart Ralston to C.G. Power, 6 August 1952, QUA, Power Papers, box 8, "Ralston, Hon. Stuart"; Bruce Hutchison to C.G. Power, 5 May 1952, QUA, Power Papers, box 6, "Hutchison, Bruce"; and R.S. Malone to Bruce Hutchison, 20 March 1952, UC, Hutchison Papers, box 2, file 15.

29 C.G. Power to Angus L. Macdonald, 15 November 1950, QUA, Power Papers, box 7, "Macdonald, Hon Angus."

30 "Fantastic Idea of Mr. King's," *Winnipeg Daily Star*, 14 October 1952.

31 Bruce Hutchison to C.G. Power, 1 April 1952, QUA, Power Papers, box 6, "Hutchison, Bruce."

32 Eugene Forsey to Arthur Meighen, 16 October 1952, LAC, Meighen Papers, MG26, I, vol. 223, "Forsey."

33 Hutchison, *The Unknown Country*, 3; Hutchison, *Incredible Canadian*, 1.

34 Quotations from Bruce Hutchison, "Bruce Hutchison's Thoughts on Mackenzie King," *Maclean's*, 15 November 1952.

35 Hutchison, "Thoughts on Mackenzie King," 32.

36 Eugene Forsey to Arthur Meighen, 14 November 1949, LAC, Meighen Papers, MG26, I, vol. 223, "Forsey."

37 Hutchison, "Thoughts on Mackenzie King," 31, 32.

38 William Arthur Deacon, "Strange, Lonely Figure of Prime Minister King," *Globe and Mail*, 22 November 1952, 14; Arthur Meighen to Eugene Forsey, 27 October 1952, LAC, Meighen Papers, MG26, I, vol. 223, "Forsey"; C.G. Power to Bruce Hutchison, 4 November 1952, QUA, Power Papers, box 6,

"Hutchison, Bruce"; and T.W., "Mackenzie King in War," *Hamilton Spectator*, 12 November 1955.

39 Eugene Forsey, "The Incredible Mr. Hutchison," *Ottawa Citizen*, 6 December 1952.

40 C.G. Power to Leslie Roberts, 12 January 1953, QUA, Power Papers, box 8, "Roberts, Leslie." Hutchison clearly felt pressure from friends in the prime minister's office concerning the story of the revolt in the army. In March 1953 he published an updated account which claimed to have definite proof that the revolt wasn't just a figment of King's – and St Laurent's – imagination. The story, though, gave no evidence and was based on confidential and unrevealed sources. Privately, Hutchison admitted that "it was represented to me most seriously that Mr. St. Laurent had been left in an odd and embarrassing position by my book which made it appear that he had fallen for Mr. King's absurd fantasy of a military strike ... I was urged, as I say, on the highest level, to do this job as a kind of favor or justification I owed the Prime Minister." Bruce Hutchison to C.G. Power, 26 May 1953, QUA, Power Papers, box 6, "Hutchison, Bruce."

41 Fred McGregor to Robertson, 5 Dec 1952, LAC, Robertson Papers, MG30, E163, vol. 3(b); "Mackenzie King Volume Draws Liberal MP's Fire," *Globe and Mail*, 2 December 1952; and "Interested Reader," letter to the editor, *Ottawa Journal*, 27 November 1952.

42 Frank Underhill, "Turning New Leaves," *Canadian Forum* (December 1952), 206–7. Of course, Underhill had been early to this style of critical analysis and had both benefited from it and suffered for it in the 1920s and 1930s – alternatively praised for his refreshing style, especially in his writing in *Canadian Forum*, and constantly attacked by members of the University of Toronto Board of Governors who thought that his acerbic tone and unconventional views should not have been supported by the university. See Dewar, *Frank Underhill and the Politics of Ideas*, esp. 97–106.

43 Borden Clarke to McGregor, 15 November 1952, LAC, WLMK, MG26, J17, J18, file 2.

44 T.A. Crerar to Bruce Hutchison, 18 December 1952, QUA, T.A. Crerar Fonds [hereafter Crerar Papers], 2117, box 88, corresp. 1953.

CHAPTER EIGHT

1 For a slightly fuller account of the controversy, see Christopher Dummitt, "Harry Ferns, Bernard Ostry and *The Age of Mackenzie King*."

2 The sketch of Ferns here largely comes from Ferns, *Reading from Left to Right*.

3 There were later rumours that Oscar Skelton, deputy minister of external affairs, allowed leftists to join the department though his biographer suggests there is no evidence for this. Hillmer, *O.D. Skelton*, 262–3.

4 R. Morgan to H.S. Ferns, 4 August 1949, LAC, H.S. Ferns Fonds [hereafter Ferns Papers], MG32, G16, box 3, file "Min. of Defence."

5 H.S. Ferns to Brooke Claxton, 14 August 1949, ibid.

6 H.S. Ferns to Charles H. Bland, 12 March 1950, ibid.

7 Bernard Ostry to H.S. Ferns, 12 January 1955, YUA, Ostry Papers, vol. 155, file 1157.

8 Ferns, *Reading from Left to Right*, 297–310.

9 There is no biography of Ostry and he did not write his memoirs so the information here is gleaned from scattered sources. See Ramsay Cook, "The Age of Mackenzie King," *Globe and Mail*, 22 January 1977, 39; Shinbane Dorfman and Kanee to Bernard Ostry, 17 July 1953, YUA, Ostry Papers, vol. 158, file 1278; and Russell W. Kerr to Bernard Ostry, 20 November 1953, ibid.

10 Julie Medlock to Joseph Barnes, 18 January 1956, YUA, Ostry Papers, vol. 156, file 1190.

11 Julie Medlock to Bernard Ostry, 9 September 1954, ibid.

12 Julie Medlock to Bernard Ostry, 8 January 1955, ibid.; Thelma Johnson to H.S Ferns, 29 December 1953, LAC, Ferns Papers, box 7 file [unnamed – various correspondents]; and W.L. Morton to H.S. Ferns, 20 May 1952, LAC, Ferns Papers, box 3, file "Morton et al crsp."

13 Bernard Ostry to W.K. Lamb, 24 February 1954, YUA, Ostry Papers, vol. 155, file 1178. On this incident, see H.S. Ferns to W.L. Morton, 6 May 1953, YUA, Ostry Papers, vol. 155, file 1157.

14 H.S. Ferns to W.L. Morton, 25 May 1953, YUA, Ostry Papers, vol. 19, file 131; and Bernard Ostry to W.K. Lamb, 24 February 1954, YUA, Ostry Papers, vol. 155, file 1178.

15 For Lamb's version of events in which Ostry was a problem to be dealt with carefully, see Lamb's correspondence with F.W. Gibson and Norman Fee in LAC, W.K. Lamb Fonds (hereafter Lamb Papers), MG31, D8, vol. 6, file "F W Gibson" and file "Norman Fee."

16 H.S. Ferns to Bernard Ostry, 23 December 1953, and R. Miliband to H.S. Ferns [with note from H.S. Ferns, passed on to Bernard Ostry], 18 January 1954, YUA, Ostry Papers, vol. 155, file 1157.

17 P.B [Peggy Blackstock], "Report on THE AGE OF MACKENZIE KING," n.d. [c. early 1954], YUA, Ostry Papers, vol. 154, file 1123. Judith Robinson eventually edited Farthing's posthumous collection of writings, which were published as *Freedom Wears a Crown*.

18 Memorandum on manuscript by Ferns and Ostry, n.d., YUA, Ostry Papers, vol. 154, file 1123; and Alan Hill to Bernard Ostry, 9 March 1954, YUA, Ostry Papers, vol. 155, file 1172.

19 The correspondence on troubles with Heinemann's and Hill is lengthy, most of which can be found in YUA, Ostry Papers, vol. 155, files 1172 (Hill) and 1157 (Ferns); and in LAC, Ferns Papers, vol. 2, file 12 (Heinemann).

20 John Stevenson to Bernard Ostry, 25 June 1955, YUA, Ostry Papers, vol. 157,

file 1239. See also H.S. Ferns to Bernard Ostry, 18 July 1954, and H.S. Ferns to Bernard Ostry, 20 July 1954, YUA, Ostry Papers, vol. 155, file 1157.

21 On the deliberateness of Ostry's approach, see H.S. Ferns to Bernard Ostry, n.d. [Saturday], YUA, Ostry Papers, vol. 155, file 1157. The correspondence itself is in YUA, Ostry Papers, vol. 154, file 1139 (T.A. Crerar); vol. 156, files 1191 (Arthur Meighen) and 1220 (Stuart Ralston); and vol. 157, file 1239 (Stevenson).

22 Arthur Blakely, "Will Mackenzie King Reveal Low Scandals in High Places?" *Winnipeg Tribune*, 16 September 1955; Bernard Ostry to H.S. Ferns, 2 February 1955, Ostry Papers, vol. 155, file 1157; Ferns and Ostry, "Mackenzie King and the First World War," 112; Colin Cameron to Bernard Ostry, 3 August 1955, YUA, Ostry Papers, vol. 154, file 1129; and John Stevenson to Bernard Ostry, 25 June 1955, YUA, Ostry Papers, vol. 157, file 1239.

23 Bernard Ostry to Arthur Meighen, 5 September 1955, and Arthur Meighen to Bernard Ostry, 7 September 1955, YUA, Ostry Papers, vol. 156, file 1191.

24 Ben Malking to Bernard Ostry, 28 November [1955], YUA, Ostry Papers, vol. 155, file 1185; and Leonard Brockington to H.S. Ferns, 15 December 1955, LAC, Ferns Papers, vol. 3, file "Brockington."

25 Ferns and Ostry, *The Age of Mackenzie King*.

26 Janet Skelton to Bernard Ostry, 19 January [1956], YUA, Ostry Papers, vol. 157, file 1235. Another account of how the Canadian reluctance to challenge authority affected response to the book is Tanis and Michael to H.S. Ferns, 10 December 1955, LAC, Ferns Papers, box 6, file 6.

27 Even Arthur Meighen, who had many reasons to appreciate the Ferns and Ostry volume, still found it lacking compared to Creighton. Arthur Meighen to Roger Graham, 8 December 1955, YUA, Ostry Papers, vol. 156, file 1191.

28 Charles Bruce, "Review [of] Mackenzie King's Early Life," *Daily News* [St John's, NL], 16 December 1955; Alan Morley, "Mackenzie King – the Debunkers March Again," *Vancouver Province*, 30 December 1955; "Pre-Conceived Ideas," *Canadian Business* (February 1956); and "W.L.M. King – Flat," *Winnipeg Tribune* 24 December 1955.

29 Grattan O'Leary, "An Historical Letter: Bared in New King Biography," *Ottawa Journal*, 5 December 1955.

30 Grattan O'Leary, "An Historical Letter," *Ottawa Journal*, 5 December 1955.

31 Grant Dexter, "Distorted Image," *Winnipeg Free Press*, 14 January 1956. See also "Pre-Conceived Ideas," *Canadian Business* (February 1956).

32 House of Commons *Debates*, 6 February 1956, 881.

33 Ibid.

34 *CBC Times*, 18–23 December 1955, YUA, Ostry Papers, vol. 17, file 116.

35 House of Commons *Debates*, 7 February 1956, 945.

36 Ann Orford to H.S. Ferns, 10 April 1956, and H.S. Ferns to Alan Hill, 27 July 1956, LAC, Ferns Papers, vol. 2, file 12 (Heinemann).

37 On Ferns's suspicions, see H.S. Ferns to Grattan O'Leary, 10 August 1956,

LAC, Ferns Papers, box 2, file 1. A contrary picture is J. Ferns to H.S. Ferns, 7 March 1956, LAC, Ferns Papers, box 6, file 6. For the *Saturday Night* episode, see Charles Gwyn Kinsey to H.S. Ferns, 5 January 1956, and Herbert Mc-Manus to H.S. Ferns, 23 February 1956, LAC, Ferns Papers, box 8, file "Crsp 1954–1957"; and H.S. Ferns to W.L. Morton, 21 January 1956, William Ready Division of Archives and Research Collections, McMaster University Archives (MUA), W.L. Morton Fonds [hereafter Morton Papers], box 9, file "H.S. Ferns."

38 Brooke Claxton to J.W. Pickersgill, 29 December 1955, LAC, Claxton Papers, MG32, B5, vol. 83, file "J.W. Pickersgill."

39 Ibid.; Brooke Claxton to J.A. Corry, 16 January 1956, LAC, Claxton Papers, vol. 72, file "C Miscellaneous."

40 Some of Claxton's role in the cancellation was described in newspapers. Claxton privately admitted his own involvement, though he saw nothing wrong with his actions. Brooke Claxton to T.W.L. MacDermott, 28 March 1956, LAC, Claxton Papers, vol. 81, file "T.W.L. MacDermott."

41 House of Commons *Debates*, 7 February 1956, 911, 945–8.

42 "Explanation Required," *Saskatoon Star Phoenix*, 9 February 1956. Orford's letter appeared in various papers, including the *Montreal Gazette*, 9 February 1956; *Hamilton Spectator*, 8 February 1956; and *Daily Packet and Times* (Orillia), 8 February 1956.

43 "No Ostry-cism," *Winnipeg Free Press*, 11 February 1956; Grant Dexter, "CBC Story," *Winnipeg Free Press*, 25 February 1956; and Blair Fraser, "Why the CBC Shunned the King Story," *Maclean's* 31 March 1956.

44 H.S. Ferns to Bernard Ostry, 30 March 1956, and [Press Statement], 20 April 1956, LAC, Ferns Papers, vol. 6, file "Ostry"; Bernard Ostry, letter to the editor, *The Times* [London], 27 April 1956, YUA, Ostry Papers, vol. 157, file 1243; [Press Statement], 28 April 1956, LAC, Ferns Papers, vol. 6, file "Ostry"; and "Advance Review," *Winnipeg Free Press*, 10 May 1956.

45 Reg Whitaker, review of Ferns and Ostry, *Age of Mackenzie King* [transcript], *Sunday Morning*, CBC, n.d. [c. autumn 1976], YUA, Ostry Papers, F0370, 1991-030, vol. 20, file 135.

CHAPTER NINE

1 On the question of how much Dawson would be able to consult the diary, see McGregor to Dawson, 19 December 1950, LAC, Lamb Papers, MG31, D8, vol. 9, file 19; McGregor to Carruthers, 29 June 1951, LAC, Markham Papers, MG32, F6, Correspond – F.A. McGregor; "Literary Executors," 4 May 1952, LAC, WLMK, MG26, J18, file 2; "Memorandum re Use of Diaries," 8 May 1952, ibid.; and F. McGregor to other executors, 4 December 1953, LAC, Robertson Papers, MG30, E163, vol. 3(b). On Robertson's hesitancy, see Roberson to McGregor, 9 May 1955, LAC, Robertson Papers, MG30, E163, vol. 3(b); and Robertson to Lamb, 13 March 1953, ibid.

2 Fred McGregor to Lamb, 17 June 1955, LAC, Lamb Papers, vol. 9, file 7.

3 It is worth noting at the outset that Daviault didn't leave any letters or diaries from which we can judge him based on his own words. Instead, everything we know comes from the files of those who investigated him, leaving their impressions of his character, his mental state, and the bad things he allegedly did. The details about Daviault here largely draw from the background checks conducted by the Security Service and the collection of documents they amassed, including Daviault's wartime medical and service records. These are part of a special RCMP file on the missing diary and the Featherbed files. See LAC, CSIS, RG146, vol. 4944, "Missing Mackenzie King Diary" and "Featherbed File," vol. 2. The Featherbed files are housed at LAC yet when I requested access the archivists could not locate them. Canadian Press reporter Jim Bronskill was kind enough to give me digital copies of the files that had been released to him. In this book, I am citing the volume numbers that appear on the pages provided. Because the archivists at LAC could not provide me with the files, and because even the finding aids to these materials are not open to researchers, I am unable to provide full archival citations.

4 "Ottawa Survivor of Corvette Tells of Tragedy in Fog," *Ottawa Citizen*, 16 December 1941.

5 Details for these incidents are in the medical report conducted by a psychiatrist and included in LAC, RCMP, "Featherbed File," vol. 2.

6 Dempson, *Assignment Ottawa*, 28.

7 McGregor, "Confidential Memorandum re Diaries," 13 September 1955, LAC, Robertson Papers, MG30, E163, vol. 3(b).

8 [Photography section staff details], n.d. [October-November 1955], LAC, WLMK, MG26, J17, vol. 10, file 6; and Lamb to Colonel L.H. Nicholson, 18 October 1955, LAC, WLMK, MG26, J17, vol. 10, file 6.

9 [Blanked out] to S/Insp. A.M. Barr, 21 February 1972, LAC, CSIS, RG146, vol. 4944, "Missing Mackenzie King Diary, November 10 to December 31 1945, part 1."

10 R.I. MacEwan to A.M. Barr, 21 February 1972, LAC, RCMP, "Featherbed File," vol. 2; and [blanked out] to S/Insp. A.M. Barr, 21 February 1972, LAC, CSIS, RG146, vol. 4944, "Missing Mackenzie King Diary, November 10 to December 31 1945, part 1."

11 R.I. MacEwan to A.M. Barr, 21 February 1972, LAC, RCMP, "Featherbed File," vol. 2.

12 The details of the project are laid out in several files in the section of King's papers that contain the papers of the literary executors.

13 Dawson to Robertson, 14 August 1956, LAC, Robertson Papers, MG30, E163, vol. 3(b).

14 On the arrangements for Neatby's and Pickersgill's roles in biography, see Blair Neatby to Pickersgill, 12 April 1958, LAC, JP, vol. 278, file 9; Neatby, [memo of meeting at home of Lamb, with Lamb, Pickersgill, McGregor, and

Dawson], 6 April 1958, LAC, WLMK, MG26, J17, vol. 10, file 9; "Hint Pickersgill King Biographer," *Globe and Mail*, 30 July 1958, 13; and Robertson to Carruthers, 24 July 1958, LAC, Robertson Papers, MG30, E163, vol. 3(b).

15 McGregor to Sarah Dawson, 16 November 1958, LAC, WLMK, MG26, J17, vol. 10, file 10.

16 Dawson, *William Lyon Mackenzie King.*

17 "Other 1958 Literary Awards," *Globe and Mail*, 6 June 1959, 16; J.B. McGeachy, "Canada's Mystical Prime Minister," *Financial Post*, 22 November 1958; and C.R. Blackburn, "Biographer Reveals Romance in Early Life of Ambitious Mackenzie King," *Globe and Mail*, 17 November 1958, 10.

18 [Notes on Karl Menninger, *Love against Hate*], n.d., Dalhousie University Archives (DUA), Robert MacGregor Dawson Fonds [hereafter Dawson Papers], MS-2-256, box 18, file 4.

19 [Notes on Karen Horney, *Our Inner Conflicts: A Constructive Theory of Neurosis*], n.d., DUA, Dawson Papers, box 18, file 4.

20 See Gleason, *Normalizing the Ideal*, 75, 89; May, *Homeward Bound*, 74; and Ehrenreich, *The Hearts of Men*. In *Rebel without a Cause*, fatherhood is also implicated, with a father character wearing an apron as just one example of a supposedly emasculated man.

21 Markham, *Friendship's Harvest*, 151.

22 [Notes on Karl Menninger, *Love against Hate*].

23 Dawson doesn't directly draw on Menninger in the biography but he pays particular attention to the way, after the Mathilde Grossert affair, King began to single out his mother for special attention. "His diary references, too, which had always displayed tenderness and appreciation beyond the practice of most children, now were burdened with the most florid encomiums. Where he had previously been a devoted son and admirer, he now worshipped at a shrine, endowing his mother with all the virtues and finer attributes of womanhood." Dawson, *William Lyon Mackenzie King*, 82.

24 Halpenny to W.K. Lamb, 16 March 1959, LAC, WLMK, MG26, J17, vol. 10, file 10.

25 The brief notes for a meeting of the literary executors from around this time show that they were still undecided. They were contemplating making an abridged version of the diary which could be released to the public. The full diary would then be locked away until the year 2000. Other notebooks, including King's binders detailing his spiritualistic activities, were to be destroyed. "Policy regarding the King Diary," n.d. [c. 1958], LAC, Lamb Papers, MG31, D8, vol. 9, file 7.

26 "Does History Belong to the Men Who Make It?" *Maclean's*, 1 December 1958.

27 "Public Men and Their Diaries," *Ottawa Journal*, 6 January 1959.

28 H.S. Ferns, letter to the editor, *Globe and Mail*, 5 January 1959, 6.

29 "Note on Sources" for *Age of Mackenzie King*, draft, n.d. [c. 1955], YUA, Ostry Papers, F0370, 1991-030, vol. 19, file 126.

30 R.A. MacDougall, letter to editor, 12 January 1959, *Globe and Mail*, 6; and "Not So Private Diaries," *Toronto Telegram*, 20 December 1958.

31 Halpenny to Lamb, 16 March 1959, LAC, WLMK, MG26, J17, vol. 10, file 10; and Lamb to Halpenny, 23 March 1959, ibid. (emphasis in original).

CHAPTER TEN

1 The sketch of Scott here largely draws on Djwa, *The Politics of the Imagination*.

2 Margaret Collingwood to F.R. Scott, 14 November 1957, LAC, Francis Reginald Scott Fonds [hereafter Scott Papers], MG30, D211, vol. 3, file "The Blasted Pine, First Edition."

3 The relative bounty of this period of economic boom is a source of political disagreement among Canadians historians, as seen by the very different views in the two standard textbooks of the period. The positive view is given in Bothwell, English, and Drummond, *Canada since 1945*. Alvin Finkel offers a Marxist critique in *Our Lives*. Given the recent work on global economic inequality and how it changed over time, the original, more optimistic view now seems more useful for making sense of what was unique about this period. See Thomas Piketty, *Capital in the Twenty-First Century*.

4 Eugene Forsey, "Why Parliament at All?" Letter to the editor, *Globe and Mail*, 9 June 1956, 6. Another Forsey letter, to the *Ottawa Journal*, was read into the record of Parliament and became a subject of debate. See House of Commons *Debates*, 31 May 1956, 4529–34.

5 Brooke Claxton to T.W.L. MacDermot, 12 June 1956, LAC, Claxton Papers, vol. 81, file "T.W.L MacDermot."

6 Bruce Hutchison to Grant Dexter, 1 July [1955], UC, Hutchison Papers, box 1, file 10.

7 C.G. Power to T.A. Crerar, 15 April 1958, QUA, Power Papers, box 5, file "Crerar, Hon. T.A."

8 Although Doug Owram emphasizes the radical shift in the 1960s, his study of the era is alive to the continuities between the 1950s and 1960s even if he focuses more on the generational experience of the Baby Boom, including such things as educational practice and parenting advice. See Owram, *Born at the Right Time*. Deborah Cohen argues that in Britain the cultural shift happened at a grass-roots level, with family members of homosexuals and the handicapped, or those who had given up their children for adoption, opting to be more open about the realities of their lives. See Cohen, *Family Secrets*.

9 Heron, *Booze*, 314–31.

10 Morton, *At Odds*. Morton argues that, in the post-war years, the issue came to be more about the uses of gambling – whether it could be made to be of

some benefit and not simply abused by organized crime. This tended to individualize the problem of gambling, making it more situational and less about gambling in general. Gambling-addiction research would follow the alcoholism model.

11 Very little has been written about this in the Canadian context though the issue is nicely dealt with in "The Good Life," an episode of the CPAC documentaries series *The Fifties*, http://www.cpac.ca/en/programs/the-fifties/ (accessed 27 June 2016). On government housing policies, see Harris, *Creeping Conformity*; and Atwood, *Payback*. The American story is told in Hyman, *Debtor Nation*. An alternative view is presented in Calder, *Financing the American Dream*.

12 On the rise and decline of the Production Code, see Leff and Simmons, *The Dame in the Kimono*.

13 Creighton, *The Forked Road*, 118.

14 MacLennan, *The Watch That Ends the Night*, 47, 266, 275, 343.

15 *The Trial of Lady Chatterley: Regina v Penguin Books Limited: The Transcript of the Trial* (London: Penguin 1961).

16 Published in Philip Larkin, *High Windows* (London: Faber and Faber 1974).

17 Quoted in Djwa, *The Politics of the Imagination*, 348. The whole trial is dealt with from 339 to 348.

CHAPTER ELEVEN

1 Interview, 20 March 1966, *This Hour Has Seven Days* (CBC Digital Archives), http://www.cbc.ca/player/play/1725906310 (accessed 19 November 2015).

2 The synopsis of the controversy over *This Hour Has Seven Days* is gleaned from Watson, *This Hour Has Seven Decades*, chapter 10; and Taras, *The Newsmakers*, 60.

3 Watson, *This Hour Has Seven Decades*, 203.

4 Dempson, *Assignment Ottawa*, 1–8; Patrick Brennan, *Reporting the Nation's Business*, chapter 5.

5 Hutchison, *The Far Side of the Street*, 220.

6 Watson, *This Hour Has Seven Decades*, 132.

7 Taras, *The Newsmakers*, 54–5.

8 Watson, *This Hour Has Seven Decades*, 139.

9 Ibid.

10 Douglas Leiterman to Lamb, 3 July 1958, and McGregor to Leiterman, 13 July 1958, LAC, Pickersgill Papers, vol. 278, file 9.

11 All citation here are from *Close Up on Mackenzie King*, 10 and 17 March 1960, LAC, Canadian Broadcasting Corporation Fonds [hereafter CBC Papers], Acc. no. 1986-0810.

12 Douglas Leiterman, "The King Nobody Knew," *CBC Times*, 5–11 March 1960, LAC, Claxton Papers, vol. 78, file "I miscellaneous."

13 Brooke Claxton to C.D. Howe, 18 March 1960, LAC, Claxton Papers, vol.

78, file "C.D. Howe"; C.D. Howe to Brooke Claxton, 28 March 1960, ibid.; Paul Fox to C.G. Power, 6 April 1960, QUA, Power Papers, box 5, file "Fox, Paul"; and C.G. Power to Paul Fox, 11 April 1960, ibid.

14 Edwin Copps, "A Distorted Image of Mackenzie King," *Saturday Night*, 16 April 1960.

15 Ibid.

16 Douglas Leiterman, letter to the editor, *Saturday Night*, 30 April 1960.

17 Ibid.

18 *Canadian Annual Review, 1960* (Toronto: University of Toronto Press 1961), 363.

CHAPTER TWELVE

1 Pickersgill and Forster, *The Mackenzie King Record, Vol 2*, vii.

2 [Advertisement for Pickersgill, *The Mackenzie King Record*], *Globe and Mail*, 15 October 1960, 17.

3 I. Norman Smith, "How Mackenzie King Fought the War," *Saturday Night*, 15 October 1960.

4 "In Vancouver," *Globe and Mail*, 24 October 1960, 25.

5 C.G. Power to J.W. Pickersgill, 21 November 1960, QUA, Power Papers, box 8, file "Pickersgill, J.W."

6 Anonymous letter sent along with C.G. Power to J.W. Pickersgill, 21 November 1960, ibid.

7 *Canadian Annual Review, 1960* (Toronto: University of Toronto Press 1961), 32.

8 Blair Neatby to T.A. Crerar, 4 September 1956, QUA, Crerar Papers, box 89, corresp. 1956.

9 For an early reflection on these changes, see Berger, *The Writing of Canadian History*.

10 H. Blair Neatby, *The Lonely Heights, William Lyon Mackenzie King, Volume II, 1924–1932*; and H. Blair Neatby, *William Lyon Mackenzie King, Volume III, 1932–1939*.

11 Neatby, *The Lonely Heights*, 175.

12 Ibid., 204–6.

13 Ibid., 204.

14 Ibid., 204–6.

15 For a thoughtful report on the slow, uneven, and incomplete process of secularization in these years, but one that nonetheless regards the era of the late 1950s and 1960s as significant, see Gidney, *A Long Eclipse*.

16 Neatby to literary executors, 4 July 1961, LAC, JP, vol. 278, file 9.

CHAPTER THIRTEEN

1 Even scholars who disagree on the meaning of the '60s in Canada agree on the general anti-authoritarian impulse. This is highlighted, for example, in

Campbell, Clément, and Kealey, "Introduction: Time, Age, Myth: Towards a History of the Sixties," in Campbell, Clément, and Kealey, eds., *Debating Dissent*, 12; Palmer, *Canada's 1960s*, 4–5, 429; Kostash, *Long Way from Home*, 247; and Milligan, *Rebel Youth*, 3.

2 Taylor, *Sources of the Self*; and *The Malaise of Modernity*.

3 On Needham, see Wente, *An Accidental Canadian*, 29–31; Obituary, Richard Needham, *Globe and Mail*, 18 July 2005, http://v1.theglobeandmail.com/servlet/story/LAC.20050718.OBBRIEF18-3/BDAStory/BDA/deaths (accessed 19 November 2015).

4 Richard J. Needham, "The Halo and the Hoodlum," *Globe and Mail*, 3 November 1965, 6, and "A Writer's Notebook (XXXI)," *Globe and Mail*, 25 March 1968.

5 Richard J. Needham, "Unspeakable Love," *Globe and Mail*, 14 February 1966.

6 Ibid. It's not clear to me if Needham just made up this play or if it really was written and performed. I have not come across the play. Yet someone did write to the University of Toronto Press in 1959 asking for permission to reproduce in a play parts of King's diary that had appeared in the sections of Dawson's biography published in *Weekend* magazine. See J. Mason Manser to UTP, 2 February 1959, LAC, WLMK, MG26, J17, vol. 10, file 10.

7 Richard J. Needham, "The Art of the Impossible," *Globe and Mail*, 28 February 1966, and "Mr. Needham Advises," *Globe and Mail*, 17 July 1967.

8 "Camp's Vision Is New Order in Politics," *Globe and Mail*, 7 October 1966.

9 Litt, "Trudeaumania."

10 On the Ouellet/Papineau case, see Rudin, *Making History in Twentieth-Century Quebec*, 149–61.

11 H.B. Neatby to Maurice Careless, 17 May 1968, LAC, Lamb Papers, vol. 3, file "CHA."

12 Ibid.

13 J.W. Pickersgill to A.R.M. Lower, 14 March 1967, QUA, A.R.M. Lower Fonds [hereafter Lower Papers], Collection 5072, box 7, file "Correspondence, Pickersgill, John Whitney."

14 Tim Reid, "Ever Absorbing, Not So Complete," *Globe and Mail*, 23 November 1968.

15 C.P. Stacey, letter to the editor, *Globe and Mail*, 30 November 1968; Tim Reid, letter to the editor, *Globe and Mail*, 16 December 1968; and J.W. Pickersgill to Lower, 4 September 1969, QUA, Lower Papers, box 7, file "Correspondence, Pickersgill, John Whitney."

CHAPTER FOURTEEN

1 It's likely not a coincidence that one of the restricted files in Jack Pickersgill's papers contained correspondence about access to King's papers and diaries. It was closed until 2007 despite the fact that it contained nothing of a sensitive

nature, except the evidence that Pickersgill had essentially cherry-picked who would have access based on his own arbitrary criteria. The files are in LAC, Pickersgill Papers, vol. 279, files 1–3. See, for example, J.W. Pickersgill to Mark J. Moher, 23 March 1972, LAC, Pickersgill Papers, vol. 279, file 3; J.W. Pickersgill to William Kilbourn, 24 March 1972, LAC, Pickersgill Papers, vol. 279, file 2.

2 [A literary executor] to James Eayrs, 6 September 1966, LAC, Pickersgill Papers, vol. 278, file 10.

3 Kenneth McNaught, "National Affairs," *Saturday Night* (February 1966), 9–10.

4 In fact, it should really read "the Neatbys' arguments" for Neatby's wife, Jacqueline (Côté) Neatby, was just as strenuous in urging the literary executors to preserve and open up King's diary. Jacqueline Neatby, "Memo re Mackenzie King Papers," 13 June 1961, LAC, Lamb Papers, vol. 9, file 8.

5 Pickersgill to Donald M. Page, 20 May 1970, LAC, Pickersgill Papers, vol. 278, file 10; Lamb to Pickersgill, 4 December 1971, LAC, Pickersgill Papers, vol. 279, file 1; Lamb to Pickersgill, 28 December 1971, ibid.; and Pickersgill to Wilfrid Smith, 30 December 1971, ibid.

6 Pickersgill to W.I. Smith, 29 December 1971, LAC, Pickersgill Papers, vol. 279, file 1.

7 In preparing to open up the diaries, Lamb reflected on the role of Daviault in necessitating this action: "The existence of the bootleg microfilm copy is a further complication; I don't see how we can destroy the original and thereby give the copy an immensely greater value." W.K. Lamb to J.W. Pickersgill, 24 May 1971, LAC, Pickersgill Papers, vol. 279, file 3.

8 [Blanked out] to S/Insp. A.M. Barr, 21 February 1972, LAC, CSIS, RG146, vol. 4944, file "Missing Mackenzie King Diary, November 10 to December 31 1945, part 1."

9 W.K. Lamb to J.W. Pickersgill, 24 May 1971, LAC, Pickersgill Papers, vol. 279, file 3.

10 Lamb to Pickersgill, 28 December 1971, LAC, Pickersgill Papers, vol. 279, file 1.

11 Lamb to Neatby, 2 July 1963, LAC, Lamb Papers, vol. 9, file 8.

12 W.I. Smith to Pickersgill, 21 January 1972, LAC, Pickersgill Papers, vol. 279, file 1.

13 Lamb to Pickersgill, 22 August 1972, ibid.

14 Pickersgill to W.I. Smith, 27 August 1974, ibid.

CHAPTER FIFTEEN

1 Geoffrey Stevens, "A Special Day," *Globe and Mail*, 1 January 1975.

2 In 1974 Pickersgill and the other literary executors still intended not to release King's diaries for his retirement years but they changed their minds later in the decade and released these as well, again thinking that to keep them private

would only encourage more criticism and questions about what they were hiding. Pickersgill to W.I. Smith, 27 August 1974, LAC, Pickersgill Papers, vol. 279, file 1; Pickersgill to W.I. Smith, 30 March 1977, ibid.

3 "Historical Notes: Diary of a Prime Minister," *Time* [Canada], 13 January 1975, 9.

4 "Mackenzie King Began World War II with a Prayer," *Toronto Star*, 2 January 1975.

5 Pickersgill to Lamb, 9 January 1975, LAC, Pickersgill Papers, vol. 279, file 1; Lamb to Pickersgill, 21 January 1975, ibid.

6 Jennifer S.H. Brown, "Some Memories of My Uncle, Charles Perry Stacey," 1 March 1990, University of Toronto Archives (UTA), Stacey Family Papers [hereafter SF], B94-0014, box 1, file 7. This portrait of Stacey is also drawn from [Obituary, C.P. Stacey], no author, n.d. [c. 1989], UTA, C.P. Stacey Fonds [hereafter Stacey Papers], B2008-005, box 1, file 2; [Obituary, C.P. Stacey], *Toronto Star*, 19 November 1989, UTA, SF, box 1, file 7; Desmond Morton, "Obituary – Charles Perry Stacey, 1905–1989," *Books in Canada* (n.d.), ibid.; and especially Stacey, *A Date with History*.

7 Stacey presents a more mixed and appreciative view of King in his memoirs, though here too he notes King's love of pomp and ceremony. See Stacey, *A Date with History*, chapter 13.

8 Ibid., 14.

9 C.P. Stacey, "Mackenzie King and His Women," public address, Massey College, 7 February 1974, UTA, Stacey Papers, box 46, 1972-02-07; and C.P. Stacey, "Mackenzie King and His Friends," public address, UBC, 14 February 1975, UTA, Stacey Papers, box 46, 1975-02-14.

10 Peter Newman, "The Nobility of Sailor Jack's Last Career – Literary Chamberlain, History's Guardian," *Globe and Mail*, 17 January 1976.

11 Ramsay Cook, letter to the editor, *Globe and Mail*, 21 January 1976.

12 H.B. Neatby, letter to the editor, *Globe and Mail*, 29 January 1976.

13 Peter C. Newman, letter to the editor, *Globe and Mail*, 14 February 1976.

14 Details can be found in UTA, Stacey Papers, box 55, "A Very Double Life Corresp, 1974–77."

15 Stacey, *A Very Double Life*, 9.

16 Bruce Hutchison, "Bruce Hutchison's Thoughts on Mackenzie King," *Maclean's*, 15 November 1952.

17 McGregor doesn't name any of the women directly. He does talk about how King would go only so far, how he was unwilling to "let himself go," even venturing to refer to his possible "mother complex." See also McGregor, *The Fall & Rise of Mackenzie King: 1911–1919*, 82–91; and H. Blair Neatby, *The Lonely Heights, William Lyon Mackenzie King, Volume II, 1924–1932*, chapter 19.

18 Stacey, *A Very Double Life*, 36–7.

19 Ibid., 37–8, 81.

20 Ibid., 38.

21 Ibid., 41–8.

22 Ibid., 42–3.

23 Ibid., 81.

24 Some have thought Stacey particularly hard on King over this point, suggesting that many pet lovers today show a great deal of feeling for their dying animals. It's worth pointing out that the literary executors themselves sensed the danger of King's entries about Pat's death. There is a note in their papers indicating that these particular entries are to be destroyed. They were not, but it does show that Stacey wasn't alone in seeing King's reaction as over-the-top.

25 Stacey, *A Very Double Life*, 142–3.

26 Ibid., 160.

27 Ibid., 174.

28 Ibid., 175–6.

29 C.P. Stacey to W.K. Lamb, 19 May 1976, UTA, Stacey Papers, box 55, file "A Very Double Life Corresp, 1974–77."

30 Harry Bruce, "Prostitution if Necessary, but Not Necessarily Prostitution," *Ottawa Journal*, 23 March 1976; and *A Very Double Life* excerpts, *Toronto Star*, 11 March 1976.

31 *A Very Double Life* excerpts, *Toronto Star*, 11 March 1976.

32 "King was a 'worried little man,'" *Hamilton Spectator*, 1 May 1976; Jim Bremner, letter to the editor, *Toronto Star*, 11 March 1976; and William French, "Sex and All, He's Still an Enigma," *Globe and Mail*, 8 April 1976.

33 William French, "Sex and All, He's Still an Enigma," *Globe and Mail*, 8 April 1976.

34 Peterboro [sic] citizen to Stacey, 11 March 1976, UTA, Stacey Papers, box 56, "ADVL Letters, etc. 1976–78"; Cec[e]lia Whelan, letter to the editor, *Ottawa Journal*, 22 March 1976; and Neatby to Lamb, n.d. [c. 1975–76], LAC, Lamb Papers, vol. 37, file 16.

35 W.K. Lamb to Stacey, 27 June 1976, UTA, Stacey Papers, box 55, "A Very Double Life Corresp, 1974–77"; and Michael Holyroyd in his introduction to Strachey, *The Illustrated Queen Victoria*, 6.

CHAPTER SIXTEEN

1 H.S. Ferns, "Mackenzie King of Canada, Part I," *Canadian Forum* (November 1948), 174–7.

2 Watkins, *Prospect of Canada*, 10.

3 Glassco, *Memoirs of Montparnasse*. On the fictional elements of the memoir, see Busby, *A Gentleman of Pleasure*, esp. chapter 9. Charles Ritchie published several memoirs, though the one that caught the most attention at this time was *The Siren Years*.

4 Christina Newman, "How the Power of the Old Establishment Was Broken," *Globe and Mail*, 15 December 1975. The reference to the Ostrys is in

Christina [surname not given] to Bernard Ostry, 3 November 1967, YUA, Ostry Papers, vol. 158, file 1292.

5 Kay Kritzwiser, "Laurier House, Mackenzie King's Old home," *Globe and Mail*, 27 March 1976. Fotheringham made this comment while appearing on a TV show alongside Maggie Trudeau, who was herself promoting her first starring role in a new film. See *90 Minutes Live*, 29 December 1977, LAC, CBC Papers, Acc. no. 1978-0318.

6 Roy MacSkimming, "King's Secrets Are Superior Court Gossip," *Toronto Star*, 14 April 1976; and "Between Privacy and Relevance," *Ottawa Journal*, 30 March 1976.

7 Hugh F. Don't, "Under the Stars" [clipping – no publication given, c. April 1976], UTA, Stacey Papers, box 1, file 1.

8 James Eayrs, "Oedipus Rex," *Canadian Forum* (June-July 1976).

9 Reg Whitaker, "The young S.O.B.?" *Canadian Dimension* (c. May 1976), 36–7.

10 On psychiatry in the 1970s and on the anti-psychiatry movement, see Edward Shorter, *A History of Psychiatry: From the Era of the Asylum to the Age of Prozac* (New York: John Wiley and Sons 1997), 274–7; Grob, *The Mad among Us*; and Paris, *The Fall of an Icon*.

11 Paul Fox, "The Right Honorable Weirdo," *Maclean's* (19 April 1976), 64, 66; and Len Tayler, "What They Said about Willie Was True," *Vancouver Province*, 11 June 1976.

12 B[ruce Hutchison] to Dexter, [report on conversation with Norman Lambert], 4 March 1951, QUA, Dexter Papers, box 6, file 3.

13 Robertson Davies, *The Manticore* (Toronto: Macmillan 1972), 87.

14 Ibid., 101; and Elspeth Cameron, "Irreverent, Imaginative Truth," *Quill & Quire* (January 1984), 27.

15 "Too Rugged a Test," Editorial, *Globe and Mail*, 14 September 1964, 6.

16 Author's interview with H. Blair Neatby, 22 August 2012.

17 Esberey, "Prime Ministerial Character: An Alternative View"; and Courtney, "Prime Ministerial Character: An Examination of Mackenzie King's Political Leadership."

18 H. Blair Neatby, "Mackenzie King and Psycho-Biography," [publication not given] 3:4 (1975): 15–16, UTA, Stacey Papers, box 38, file "King – Press Clippings, Notes, 1950–76."

19 Neatby, "Mackenzie King and Psycho-Biography."

20 Reginald Whitaker, "Mackenzie King in the Dominion of the Dead," *Canadian Forum* (February 1976), 6–11.

21 Ibid.

22 Stacey, *A Very Double Life*, 13, 64.

23 David Lewis, "His Privy Parts: On Perusing the Diaries of Mackenzie King, Self-Anointed Leader and Most Peculiar Man," *Books in Canada* (June

1976), 3–4; and J.E. Esberey, [review of *A Very Double Life*], *Histoire Sociale/ Social History* 9:19 (1977): 177–8.

24 Lynn McIntyre and Joel J. Jeffries, "The King of Clubs: A Psychobiography of William Lyon Mackenzie King, 1893–1900," 22, University of Manitoba Archives [UMA], Heather Robertson Fonds [hereafter Robertson Papers], MSS77, PC7, TC67, box 1, file 2.

25 Joy Esberey, *Knight of the Holy Spirit*, 3–4, 14.

26 A later, fuller version is Roazen, *Canada's King*.

CHAPTER SEVENTEEN

1 Details on Daviault's death along with the letter, A.M. Barr to [blank], 6 March 1972, LAC, RCMP, "Featherbed File," vol. 2; and Lamb's comments in Lamb to Pickersgill, 22 Aug 1972, LAC, Pickersgill Papers, vol. 279, file 1.

2 On the Featherbed investigation, see Whitaker, Kealey, and Parnaby, *Secret Service*, chapter 8.

3 Memorandum for File re: Featherbed, 14 August 1969, LAC, CSIS, RG146, vol. 4944, file "Missing Mackenzie King Diary, November 10 to December 31 1945, part 1."

4 On meeting with Lamb and Pickersgill, see ibid. Although the Security Service agents didn't specifically tell Lamb and Pickersgill whom they hoped to investigate in the matter of the King diary, an internal Security Service report a few weeks later suggests that it was none other than Norman Robertson, their fellow literary executor, and a man who had headed External Affairs and the Canadian civil service. Lamb had allowed the agents to view King's special Gouzenko diary. This was separate from his regular diary. In reviewing the events of the Gouzenko scandal from King's perspective, the agents were reassured that Robertson "exhibit[ed] an approach to the problem entirely consistent with the best interests of the country and security in general." The Mounties had been suspicious of Robertson because of some of his decisions. They particularly wondered about the security clearance he granted for George Vickers Haythorne. But apparently, the King diary made Norman Robertson seem better to the Mounties.

5 [Name blanked out] to S/Insp. A.M. Barr, 21 February 1972, LAC, CSIS, RG146, vol. 4944, file "Missing Mackenzie King Diary, November 10 to December 31 1945, part 1."

6 [Name blanked out] to S/Insp. A.M. Barr, 21 February 1972, ibid.

7 S/Insp A.M. Barr to [blank], 13 April 1972, LAC, RCMP, "Featherbed File," vol. 3.

8 Details of the Security Service investigation, including the report of the medical doctor regarding Daviault's death, are collected in LAC, RCMP, "Featherbed File," vol. 2.

9 A.M. Barr to Cpl. MacKinnon, 14 September 1972, LAC, RCMP, "Featherbed

File," vol. 3; Cpl. D.L. MacKinnon to S/Insp A.M. Barr, 19 January 1973, ibid.; and [name unclear] to Dave, transit slip, 4 July 1974, ibid.

10 The classic text here is Lipsett, *Continental Divide*. See also Horowitz, *Canadian Labour in Politics*, esp. chapter 1; and Friedenberg, *Deference to Authority*.

11 For a good recent account of the transformation of American politics and culture in the 1970s that recognizes the common ground on left and right in the decade, centring on a culture of individualism, see Borstelmann, *The 1970s*. Also useful on how Watergate fit into the broader culture of the decade is Jenkins, *Decade of Nightmares*.

12 Porter's book, *The Vertical Mosaic*, was the University of Toronto Press's best-selling title to that date, selling over 100,000 copies. See also MacSkimming, *The Perilous Trade*, 102; and Berton, *The Smug Minority*. In his biography of Berton, Brian McKillop notes that the book generated a huge amount of controversy but sold especially well in smaller centres. See McKillop, *Pierre Berton*, 478–9.

13 Richard J. Needham, "The Rulers and the Ruled," *Globe and Mail*, 10 June 1965, 6.

14 "Canada Has Its Secrets, Too," editorial, *Globe and Mail*, 2 July 1971.

15 Donald C. Rowat, "How Much Administrative Secrecy?" *Canadian Journal of Economics and Political Science* 31:4 (1965): 480, 482. It's becoming clearer that others around King did know of his activities but remained silent. King's visits to the Kingston fortune-teller Mrs Bleaney were already gossiped about (and fretted over) by Liberal Party insiders at the time of the 1926 election. Hillmer, *O.D. Skelton*, 150.

16 "Historical Notes: Diary of a Prime Minister," *Time* [Canada], 13 January 1975, 9; John K. Elliott, "Fortunate Diaries of King Preserved," *London Free Press*, 1 May 1976.

17 Harry Ferns to Bernard Ostry, 16 May 1976, YUA, Ostry Papers, vol. 20, file 138.

18 On Lorimer's place in Canadian publishing, see MacSkimming, *Perilous Trade*, 208–17.

19 Bernard Ostry to James Lorimer, 29 July 1976, YUA, Ostry Papers, vol. 20, file 138.

20 A fuller account of the republishing of *Age of Mackenzie King* is provided in Dummitt, "Harry Ferns, Bernard Ostry and *The Age of Mackenzie King*."

21 Dalton Camp, "Liberals Shielded Mackenzie King from Biographers," *Toronto Star*, 5 November 1976; and John Meisel, [draft introduction], 21 June 1976, YUA, Ostry Papers, vol. 20, file 138.

22 Peter Newman, "The King of Kings," *Maclean's*, 29 November 1976; David McIntosh, letter to the editor, *Globe and Mail*, 26 March 1976; and "Historian Tells of Flesh-and-Blood PM," *The Liberal*, 5 May 1976.

23 Heather Robertson, "Chills," *Saturday Night* (November 1976), 39–40.

24 See, for example, Ostry's appearance on *The Larry Solway Show*, [Interview with Bernard Ostry], *Larry Solway Show*, n.d. [c. 15 February 1977], LAC, Columbia Pictures Television Canada Fonds, Acc. no. 1987-0373.

25 Tom Barrett, "Former Archivist Admits Denying Writer King Papers," *Vancouver Sun*, 22 November 1976.

26 Bernard Ostry to Harry Ferns, n.d. [c. 22 November 1976], YUA, Ostry Papers, vol. 20, file 138. On the scandal, see Regehr, *The Beauharnois Scandal*.

27 Richard Gwyn, "King Received $25,000 from his Fundraisers," *Toronto Star*, 6 January 1977, 4; and Barbara Yaffe, "King Knew What Donations Were about, Was a Snake in Grass: Donor's Niece," *Globe and Mail*, n.d. [7 January 1977], YUA, Ostry Papers, vol. 20, file 136.

28 "King Had Great Faith in His Own Incorruptibility, Author Says," *Globe and Mail*, 6 January 1977, 9, YUA, Ostry Papers, vol. 20, file 136.

29 J.L. Granatstein, "Was King Really Bribed? Diaries Cast Doubt on It," *Globe and Mail*, 18 January 1976; Ramsay Cook, "The Age of Mackenzie King," *Globe and Mail*, 22 January 1977, 39; and Bernard Ostry, letter to the editor, *Globe and Mail*, 18 January 1977, YUA, Ostry Papers, vol. 19, file 132.

30 Hugh Winsor, "The Tea That Aided the Party in Boston and Other Questions from an Old Affair," *Globe and Mail*, [7 January 1977], YUA, Ostry Papers, F0370, 1991-030, vol. 20, file 136; Bernard Ostry, letter to the editor, *Globe and Mail*, 22 January 1977; and Bernard Ostry, letter to the editor, *Globe and Mail*, 18 January 1977, YUA, Ostry Papers, vol. 19, file 132.

31 Bernard Ostry, letter to the editor, *Globe and Mail*, 22 January 1977.

32 "Ostry: How King Screwed Canada," *Georgia Straight*, 17–24 February 1977.

33 [Statement by Blair Neatby], 18 January 1977, LAC, JP, vol. 279, file 1.

34 House of Commons *Debates*, 9 December 1975, 9847-8.

35 Ibid., 15 November 1977, 873; and Lawrence Martin, "Leaked RCMP Dossier on Trudeau Going at $100,000, Sources Say," *Globe and Mail*, 17 November 1977, 2.

36 D.B. Smith, S/Sgt International Obligations, to Officer i/c B Operations, 9 October 1980, LAC, RCMP, "Featherbed File," vol. 5. On the controversy over Trudeau's alleged homosexuality and the Kissinger/Nixon comments, see English, *Just Watch Me*, 118.

37 Cossitt frequently put questions about the Featherbed files on the order paper in the late 1970s and early 1980s. On the controversy over the Gouzenko papers, see 1981 documents in "Missing Mackenzie King Diary, November 10 to December 31 1945, part 1," and vol. 5 of "Featherbed File."

38 [Transcript, CJOH Nesline, Missing Espionage Documents], 6 May 1981, LAC, CSIS, RG146, vol. 4944, "Missing Mackenzie King Diary, November 10 to December 31 1945, part 1."

39 "Spying Papers Not Missing, Kaplan States," *Globe and Mail*, 28 May 1981, n.p., LAC, CSIS, RG146, vol. 4944, "Missing Mackenzie King Diary, November

10 to December 31 1945, part 1"; LAC, CSIS, RG146, vol. 4944, Memo, Officer i/c B Operations H.W. Brandes to Officer i/c Secretariat to the DG, ATTN. c/M S. Kelley, 22 April 1981; and o i/c SDG [Supt. Schultz?] to o i/c B Ops and [blanked out], 16 April 1981, LAC, CSIS, RG146, vol. 4944, "Missing Mackenzie King Diary, November 10 to December 31 1945, part 1."

40 "Ostry: How King Screwed Canada," *Georgia Straight*, 17–24 February 1977; and Julianne Labreche, "The Once and Future King," *Maclean's*, 15 January 1979, 15–17.

41 Pickersgill to W.I. Smith, 15 March 1977, LAC, JP, vol. 279, file 1.

CHAPTER EIGHTEEN

1 Cheryl Sutherland, "King's Diaries Basis for Novel," *Star-Phoenix* [Saskatoon], 19 November 1983; Elspeth Cameron, "Irreverent, Imaginative Truth," *Quill & Quire* (January 1984), 27; and Barbara Wade Rose, "Fact and Fiction," *Books in Canada* (August/September 1986), 7–10;

2 *The King Chronicle* (Dir. Donald Brittain, 1988); Dennis Lee, *Alligator Pie*.

3 Norman Hillmer and J.L. Granatstein, "Historians Rank the BEST AND WORST Canadian Prime Ministers," *Maclean's*, 21 April 1997.

4 Granatstein and Hillmer, *Prime Ministers*, 6.

5 Ibid., 84, 101.

6 Ibid., 2, 227.

7 Bliss, *Right Honourable Men*, 123, 124–5.

8 Ibid., 128.

9 Ibid., 128, 129.

10 Stephen Azzi and Norman Hillmer, "Ranking Canada's Best and Worst Prime Ministers," *Maclean's*, 7 October 2016.

11 In the midst of early multiculturalism policies, the rights revolution, and a rethinking of Canada's racial history, some of Mackenzie King's policies that were not seen as significant in the 1950s would take on greater importance. See Adachi, *The Enemy That Never Was*; and Abella and Troper, "*None Is Too Many*."

12 Even as Bliss and Hillmer and Granatstein were writing about the relative greatness of Canada's prime ministers, the historical profession was itself turning its back on a notion of politics that emphasized the leading role of the men who headed governments. Bliss himself reflected on this in the midst of the transformation. See Bliss, "Privatizing the Mind."

CONCLUSION

1 See, for example, Frank Graves, "The Trust Deficit: What Does It Mean?" http://www.ekospolitics.com/wp-content/uploads/full_report_may_14_2013.pdf (accessed 1 July 2015).

2　See, for example, the excellent work being done by the Samara institute on educating citizens and encouraging democratic reform at www.samara canada.com and in particular its book on the experience of members of Parliament: Loat and MacMillan, *Tragedy in the Commons*.

3　Nevitte, *The Decline of Deference*. Nevitte was building on the seminar work of Ronald Inglehart and his discussion of the rise of "post-materialist" values as a force in Western democracies. See Inglehart, *The Silent Revolution*, and *Cultural Shift in Advanced Industrial Society*. This idea of value change has been part of a larger discussion of the so-called democratic deficit in Western democracies and the possible explanations for it. On the democratic deficit, the key resource is Norris, *Democratic Deficit*. Norris is skeptical about the extent of the democratic deficit, but see also the essays in Lenard and Simeon, eds., *Imperfect Democracies*.

4　On the mid-century turn against shame and toward a culture of openness in Britain, see Cohen, *Family Secrets*, and, with a focus on political scandal, Davenport-Hines, *An English Affair*.

5　On Macdonald, see Ged Martin, "John A. Macdonald and the Bottle." The relationship between Laurier and Émilie Barthe (Lavergne), as well as a brief note on when the information appeared, can be found in Réal Bélanger's entry for her in the *Dictionary of Canadian Biography*. On the Trudeau marriage stories, see English, *Just Watch Me*, 325–9.

6　T.J.A. "Mackenzie King in Candour," *Kingston Whig-Standard*, 3 December 1952.

POSTSCRIPT

1　"U of T Shocked at Death of New Chief," [clipping, newspaper title not given], 9 August 1983, LAC, RCMP, "Featherbed File," vol. 5; and author's interview with Lucile McGregor, 22 February 2008.

2　Memo, Head [blank] to DG CI, 9 January 1985, LAC, RCMP, "Featherbed File," vol. 2.

3　Pickersgill and Forster, *The Mackenzie King Record: Volume 3, 1945–1946*, vi.

4　"Mr. King's Diaries: Archives – Photostating [sic]," n.d. [c. January 1956], LAC, WLMK, MG26, J17, vol. 10, file 6.

Bibliography

ARCHIVAL SOURCES

Clara Thomas Archives, York University (YUA)
  Bernard Ostry Papers
Cork County Archives, Ireland (CCA)
  Geraldine Cummins Papers
Dalhousie University Archives (DUA)
  Robert MacGregor Dawson Papers
Library and Archives Canada (LAC)
  Canadian Broadcasting Corporation Fonds
  Canadian Security Intelligence Service Papers
  Brooke Claxton Papers
  Columbia Pictures Television Canada Fonds
  H.S. Ferns Papers
  Jessie Kinsey Papers
  W.K. Lamb Papers
  William Lyon Mackenzie King Papers
  Violet Rosa Markham Carruthers Papers
  Arthur Meighen Papers
  Norman Robertson Papers
  Francis Reginald Scott Papers
  John Stevenson Papers
Queen's University Archives (QUA)
  T.A. Crerar Papers
  Grant Dexter Papers
  A.R.M Lower Papers
  C.G. Power Papers
University of Calgary, Special Collections (UC)
  Bruce Hutchison Papers
University of Toronto Archives (UTA)
  C.P. Stacey Papers
  Stacey Family Papers

William Ready Division of Archives and Research Collections, McMaster
University (MUA)
W.L. Morton Papers

SECONDARY SOURCES

Abella, Irving, and Harold Troper. *"None Is Too Many": Canada and the Jews of Europe, 1933–1948*. Toronto: Lester and Orpen Dennys 1983.

Adachi, Ken. *The Enemy That Never Was: A History of the Japanese Canadians*. Toronto: McClelland and Stewart 1976.

Appiah, Kwame Anthony. *The Honor Code: How Moral Revolutions Happen*. New York: W.W. Norton 2010.

Atwood, Margaret. *Edible Woman*. Toronto: McClelland and Stewart 1969.

– *Payback: Debt and the Shadow of Wealth*. Toronto: Anansi 2010.

Azoulay, Dan. *Hearts and Minds: Canadian Romance at the Dawn of the Modern Era, 1900–1930*. Calgary: University of Calgary Press 2012.

Bailey, Beth, and David Farber, eds. *America in the 70s*. Lawrence: University of Kansas Press 2004.

Bedore, Margaret Elizabeth. "The Reading of Mackenzie King." PhD thesis, Queen's University, 2008.

Berger, Carl. *The Writing of Canadian History: Aspects of English-Canadian Historical Writing since 1900*. 2nd ed. Toronto: University of Toronto Press 1986.

Berton, Pierre. *The Smug Minority*. Toronto: McClelland and Stewart 1968.

Betcherman, Lita-Rose. *Ernest Lapointe: Mackenzie King's Great Quebec Lieutenant*. Toronto: University of Toronto Press 2002.

Binkley, Sam. *Getting Loose: Lifestyle Consumption in the 1970s*. Durham, NC: Duke University Press 2007.

Bliss, Michael. "Privatizing the Mind: The Sundering of Canadian History, the Sundering of Canada." *Journal of Canadian Studies* 26:4 (1991–92): 6–11.

– *Right Honourable Men: The Descent of Canadian Politics from Macdonald to Chrétien*. Rev. ed. Toronto: Harper Collins 2004.

Boorstin, Daniel. *The Image, or What Happened to the American Dream*. New York: Atheneum 1962.

Borstelmann, Thomas. *The 1970s: A New Global History from Civil Rights to Economic Inequality*. Princeton, NJ: Princeton University Press 2012.

Bothwell, Robert. "Let Us Now Praise Famous Men": Political Memoirs and Biography in Canada." In George W. Egerton, ed., *Political Memoir: Essays on the Politics of Memory*. London: Frank Cass 1994. 121–30.

Bothwell, Robert, John English, and Ian Drummond. *Canada since 1945: Power, Politics, Provincialism*. Rev. ed. Toronto: University of Toronto Press 1989.

Bowman, James A. *Honor: A History*. New York: Encounter Books 2006.

Brandon, Ruth. *The Spiritualists: The Passion for the Occult in the Nineteenth and Twentieth Centuries*. Buffalo, NY: Prometheus Books 1983.

Brennan, Patrick. *Reporting the Nation's Business: Press-Government Relations during the Liberal Years, 1935–1957*. Toronto: University of Toronto Press 1994.

Burtch, Michale. *Jack Bush: Hymn to the Sun, Early Work*. Sault Ste Marie, ON: Art Gallery of Algoma 1997.

Busby, Brian John. *A Gentleman of Pleasure: One Life of John Glassco, Poet, Memoirist, Translator and Pornographer*. Montreal and Kingston: McGill-Queen's University Press 2011.

Calder, Lendol. *Financing the American Dream: A Cultural History of Consumer Credit*. Princeton, NJ: Princeton University Press 2001.

Campbell, Laura, Dominique Clément, and Gregory S. Kealey, eds. *Debating Dissent: Canada and the 1960s*. Toronto: University of Toronto Press 2012.

Carr, E.H. *What Is History?* New York: Knopf 1961.

Chapnick, Adam. "A 'Conservative' National Story?: The Evolution of Citizenship and Immigration's *Discover Canada.*" *American Review of Canadian Studies* 41:1 (2011): 20–36.

Coates, Colin M., and Cecilia Morgan. *Representations of Madeleine de Verchères and Laura Secord*. Toronto: University of Toronto Press 2002.

Cohen, Deborah. *Family Secrets: Living with Shame from the Victorians to the Present Day*. London: Viking 2013.

Collier, James Lincoln. *The Rise of Selfishness in America*. New York: Oxford University Press 1991.

Cook, Ramsay. *The Regenerators: Social Criticism in Late Victorian English Canada*. Toronto: University of Toronto Press 1985.

Cook, Terry. "An Archival Revolution: W. Kaye Lamb and the Transformation of the Archival Profession." *Archivaria* 60 (2006): 185–234.

Cook, Tim. *Warlords: Borden, King and Canada's World Wars*. Toronto: Allen Lane 2012.

Courtney, John C. "Prime Ministerial Character: An Examination of Mackenzie King's Political Leadership." *Canadian Journal of Political Science* 9:1 (1976): 77–100.

Cousins, Wendy. "Writer, Medium, Suffragette, Spy? The Unseen Adventures of Geraldine Cummins." *Paranormal Review* 45 (2008): 3–7.

Creighton, Donald. *The Forked Road: Canada, 1939–1957*. Toronto: McClelland and Stewart 1976.

– *John A. Macdonald: The Old Chieftain*. Toronto: MacMillan 1955.

– *John A. Macdonald: The Young Politician*. Toronto: MacMillan 1952.

– "Sir John A. Macdonald and Canadian Historians," *Canadian Historical Review* 39 (March 1948): 1–13.

Crowley, Brian Lee. *Fearful Symmetry: The Rise and Fall of Canada's Founding Values*. Toronto: Key Porter 2009.

Cummins, Geraldine. *Unseen Adventures: An Autobiography Covering Thirty-Four Years of Work in Psychical Research*. London: Rider 1951.

Davenport-Hines, Richard. *An English Affair: Sex, Class and Power in the Age of Profumo*. London: William Collins 2013.

Davies, Robertson. *The Manticore*. Toronto: Macmillan 1972.

Dawson, R. MacGregor. *William Lyon Mackenzie King: A Political Biography, Volume 1, 1874–1923*. Toronto: University of Toronto Press 1958.

Dempson, Peter. *Assignment Ottawa: Seventeen Years in the Press Gallery*. Toronto: General Publishing 1968.

Dewar, Kenneth C. *Frank Underhill and the Politics of Ideas*. Montreal and Kingston: McGill-Queen's University Press 2015.

Djwa, Sandra. *The Politics of the Imagination: A Life of F.R. Scott*. Toronto: McClelland and Stewart 1987.

Dryden, Jean E. "The Mackenzie King Papers: An Archival Odyssey." *Archivaria* 6 (summer 1978): 40–69.

Dummitt, Christopher. "Harry Ferns, Bernard Ostry and *The Age of Mackenzie King*: Liberal Orthodoxy and Its Discontents in the 1950s." *Labour/Le Travail* 66 (autumn 2010): 107–39.

– "Mackenzie King Wasn't a Libertarian: Drug History and the Forgotten Sixties." *BC Studies* 153 (spring 2007): 107–15.

– "The 'Taint of Self': Reflections on Ralph Connor, His Fans, and the Problem of Morality in Recent Canadian Historiography.' *Histoire Sociale/Social History* 46:91 (2013): 63–90.

Dyck, Erika. *Psychedelic Psychiatry: LSD on the Canadian Prairies*. Winnipeg: University of Manitoba Press 2012.

Ehrenreich, Barbara. *The Hearts of Men: The American Dream and the Flight from Commitment*. Garden City, NJ: Doubleday 1983.

Engel, Marian. *Bear: A Novel*. Toronto: McClelland and Stewart 1976.

English, John. *Just Watch Me: The Life of Pierre Elliott Trudeau, 1968–2000*. Toronto: Knopf 2009.

Esberey, J.E. *Knight of the Holy Spirit: A Study of William Lyon Mackenzie King*. Toronto: University of Toronto Press 1980.

– "Prime Ministerial Character: An Alternative View." *Canadian Journal of Political Science* 9:1 (1976): 101–6.

Fahrni, Magda, and Robert Rutherdale, eds. *Creating Postwar Canada: Community, Diversity and Dissent, 1945–1975*. Vancouver: UBC Press 2007.

Farber, David. *The Sixties: From Memory to History*. Chapel Hill: University of North Carolina Press 1995.

Farley, John. *Brock Chisholm, the World Health Organization, and the Cold War*. Vancouver: UBC Press 2008.

Farthing, John. *Freedom Wears a Crown*. Toronto: Kingswood House 1957.

Ferns, H S. *Reading from Left to Right: One Man's Political History*. Toronto: University of Toronto Press 1983.

Ferns, H.S., and Bernard Ostry. *The Age of Mackenzie King: Rise of the Leader*. Toronto: British Books 1955.

– "Mackenzie King and the First World War." *Canadian Historical Review* 36:2 (1955): 93–112.

Finkel, Alvin. *Our Lives: Canada after 1945*. Toronto: Lorimer 1997.

Forsey, Eugene. *A Life on the Fringe: The Memoirs of Eugene Forsey*. Toronto: University of Toronto Press 1990.

– *The Royal Power of Dissolution of Parliament in the British Commonwealth*. Toronto: Oxford University Press 1943.

Forsey, Helen. *Eugene Forsey: Canada's Maverick Sage*. Toronto: Dundurn 2012.

"Forum: History under Harper." *Labour/Le Travail* 73 (spring 2014): 195–238.

Fraser, John, and Graham Fraser, eds. *Blair Fraser Reports: Selections, 1944–1968*. Toronto: Macmillan 1969.

Friedenberg, Edgar Z. *Deference to Authority: The Case of Canada*. White Plains, NY: M.E. Sharpe 1980.

Fukuyama, Francis. *The Great Disruption: Human Nature and the Reconstitution of Social Order*. New York: Free Press 1999.

Gidney, Catherine. *A Long Eclipse: The Liberal Protestant Establishment and the Canadian University, 1920–1970*. Montreal and Kingston: McGill-Queen's University Press 2004.

Gidney, Catherine, and Michael Dawson, "Persistence and Inheritance: Rethinking Periodization and English Canada's 'Twentieth Century.'" In Christopher Dummitt and Michael Dawson, eds., *Contesting Clio's Craft: New Directions and Debates in Canadian History*. London: Institute for the Study of the Americas 2009. 47–74.

Glassbert, David. *Sense of History: The Place of the Past in American Life*. Amherst: University of Massachusetts Press 2001.

Glassco, John. *Memoirs of Montparnasse*. Toronto: Oxford University Press 1970.

Gleason, Mona. *Normalizing the Ideal: Psychology, Schooling and the Family in Postwar Canada*. Toronto: University of Toronto Press 1999.

Gordon, Alan. *The Hero and the Historians: Historiography and the Uses of Jacques Cartier*. Vancouver: UBC Press 2010.

Graham, Roger. *The King-Byng Affair, 1926: A Question of Responsible Government*. Toronto: Copp Clark 1967.

Granatstein, J.L. *A Man of Influence: Norman A. Robertson and Canadian Statecraft, 1929–1968*. Toronto: Deneau 1981.

– *The Ottawa Men: The Civil Service Mandarins, 1935–1957*. Toronto: Oxford University Press 1982.

Granatstein, J.L., and J.M. Hitsman. *Broken Promises: A History of Conscription in Canada*. Toronto: Oxford University Press 1977.

Granatstein, J.L., and Norman Hillmer. *Prime Ministers: Ranking Canada's Leaders*. Toronto: Harper Collins 1999.

Greenberg, David. *Nixon's Shadow: The History of an Image*. New York: W.W. Norton 2003.

Grierson, Frank. *William Lyon Mackenzie King: Histology and Vision*. Ottawa, 1952.

Grob, Gerald. *The Mad among Us: A History of the Care of America's Mentally Ill.* New York: Free Press 1994.

Halbwachs, Maurice. *On Collective Memory.* Ed and trans. Lewis A. Coser. Chicago: University of Chicago Press 1992.

Hale, Nathan G. *The Rise and Crisis of Psychoanalysis in the United States: Freud and the Americans, 1917–1985.* New York: Oxford University Press 1995.

Hardy, H. Reginald. *Mackenzie King of Canada: A Biography.* Toronto: Oxford University Press 1949.

Harris, Richard. *Creeping Conformity: How Canada Became Suburban.* Toronto: University of Toronto Press 2004.

Heath, Joseph, and Andrew Potter. *The Rebel Sell: Why the Culture Can't Be Jammed.* Toronto: Harper Perennial 2004.

Henderson, George F. *W.L. Mackenzie King: A Bibliography and Research Guide.* Toronto: University of Toronto Press 1998.

Heron, Craig. *Booze: A Distilled History.* Toronto: Between the Lines 2003.

Hillmer, Norman. *O.D. Skelton: A Portrait of Canadian Ambition.* Toronto: University of Toronto Press 2015.

Himmelfarb, Gertrude. *The De-Moralization of Society: From Victorian Virtues to Modern Values.* New York: Vintage Books 1994.

Hodgetts, J.E., ed. *The Sound of One Voice: Eugene Forsey and His Letters to the Press.* Toronto: University of Toronto Press 2000.

Hodgetts, J.E., et al. *The Biography of an Institution: The Civil Service Commission of Canada, 1908–1967.* Montreal and Toronto: McGill-Queen's University Press 1972.

Horowitz, Gad. *Canadian Labour in Politics.* Toronto: University of Toronto Press 1968.

Hutchison, Bruce. *The Far Side of the Street.* Toronto: Macmillan 1976.

– *The Incredible Canadian: A Candid Biography of Mackenzie King, His Works, His Times and His Nation.* Toronto: Longman, Green 1952.

– *The Unknown Country: Canada and Her People.* Toronto: Longmans, Green 1942.

Hyman, Louis R. *Debtor Nation: The History of America in Red Ink.* Princeton, NJ: Princeton University Press 2011.

Inglehart, Ronald. *Cultural Shift in Advanced Industrial Society.* Princeton, NJ: Princeton University Press 1990.

– *The Silent Revolution.* Princeton, NJ: Princeton University Press 1977.

Jang, Sarah. "The Pitfalls of Using Google Ngram to Study Language." *Wired* (12 October 2015), http://www.wired.com/2015/10/pitfalls-of-studying-language-with-google-ngram/ (accessed 2 May 2016).

Jenkins, Keith. *On "What Is History?": From Carr and Elton to Rorty and White.* London: Routledge 1995.

Jenkins, Philip. *Decade of Nightmares: The End of the Sixties and the Making of Eighties America.* Oxford: Oxford University Press 2006.

Jochelson, Richard, and Kirsten Kramar. *Sex and the Supreme Court: Obscenity and Indecency Law in* Canada. Halifax: Fernwood 2011.

Johnston, Russell T. *Selling Themselves: The Emergence of Canadian Advertising.* Toronto: University of Toronto Press 2001.

Jones, Esyllt, and Adele Perry. *The People's Citizenship Guide: A Response to Conservative* Canada. Winnipeg: ARP Books 2011.

Kinsman, Gary, and Patrizia Gentile. *The Canadian War on Queers: National Security as Sexual Regulation.* Vancouver: UBC Press 2009.

Kostash, Myrna. *Long Way from Home: The Story of the Sixties Generation in Canada.* Toronto: Lorimer 1980.

Krause, Sharon R. *Liberalism with Honor.* Cambridge, MA: Harvard University Press 2002.

Lapalme, Georges-Émile. *Le bruits des choses reveilles.* Montreal, 1970.

Laurendeau, André. *La crise de la conscription, 1942.* Montreal: Les éditions du jour 1962.

Lee, Dennis. *Alligator Pie.* Toronto: Macmillan 1974.

Leff, Leonard J., and Jerold L. Simmons. *The Dame in the Kimono: Hollywood, Censorship, and the Production Code.* 2nd ed. Lexington: University of Kentucky Press 2001.

Lenard, Patti Tamara, and Richard Simeon, eds. *Imperfect Democracies: The Democratic Deficit in Canada and the United States.* Vancouver: UBC Press 2012.

Levine, Allen. *King: William Lyon Mackenzie King: A Life Guided by the Hand of Destiny.* Toronto: Douglas and McIntyre 2012.

Lipsett, Seymour Martin. *Continental Divide: The Values and Institutions of the United States and Canada.* New York: Routledge 1990.

Litt, Paul. "Trudeaumania: Participatory Democracy in the Mass-Mediated Nation." *Canadian Historical Review* 89:1 (2008): 27–53.

Loat, Alison, and Michael MacMillan. *Tragedy in the Commons: Former Members of Parliament Speak out about Canada's Failing Democracy.* Toronto: Random House 2014.

Lowenthal, David. *Possessed by the Past: The Heritage Crusade and the Spoils of History.* New York: Free Press 1996.

MacLennan, Hugh. *The Watch That Ends the Night.* New York: Charles Scribners' Sons 1959.

MacSkimming, Roy. *The Perilous Trade: Book Publishing in Canada, 1946–2006.* Toronto: McClelland and Stewart 2007.

Markham, Violet. *Friendship's Harvest.* London: Max Reinhardt 1956.

Martel, Marcel. *Canada the Good: A History of Vice in Canada Since 1500.* Waterloo, ON: Wilfrid Laurier University Press 2014.

– *Not This Time: Canadians, Public Policy and the Marijuana Question.* Toronto: University of Toronto Press 2006.

Martin, Ged. "John A. Macdonald and the Bottle." *Journal of Canadian Studies* 40:3 (2005): 162–85.

May, Elaine Tyler. *Homeward Bound: American Families in the Cold War Era.* New York: Basic Books 1988.

McGillicuddy, Owen E. *The Making of a Premier: An Outline of the Life Story of the Right Hon. W.L. Mackenzie King,* C.M.G. Toronto: Musson Book Company 1922.

McGregor, Frederick Alexander. *The Fall and Rise of Mackenzie King.* Toronto: Macmillan 1962.

McKillop, A.B. *Pierre Berton: A Biography.* Toronto: McClelland and Stewart 2008.

McMullen, Stan. *Anatomy of a Seance: A History of Spirit Communication in Central Canada.* Montreal and Kingston: McGill-Queen's University Press 2004.

McNairn, Jeffrey L. *The Capacity to Judge: Public Opinion and Deliberative Democracy in Upper Canada, 1791–1854.* Toronto: University of Toronto Press 2000.

Milligan, Frank. *Eugene A. Forsey: An Intellectual Biography.* Calgary: University of Calgary Press 2004.

Milligan, Ian. *Rebel Youth.* Vancouver: UBC Press 2015.

Moher, Mark. "The 'Biography' in Politics: Mackenzie King in 1935." *Canadian Historical Review* 55:2 (1974): 239–47.

Morgan, Cecilia. *Creating Colonial Pasts: History, Memory and Commemoration in Southern Ontario, 1860–1980.* Toronto: University of Toronto Press 2015.

Morton, Suzanne. *At Odds: Gambling and Canadians.* Toronto: University of Toronto Press 2003.

Mount, Ferdinand. "The Doctrine of Unripe Time." *London Review of Books* 28:22 (16 November 2006).

Neatby, H.B. *The Lonely Heights, William Lyon Mackenzie King, Volume II, 1924–1932.* Toronto: University of Toronto Press 1963.

– *The Prism of Unity, William Lyon Mackenzie King, Volume III, 1932–1939.* Toronto: University of Toronto Press 1976.

Nevitte, Neil. *The Decline of Deference: Canadian Value Change in Cross-National Perspective.* Peterborough, ON: Broadview Press 1996.

Noel, S.J.R. *Patrons, Clients, Brokers: Ontario Society and Politics, 1791–1896.* Toronto: University of Toronto Press 1990.

Nolan, James L., Jr. *The Therapeutic State: Justifying Government at Century's End.* New York: New York University Press 1998.

Nora, Pierre. *Les lieux de mémoires.* Paris: Gallimard 1984 [vol. 1], 1987 [vol. 2], 1992 [vol. 3].

Norris, Pippa. *Democratic Deficit: Critical Citizens Revisited.* Cambridge: Cambridge University Press 2011.

Oppenheim, Janet. *The Other World: Spiritualism and Psychical Research in England, 1850–1914.* Cambridge: Cambridge University Press 1985.

Owram, Doug. *Born at the Right Time: A History of the Baby Boom Generation.* University of Toronto Press 1996.

Palmer, Bryan. *Canada's 1960s: The Ironies of Identity in a Rebellious Era*. Toronto: University of Toronto Press 2009.

Paris, Joel. *The Fall of an Icon: Psychoanalysis and Academic Psychiatry*. Toronto: University of Toronto Press 2005.

Pickersgill, J.W. *Seeing Canada Whole: A Memoir*. Toronto: Fitzhenry and Whiteside 1994.

Pickersgill, J.W., and Donald Forster. *The Mackenzie King Record, Volumes 1–4*. Toronto: University of Toronto Press 1961, 1968, 1970.

Piketty, Thomas. *Capital in the Twenty-First Century*. Cambridge, MA: Harvard University Press 2013.

Pope, Peter E. *The Many Landfalls of John Cabot*. Toronto: University of Toronto Press 1997.

Porter, John. *The Vertical Mosaic: An Analysis of Social Class and Power in Canada*. Toronto: University of Toronto Press 1965.

Potter, Andrew. *The Authenticity Hoax: How We Got Lost Finding Ourselves*. Toronto: McClelland and Stewart 2010.

Prentice, Alison L. *The School Promoters: Education and Social Class in Mid-Nineteenth Century Upper Canada*. Toronto: McClelland and Stewart 1977.

Prentice, Alison L., and Susan Houston. *Schooling and Scholars in Nineteenth-Century Ontario*. Toronto: University of Toronto Press 1988.

Pyne, Stephen J. *Voice & Vision: A Guide to Writing History and Other Serious Non-Fiction*. Cambridge, MA: Harvard University Press 2009.

Rasmussen, Ken. "Administrative Reform and the Quest for Bureaucratic Autonomy, 1867–1919." *Journal of Canadian Studies* 29:3 (1994): 45–62.

Regehr, T.D. *The Beauharnois Scandal: A Story of Canadian Entrepreneurship and Politics*. Toronto: University of Toronto Press 1990.

Richler, Mordecai. *Joshua Then and Now: A Novel*. Toronto: McClelland and Stewart 1980.

Ritchie, Charles. *The Siren Years: A Diplomat Abroad, 1937–1945*. Toronto: Macmillan 1974.

Roazen, Paul. *Canada's King: An Essay in Political Psychology*. Oakville, ON: Mosaic Press 1998.

Robertson, Gordon. *Memoirs of a Very Civil Servant: Mackenzie King to Pierre Trudeau*. Toronto: University of Toronto Press 2000.

Rodgers, Daniel T. *Age of Fracture*. Cambridge, MA: Belknap Press of Harvard University Press 2011.

Rogers, Norman McLeod. *Mackenzie King*. Toronto: George N. Morang 1935.

Rotskoff, Lori. *Love on the Rocks: Men, Women, and Alcohol in Post-World War II America*. Chapel Hill: University of North Carolina Press 2002.

Rudin, Ronald. *Making History in Twentieth-Century Quebec: Historians and Their Society*. Toronto: University of Toronto Press 1997.

Rutherford, Paul. *A World Made Sexy: Freud to Madonna*. Toronto: University of Toronto Press 2007.

Shorter, Edward. *A History of Psychiatry: From the Era of the Asylum to the Age of Prozac*. New York: John Wiley and Sons 1997.

Stacey, C.P. *Canada and the Age of Conflict: A History of Canadian External Policies, Volume 2, 1921–1948: The Mackenzie King Era*. Toronto: University of Toronto Press 1981.

– *A Date with History: Memoirs of a Canadian Historian*. Ottawa: Deneau 1982.

– *A Very Double Life: The Private World of Mackenzie King*. Toronto: Macmillan 1976.

Strachey, Lytton. *The Illustrated Queen Victoria*. Bloomsbury, UK: Albion 1987 [orig. 1921].

Stratton, Allen. *Rexy! A Play*. Toronto: Playwrights Canada 1981.

Taras, David. *The Newsmakers: The Media's Influence on Canadian Politics*. Toronto: Nelson 1990.

Taylor, Charles. *The Malaise of Modernity*. Toronto: Anansi 1991.

– *Multiculturalism and the Politics of Recognition: An Essay*. Princeton, NJ: Princeton University Press 1992.

– *A Secular Age*. Cambridge, MA: Belknap Press of Harvard University Press 2007.

– *Sources of the Self: The Making of Modern Identity*. Cambridge: Cambridge University Press 1989.

The Trial of Lady Chatterley: Regina v Penguin Books Limited: The Transcript of the Trial. London: Penguin 1961.

Ward, Norman. *Dawson's The Government of Canada*. Toronto: University of Toronto Press 1987.

Ward, W. Peter. *Courtship, Love and Marriage in Nineteenth-Century English Canada*. Montreal and Kingston: McGill-Queen's University Press 1990.

– *A History of Domestic Space: Privacy and the Canadian Home*. Vancouver: UBC Press 1999.

Wardhaugh, Robert A. *Behind the Scenes: The Life and Work of William Clifford Clark*. Toronto: University of Toronto Press 2010.

Watson, Patrick. *This Hour Has Seven Decades*. Toronto: McArthur 2004.

Welsh, Alexander. *What Is Honor? A Question of Moral Imperatives*. New Haven, CT: Yale University Press 2008.

Wente, Margaret. *An Accidental Canadian: Reflections on My Home and (Not) Native Land*. Toronto: Harper Collins 2005.

Whitaker, Reginald. *The Government Party: Organizing and Financing the Liberal Party of Canada*. Toronto: University of Toronto Press 1977.

Whitaker, Reginald, Gregory S. Kealey, and Andrew Parnaby. *Secret Service: Political Policing in Canada from the Fenians to the Fortress America*. Toronto: University of Toronto Press 2012.

Wood, James. *How Fiction Works*. New York: Picador 2008.

Woodruff, Paul. *Reverence: Renewing a Forgotten Virtue*. London: Oxford University Press 2001.

Wright, Donald. *Donald Creighton: A Life in History*. Toronto: University of Toronto Press 2015.

Wright, Robert. *Three Nights in Havana: Pierre Trudeau, Fidel Castro and the Cold War World*. Toronto: Harper Collins 2007.

Index

"colony to nation." *See* Canada's relations with Britain
conscription, 18–19, 23–7, 100–2, 208
Cook, Jack Kent, 140
Cook, Ramsay, 180, 210–11, 250
Cossitt, Tom, 252–3
Côté, Jacqueline (Neatby), 181–2
Courtney, John, 230
Creighton, Donald, 96, 125, 267
Crerar, T.A., 97, 107–8, 122, 161
Cummins, Geraldine, 56–62, 64, 69–70, 248

Daviault, Jean-Louis, 137–42, 199, 236, 239–41, 271–2
Davies, Robertson, 227–9
Dawson, Robert MacGregor, 50, 136, 143–4, 178, 181, 194, 212–13, 230, 248
debt, attitudes toward, 162–3
Deep Throat, 4, 226
deference: decline of in politics, 241–4, 246, 251, 258–9, 262–9; as part of Canadian political tradition, 241–2
democracy, Canadian history of, 80–6
Dempson, Peter, 239
Dexter, Grant, 11, 94, 127–8, 132–3
diary of Mackenzie King: arguments for access to, 148–51, 180, 186, 194–6, 200; comparison to Watergate White House tapes, 244–7; excitement over release of, 205–6; history of, 8–9, 51; King's wishes for, 9; missing volume of, 238–41, 252, 254–5, 270–2; plans for destruction or preservation, 9, 52–5, 136–7, 139, 148–51, 196–201, 210; special spiritualism binders, 200, 206, 256–7; stolen copies of, 137–42, 199, 236, 239, 271–2; use in the writing of official biography, 38–9, 53–4, 136–7, 142, 178–9, 181–2, 183–7, 194

Diefenbaker, John G., 159, 180
drinking, changing attitudes toward, 161–2
Dunton, Davidson, 131–3

Eayrs, James, 143, 197, 225–6
Edible Woman, 222
education, changing attitudes toward, 92–3
election of 1917, 18
Engel, Marian. *See* Bear
Erikson, Erik, 230
Esberey, Joy, 230, 233
espionage, connection of King diary to, 141, 237–41
"Establishment," critiques of, 188–92, 197, 223–4, 241–4, 247, 255–6, 262

Ferns, H.S. (Harry): background of, 109–14; conflict with Ostry, 133–4; earlier writing on King, 221; fears of censorship, 118–19, 129; involvement in 1976 republication of *Age of Mackenzie King*, 245; views on King's diary, 150
Ford, Rob, 268
Forsey, Eugene: background of, 73–6; concern with Canada's British traditions, 120; criticism of Liberal Party, 158–9; criticism of Mackenzie King, 73–4, 76–80, 158, 183; relationship with Arthur Meighen, 78–9; response to *The Incredible Canadian*, 98–9, 102; views on education, 92
Forster, Donald, 188, 270–1
Fotheringham, Allan, 224
Fox, Paul, 227
Fraser, Blair, 62–4, 76, 133, 170, 216
French-English relations in Canada, 18–19, 23–4, 260–1
Freud, Sigmund, popularization of his ideas, 6–7, 88–94, 186–7, 226–35

Freudian ideas: alternative versions of psychoanalysis, 92; connection to a more authentic culture, 91, 105, 179, 226–7; influence on interpretations of Mackenzie King, 227–35; role in anti-Victorianism, 91, 224, 226–35. *See also* Oedipus Complex

Fukuyama, Francis, xvii

gambling, changing attitudes toward, 162
Gibbes, Beatrice, 61
Gibson, Frederick, 143
Glasco, John, 222–3
Gordon, Alan, xiii
Gouzenko spy scandal, 170, 238, 252, 254–5
government secrecy, 243–4, 252–6
Granatstein, J.L., 250–2, 259–60
Gray, David, 58–9
Grossert, Mathilde, 145, 148, 174, 213, 232

Hamilton, Duchess of, 33
Handy, J. Edouard, 52–4, 69–70, 271
Hardy, H. Reginald, 43, 104
Harper, Bert, 74, 213–15
Haydon, Andrew, 249
Heineman's, 119
Herridge, Marjorie, 215
Hill, Alan, 119–20
Hillmer, Norman, 259–60
Himmelfarb, Gertrude, xvii
historical memory, xiii
Hollis, Roger, 254
honour, role in politics, 80–6
Horney, Karen, 145–6
Hughes, Helen, 67
human rights. *See* rights revolution
Hutchison, Bruce, 50, 87, 94–5, 119, 170, 227

The Incredible Canadian, 87, 97–105; response to, 105–8, 267
independence of Canada. *See* Canada's relations with Britain
individualism, xv–xviii, 7–8, 188–9, 265
Industry and Humanity, 124
Institut Canadien Français, 139

Jaws, 236
Joshua Then and Now, 258
journalism: deference of, 67–8, 170, 251; history of 7, 168–70, 190–2; investigative, rise of, 171–2, 241–2
Jung, Carl 7, 227–8

Keable Inquiry, 252
"King, Mary Mackenzie," 56
King, William Lyon Mackenzie: activities during First World War, 18–29, 122–3, 126; attachment to his dogs, 67, 206, 215–16; connection to John D. Rockefeller, 18; connection with rebel grandfather, 16, 41; and conscription, 22–7, 100–2; corruption of, 249–51; as deputy minister, 17, 124; earlier biographies, of 16, 41–4; election as Liberal Party leader, 19; as enigma, 29–30, 103; interest in spiritualism, 4–5, 33–7, 43–4, 52, 56–8, 60, 62–7, 70, 175, 205, 216–18, 256–7; involvement with labour unions, 16–17, 120, 124; partisanship of, 180; plans for his memoirs, 38–41; policies regarding Quebec, 23–5, 260; as political genius, 97–100, 259–60; praise for, 12–14, 27, 98; private life of, 145, 183–6, 191, 194, 206, 212–20, 232, 260; psychoanalytic interpretations of, 144–8, 183–7, 229–35; racism of, 124, 194–5; reactions to the death of, 11–15; relations with prostitutes, 5, 212–15,

223–4, 225–6, 261; relationship with mother, 65, 146–8, 205, 213, 216, 231–2; romances with women, 144–5, 148, 174, 209, 212–15, 218, 261; secret life, 3, 5, 73–4, 102–5, 191, 206, 209, 211–20, 223–4, 229, 230–1, 233, 243, 251, 255–6, 261, 266; as symbol of the Establishment, 243–4; unpopularity of, 15, 29–30; use of spiritualism in politics, 34, 67; views of Canadians toward, 29–30; views of him as a man, 29, 87, 106, 146, 174; wartime policies of, 27–8, 208; Weird Willie phenomenon, 3–4, 205–6, 232, 258–9, 261–2; youth, 16, 74, 144. *See also* diary of Mackenzie King; literary executors of Mackenzie King

King-Byng controversy, 21–2, 76–80, 97–100

Kinsey Reports, 93

Lady Chatterley's Lover, trial, 166–7
Laing, R.D., 231
Lamb, W. Kaye, 47–8, 118, 151, 219, 236, 238–9, 248
Lambert, Norman, 227
Lapierre, Laurier, 168
Lapointe, Ernest, 24, 68–9
Larkin, P.C., 250–1
Larkin, Philip, 167
Laurendeau, André, 25
Laurier, Wilfrid, 17–8, 23, 126, 266–7
Lee, Dennis, 259–60
Leiterman, Douglas, 169–72, 176
Lewis, John, 42
liberalism, changes to, 161, 190
Liberal Party of Canada: changes to by 1970s, 223; status of in 1950s, 115–16, 118–19, 133, 157–9;
literary executors of Mackenzie King: appointment of, 45–8; attempts to

minimize attention given to King's interest in spiritualism, 58–62; criticisms of, 194–5, 209–11, 247–51; decision to open up King's diary, 197–9; decisions regarding King's diary and other papers, 9, 51–5, 136–7, 139, 142, 148–51, 196–201, 208–10, 256–7, 271–2; role in King's official biography, 49–51, 95

London Spiritualist Alliance, 67

Macdonald, John A., 267
The Mackenzie King Record, 178–81, 186, 188, 194–6, 238, 270–1
Maclean's magazine, 62–3, 143
MacLennan, Hugh, 164–5
MacTavish, Duncan, 61, 140
The Manchurian Candidate, 147
The Manticore, 227–8
Markham, Violet, 38–9, 136, 147
McAree, J.V., 36–7
McDonald Commission, 252–3
McDougald, Wilfrid, 249
McGill University, 75–6
McGillicuddy, Owen Ernest, 41–2
McGregor, Fred, 45, 52–4, 136–7, 140–1, 143, 172, 201, 212, 270
McKinnon, Corporal D.L., 240–1
McNaughton, General Andrew, 26, 101–2
Mead, Margaret, 7
Meighen, Arthur, 19, 21, 23–4, 77–9, 121–2
Meisel, John, 246
Memoirs of Montparnasse, 222–3
Menniner, Karl, 145, 147–8
Menninger, Karl, 91
Menon, Krishna, 114–15
mental illness, changing attitudes toward, 90
money, changing attitudes toward, 162–3

morality, changing views of, 159–67, 172, 190–2, 221–35
Mulock, William, 17
Mulroney, Brian, 260
Murphy, Charles, 250

narrative history, xi–xii
National Film Board, 239
National Resource Mobilization Act, 24
Neatby, H. Blair, 181–7, 192–4, 198–9, 210, 219, 229–30, 251, 257
Neatby, Hilda, 92
Needham, Richard 189–92, 243
neo-liberalism, similarity to 1960s radicalism, xv–xvi
Nevitte, Neil, 264
Newman, Peter, 209–11, 247
Nicholson, Colonel L.H., 141
Nixon, Richard, 4, 236, 244, 254
Norman, Herbert, 237

Oedipus Complex, 146–8, 233
official biography of W.L. Mackenzie King, 49–50, 136, 142–8, 178–80, 181–7
O'Leary, Grattan 126–7, 250
Operation Featherbed, 237–41, 253–6, 270–1
Ostry, Bernard: background, 114–17; denial of access to papers in archives, 117–18; involvement in 1976 republication of Age of Mackenzie King, 245, 248–52; relations with Ferns, 133–4; as representative of new Ottawa, 223; role in promoting Age of Mackenzie King, 129–30; role in writing Age of Mackenzie King, 117–18, 121–2
Ostry, Sylvia, 223
Ouellet, Fernand, 192–4

Papineau, Julie, 193

patronage, 83–4
Patteson, Joan, 43, 54, 215–16
Pearson, Lester, 250
Pentagon Papers, 243
Pickersgill, J.W., 45–6, 95, 101, 117–18, 132, 143–4, 178–80, 188, 194–5, 209–10, 238–9, 248, 257, 270–1
Pincher, Chapman, 254
plebiscite. See conscription
Pollitt, Nan, 249–50
Porter, John, 242
post-war era, history of, xiv, xviii
Power, Charles Gavan (Chubby), 97, 101, 106, 160–1
privacy, right of politicians to, 149–51
psychiatry, 88–90
Psychic News, 34, 60, 64
psychic research. See King, William Lyon Mackenzie, interest in spiritualism; spiritualism
psychoanalysis. See Freud, Sigmund
psychobiography, 230–3

Ralston, J.L., 26–7, 101–2
Rebel without a Cause, 147
Reid, Tim, 194–5
respectability, role in politics, 80–6, 176–7
revolt of army during Second World War, story of, 100–2
Rexy! 258
Richler, Mordecai, 258
rights revolution, 7–8, 188–9
Riordan, Kitty, 213
Ritchie, Charles, 223
Robertson, Gordon, 257
Robertson, Heather, 247, 258–9
Robertson, Norman, 46–7, 54, 111, 119, 136, 198
Rockefeller Foundation, 39, 142
Rodgers, Daniel T., xvi
Rogers, Norman, 42